Hegel and the Other

SUNY series in Hegelian Studies
William Desmond, editor

Hegel and the Other

A Study of the
Phenomenology of Spirit

Philip J. Kain

STATE UNIVERSITY OF NEW YORK PRESS

Published by
State University of New York Press, Albany

© 2005 State University of New York

For information, address State University of New York Press,
194 Washington Avenue, Suite 305, Albany, NY 12210-2365

Production by Marilyn P. Semerad
Marketing by Susan M. Petrie

Library of Congress Cataloging-in-Publication Data

Kain, Philip J., 1943–
    Hegel and the other : a study of the phenomenology of spirit / Philip J. Kain.
        p. cm. —(SUNY series in Hegelian studies)
    Includes bibliographical references and index.
    ISBN 0–7914–6473–3 (hardcover : alk. paper) — ISBN 0–7914–6474–1
(pbk. : alk. paper)
    1. Hegel, Georg Wilhelm Friedrich, 1770–1831. Phänomenologie des Geistes.
    2. Spirit. 3. Consciousness. 4. Truth. I. Title. II. Series.

B2929.K27 2005
193—dc22
                                                                    2004016481

10 9 8 7 6 5 4 3 2 1

For Don Beggs,
friend and critic

Contents

Acknowledgments

I would like to thank the following for reading and commenting on earlier portions of this book: Robert Audi, Calvin Stewart, James Felt, Tom Powers, S. Robert Smith, and especially Don Beggs. I would also like to acknowledge my debt to the late Stanley Moore, in whose seminars during the 1970s I first learned Hegel.

Parts of the introduction and chapter 1 first appeared as "The Structure and Method of Hegel's *Phenomenology*" in *Clio* 27 (1998): 593–614. Parts of chapter 2 first appeared as "Self-Consciousness, the Other, and Hegel's Dialectic of Recognition: Alternative to a Postmodern Subterfuge" in *Philosophy & Social Criticism* (SAGE Publications) 24 (1998): 105–126. Parts of chapter 3 first appeared as "Hegel, Reason, and Idealism" in *Idealistic Studies* 27 (1997): 97–112. Other parts of chapter 3 first appeared as "Hegel's Critique of Kantian Practical Reason" in *Canadian Journal of Philosophy* 28 (1998): 367–412. Parts of the introduction, chapter 3, and chapter 4 first appeared as "Hegel's Political Theory and Philosophy of History" in *Clio* 17 (1988): 345–68. Parts of chapter 4 first appeared as "Hegel, Antigone, and Women" in *Owl of Minerva* 33 (2002): 157–177.

Abbreviations

A	Hegel, *Aesthetics*
CPR	Kant, *Critique of Pure Reason*
CPrR	Kant, *Critique of Practical Reason*
CR	Herskovits, *Cultural Relativism: Perspectives in Cultural Pluralism*
DFS	Hegel, *Difference Between Fichte's and Schelling's System of Philosophy*
EGP	Hegel, *Einleitung in die Geschichte der Philosophie*
F	Kant, *Foundations of the Metaphysics of Morals* (Beck translation)
F&K	Hegel, *Faith and Knowledge*
FIH	Mills, ed., *Feminist Interpretations of G. W. F. Hegel*
FP	Kant, *Fundamental Principles of the Metaphysic of Morals* (Abbott translation)
FPS	Hegel, *First Philosophy of Spirit*
GW	Hegel, *Gesammelte Werke*
H	Taylor, *Hegel*
HL	Harris, *Hegel's Ladder*
HP	Hegel, *Hegel's Lectures on the History of Philosophy*
HP&S	Harris, *Hegel: Phenomenology and System*
HTJ	Hegel, *Hegels theologische Jugendschriften*
ILHP	Hegel, *Introduction to the Lectures on the History of Philosophy*

IUH   Kant, "Idea for a Universal History"

JS   Hegel, *Jena System, 1804-5*

KGS   Kant, *Kant's gesammelte Schriften*

KTF   Allison, *Kant's Theory of Freedom*

KTI   Allison, *Kant's Transcendental Idealism*

L   Hegel, *Logic of Hegel*

MEJ   Kant, *Metaphysical Elements of Justice: Part I of the Metaphysics of Morals*

MPV   Kant, *Metaphysical Principles of Virtue: Part II of the Metaphysics of Morals*

NE   Aristotle, *Nicomachean Ethics*

NL   Hegel, *Natural Law*

OR&T   Rorty, *Objectivity, Relativism, and Truth: Philosophical Papers, vol. I*

PCR   Hegel, *Positivity of the Christian Religion*

PH   Hegel, *Philosophy of History*

PhM   Hegel, *Phenomenology of Mind* (Baillie translation)

PhS   Hegel, *Phenomenology of Spirit* (Miller translation)

PM   Hegel, *Hegel's Philosophy of Mind*

PN   Hegel, *Hegel's Philosophy of Nature* (Miller translation)

PP   Kant, *Perpetual Peace*

PR   Hegel, *Hegel's Philosophy of Right*

PRel   Hegel, *Lectures on the Philosophy of Religion*

PW, I   Hegel, *Vorlesungen über die Philosophie der Weltgeschichte*, vol. 1

PW, II   Hegel, *Vorlesungen über die Philosophie der Weltgeschichte*, vols. 2–4

PWHI   Hegel, *Lectures on the Philosophy of World History: Introduction*

R   Kant, *Religion Within the Limits of Reason Alone*

SC   Rousseau, *On the Social Contract*

SCF   Hegel, *Spirit of Christianity and Its Fate*

SEL   Hegel, *System of Ethical Life*

SL   Hegel, *Hegel's Science of Logic*

SS   Hegel, *System der Sittlichkeit*

SW   Hegel, *Sämtliche Werke*

VPRel   Hegel, *Vorlesungen über die Philosophie der Religion*

Introduction

Structure and Method of the *Phenomenology*

Hegel's *Phenomenology of Spirit* is a long, difficult, and obscure text. In this introduction I want to begin with a broad overview of its structure, approach, and method so as to try, as clearly and simply as possible, to explain how I think it is organized, what it is trying to do, and where it is trying to go. I want to introduce issues, questions, and problems that will be taken up in subsequent chapters. At this point, I do not intend to find solutions or reach conclusions.

In my view, the *Phenomenology* should be thought of as divided into three parts: part 1 (Individual Consciousness), part 2 (Cultural Consciousness), and part 3 (Absolute Consciousness). These are my divisions; Hegel himself divides the text into a preface, an introduction, and eight chapters that are arranged under three sections. My part 1 (Individual Consciousness) includes chapters I through V. The first three of these chapters, "Sense-Certainty," "Perception," and "Force and the Understanding," Hegel gathers together as Section A, which he entitles "Consciousness." Chapter IV, "The Truth of Self-Certainty," alone makes up Hegel's Section B, which he entitles "Self-Consciousness." Chapter V, "The Certainty and Truth of Reason," together with the rest of the chapters (chapters VI through VIII) make up Hegel's Section C, which he did not give a title of its own.

Under my part 2 (Cultural Consciousness), I include one chapter, chapter VI, entitled "Spirit." And under my part 3 (Absolute Consciousness), I include two chapters, chapter VII, "Religion," and chapter VIII, "Absolute Knowing."

1	2	3
Individual Consciousness	Cultural Consciousness	Absolute Consciousness
I. Sense-Certainty	VI. Spirit	VII. Religion
II. Perception		VIII. Absolute Knowing
III. Force and the Understanding		
IV. Self-Consciousness		
V. Reason		

The expressly proclaimed task of the *Phenomenology* is to educate ordinary consciousness—to raise it to the level of what Hegel calls "science" (*PhS*, 3, 15–16, 50/*GW*, IX, 11, 24, 56).[1] What we have in the *Phenomenology*, then, is a movement from the simplest form of knowledge—sense knowledge, sensation (Hegel calls it "sense-certainty")—all the way to absolute knowing, that is, total, complete, all-encompassing knowledge. But "knowledge" is really too narrow a term. "Consciousness" would be better. What Hegel explores in the *Phenomenology* is not just epistemology, metaphysics, natural science, and theology, but desires, attitudes, and morality, as well as social, cultural, political, and religious practices, values, awareness, and aspirations.

Part 1 deals with individual consciousness—its attitudes, awareness, vision, behavior, and so forth. Part 2 deals with society, politics, a culture, a whole world and its consciousness. Here, the "I" becomes a "we" (*PhS*, 110/*GW*, IX, 108), and we get a much more complex collective awareness— the attitudes, behavior, visions, practices, consciousness, and aspirations of a culture. Part 3 deals with absolute consciousness, which gives us an even higher, more universal and total perspective, seemingly a God's eye perspective—the religious consciousness, identity, and groundedness of a culture.

At this point it is impossible to define or explain the absolute. But we might provisionally point out that it is usually taken to be absolute in several senses: (1) As for the traditional conception of God, absolute knowing grasps absolutely all reality—it is total. There is no reality except what is present to absolute consciousness, no thing-in-itself left outside, nothing at all outside. (2) It is also absolutely true, not just in the sense that it involves no errors or illusions, but in the older sense of "true," as when one speaks of a "true friend," that is, one who lives up to the concept, the ideal, the essence, of friendship (*L*, 51–2, 305, 354/*SW*, VIII, 89–90, 372–3, 424). It is truth fully realized—the highest truth. There is nothing higher. (3) It is also absolutely present to consciousness. It is not merely implicit or in potential. It has been actualized, fully manifested, in appearance. (4) It is also absolute freedom. It is not other to me, outside, an obstacle. It is not heteronomous. I am fully at home with it. It is absolutely mine—my very identity.

The *Phenomenology*, as it proceeds, sets out different forms of consciousness for our examination. It orders them from the simplest to the most complex, from individual consciousness to absolute consciousness, and it tries to move ordinary consciousness along until it finally reaches and accepts the absolute. That is the way the *Phenomenology* is set out. But that is not the real order of things for Hegel. The absolute is not a last step that comes only at the end. The absolute is primary and total. As we shall see more clearly as we proceed, the absolute is a necessary presupposition for all earlier, lesser, simpler forms of consciousness. After all, nothing is outside the absolute. It may require the whole course of the *Phenomenology* for ordinary consciousness to become aware of the absolute, but once it does so, it sees that from the very first step of the *Phenomenology*, in the simplest form of awareness, it never existed outside the absolute.

Thus, we must come to see that part 2 (Cultural Consciousness) cannot really exist apart from, without, or before part 3 (Absolute Consciousness). The development of cultural consciousness, in Hegel's view, is fundamentally tied up with, produces, and is produced by religious consciousness. Society, politics, and culture mold, and are molded by, religious consciousness, practices, and ideals—by God or the absolute.

So also, part 1 (Individual Consciousness) cannot really exist apart from, without, or before part 2 (Cultural Consciousness), and thus not before part 3. The development of individual consciousness is fundamentally tied up with, produces, and is produced by the development of cultural consciousness and also religious consciousness. This is one of the fundamental claims that Hegel is making—that the simplest knowledge, all individual consciousness, cannot ultimately be understood except as a part of the development of a sociocultural consciousness as well as a religious or absolute consciousness.

All of this will have to be explained as we proceed, but if we turn for a moment to another of Hegel's texts, the *Philosophy of History*, we notice immediately that Hegel is there concerned with a relationship between three things—God, nations, and individuals, that is, absolute consciousness, sociocultural consciousness, and individual consciousness. In Hegel's view, historical reality involves an interaction between these three elements. If so, then it follows that in the *Phenomenology* it will only be at the very end of the text (in part 3) that we raise ourselves to, that we arrive at the actual historical world. We do so only when we have the presence of all three of these elements—individual consciousness, cultural consciousness, and religious consciousness. The development that occurs in the *Phenomenology*, then (before the very end of the text), cannot be historical. There can be historical allusions, but not historical development proper—at least as Hegel understands such development.

We only have full actuality when we get to the whole—to the absolute. Short of that, something is missing. Throughout part 2, we only have cultural consciousness and individual consciousness. We have not yet taken up religious consciousness. Throughout part 1 we only have individual consciousness. We have not yet taken up cultural consciousness or religious consciousness. Individual consciousness, cultural consciousness, and religious consciousness have been separated, isolated, assigned to different parts of the text. The separation is artificial—for purposes of analysis (*PhS*, 264/*GW*, IX, 239). Why does Hegel do this? Precisely to show us that in reality these forms of consciousness *cannot* exist in separation.

Thus, the *Phenomenology* does not start with individual consciousness in the way that a Hobbes, Locke, or Kant would, and from there go on to try to deduce the absolute. In Hegel's view such an individual consciousness radically apart from the absolute is impossible. We only start with such a stance in order to show that it must fail.

Hegel holds a doctrine of internal relations. "Everything that exists stands in correlation, and this correlation is the veritable nature of every existence" (*L*, 245; see also 231/*SW*, VIII, 305, 289; see also *SL*, 86/*GW*, XXI, 72–3). To adequately understand anything, what it really is, its essence, we must understand its relationship to other things, the whole, the absolute.[2] The central argument of the *Phenomenology* is that if we start by trying to understand the simplest form of consciousness we will be unable to adequately explain it without bringing in more and more complex forms of consciousness, and ultimately that we will be forced all the way to the absolute.

Hegel wants to argue that individual consciousness cannot hold up without cultural consciousness and that cannot hold up without absolute or religious consciousness. So Hegel sets out as many forms of consciousness as he can. He lays them out from the simplest to the most complex. Each form of consciousness echoes traditional philosophical views—those of empiricism, or Kant, or Fichte, or Rousseau, or others. Each echoes some position in traditional epistemology, or metaphysics, or ethics, or political theory, or philosophy of religion. And Hegel tries to show that no one of these positions will hold up, avoid contradiction, escape some difficulty or inadequacy, some shortcoming, until we move all the way to the absolute.

The need for the absolute is a need for an adequate paradigm. Each stage of the *Phenomenology*, we will discover, lacks something. To handle what is missing will require a more complex and inclusive conceptual scheme that will include all that the earlier scheme did plus what it could not. In this way we gain the presuppositions necessary to explain our experience. And to do so adequately, Hegel thinks, will ultimately require a paradigm that includes all reality.

If the absolute includes all of reality, if we cannot avoid it, if we cannot even get outside it, why doesn't the *Phenomenology* just start with the absolute right off? In the *Philosophy of History*, the absolute is there before us from the first pages; whereas, in the *Phenomenology* we have to wait for more than four hundred pages before we get to the absolute. This is because the task of the *Phenomenology* is to introduce ordinary consciousness to and to prove the absolute. We cannot start by assuming the existence of this monster—who would believe us? If we want to prove the absolute, we cannot start with it—with a definition, a principle, an intuition, "a shot from a pistol" (*PhS*, 16/*GW*, IX, 24; see also *SL*, 67/*GW*, XXI, 53).

Hegel starts with the most basic sort of awareness, namely, simple sensation. From there he moves step by step through ever more complex forms of experience, and he carefully examines each one of them. He watches each try to explain itself, justify itself, give an adequate account of itself. Each and every one fails to do so and each time we must move on to a more complex form of consciousness—one that tries to account for all that the earlier form did as well as what the earlier form was unable to account for.

If any of these earlier forms of consciousness were actually able to justify itself, hold up, adequately explain experience, and solve all its problems, then Hegel's project would fail. We would stop there and would need go no further. We would have a philosophical account of experience that did not require the absolute. But for Hegel, each of these stages does fail and we must move on until we reach the absolute. Only the absolute will be able to hold up.

In the *Science of Logic*, Hegel claims that the *Phenomenology* gives us a justification (*Rechtfertigung*), a deduction (*Deduction*), of the absolute. What Hegel is saying here, I think, is that the mode of argument that the *Phenomenology* uses to establish the absolute is the same sort of argument that Kant called a transcendental deduction (*Deduction*), and which Kant used to establish the legitimacy (*Rechtmässigkeit*) of the categories (*SL*, 48–9/*GW*, XXI, 32–3; *CPR*, B116–A85).[3] For Kant, we have ordered experience—that is something it is simply impossible to deny. His transcendental deduction proceeds, then, by asking *how* we have this experience; we seek the transcendental conditions that make this ordered experience possible. The categories of the understanding, Kant thinks, are those conditions. If we can show, then, that the only possible way to have ordered experience is through the categories of the understanding, then we have given a deduction of the categories, justified them, proven them (*CPR*, B126–A94, A97, A125, B161). This is the sort of thing that Hegel is doing in the *Phenomenology*. We begin by setting out our experience, though it turns out that we end up setting out far more complex forms of experience than Kant attended to. As we set out these forms of experience, we try to explain how we can have them, we seek the conditions that make these experiences possible, we seek to justify them, and ultimately we are led all the way to the absolute. Anything short of that will fail to adequately account for the total range of our experience. That is the argument.[4]

The doctrine of internal relations holds that we cannot abstract a bit of reality out of the whole, isolate it, and understand it adequately on it own. Russell ridiculed this doctrine—largely by mischaracterizing it.[5] An extremely radical version of this doctrine might hold that it is not possible to understand anything about a thing unless we understand its relations to *all other things*. That, of course, would make an understanding of anything quite impossible. One might also hold that unless one understands a thing's relations to all other things one can understand *nothing at all* about the thing. Hegel, I think, does not hold either of these extreme positions; his view is much less radical. Either of these positions would make it impossible ever to start philosophizing. We would simply and immediately have to know all reality, all relations, the absolute, or we could not take the first step—because anything short of the absolute could not be known at all. To introduce his philosophy, then, Hegel proceeds by taking up isolated forms of experience and shows us that we cannot know, cannot explain these forms of experience fully and adequately—not that we cannot know them at all. We certainly can, in Hegel's view, understand them enough to see that we do not understand them adequately. He wants to show us that, try as we might, we will not be able to adequately explain these isolated bits of experience without the whole—the absolute. He tries to show us that if we do not understand the thing's relations to other things, some problem will arise and our explanation will be flawed and incomplete. Hegel *does* think that we can only gain an adequate understanding of a thing by understanding its relation to the absolute, but he thinks that without yet being convinced of the absolute we can see that our explanation of the thing comes up short, and he also thinks that it is precisely continuous failure of this sort that will finally drive us to see the need for the absolute.

On the other hand, Hegel does not have to hold that it is possible or necessary, once we have accepted the absolute, to actually spell out every last relation between each and every thing. The absolute allows us to understand the connection between things the way a scientific paradigm allows us to understand the connection between the parts of nature with which it deals. A finite mind could never exhaustively explain all the relations involved, but the paradigm tells us how any details we are going to come across should be related, and we must find that any details we do take up actually can be related in that way.

After all, how can one prove the absolute? How can one prove a first principle? We certainly cannot deduce it in the sense of logically derive it from other principles.[6] If we think the absolute is buried in the premises we start with, and we try to draw the absolute out of them, logically deduce it, can we succeed in proving the absolute? Not unless the starting premises have been proven. But if they are starting premises they obviously have not been proven. To prove them, the starting premises would have to be derived from other premises, and those in their turn from others, and so on ad infinitum. We would have an unproven and unprovable starting point—as Fichte thinks we must (*DFS*, 103, 105/*GW*, IV, 23, 24).[7] If there were some other way to establish the necessity of a starting point, find some sort of Cartesian, indubitable, Archimedian point, then we would have to consider such an approach. But, as we shall see in "Sense-Certainty," Hegel does not start in this way. He does not start off with something undeniable and indubitable. In fact, he almost instantly finds sense-certainty quite deniable and doubtable, as he does every other stage until the absolute. Moreover, the *Phenomenology* just does not proceed by laying down and establishing true propositions from which we go on to logically deduce further true propositions. Nor does it even proceed as Fichte did, by laying down fundamental and true principles and then showing them to be impossible unless we go on to presuppose further conditions.[8] In short, the *Phenomenology* is not a "progressive discovery of *truth*," as Harris has it (*HP&S*, 19). Instead, what happens is that at every stage we find that our explanation will not hold, that it is somehow inadequate, incomplete, false at least in certain respects, and that we must go on to more complex presuppositions, until we finally reach the absolute. The *Phenomenology*, Hegel says, is a "pathway of doubt," a "way of despair," a "thoroughgoing scepticism" (*PhS*, 49–50/*GW*, IX, 56).

Like Kant, Hegel starts out from experience. We cannot deny that we experience a tree, a white cube of salt, a force, a desire for recognition, religious devotion, and so forth. Hegel does not think that there is nothing to question and no room for deception in such experience—in fact, he very obviously thinks there is a great deal of deception and a lot to question. We may even have it completely wrong. But in any experience there is something that cannot be gotten around. There is something that demands explanation—there is something we must try to understand. So Hegel sets these experiences out from the simplest to the most complex and examines traditional attempts to understand and explain them. Each explanation fails. In this way, Hegel's approach is a negative one. And thus, unlike Fichte, he does not have the burden of justifying any principle, position, or theory; he does not have to give us, or defend, his own explanation—until the very end when he arrives at the absolute. His strategy, then, his method for proving the absolute, is to keep setting out more and more complex forms of experience, ones that demand explanation, and to demolish any explanations of this experience that are simpler than the absolute—thus to show us that the absolute is the only explanation of our experience.

As long as we can point to something that counts as experience, we can ask what makes that experience possible, we can seek the conditions necessary for that experience to be possible. We must account for every sort of experience that can be brought up and we must give the conceptual presuppositions sufficient to explain the possibility of that experience. Each stage fails, but it does not fail in every sense. Along the way, we accumulate a good deal of explanation—or potential explanation. It is just that experience has not been explained completely. We finally need a paradigm with enough scope to include everything, take it all up, make it a part of a whole, and leave nothing out. Hegel's approach is a bit like Plato's. We cannot logically deduce the forms. Instead we use dialectic. We seek the necessary presuppositions for any type of knowledge. We move backward through these presuppositions until we reach the forms.[9]

This is crucially important because many readers assume that the *Phenomenology* proceeds by necessary logical deduction, that each successive stage is logically derived from what precedes. Kojève and Hyppolite hold such views. So do Stace and Norman, but then they find that such logical necessity fails, or seems arbitrary or obscure.[10] Readers notoriously are unable to see the necessity involved in moving from one form of consciousness to the next. This perplexity arises, in my view, from mistakenly assuming that each stage is supposed to be logically deduced from the preceding.

Other commentators give up on logical deduction and try to find different forms of necessity in the movement from one stage to the next. Harris suggests that each stage "generates a new 'shape'" and that the "transition is necessary." It is "actually a logical *result*" in the sense that it is "the answer to the problem that emerged as critically important in our lives when we were living within the earlier categorical framework" (*HP&S*, 18–19, 34–5; see also *HL*, I, 67, 263). For Lukács, Pinkard, Stewart, and Forster, the necessity is dialectical—each stage resolves contradictions found on a lower level. For Butler, it is desire that necessarily drives the Hegelian subject on toward the absolute. We might argue that the necessity is presuppositional, that the *Phenomenology* sets out the presuppositions necessary to explain our experience. Verene admits that one stage is not logically deduced from another, but thinks there is still necessity to be found in the *Phenomenology*. He argues that we move from one stage to the next by ingenuity, wit, by Hegel acting behind the scenes as a stage hand.[11] Verene is quite correct about how the *Phenomenology* moves from one stage to the next, I think, but how this involves necessity, and what sort of necessity it is, he does not make clear. I also have no objection to dialectic or desire. In fact, for Hegel, all we need do is present reason with something that it does not know and reason will necessarily be driven to grasp it, encompass it, and will never be satisfied short of totality. Indeed, a claim for totality can be found at every stage of the *Phenomenology*. Each form of consciousness implies that it will give us all knowledge that is possible, significant, or meaningful. Anything else is irrelevant and unimportant. Ordinary consciousness comes on the stage quite sure of itself, unaware of any problems, feels that it knows all there is to know, and naively thinks it can explain it all perfectly well without anything so elaborate as the absolute being necessary. And when it fails, another form of consciousness will rush in to show that it can do better. We do have some sort of necessity here—something that will keep us moving on toward the absolute, something that generates a new shape or gives us an answer to an earlier problem. Moreover, I myself have already argued that the *Phenomenology* tries to get at the presuppositions necessary to explain our experience. But the fact that we are driven to go on to another stage after each stage fails, or the fact that later stages resolve contradictions in earlier stages, even the fact that later stages give us the presuppositions necessary for the possibility of experience described at earlier stages—none of this logically deduces the next stage, none of this tells us ahead of time what we must move on to, none of this gives us ahead of time the specific details of what the next stage must look like. And this is not at all surprising. Hegel himself admits that the movement from stage to stage is presented to consciousness without it understanding how it happened—it proceeds behind the back of consciousness (*PhS*, 56/*GW*, IX, 61).

Moreover, whatever sort of necessity might be involved in desire or dialectic, which keeps us moving on toward the absolute, it certainly could not be taken to *prove* the absolute. Desire, dialectic, consciousness in general lead on to a lot of things in the course of the *Phenomenology*. None of them hold up for very long. Just because consciousness leads to something does not establish that thing in any adequate way. If logical deduction is ruled out, then to have a proof we need a transcendental deduction—we must show that without the absolute we cannot have the sort of experience we do have. We must show that the absolute is a necessary presupposition of our experience. Presuppositional necessity, then, is fundamental in the *Phenomenology*—without it we would have no proof of the absolute.

Nevertheless, presuppositional necessity is not enough to explain the transitions from stage to stage in the *Phenomenology*. Just as unresolved contradictions set up some sort of necessity that they be dialectically resolved, but do not tell us ahead of time anything specific concerning what the resolution must look like, so also the fact that cultural consciousness, religious consciousness, or the absolute are necessary presuppositions for the simplest individual consciousness to finally hold up does not ahead of time give us or allow us to deduce from individual consciousness anything specific concerning cultural consciousness, religious consciousness, or the absolute.

What else do we need, then, to understand the sort of necessity that moves us along from stage to stage in the *Phenomenology*? Bergmann draws our attention to an important form of necessity that we find in Hegel, namely, necessity for a purpose—necessity in order to reach a goal.[12] We might call this strategic necessity. If we want to get to X, then it is necessary to discover the steps that can get us there. If we want to reach the absolute, it is necessary to find our way through such and such stages. If we are to give a transcendental deduction of the absolute, it is necessary to uncover the conceptual presuppositions needed to explain experience. If we are to explain the sort of necessity found between stages in the *Phenomenology*, we cannot ignore strategic necessity. Once we get to the absolute, we can look back and see that the steps that got us there were necessary. We would not have made it if we had taken a wrong turn, left out this or that crucial step, or ignored religion, or culture, and so forth. This sort of necessity, completely unlike logical deduction, tells us nothing ahead of time about the details of what the next stage must be. Moreover, in this sort of necessity it is not the case that every little detail that Hegel included in each stage was necessary. The stages used to move us on to the absolute could be different from the ones Hegel used. Details could be improved upon. Things could certainly be clearer. Hegel must simply go through enough stages in enough detail to convince us that nothing short of the absolute will explain our experience. If someone comes up with an explanation of our experience short of the absolute that has not occurred to Hegel, he would have to show that it will not work.

What has to be done is to show that each stage fails. But nothing specific necessarily follows from that failure—certainly the next stage is not logically deduced. As each stage fails, we simply take up another form of consciousness. We look for more complex presuppositions that can include the accomplishments of the earlier stages and overcome their failures. It is we who make the leap to the next stage in order to overcome the inadequacies of the preceding stages. There is no problem with transitions from stage to stage. Hegel strategically thinks up the next stage himself. He selects the example he thinks will work best to make his point. He selects the sort of experience that will lead us to realize that more complex conceptual presuppositions are necessary. Hegel does whatever he wants; the only *necessity* here is that he must arrange things so as to lead us to see that the absolute is ultimately necessary to explain all our experience.

The strategic necessity operating in the *Phenomenology* attempts to reveal the presuppositional necessity of the absolute. This might be seen even more clearly perhaps by considering mathematicians and mathematical proofs. It is completely up to the mathematician to decide how to set out a proof, how to develop it, what stages to go through, and so forth. This is strategic necessity. But if the proof is to work, the mathematician's strategy must finally reveal to us the necessary logical deduction of the conclusion. There can be many different strategies for reaching the same logical conclusion. In the *Phenomenology*, it is strategic necessity that allows Hegel to steer his course (here *without* relying on logical deduction) to the conclusion, the absolute, the presupposition or set of presuppositions necessary to explain our experience.[13]

Some Hegelians would like to think that the second form of necessity regulates, determines, or replaces the first, that the necessity of the absolute (whether for them it is logical, presuppositional, dialectical, or whatever) regulates and determines the approach, the stages of the proof, and the strategy followed. Of course it does as a final goal, but these Hegelians often sound as if does so much more directly. Houlgate, for example, claims that the method of the *Phenomenology* does not depend at all upon strategic assumptions made by Hegel. Hegel need assume nothing. All he need do is attend to the ways in which the various forms of consciousness criticize and transform themselves—Hegel simply looks on as they call themselves into question.[14] These metaphors do capture something about the experience of reading Hegel—one category or form of consciousness just seems to transform itself into another on its own.[15] Harris speaks of their evolution or generation (*HP&S*, 18; *HL*, I, 184–5). But to take these metaphors literally, or even to take them very far, will reify thought. They already make Hegel a passive onlooker and his thought something that merely happens to him. They cloak Hegel's very real strategic activity. Hegel very definitely decides a great many things himself. He decides in what order to take things up. He decides what examples of consciousness will best lead toward the presuppositions he thinks we must make—for example, he chooses fighting and lordship and bondage rather than love to get us to self-consciousness. In fact, most of the examples he takes up could have been different. To get where he wanted to go, he could have chosen something else besides Stoicism, scepticism, unhappy consciousness, physiognomy, phrenology, Antigone, the French Revolution, and so forth. Moreover, Hegel interprets each stage and picks out the specific problems he wants to focus on. The stages themselves do not show us every problem they can or do have. Hegel strategically selects and he selects in order to lead us toward the absolute—and that is something each stage does not do on its own, or does not do very effectively. Once we adopt the perspective of the absolute, we must not let it absorb and blind us to the strategic activity of the individual philosopher. Rather, we must see that the absolute accommodates and makes room for it.

After each stage fails, Hegel is perfectly free to introduce us to whatever he thinks will move us closer to the absolute. On the other hand, each stage fails on its own—in the sense that we do not need to import an external criterion of truth (*PhS*, 53–4/*GW*, IX, 59). We do not judge each stage against a norm of absolute truth that Hegel brings onto the scene to show us what has gone wrong. That would be to presuppose this norm—ultimately it would be to merely presuppose the absolute. Whereas, we must prove the absolute— we must show it to be a necessary presupposition. At each stage, Hegel will take up a more complex conceptual scheme, paradigm, philosophical theory, or set of presuppositions in order to explain experience, and each time the explanation will fail on its own terms. Something will not fit, something will be left out, something will be unexplained, and we will have to go on to try a more complex explanation. Only the absolute will finally succeed.

At each stage of the *Phenomenology*, consciousness discerns what it takes to be essential about reality as opposed to what it takes to be inessential, accidental, or unimportant. Ordinary consciousness may not always be able to articulate this, but it indicates by the way it acts what it takes—and what it does not—to be essential and important about the perceptual world, nature, ethics, culture, religion, and so forth.[16] Consciousness pursues this essence, acts on it, concerns itself with it. Consciousness claims that it is reality or claims it as real knowledge. But we find that it will not work. What the consciousness on the stage takes to be essential is always too limited. Reality contradicts it in some way. Something other which should be inessential emerges as something that must be taken as essential. Ordinary consciousness always claims to be adequate, comprehensive, total, but it always meets an outside that escapes it, contradicts it, limits it—until it finally reaches the absolute which has no outside.

However, it is not as if we first hear of the absolute only at the end of the *Phenomenology*. We get shots at it all along the way. Each form of consciousness comes on the stage acting as if it were the absolute. Each tries to explain all that is real, or at least the essence of all that is real. The rest, it claims, is irrelevant. At every stage, the question we must ask is whether this form of consciousness explains all experience—or, if its principle were extended and developed, could it do so? And the answer is always no. Each form of consciousness operates with fixed concepts and categories that are too narrow and inflexible to handle the wealth, complexity, fluidity, growth, and development of reality. Thus we must move on toward the absolute.

Hegel operates with a distinction between a somewhat naive ordinary consciousness, there, as it were, on the stage, and *we* (Hegel graciously includes us, his philosophical readers, in his project): we who philosophize, we who watch that consciousness on the stage, analyze it, compare it to earlier forms of consciousness, and see things it does not see. There may also be a big distinction within this "we," a big distinction between Hegel and his philosophical reader (depending on the sophistication of the particular reader), because one of the things that soon becomes clear is that while ordinary consciousness and perhaps even the reader are being led to the absolute, Hegel himself has *already* been there. And thus, he sees each stage quite differently, certainly, than does the consciousness on the stage. That consciousness takes itself to be total. Hegel sees it as a mere fragment. Moreover, it is Hegel who must make the choices and design the strategy to move that consciousness on toward the absolute, and, depending on the sophistication of the reader, Hegel may have to lead the reader as much as the consciousness on the stage.

But again, it is not accurate to suggest, even granting that Hegel has already been there, that the absolute is off somewhere at the end of the road. Nothing is outside the absolute. Not Hegel, not us, not even the consciousness on the stage—though, of course, we are not about to accept this, or even see it, until the absolute has been proven to us. But if the *Phenomenology* is finally able to give a deduction of the absolute, if the absolute exists, then nothing exists outside the absolute, not even the *Phenomenology* itself. After all, on the first page of the introduction, Hegel begins by telling us that knowledge can be neither an instrument nor a medium (*PhS*, 47/*GW*, IX, 53). Knowledge is not over against the absolute as if the absolute were an object, an other, to knowing. Our knowing is a part of the absolute. The stages of the *Phenomenology*, we would then have to say, are the absolute moving to itself. Or as Walker has it, "there is no 'way in' to the truth which is not already part of the truth."[17]

For Hegel, therefore, philosophy must form a circle. As Norman puts it, Hegel shows us that we cannot know before we know. Any attempt to demonstrate an epistemological criterion that would claim to tell us what we can and cannot know would already *be* a knowing and thus would presuppose the criterion it was supposed to demonstrate (see also *L*, 17, 84/*SW*, VIII, 54, 124–5).[18] And so, for Hegel, all philosophy must start without such a criterion—it must start with something unproven (*PR*, 225/*SW*, VII, 39). In the *Phenomenology*, the unproven that we start with is the absolute, since it is impossible to be outside it. We abstract from the absolute, we try to, but in order to show that we cannot really abstract from it. Only at the end do we circle back to and justify our beginning—we realize we have been within the absolute all along and could not have taken a step without it (*PhS*, 10/*GW*, IX, 18).

Once we see this, it will give us an additional perspective on the sort of necessity we find in the movement from one form of consciousness to the next in the *Phenomenology*. From the perspective of the consciousness on the stage, even from the perspective of Hegel the individual philosopher, we have seen, there is no necessity of the sort found in a logical deduction. Hegel himself decides how to move us from one stage on to the next. He chooses a suitable example and tries to lead us to the absolute as strategically as possible. Nevertheless, despite the fact that all of this is the result of decisions and choices made by the individual philosopher, we must now begin to realize that everything, even the individual philosopher, is part of the absolute and thus that even the philosopher's decisions and choices must also be seen as the absolute working through philosophy and guiding consciousness to itself. The absolute draws each stage of itself to itself.

I do not at all mean to go back on what I have said. From the perspective of the consciousness on the stage, and even from the perspective of the individual philosopher, there is no way to deduce the next stage. But once we come to understand the absolute, once we begin to see that things are internally related, that they are constituted by other things, that they are formed by the whole, then we can begin to see that there is an additional level of necessity operating in the *Phenomenology*. If we attempt to isolate things from their web of internal relations—if it is the case that things essentially are their relations, if they essentially are their relations to the whole—then the whole will have an effect on these isolated parts. The bit we have abstracted will have conceptual threads attaching it to the rest that we will not be able to purge from our thinking. They will creep into our thought, undermine it, show us that our notion is too narrow, that we have left out something essential, and we will be forced to move on. It will be as if the absolute is exerting a pull on us, exciting a drive, a desire, a dialectic, in the isolated stage of consciousness that we are considering. We will feel a necessity to make certain presuppositions; we will feel that our goal incites our strategic action.

From this perspective, Hegel's infamous notion of determinate negation begins to make some sense. If we have the whole clearly before us, then when one stage fails to meet its own standards, it is not implausible to say that we can see what the next stage must be in our attempt to lay out the absolute. But if we do not have the whole clearly before us, it makes no sense at all to say that from the failure of one form of consciousness, we are led to the next, and certainly not that we can logically deduce the next. The negation of the concept A cannot alone and of itself engender a completely new concept B— which is what Hegel's notion of determinate negation is often taken to mean (*PhS*, 36, 51/*GW*, IX, 42, 57).[19] However, if concept A is seen to be part of a whole, and if we have that whole clearly before us, then the negation of concept A, the denial that it is the whole, may well lead us to concept B, that is, may allow us to see more clearly than before what yet has to be grasped in our attempt to grasp the whole.

Before we get carried away with the absolute, however, there is something else that we must notice about it. As the *Phenomenology* proceeds, it becomes quite clear, I shall argue, that the absolute not only develops but is a sociocultural construction. One of my main concerns in this book will be to counter the traditional interpretation of the absolute as the greatest dogmatism of rationalist metaphysics, the final closed system, the ultimate totalization. At the other extreme, Pippin argues that most scholars who reject this traditional metaphysical interpretation of the absolute reject the absolute altogether and accept only Hegel's theory of culture, his concept of spirit, and his philosophical anthropology.[20] I certainly reject the traditional interpretation of the absolute, the right Hegelian view, and I am definitely sympathetic to the left Hegelian interest in culture, spirit, and philosophical anthropology, but I do not think it follows from this that the absolute, if properly understood, must be discarded.

I will spend a good deal of time arguing that for Hegel the absolute is constructed; at this point, however, simply notice that in an earlier text Hegel himself said, "The task of philosophy is to construct the Absolute for Consciousness." And again, that in philosophizing, "the Absolute gets produced by reflection for consciousness, it becomes thereby an objective totality, a whole of knowledge" (*DFS*, 94, 98/*GW*, IV, 16, 19). In a later text, Hegel says, "God is God only so far as he knows himself." However, this self-knowledge that God has is "man's knowledge of God" (*PM*, 298/*SW*, X, 454). In other words, it is our knowing that constructs God (*PhS*, 11–12/*GW*, IX, 19–20). Hegel was also fond of Meister Eckhart's claim that the "eye with which God sees me is the eye with which I see him; my eye and his eye are one and the same....If God did not exist nor would I; if I did not exist nor would he"(*PRel*, I, 347–8/*VPRel*, I, 248).

The claim that God is constructed, which seems obvious to nonbelievers (of which I count myself one), is objectionable to most believers, and both believers as well as nonbelievers usually think that such construction implies atheism. That is a serious mistake that will make it impossible for us to understand Hegel. The claim that God is constructed is absolutely neutral with respect to belief or disbelief—indeed, is totally irrelevant to the question of God's existence. Even the believer must admit that for God to make any sense to human beings, God must be constructed. Each culture must find the language, concepts, practices, and institutions that make their God understandable to them. This is true even if the believer thinks that God contributed to all of this, dictated every syllable, comma, and period. No serious religious believer thinks that creation, for example, happened literally and precisely the way it is described in Genesis. No human language could describe the way it actually happened. Believers must tell a story that makes sense to human beings in a particular culture at a particular historical period and that hopes to grasp some of the truth of what happened.

On the other hand, the nonbeliever will find such construction to be perfectly compatible with disbelief. Yet, to be sensible, the nonbeliever must admit that any culture, in a very significant way, is a product of its God—whether or not God exists. Even if there is no God, the religious language, concepts, values, practices, and institutions that a culture has developed over time will react back upon it, influence it, mold it, and at least in certain ways may benefit this culture, improve it, do it good. Moreover, this could continue to occur long after the last believer.

As we proceed in the *Phenomenology*, we will see not only that the absolute exists only in so far as it is constructed by a culture, but that this implies cultural relativism. Hegel says:

> Metaphysics is...the diamond-net into which we bring everything in order to make it intelligible. Every cultured consciousness has its metaphysics, its instinctive way of thinking....All cultural change reduces itself to a difference of categories. All revolutions, whether in the sciences or world history, occur merely because spirit has changed its categories in order to understand and examine what belongs to it, in order to possess and grasp itself in a truer, deeper, more intimate and unified manner.[21]

Hegel also says, "Each individual is the son of his own nation at a specific stage in this nation's development. No one can escape from the spirit of his nation." (*PWHI*, 81/*PW*, I, 95). "It is just as absurd to fancy that a philosophy can transcend its contemporary world as it is to fancy that an individual can overleap his own age, jump over Rhodes" (*PR*, 11/*SW*, VII, 35). If, as has been suggested above, all criteria are internal to the process of knowing, then as a culture goes through the process of constructing and coming to know its absolute—through its art, religion, and philosophy—the criteria of the absolute will not transcend this cultural process. A culture may well take the absolute to be true in and for itself above and beyond any particular culture. That is fine. There are no problems with that. We must just remember, though, that that is so for-this-culture.

In my view—and I shall argue it at length—cultural relativism is radically misunderstood by most of those who attack it. Because cultures differ, these opponents think, cultural relativists hold that there is no real right or wrong, no objective truth or falsity. That is not the view of serious cultural relativists,[22] and it is not the view of Hegel. All consciousness develops within a specific cultural context and a specific historical era, but this in no way precludes the possibility that a culture has access to truth. After all, from the fact that there have been different scientific paradigms, must we conclude that there is no truth or that one paradigm is as good as any other?

What are we to conclude? Is the absolute true? That is the only conclusion we can reach for Hegel. He thinks all philosophy contains truth. It expresses the spirit of its age—it expresses the absolute. All philosophy also contains some falsity. As we have seen above, truth is the whole. We have truth in so far as we grasp all of reality—that is, in so far as we grasp the absolute. In so far as our concepts fall short of the whole, they are false (*PhS*, 2, 11/*GW*, IX, 10, 19; *L*, 24, 160/*SW*, VIII, 60, 205–6). The trouble here is that if the absolute includes the whole of reality, if there is no outside, then the truth of the absolute cannot involve a correspondence between it and some object outside it. Hegel's view is that we have truth when the thing corresponds to its concept, its essence—which is to say that we have truth when the thing corresponds to *itself*. True friends, for example, are those who realize, manifest, exemplify—in *themselves*—the ideal of friendship (*L*, 51–2, 304–5, 354 /*SW*, VIII, 89–90, 372–3, 424). The absolute includes all of reality fully realized, fully actualized, fully corresponding to its concept, and fully expressed to itself. If we ask whether the absolute is true, the only answer possible is: *only* the absolute is true. The absolute *is* what is true. We will have to struggle with this as we proceed.

Still, if it is the task of the *Phenomenology* to prove the absolute, to give a transcendental deduction of it, to show that without the absolute we cannot explain the possibility of our experience, can we admit that the absolute is a sociocultural construction? While that will make the absolute easier to accept than the absolute traditionally understood as God, nevertheless doesn't it dissolve the absolute into irreality and illusion? This is a matter that we will have to deal with at length in what follows. At this point we can at least begin to say the following. For Kant, we have ordered experience. If we can state the conditions, the necessary presuppositions, for our having this ordered experience, we can give a deduction of those presuppositions. For Kant they are the categories of the understanding. So also, for Hegel, categories or concepts, though of a much more complex sort, are necessary for ordered experience to be possible. But we must begin to notice that for Hegel we will need a great deal more order and ordering than for Kant.

To see why this is the case, we must notice that Hegel rejects a Kantian unknown thing-in-itself. For Hegel, as we shall see, this thing-in-itself is simply a product of our thought. It is the abstract concept of an object shorn of any content. Nothing is more easily known. We mistakenly think it cannot be known because we find no content there to know (*L*, 91–2/*SW*, VIII, 133). There is no content there to be known and thus no content can be known because we thought away all the content. All that is left, and what *is* there, the bare *concept*, the concept of an object, is obviously and easily known. If we hold, then, as both Kant and Hegel do, that we construct our experience, that we constitute the object, and if we also hold, as Hegel will argue, that the thing-in-itself is known, then we certainly cannot hold that what we constitute is phenomenal appearance, that is, mere appearance cut off from a thing-in-itself that remains behind as unknown. In constituting experience, we will sooner or later find it impossible to deny, we constitute reality. There is no way around it—Hegel is a thoroughgoing idealist.

As soon as Hegel takes this step, he must take another. If all of reality is constituted by consciousness, it cannot be constituted by individual consciousness. If I constitute my reality, you yours, and everybody else theirs, we would have a subjectivist chaos. Nor could this explain how we have a common culture. For Hegel, individual consciousness must be raised to the level of absolute consciousness—which constitutes all of reality and which we participate in culturally.

As soon as Hegel makes this move, it becomes clear that consciousness must be responsible for the constitution of a great deal more order in experience than was the case for Kant. In the first place, we cannot get off with accounting for this order as an order in mere Kantian phenomenal appearance. If we construct reality, we must account for the order found in reality. Consciousness is responsible for all order in nature, culture, history, and the religious sphere. There is no other source for that order. The question, then, is what sorts of presuppositions must we make to explain this enormous amount and scope of order? This should begin to make it clearer why we cannot get along with less than the absolute. We must account for a great deal of order, order of enormous scope. The whole of experienced reality is ordered. How did it get that way? Individual consciousness could not be responsible for it. Individual consciousness might be able to order its own experience understood as Kantian appearance, but not all of *reality*. Nothing short of the absolute will be able to explain the totality of this order.

Let me try to explain this further. For Kant, the categories of the understanding constitute experience, but, as it were, only local experience. Everything that can appear to us must appear to us as ordered by the categories. But the only things that ever appear to us are bits of nature. Nature as a whole never appears to us. And so while any bit of nature that appears to us will be unified by the categories of the understanding, the categories cannot give us the unity of nature as a whole. To think they can would be to think the categories can be applied beyond experience, which would result in transcendental illusion. Nevertheless, for Kant, it is necessary to assume that nature as a whole is unified. The very possibility of natural science, to say nothing of ordinary experience, depends upon it. We must assume that the laws of nature that hold in one part of nature are not arbitrarily suspended but also hold in the rest of nature that we have not yet experienced. We assume nature to be consistent. It cannot be the case that laws of nature contradict each other. Science as well as ordinary experience would flounder. For Kant, therefore, we must think of nature as-if it were designed by a divine intelligence. We cannot know this. It is not given by the categories. We cannot apply the categories to the whole of nature, but we must take the unity and consistency of nature as a regulative idea (CPR, A644=B672, A653–B682, A670–B699, A672–B701, A677–B707, A686–B715).

One can almost hear Hegel chuckling in the background. Kant's move is perfectly transparent. Consciousness constructs this unity that we need in nature. It just insists that an unknown thing-in-itself remains behind so it can get away with holding that this order is to be taken as a mere regulative idea, mere phenomena, mere appearance, not reality. But if the thing-in-itself is our construction just as much as the regulative idea, if we are unable to deny that, then we must face up to what we are doing. There is only one possible source of all this order, and that is us. And if we cannot get away with claiming that what we order is mere appearance, because we cannot pretend that the thing-in-itself remains unknown, if we must admit that we order reality, then we must also go on to admit that we cannot order it as individual consciousnesses, but only as participating in absolute consciousness. If that is the only way to explain the order of nature, if all other attempts fail, as Hegel will try to show, then we must accept the absolute.

Does this convince us to accept the absolute? Do we still resist? If so, why? The absolute is a paradigm, and for Kuhn we cannot prove or disprove a paradigm directly, certainly not in the sense of measuring it against external reality or by some other independent criterion.[23] It is the paradigm itself that allows us to study reality, establish a measure, form a criterion. If paradigms do not bother us in science, why should the absolute be so problematic? Part of the reason, perhaps, stems from a resistance to the notion of sociocultural construction, a belief that anything socioculturally constructed is false or illusory. Scientific paradigms are socioculturally constructed. Are they false? Are they illusory? Surely our government is nothing but a sociocultural construction, a complex set of ideas, values, practices, procedures, and commitments that we serve, obey, believe in, criticize, try to change, and so forth. Is government an illusion?

If we do decide to accept the absolute, however, other problems set in. If the absolute is constructed culturally and historically, if it undergoes change and development, if the absolute in ancient China, ancient Greece, and nineteenth-century Germany differ, how can they all be called "absolute"? Aren't we misusing the term? What sense does it make to call the absolute of one era "absolute" if it differs from the absolute of another era? The answer requires us to see that for Hegel reality *itself* is actually constructed by culture. The absolute of any given era *will* grasp all reality, everything that can be real for that era, everything it is capable of recognizing as of any importance. All else for it will fall outside the absolute and cannot but be unimportant, inessential, nothing. The absolute of any past era really was absolute. At the same time, as a culture works on its world, transforms it, constructs it, sooner or later we will find that something that was inessential, unreal, or marginal starts to become central, important, and quite real. And if our absolute, our paradigm, cannot accommodate this new reality—and sooner or later it will not be able to— then we will find that our absolute is no longer *all* of reality, not absolute, that it has been subverted. At that point we will be in need of a new absolute and culture will set about constructing it. Hegel speaks of "the tragedy which the absolute eternally enacts with itself, by eternally giving birth to itself into objectivity, submitting in this objective form to suffering and death, and rising from its ashes" (*NL*, 104/*GW*, IV, 458–9). This will be of crucial and central importance as we proceed, but at this point I think we are getting a bit ahead of ourselves. My task in this introduction has been to set out some of the problems and issues we will take up, not solve them.

Let me add one last thing in closing. Hegel is often studied by scholars in opposition to other philosophies. Hegel is often studied in opposition, especially, to Marxist philosophy. Here he is studied in order to reclaim him from the complex process of appropriation, criticism, and transformation he underwent at the hands of Marx. Scholars who study Hegel in this way often write as if Marx had no business appropriating "their" Hegel. They somehow fail to recognize that Marx was a Hegelian—perhaps more so than they. While I certainly do not want to reduce Hegel to somebody's precursor, neither do I want to reclaim him from anyone. If Hegel is a first-rate philosopher, as he certainly is, he can and should be appropriated, used, even transformed by other philosophers. In the long run, this will bring Hegel to life rather than kill him.

A similar relationship exists between Hegel and what has come to be called postmodern philosophy. It too has appropriated Hegel, or at least it developed out of a world that had been deeply Hegelianized,[24] and it too has been quite critical of, even hostile to Hegel. One gets the feeling at times that Hegel is taken as the epitome of all that postmodernism is against. Jameson writes, "The rhetoric of totality and totalization that derived from what I have called the Germanic or Hegelian tradition is the object of a kind of instinctive or automatic denunciation by just about everybody."[25] Hegel is the arch totalizer, the advocate of the ultimate closed system, the purveyor of a grand narrative of historical evolution and the ranking of cultures.

I do want to spend at least a bit of time talking about relations between Hegel and postmodernism. Again, I do not want to present Hegel as postmodernism's precursor, though he is that in many ways. Neither do I want to reclaim him from postmodernism as if it has no business appropriating and criticizing Hegel. I should say at the start, however, that this is a book about Hegel, not about postmodern critiques of Hegel. In order to better understand Hegel, I want to consider some postmodern criticisms of him, and in the process I hope to illuminate some contributions Hegel might make to postmodern thought.

Enough then of introducing, let us actually begin our approach to the absolute.

1

Consciousness and the Transcendental Deduction

Every stage of the *Phenomenology* is filled with obscure allusions to other texts—both philosophical and literary. Lauer thinks we should be slow in concluding just which texts Hegel has in mind. He suggests that Hegel may not have been sure himself or that he wanted to refer to an amalgam of positions. Pippin suggests that Hegel refrains from giving us specific references because he wants to sketch the position he is criticizing in as abstract a way as possible, so as to include all partisans of such a position.[1] These points are well taken. Hegel's allusions are like those found in a novel. They are not specific, precise, and limited. They are general, open, even symbolic—as if they were trying to refer to as much as possible.

Nevertheless, I will spend considerable effort trying to identify at least some of the texts that Hegel is alluding to. One of the reasons for this is that Hegel alludes to Kant in many more cases than has been recognized; and if we notice this it will change, it will clarify and improve our understanding of Hegel. I intend to pay a great deal of attention to Hegel's reliance on Kant. I do not mean to imply by this that Hegel was not significantly influenced by other philosophers—Fichte, Schelling, Aristotle, Spinoza, Rousseau, and others. He certainly was. Nor do I want to suggest that Hegel is alluding only, or even primarily, to Kant, and not to other philosophers. And I certainly do not want to suggest that by establishing a connection to Kant we will be able to explain everything that is going on in the *Phenomenology*. I only want to suggest that we can learn something important by seeing connections to Kant.

I. Kant's Transcendental Deduction

I want to argue that right from the start, in the first three chapters of the *Phenomenology*, and in each and every one of them—"Sense-Certainty,"

"Perception," and "Force and the Understanding"—Kant is at the conceptual center of the issues treated. These three chapters are included in what I have called part 1 of the *Phenomenology*, which deals with individual consciousness. It is my contention that these three chapters begin Hegel's deduction and that they closely follow Kant's "Transcendental Deduction," especially as Kant laid it out in the first edition of the *Critique of Pure Reason* (CPR, A95–130).

Kant says, "If each representation were completely foreign to every other, standing apart in isolation, no such thing as knowledge would ever arise. For knowledge is [essentially] a whole in which representations stand compared and connected."[2] For knowledge to be possible, the manifold of sensation must be run through and held together. Coherent experience, Kant argues in the first edition, requires a threefold synthesis: a synthesis of apprehension in intuition, a synthesis of reproduction in imagination, and a synthesis of recognition in a concept. These are not three separate steps; they are inseparable moments of one synthesis. In the synthesis of apprehension, for Kant, the imagination takes up impressions, apprehends them, forms them into an image, and makes them modifications of the mind belonging to inner sense and thus subject to time. Inner intuition is thoroughgoingly temporal. Our representations appear to us successively in time. They are ordered, connected, and related in time (CPR, A98–100, A102, A120–1).

This synthesis of apprehension, however, cannot by itself give us ordered experience. A second synthesis is also necessary. The mind must be able to reinstate preceding perceptions alongside subsequent perceptions and hold them together in a temporal series. We need to retain, remember, and reproduce perceptions. We need a synthesis of reproduction in imagination (CPR, A100–1, A121). If I try to "think of the time from one noon to another," Kant tells us, and "if I were always to drop out of thought the preceding representations... [if I] did not reproduce them while advancing to those that follow," then, he says, "not even the...most elementary representations...could arise"(CPR, A102). We must be aware that what we think is the same as what we thought a moment before (CPR, A103). Otherwise we would have nothing but disjointed chaos. We would not be able to connect earlier with later perceptions of an event or object—they would not belong together for us. One sentence of a speech, even one word, since it would not be remembered, could not be connected with the next. We would have no coherent experience.

Still, even this is not enough. Representations, if they are to give rise to knowledge, cannot be reproduced in any old order just as they happen to come together. The reproduction must conform to a rule according to which a perception is connected with some one representation rather than another (CPR, A121). The concepts or categories of the understanding provide these rules—rules for the necessary reproduction of the manifold (CPR, A103, A106; also B233–A201). A third synthesis, then, is also necessary. A synthesis of recognition in a concept is necessary to determine the specific order and relation of the reproduction of representations. The only way to grasp these successive and remembered moments in one cognition and the only way to unify these sensations into one object is through concepts that embrace, organize, and unify them. Otherwise we would not have an object, but merely a disjointed series of isolated, remembered sensations.

Furthermore, this threefold synthesis requires a unity of consciousness— Kant calls it the "transcendental unity of apperception" (CPR, A106–7). For Hume, there was no fixed, stable, unified self that could be experienced. When we turn to inner sense, we experience nothing but a flux of shifting ideas, images, and impressions.[3] Kant agrees with Hume that we never experience a unified self (CPR, A106–7). But for Kant there must be a unified self. If not, then the diverse multitude of sensations, the temporal flux that constitutes inner sense, would not belong to a single consciousness and thus could not belong to me. The flux must be unified within a single self for experience to be possible—or else this flux of images could not be *my* flux of images. It could not be *my* experience. I would then have no experience— "merely a blind play of representations, less even than a dream" (CPR, A112, A122, B132–3).

At the very same time, there is also a second unity involved here—that of the object. For the manifold of sensations to be unified as one object, it is also the case that this manifold must be contained in a unified self. If we cannot presuppose a transcendental unity of apperception, there is no way to understand the possibility of a unified object. The transcendental unity of apperception through the categories forms a unified object. Thus the transcendental unity of apperception is an objective condition of all knowledge. It is not merely a subjective condition that I require in order to have knowledge of an object. It is an objective condition under which representations must stand in order to become an object for me (CPR, A105, A108, A111–12, A125, B138–9, B143). Representations for their part must be capable of association; they must have what Kant calls an "affinity." They must be able to enter the mind, conform to the unity of apperception, and be subject to the rules of the categories (CPR, A122).

This might all seem to be just a bizarre problem that idealists are stuck with and that other "sensible" philosophers need not be bothered by. But that is not the case at all. Kant, it is true, suggests that our experience is constructed out of unconnected elements. This might seem to be an odd and unacceptable view, but for Kant to be right, we must see, it need not at all be the case that things-in-themselves are unconnected. Let us assume, just as a materialist or a realist might, that things are fully organized and connected independently of our perception. Nevertheless, we must still *apprehend* these things, and in doing so we would have to organize and connect *our various representations*—whatever the character of the thing itself.

Suppose a house exists before us. We apprehend a foundation, walls, roof, chimney, doors, and so forth. Even if they are organized and connected in themselves as for the best realist, we must still organize and connect them in our apprehension, or for us there would only be disconnected chaos. Each shingle on the roof, brick of the chimney, pane of the window—all the way down to the minutest details—would have to be grasped in our apprehension, reproduced in memory, subsumed under concepts, and brought under the unity of apperception. If not, we would have unconnected chaos (CPR, A98–101, A122, B134, B154, A156). Our senses separate things. We apprehend the roof separately from the foundation; we can fail to remember one moment of the walls as connected with other moments. We might think of our experience as recorded on a series of videos—one of the roof, another of the windows, and so forth. Moreover, each and every frame of film would be a separate representation. We must organize each of these representations in our inner experience—and whatever the world in itself might be like is irrelevant.[4] A threefold synthesis and a transcendental unity of apperception are necessary to have ordered experience for any sort of theory of experience.[5]

I want to argue that the first three chapters of the *Phenomenology* follow and comment on Kant's treatment of the threefold synthesis of the imagination. At the same time, they criticize Kant and try to get beyond his unknown thing-in-itself. Chapter I, entitled "Sense-Certainty," takes up immediate sensation and treats it simply as apprehended, that is, it treats it as if we had a synthesis of apprehension, the first moment of the threefold synthesis, but without going any further, without yet having a synthesis of reproduction or a synthesis of recognition in a concept. And we quickly see that this fails. We cannot even hold impressions together through time. So in chapter II, entitled "Perception," we go on to include a synthesis of reproduction, the second moment of the threefold synthesis, memory holding together a series of representations through time. Here we get a thing and its properties—which recalls the empiricism of Locke. This runs into various troubles because we have not as yet included a synthesis of recognition in a concept. In chapter III, entitled "Force and the Understanding," we finally arrive at Kant's categories or concepts of the understanding, we include the third part of the threefold synthesis, and we come to see that we must understand objects as conceptual relations.

At first sight this might appear to be a bizarre overinterpretation, but it is quite clear from other texts that Hegel is fully aware of the Kantian threefold synthesis (F&K, 69–70/GW, IV, 327; PM, 208/SW, X, 337), and I suggest that seeing this relationship to Kant's transcendental deduction will make the first three chapters of the *Phenomenology* a good bit clearer as well as help us to understand the beginnings of Hegel's own deduction.

II. Sense-Certainty

Taylor (*H*, 141) and Rockmore argue that sense-certainty resembles empiricism.[6] I do not think that is correct. While it is true that sense-certainty, like empiricism, limits knowledge to sensation of particulars, nevertheless, unlike empiricism, it embodies no notion of appearances, impressions, sense-data, or anything of the sort. Rather, sense-certainty takes itself to be immediate knowledge that grasps things as they are—without altering them in any way (*PhS*, 58/*GW*, IX, 63). What Hegel has in mind here, I think, is traditional metaphysics—which in the *Logic* he says is a form of thought that never became aware of the modern antithesis between the subjective and the objective. It claims to take the material furnished by sense and bring it before the mind as it really is. It takes the laws and forms of thought to be the laws and forms of things. Thought grasps the very nature of the thing—without distortion (*L*, 60–1/*SW*, VIII, 99–100).

This form of knowledge, immediate knowledge of particulars, fails for Hegel, and indeed fails in much the same sort of way it was thought to fail in the ancient world. Sense-certainty is the sort of knowledge that Plato attacks throughout the *Theaetetus*. Plato concludes that particulars are too shifting and changeable to be objects of knowledge and that we cannot give an account of primary things taken by themselves.[7] Aristotle, too, argues that there can be neither definition nor demonstration about sensible individuals.[8] As I have already suggested, sense-certainty also corresponds to what Kant calls a "synthesis of apprehension," and it would not work for Kant either, because we have left out the rest of the threefold synthesis. Pippin thinks there are no clear philosophical precedents for sense-certainty.[9] I suggest there are several.

It might seem odd, however, to think that Hegel would decide to link traditional metaphysics with Kantian epistemology when these philosophical outlooks are so opposed. But from another perspective it is not really so odd. Plato, Aristotle, and Kant at some place in their theory must attend to, and ordinary consciousness (perhaps in any age) just seems to begin with, the simplest and naivest notion of knowledge—knowledge as a direct grasp of sense particulars (*L*, 60/*SW*, VIII, 99). Perhaps any theory must start with some sort of simple apprehension. But from there we quickly find that there is much more to it. At any rate, I want to focus on the parallel here between Hegel and Kant.

In "Sense-Certainty," we start with simple, immediate, and seemingly indubitable sensation, as if we only had an as yet unorganized manifold of isolated sensations. We certainly do not have conceptually organized objects, but, as Hegel puts it, merely a "this." We have a "here" and a "now"—a spatial here and a temporal now—making up a this. We point to it, indicate it, mean it—we can say no more about it at this stage (*PhS*, 59-60/*GW*, IX, 64–5).

But even as we try to indicate a this we soon discover that we do not really have such a pure immediacy before us—we do not really have a simple here or a now, but only *instances* of them. The here and the now change. Night changes into day. As I turn my head the tree disappears and I see a house. The indicated referent does not remain, it will not hold stable, it is not preserved. If now is night, Hegel says, let us write it down: "A truth cannot lose anything by being written down, any more than it can lose anything through our preserving it." But the next time we look, it is noon and our truth "has become stale" (*PhS*, 59–60/*GW*, IX, 64–5). The now changes, it is different, it has a different referent. We have ignored the role of time. Indicating a this will not indicate the same this through time. The this will not indicate the unity of an object through time. We have left out a synthesis of reproduction in imagination. We have ignored memory—we forget (*PhS*, 64/*GW*, IX, 68–9).

Hegel wants us to see that any here, now, or this is really a universal. No this will indicate a sensuous particular. Any this can only indicate any and all heres, nows, thises. Language can never say, can never express in words, the sensuous particular that we mean (*PhS*, 60/*GW*, IX, 65; *L*, 8–9/*SW*, VIII, 74–5). Hegel is headed in the same direction as Kant here. We cannot have knowledge simply of isolated, given sensations. Knowledge involves universals—it requires concepts.

What if, in order to understand sense-certainty, we do not focus on the sensation, as we have been doing up to now, but focus instead on the knowing "I"? It is the I that holds the this fast. Now is night rather than day because I see night, not day. Here is a tree rather than a house because I see a tree, not a house. The only problem with this, however, is that the I too is a universal. One I sees day. Another I sees night. The I refers to any I (*PhS*, 61/*GW*, IX, 66). This will soon become very important. Hume has shown us that we cannot experience a single unified self. Hegel shows us that language cannot even indicate such a self. Indeed, very much in opposition to Kant (*CPR*, B406–7), Hegel will argue that such a self—certainly a Kantian transcendental self—does not exist. In chapter IV of the *Phenomenology*, in the section entitled "Lordship and Bondage," we will see that for Hegel the self, like all else, is nothing but a conceptual relation. At any rate, sense-certainty does not overcome its difficulties in this direction.

What we are driven to, for Hegel, is a now of many nows, a here of many heres, an I of many I's—a plurality holding together as a universal. We have I's sensing a now that is a process, a passing of nows in time (*PhS*, 64, 66/*GW*, IX, 68, 70). Time, then, is an inescapable element of any sensation. And thus a synthesis of reproduction is a necessary element of any organized experience. The series of isolated sensations must be held together, remembered, reproduced, through time.

Why does Hegel begin with sense-certainty? One reason is that this is where Kant's deduction starts in the first edition. It is also where ordinary consciousness starts. But perhaps most importantly, Hegel starts with sense-certainty because it is about as far as possible from where he wants to end up—with the whole, the absolute. Sense-certainty is as opposed to a doctrine of internal relations as anything can be. It is Hegel's view that adequate knowledge cannot be had about particulars. The part can only be understood in relation to the whole. Hegel rejects the notion of a world that is just there, given, outside, other, over against consciousness, with everything in it externally related. So Hegel starts with precisely that, in order to undermine it, to move us away from it, to show us that such particulars have been abstracted from the whole.[10]

According to Stern, a holist argues that the world contains concrete objects that cannot be treated as compounds made up of more fundamental self-subsistent elements. These objects have a unity that is not properly analyzable into a plurality of self-subsistent and externally related parts. Pluralists, on the other hand, think the world contains fundamental self-subsistent elements that are ontologically prior to and independent of their instantiation in the whole, and so pluralists can explain the whole through a combination of separable elements.[11]

What Hegel does again and again in the *Phenomenology* is to focus on specific relations. And each time he shows us that we cannot understand these relations alone and in isolation. Each time we must move on to a more general relation that takes up and includes within it the earlier, more particular relation. In "Sense-Certainty," then, the fact that language will not express particulars is not due merely to a failure on the part of language. Rather, particular objects themselves fail to hold up for us. Hegel rejects the notion that brute particulars are simply there, given, for sense experience. As we shall see, for Hegel, we must come to understand objects themselves as conceptual relations.

As Taylor (*H*, 142) puts it, being aware of something, being able to say something about it, involves grasping aspects that things have in common, rather than just their particularity. For Hegel, we shall see, all particularity, all difference, is difference within a commonality. Ultimately we have differences *within* the absolute. All differences *from* the absolute would subvert the absolute. It would mean there was something other than, outside, the absolute, and thus the absolute would not include all of reality—it would not be absolute.

However, there is something else in "Sense-Certainty" that we ought to notice, as it will become a source of difficulty for the conceptual. The way Hegel puts it in the *Logic* is that everything finite is unstable, changeable, transient, implicitly other than what it is, suddenly turning into its opposite—as night turns into day (*L*, 150/*SW*, VIII, 192–3). Thus, while we must admit that nothing escapes the conceptual, we must also admit that fixed concepts always have a very difficult time holding on to things.

III. Perception

In chapter II, "Perception," we begin with what "Sense-Certainty" drove us to—a this of many thises, a now of many nows. In other words, we have an entity that holds together—particular sensations holding together as a universal. To use the language of empiricists, we have a thing of many properties (*PhS*, 66–7/*GW*, IX, 70–1). Empiricism, Hegel claims in the *Logic*, elevates the brute facts of sensation to general ideas (*L*, 77/*SW*, VIII, 117). What Hegel means here, I think, is that we have the idea of many sensations, qualities, or properties held together as a thing; in other words, basically a Lockean substance—an idea (signifying we know not what, as Locke put it) holding together many properties.[12] Or, to use Kant's language, we have now included the second moment of the threefold synthesis—a synthesis of reproduction in imagination. We have a holding together, a remembering, a reproducing, of sensations through time. However, as we shall see, we do not yet have the third moment—a synthesis of recognition in a concept. In other words, the Lockean idea of a substance signifying we know not what falls short of Kantian categories. Hegel, in *Faith and Knowledge*, claims that Kant's views are an extension of Locke's (*F&K*, 78/*GW*, IV, 333).[13]

So Hegel takes up a suitable example, a bit of salt, a thing that has several properties—it is white, tart, cubical. These properties are taken to be separate, distinguishable, and indifferent to each other as well as to the salt as a whole. As Hegel puts it, they are connected by an indifferent "also"—the salt is white, *also* tart, *also* cubical. But at the same time, these properties are all held together in a unity. And so, besides these alsos, we have a "one" (*PhS*, 68–9/*GW*, IX, 72–3).

How do we explain how these properties are unified in the salt, are a one, yet at the same time are alsos, are separate, distinguishable (we can distinguish the color from the taste, the taste from the shape, and so on)? Hegel wants to show us here that if the thing-property model, the substance-accident model, will not explain things, we will have to move toward a doctrine of internal relations.

Let us try, as empiricism did, to attribute the separateness to the subject. It is the subject's perception that distinguishes the whiteness from the tartness and from the cubicalness; and the subject will also accept responsibility for any distortion of the object brought about in this process. What we have is Locke's notion of secondary qualities.[14] The thing is white only to our eyes, tart only to our tongue, and so forth. Secondary qualities (that is, colors, sounds, tastes) exist only in the mind and are not thought to resemble anything in the object (PhS, 70, 72/GW, IX, 73–5). On the other hand, the unity we will attribute to the thing or substance itself—made up of primary qualities (solidity, extension, mobility, figure) that are supposed to exist independently on their own in the thing just as they appear to us.[15]

The problem, however, is that while we can attribute the unity to the substance, we cannot, as Berkeley pointed out, perceive that unity. All we perceive are the secondary qualities, the alsos, the whiteness, the tartness. Primary qualities cannot be perceived except through secondary qualities—for example, we cannot, without color, identify shape or distinguish movement against a background. Even the primary qualities are separable. So, we never perceive the substance, the unity, the salt itself, as something beneath the whiteness, tartness, and cubicalness. Hegel concludes, as did Berkeley, that we can dispense with this substance. The thing itself is nothing but the qualities—the whiteness, tartness, cubicalness (PhS, 73/GW, IX, 76).[16]

At this point, we have completely reversed ourselves. We can no longer say that the diversity, the separateness, is due to the subject and the unity to the object. We find no unity in the object—it is nothing but a diversity, the alsos. We find that the subject has merely projected a unity into the object (PhS, 73–4/GW, IX, 76–7). The substance is merely an idea we add to the distinguishable qualities. The unity then is due to the subject and the diversity to the object—precisely the opposite of what we started with.

Let us, then, try a different tack. Let us try making the subject responsible for both sides—for the unity, the unifying, of the object, and also for distinguishing the various qualities or properties (PhS, 74/GW, IX, 77). This is no longer a Lockean substance but merely a Berkeleyan perception. Hegel also has Kant in mind (see L, 89–90/SW, VIII, 130–1). The thing is merely what appears, what can be perceived, and that is all. The thing is whiteness, tartness, cubicalness, and the oneness is produced by our perception, the unity of our consciousness, that holds it all together. As Pippin points out, Hegel is here rejecting the Lockian or empiricist notion that there are external, nonschematized contents or substances just given to us in intuition to which we can apply a conceptual scheme.[17] There are no such givens—we cannot successfully make out the case that they exist. They are always already schematized or conceptualized.

What we have then is a thing that presents itself as a unity for-consciousness, but in-itself it is seen as diverse. This raises problems. The thing is taken both as something in-itself and as something for-consciousness. And the thing is something *different* for-consciousness than it is in-itself. It is a one for-consciousness but diverse in-itself. Moreover, the thing is one only for-*another*. The thing only gets its oneness for-itself through another. It is only one for-consciousness. But this means that to be one the thing must be *other* than itself. In other words, to get its oneness it must *not be one*, it must be something *besides* itself, it must also be something for-consciousness, for-another (*PhS*, 74–6/*GW*, IX, 77–9).

This is a problem that empiricism cannot handle. It is not at all a problem for Hegel. It is just what he wants. It shows us that the substance-accident or thing-property model will not work. It will not explain the thing's oneness that exists only for-another—its unity that exists only for-consciousness. The only way to understand this is as a *relation*—a relation grasped by *concepts*.

As Stern points out, relations do not fit easily within an ontology in which properties belong to individual things. Relations do not belong to single things. They belong to two things or they float between with one foot in one and the other foot in the other.[18] At any rate, they do not behave like properties. For Hegel, then, the only way to grasp a thing's oneness-for-consciousness together with its diversity-in-itself is as a conceptual relation, not as a thing with properties. The thing-property model is supposed to give us a unified thing with diverse properties. But we have no unified thing. Consciousness provides the unity—our *concept* provides the unity. And the thing is only a unity in *relation* to our consciousness. We are forced, then, to move on to the third moment of the threefold synthesis.

IV. Force and the Understanding

In chapter III, "Force and the Understanding," we reach the third moment of the threefold synthesis—the synthesis of recognition in a concept. However, the consciousness there on the stage has not yet become aware of the transcendental unity of apperception. In other words, consciousness does not yet see that the unity of the object is due to the unity of consciousness, which is to say that consciousness does not yet see that consciousness constitutes the object. We still have an understanding that sits back and observes its object as if the object were just given to it from outside, or as if the object were anchored in an unknown thing-in-itself—a view that Hegel also wants to undermine as he proceeds in this chapter. He wants to begin to move beyond Kant.

But the first question that arises in this chapter, I suppose, is why in the world Hegel discusses force. I have been arguing that Hegel moves from simple experience to more complex experience and at each stage chooses to take up an example appropriate to the point he wants to make. Here he chooses force for two reasons. First, it is a perfect example of a phenomenon that is unexplainable on the substance-accident or thing-property model. It can only be understood as a relation grasped by concepts. Second, in this section we are also working toward showing the necessity of Kant's categories. Force is a perfect example because we are also, with Kant, combating Hume's attack on causality. This can be seen explicitly in Hegel's earlier *Jena System of 1804–5* (JS, 53–5/GW, VII, 49–52; see also L, 42, 89–90/SW, VIII, 78–9, 130–1).[19] In force, no causal connection can be perceived as a sense impression, yet the interaction of forces is inescapably causal. The only way to grasp this causal interaction is to understand it as a conceptual relation.

What is force? Force is something that appears, is expressed, when another object approaches and attracts, repulses, or excites it. Think of two magnets. There is no actual contact between the two as with Hume's billiard balls. The influence (the attraction or repulsion) is not a mechanical operating on the other. It makes no sense to speak of a thing or substance transmitting motion as a property to another thing (PhS, 85/GW, IX, 87). We can only speak of interaction—relations—within a field. In *The Jena System of 1804–5*, Hegel explicitly claims that force is not a substance but a relation. Moreover, in force we are unable to distinguish a cause from an effect. There is no difference between force and its utterance (JS, 49–51, 55/GW, VII, 45–8, 51–2). The lightning cannot be separated from the flash. What sense does it make for Hume to ask us for an impression of the secret power that the cause imparts to the effect if we cannot distinguish the two?[20] Hume is not conceiving the issue correctly.

Force is solely—is nothing but—an interaction occurring in a field. Force exists only when it is expressed. When the magnets come close enough together, force appears. When they are far enough apart, force disappears. Perception was unable to handle the conflict between being in-itself and being for-another—being one for-another and being diverse in-itself. Force has not the slightest difficulty with this. What force is in-itself, it is through its expression, through its relation to another. It expresses itself only when the other magnet approaches. Thus, only in so far as force is for-another is it what it is in-itself. Moreover, when force is expressed it is diverse; when it is driven back into itself it is one (PhS, 80–2, 86/GW, IX, 83–5, 87; JS, 54/GW, VII, 51). Thus, it is one in-itself and diverse for-another. Yet it is only what it is in-itself (one), it is only a force, through its relation to another (diversity).

Force is a complex relation between the two magnets. It is not a perceivable thing or substance or secret power. It is a relation. Moreover, force is not an *external* relation. We do not have two things or substances that can be related externally as with Humean billiard balls. Force is quintessentially an *internal* relation—and, as I have been suggesting, that is what Hegel is after. The very essence of force is that it exists through the other. Force cannot be what it is except in its relation to another (*PhS*, 86, 82, 100/*GW*, IX, 87, 84, 99). The other is internally related to it as part of its very essence.

All we experience, then, for Hegel, is a play of forces. We see forces appear and vanish—a flux of forces. That is all. It can do us no good to project a substance behind this appearance. We have seen that that will not explain anything. What understanding grasps, then, is only relations and their relata—a flux of appearance. Nor does understanding grasp any inner workings or inner mechanism. Nevertheless, Hegel suggests, it just yearns to project something behind this appearance—not a substance as for perception but the *concept* of an unknown thing-in-itself. Consciousness just assumes something must be there. Consciousness wants something to be there. Consciousness needs it. Consciousness posits an inner as an explanation of the manifestation of force. The inner is supposed to explain the unity—the connection—of forces. The appearance is pure flux—interactions appearing and disappearing. The inner is the unity that continues through the flux—a lawlike inner unity. Consciousness takes this inner to be the in-itself, a supersensible world, the true world. Hegel says that this is the first dim appearance of reason in the *Phenomenology* (*PhS*, 86–8/*GW*, IX, 88–9). He is referring, I think, to Kant's ideas of reason—regulative ideas that allow us to treat nature as-if it were unified and consistent. Moreover, as we shall see, for Hegel there is something like a transcendental illusion involved here, as there is for Kant, though, for Hegel, in a sense very much the opposite of Kant (*CPR*, A297–B354, A314–B371, A644–B673, A653–B682, A698=B726).

In both the *Phenomenology* and the *Logic*, Hegel suggests that we are driven to go behind, within, to find a unity, a set of laws, a lawlike explanation (*L*, 42/*SW*, VIII, 78–9). Hegel calls it a *Reich der Gesetze*, which Miller translates as a "realm of laws" (*PhS*, 91/*GW*, IX, 91). I prefer Baillie's translation of a "kingdom of laws" (*PhM*, 195). Why does Hegel call it a kingdom? Kant often speaks of a kingdom of nature (e.g., *FP*, 55/*KGS*, IV, 438), but I must admit that I am also reminded of Kant's notion in the moral sphere of a kingdom of ends (*FP*, 50/*KGS*, IV, 433). I think that in this section of the *Phenomenology* Hegel is trying to draw a lot of things together in a very suggestive fashion. Let me slowly try to explain this.

In the first place, let us remember that for Kant the unknown thing-in-itself is found not only behind any experience of particular things, but also, in the "Transcendental Dialectic," behind the unity of nature as a whole (e.g., *CPR*, A677=B705-A678=B706; *CPrR*, 111/*KGS*, V, 107). This unity can never be experienced, can never be known, but must be assumed as a regulative idea. Understanding and natural science need the concept of a unified nature. For science to be possible, for the understanding to carry out its work, Kant thinks, we must assume that nature is unified and consistent (*CPR*, A653–B682, A670–B701, A686=B715, A698=B726). We must assume that laws of nature which hold in one part of nature also hold in the rest of nature that we have not experienced. It cannot be the case that laws of nature contradict each other—or science would be impossible. The same laws that explain terrestrial motion must be consistent with the laws that explain planetary motion. One set of laws must be subsumable under higher sets of laws— this is part of what Hegel means by a "kingdom" of laws (*PhS*, 91/*GW*, IX, 92).

Understanding demands this regulative idea, this kingdom of laws. Understanding must assume it. The only trouble is, if we admit that consciousness assumes this kingdom of laws, how can we say that it is unknown? It is a need, a creation, an assumption, of the understanding. The distinction between a flux of appearance and an inner world is just a distinction made by consciousness. To organize the flux of appearance, understanding posits an inner world, a beyond, a unity, a kingdom of laws. In doing this, of course, consciousness takes itself to be talking about a different, independent, inner world, there behind the scenes. But we who are philosophizing with Hegel see that consciousness simply made a distinction between outer appearances and an inner, between phenomena and a supersensible thing-in-itself. We see that the supersensible beyond is simply our assumption and, as Hegel puts it, that appearance is its essence and only filling (*PhS*, 89/*GW*, IX, 90)—all we have is an empty concept of unity that we project behind the flux of appearance. Hegel will resist this drive of consciousness to project a world beyond, a supersensible world, as an unknown thing-in-itself. In the *Phenomenology*, he says, "behind the so-called curtain which is supposed to conceal the inner world, there is nothing to be seen unless *we* go behind it ourselves, as much in order that we may see, as that there may be something behind there which can be seen" (*PhS*, 103/*GW*, IX, 102).

Hegel does not deny the existence of a thing-in-itself, as Fichte (at least at times) did.[21] Hegel just denies that the thing-in-itself is unknown. It is not unknown because we construct it. There is nothing there unless we ourselves go behind the curtain and construct it. And what is it we construct? The concept of an inner, a beyond, an other world, an empty abstraction. It looks like an unknown thing-in-itself because it has no content to be known. But nothing is more easily known—it is merely a *concept*, the bare abstract concept of an object, an empty concept whose only filling is ordinary appearance (*L*, 91–2/*SW*, VIII, 133; *PhS*, 89/*GW*, IX, 90).[22] In short, all we actually have is the flux of appearance, but we cannot accept that that is all we have. We are driven to assume, construct, posit an unknown thing-in-itself behind this content.

There is another way to approach this matter that might make Hegel's position a bit clearer. Allison distinguishes between a "two worlds" and a "two aspects" interpretation of Kant. The two worlds view, the standard view of Kant held by most, is that "there is a straightforward ontological distinction between two classes of entity: knowable and mind-dependent appearances and unknowable and mind-independent things in themselves." The two aspects view, on the other hand, rejects such an ontological distinction and holds instead that "Kant's transcendental distinction is between the ways in which things (empirical objects) can be 'considered' at the metalevel of philosophical reflection rather than between the kinds of things that are considered in such reflection."[23] Allison admits that sometimes Kant's language sounds as if he is committed to the two worlds view and in certain places there even seems to be no way around the fact that Kant really is committed to such a view (KTI, 31; KTF, 138). Nevertheless, Allison argues that we should adopt the two aspects view of Kant.

Where does Hegel stand on this? It cannot be shown that Hegel understands the distinction between a two worlds and a two aspects view with all the refinement of a contemporary scholar like Allison, but I think it is very definitely the case that Hegel is attacking a two worlds view, the standard view of what Kant holds, and that Hegel is arguing for what is basically a two aspects view. Hegel rejects the existence of another world, a supersensible world, a true world, a beyond, or whatever we wish to call it. The other world, or the distinction between two worlds, for Hegel, is nothing but a product of thought. It is the result of a distinction that is posited by consciousness. It is a conception, a different perspective, another aspect, a construction. There is nothing behind the curtain unless we go behind it ourselves so that there may be something there to be seen (PhS, 87–9, 102–3/GW, IX, 89–90, 101–2; L, 91–2/SW, VIII, 133).

Now, of course, Hegel's whole thrust here—and insofar as we do reject a two worlds for a two aspects view we play right into his hands—is to deny that the thing-in-itself can be unknown. If the thing-in-itself is not an entity in a distinct ontological realm, if it is just a different aspect of, a different way of conceiving, a different perspective on the sensible object, then, Hegel wants to know, what can there be here that is not known? Nothing is more easily known. We abstract away everything sensible, all content, and we are left simply with a conception—a conception of a bare it, the contentless concept of an object. What could more easily be known?

At this point, Hegel says, we have moved from consciousness on to self-consciousness (PhS, 103/GW, IX, 102). This is so because we see that the thing-in-itself, the inner, the kingdom of laws, is a construction of consciousness. Self-consciousness grasps appearances-for-consciousness as well as the thing-in-itself, which we now see is just another kind of appearance-for-consciousness. The content of self-consciousness is completely within consciousness. We have—though the consciousness there on the stage does not see all of this yet—a transcendental unity of apperception. All objects are within this unified consciousness, as for Kant, but in opposition to Kant, there is no unknown thing-in-itself. The transcendental illusion involved here, then, is not what Kant thought it was. It is not that—in trying to go beyond experience, in trying to know the whole of nature, in assuming that nature is a unified and consistent kingdom of laws—we mistakenly claim to know the thing-in-itself which must remain unknown. The transcendental illusion is rather that—in going behind the curtain, in constructing the thing-in-itself, the beyond, the kingdom of laws—we do not notice that it is we ourselves who do the constructing and that nothing is more easily known than what is constructed.[24]

We still must finish dealing with the various possible meanings that the term "kingdom of laws" might have. I said earlier that it reminds me of Kant's notion of a kingdom of ends. And, indeed, I think we can now see that there is at least a strong parallel between these two kingdoms. In the *Fundamental Principles of the Metaphysic of Morals,* Kant says that a kingdom is a union of different rational beings in a system of common laws. A kingdom of ends is a situation in which we abstract from the private interests of individuals and conceive their universal and rational ends combined in a systematic whole— including these rational beings as ends in themselves. A kingdom of ends, then, would be similar to a kingdom of laws in that both involve a system of laws, though in one case we have moral laws and in the other case natural laws (FP, 50/KGS, IV, 433). We must also notice that in a kingdom of ends, each individual is the source of these rational moral laws—the source of the categorical imperative. Thus each individual, Kant says, is a supreme lawgiver (FP, 49–50/KGS, IV, 432–3). Individuals, Hegel would say, are also supreme lawgivers in the realm of natural laws—they construct the kingdom of laws. Even Kant holds that the understanding is the "lawgiver of nature" (CPR, A126–7).

Furthermore, these two kingdoms must be brought into reconciliation. In the *Fundamental Principles,* Kant suggests that the kingdom of nature and the kingdom of ends should be united. In the "Transcendental Dialectic" of the *Critique of Pure Reason,* he says that ideas of reason are to make possible a transition from the concepts of nature to practical concepts. In the section on the "Postulates of Pure Practical Reason" in the *Critique of Practical Reason,* Kant says that the realization of the highest good requires the harmony of morality and nature—and that this is called the "kingdom of God." (FP, 56/ KGS, IV, 439; CPR, B386, A569–B598; CPrR, 115, 129–30, 133/KGS, V, 111, 124–5, 128). Much of this will only become clear as we proceed, but for it eventually to do so we must begin to notice a series of connections. It is very important to see Kant's influence on Hegel in these matters. Unless we do so, Hegel's thought will seem much more scattered, arbitrary, and aimless than it is. It will be especially important to notice that Hegel pays a great deal of attention to the "Transcendental Dialectic" of the *Critique of Pure Reason* and to the "Postulates of Pure Practical Reason" in the *Critique of Practical Reason*, that is, to sections that especially deal with the reconciliation of nature and morality. This is an issue, we will see, that Hegel takes up and returns to again and again in the *Phenomenology*: here in "Force and the Understanding," again in "Unhappy Consciousness," in the second half of the chapter on "Reason," and in the last part of the chapter on "Spirit." Hegel wants to weaken hard and fast boundaries between the natural realm and the spiritual (moral, cultural, political, religious) realm. He wants to reconcile these two realms in a more thoroughgoing way than Kant did. Consequently he returns to these issues at several different levels of his thought.[25]

To take the first step in trying to understand all of this, then, we must see that the connection between the "Transcendental Dialectic" and the "Postulates of Pure Practical Reason" is not unconnected to Hegel's rather mysterious notion in "Force and the Understanding" of an inverted world. He says that what in one world is the North Pole, in the other becomes the South Pole, what is black becomes white, what is sweet becomes bitter [*sauer*], and what is justice becomes crime (*PhS*, 97/*GW*, IX, 97–8). This is extremely obscure, but one thing that is quite clear is that it mixes the moral and the natural. Hegel also says that we have *two* supersensible worlds here. One of them he explicitly identifies as the kingdom of laws, which thus refers to Kant's notion in the "Transcendental Dialectic" of a supersensible realm behind the unity of the totality of nature. The other supersensible world Hegel does not identify, but it would certainly seem to be the noumenal realm of freedom behind the moral agent dealt with in Kant's moral writings (*PhS*, 96/*GW*, IX, 96).[26] These two realms, we have seen, must be brought together. How does this occur? In the "Postulates of Pure Practical Reason," the highest good requires this reconciliation. Kant says that the highest good for human beings, of course, requires virtue. But it also requires happiness. A life without happiness simply could not be considered to be the highest good for a human being. The trouble is, though, that virtue and happiness would seem to be irreconcilable. Happiness, for Kant, is a natural phenomenon that requires the regular satisfaction of our needs, interests, and desires. But to be virtuous, we certainly cannot be determined by—it is even unlikely that we can be determined in accordance with—needs, interests, or desires. We must be determined by the moral law. If we lived solely in one world, then, virtue and happiness would be irreconcilable. Only if we live in two worlds, Kant thinks, can they be reconciled. Virtue will not likely lead to happiness in the ordinary world of natural laws and causal determinism. But if we think of ourselves as also living in a noumenal world, Kant says, then virtue could lead to happiness if mediated by an Author of nature; and indeed, Kant goes on to argue that we must postulate a God who sees to it that nature is ordered such that our desires are satisfied (and thus that we can be happy) while acting virtuously (CPrR, 111–19, 128–33/KGS, V, 107–15, 124–8). At any rate, Hegel's notion of an inverted world, I suggest, grows out of Kant's concept of two opposed worlds: one of freedom, the other of nature; one of autonomy, the other of determinism; one of virtue, the other of happiness— two worlds that require a God to invert one into the other.

If Hegel rejects Kant's notion that the thing-in-itself is unknown, if he rejects the existence of two worlds, as we have seen that he does, then it follows that it will be impossible for him to accept a noumenal realm beyond and different from the phenomenal realm. If this is so, then we would expect—and we will see it confirmed as we proceed in the *Phenomenology*— that Hegel will not accept a realm of morality sharply distinguished from a realm of nature, nor of practical reason separate from theoretical reason. If we are supreme legislators in both the natural and the moral sphere, if we construct both of these realms, it is not very likely that we will ultimately be able to keep them apart. And so the Kantian opposition between two worlds, which gives rise to an inverted world, in Hegel's view, is a mistake that can and must be corrected.

Hegel says that we must eliminate the tendency to handle such differences by splitting, creating different elements, different worlds. Instead, we must grasp such differences as conceptual relations—as *inner* difference, difference within a unity (PhS, 98–9/GW, IX, 98). And that, if we pursue it far enough, will lead us to the absolute, which, after all, is all of reality, all difference, within a unity. An inverted world results from concepts that are too limited, that are not complex enough to grasp all of reality. Reality is too rich, it always exceeds, is other than, different from, contradicts, inverts, our concepts. All of this will become progressively clearer as we proceed.

2

Self-Consciousness
and the Other

I. Self-Consciousness

We have now arrived at "self-consciousness," which is Hegel's term for
the Kantian notion of a transcendental unity of consciousness, the
notion that in knowing its object, consciousness need not go outside itself.
All objects are within my consciousness; they are objects-of-my-consciousness. They have been constituted by my consciousness and are unified by my
consciousness. The way that Hegel puts it is to say that self-consciousness
"has a double object: one is the immediate object, that of sense-certainty
and perception, which however *for self-consciousness* has the character of a
negative; and the second, viz. *itself*, which is the true *essence*" (*PhS*, 105/GW,
IX, 104). What Hegel means by the claim that for self-consciousness the
object is negative is that in itself the object is taken to be nothing—it is
nothing but a thing-for-my-consciousness. Self-consciousness takes itself to
be the thing of significance. *I* am what is important and essential; the object
is nothing but a thing-for-me. Looking back to "Force and the
Understanding," we might say that self-consciousness takes itself to be the
lord who reigns over the kingdom of laws, that is, who reigns over all of natural reality that it has constructed. It is all nothing but my object. The trouble, however, is that my kingdom contains not only inanimate objects, but
other human beings as well. Or perhaps we are getting ahead of ourselves;
my kingdom contains other self-consciousnesses. Perhaps that is even to go
further than can be justified at this stage; it contains others who merely
claim to be self-consciousnesses.

Put in different language, it is Hegel's view that Kant has on his hands a fundamental contradiction between theoretical reason and practical reason. Practical reason gives us the categorical imperative, one form of which requires that we treat humanity in every case as an end, never as a means only (F, 46/KGS, IV, 428; CPrR, 90/KGS, V, 87). The moral law prohibits us from treating persons as things, as objects, as mere means to be used toward our ends. But what does theoretical reason imply if not that I have constructed all experience, that it is my object? And if it is *my object*, what legitimate objection can there possibly be to treating it *as my object*, as a mere means to my ends?

Kant's way out of this, of course, is the unknown thing-in-itself. If there were only one world, there would be no way out. But if there are two, and if we construct only the realm of phenomenal appearance, if there is a second realm, a noumenal realm, then Kant can argue that insofar as persons are part of the noumenal sphere they are, and must be treated as, ends in themselves. Kant says one has "knowledge of himself though inner sense and consequently only through the appearance of his nature.... But beyond ... these mere appearances, he necessarily assumes something else as its basis, namely, his ego as it is in itself.... He must reckon himself as belonging to the intellectual world" (F, 70/KGS, IV, 451; see also F, 71–4/KGS, IV, 452–5).

But this will not work. As we have seen, for Hegel, we must reject the notion of two worlds and we must reject the notion of an unknown thing-in-itself. The thing-in-itself is as much our construction as is the phenomenal world of appearance. If that is the case, then what legitimate objection can we possibly raise when theoretical reason takes all of reality as its object, when it is imperial, dominating, oppressive of others, fundamentally at odds with the obligations of practical reason? If the other is nothing but my object, nothing in itself, then even slavery, it would seem, would be a likely consequence of theoretical reason, and we will simply have to face this problem.

If we look inside, Hume insisted, we find nothing but a flux of changing sensations, images, and feelings. We never experience a unified self. In "Sense-Certainty," Hegel argued that language cannot even indicate such a self. If we reject an unknown thing-in-itself, if we reject the existence of a noumenal realm, there will be no way to establish the existence of a transcendental self above and beyond the empirical self. We will just have to give up such a notion.

Yet, to account for ordered experience, we saw in chapter 1 above, we must presuppose a threefold synthesis of the imagination and a transcendental unity of apperception—we must, for Kant, presuppose a unified self. Without a unified self, we could not have unified experience. Even for Hegel we must presuppose a unified self. But for Hegel there can be no *transcendental* self—an unknown thing-in-itself residing in a realm apart. A transcendental self does not exist behind the curtain of appearance just patiently waiting there to help us out.[1] There is nothing at all behind the curtain—unless we project something behind it. For Hegel as for Kant we must presuppose a unified self, but for Hegel it is *we* who *presuppose* it. We construct it. If it is the case that all of reality—the thing-in-itself as well as appearance—is constructed, and if reality contains not just objects but self-consciousnesses, then sooner or later we are going to have to admit that self-consciousness, the self, cannot be a simple unity that is just there, given, unproblematically assumed. We are going to have to admit that it too is constructed.

But if the self is merely a construction, if we concede this, what reality can it have? For Hegel's idealism, this is a problem in general. What reality does *anything* have? What we have seen in "Force and the Understanding" is that we construct reality—we construct the thing-in-itself. Or, put another way, our *recognition* of a thing makes it real. After all, we could even say that this was Kant's view of experience. For Kant, recognition was the third moment of the threefold synthesis of the imagination. Subsuming representations under categories gives us recognition, it allows us to acknowledge, to construct, to know, the object.[2]

Hegel's claim that recognition constructs reality is not without problems that we will have to wrestle with and explain, but right at this point it gives us a particular problem. If the self is constructed through recognition, then it definitely cannot be the case that I construct my self, certainly not if Hume is correct in holding that nothing but the flux of the empirical self ever appears to me. If no unified self ever appears to me, then I obviously cannot recognize such a self, and if I cannot recognize it, how could I have constructed it?

It must be, then, it can only be, that the construction of my self is dependent on the other. The other must construct me. Indeed, for Hegel, "Self-consciousness exists in and for itself when, and by the fact that, it so exists for another; that is, it exists only in being acknowledged" (*PhS*, 111/*GW*, IX, 109). For self-consciousness to be real, it must at the very least be recognized by another. How else can it be something objective—something more than a mere fancy? There is no other way once we have given up the unknown thing-in-itself.

The other, of course, even less than I, can find in me a unified self beyond the flux of the empirical self. What the other can do, however, is recognize and thus constitute me as a master, or a monarch, or a citizen, or an individual, or something else of the sort. It is certainly true that besides being a reality for itself, the self is also a reality *for-others*, and thus I must admit that at least in part my self is constructed by others.

However, this will lead to even greater problems. If I alone lack self-certainty, if I alone have difficulty in being sure of myself, what will happen if the other disagrees with whatever positive self-assessment I can muster?

What if others take me to be not at all a subject but merely an *object*-of-their-self-consciousness—the view that all self-consciousnesses tend to take of each other?

Despite all these problems, we must see that Hegel knows what he is doing and where he is going. Let me try to explain. We have started to see how radical an idealist Hegel is. It is not only phenomenal appearance that is constructed by consciousness; the thing-in-itself is also constructed by consciousness. It would seem that we are headed toward a radical subjective idealism. It would seem that Hegel has eliminated all external anchors that might keep his idealism from imploding inward into solipsism. He refuses to shore up his idealism by appealing to an outside—to an unknown thing-in-itself. There is nothing but consciousness and its objects. How then do we avoid radical subjectivity and solipsism? The key to an answer is already here, namely, *others*. On the one hand, others are nothing, nothing but objects-of-my-consciousness—my constructions. The other, then, is radically immanent. The other is thus perfectly compatible with idealism. At the same time, however, the other is also the beginning of a solution to the problem of solipsism. I am dependent on this other for recognition. I am only a self-consciousness *for-another*. Without the other I could not exist as a solid self. The other, then, is part of my essence. The self that constitutes all of reality, in short, could not exist without the other. This will allow us to avoid solipsism, as we shall see, but in the meantime it generates even further problems.

If self-consciousness fundamentally depends on an other, if the transcendental unity of apperception is fundamentally for-another, can we really claim then that it is unified, autonomous, independent? Haven't we introduced heteronomy into our concept of the transcendental unity of consciousness? How can we possibly avoid this conclusion? The only way to avoid it, we will eventually see, will be to deny that consciousness is to be understood as individual consciousness. We will be forced to move on to spirit—to a cultural consciousness—where I and the other in our very essence are parts of one spiritual or cultural unity. We have no other option. We certainly cannot, for Hegel, abandon unified consciousness. Kant has shown us why. We cannot deny that we have experience that is ordered and unified. And, as we have seen (in the first section of chapter 1), Kant shows us that it is impossible to have unified experience, a unified object, without a unified consciousness. The object would not be a single object that is my object, a single experience that is my experience, without a single unified "I." If this I, then, contains an other that it depends on for recognition, depends on for its reality, then the other cannot really—cannot essentially—be other.

The quickest and cheapest way to handle this problem might seem to be to deny the other, negate it, make it inessential and irrelevant. In fact, as we have seen, theoretical consciousness has a strong tendency in this direction, and, indeed, this is exactly what the master will try to do to the slave. But if we are dependent on the other in essence, then in negating the other, we will negate *ourselves*. If our reality depends on recognition by an other, and we consider that other a nobody, an inessential nothing, how important, significant, or real can the other's recognition make us? In fact, the very opposite would seem to be the case. The *more* important, significant, and essential we consider the other, the more real the other's recognition can make us.

This will all give rise to a great deal of conflict that will play itself out around a connected series of problems: how do we get consciousnesses capable of granting each other solid recognition so that we can have solid selves that are not mere inessential objects? We will finally have to admit that I and the other are equally and essentially parts of a larger consciousness—that we are not related heteronomously but are internally related as members of a single community. We will be driven beyond individual consciousness to spiritual or cultural consciousness. We will find that we are formed by the recognition that institutions like the family, law, the state, and religion can give us. Ultimately we will need the absolute. Only then will we achieve recognition with enough scope and substance to give us solid reality and secure self-certainty without heteronomy.

Robert R. Williams has set out some very interesting obstacles that are quite relevant to the interpretation of Hegel that I will develop. I want to indicate from the start how I will try to step around these obstacles. Williams points out that one prominent reading of Hegel sees his theory of Geist or spirit as a direct descendant of Kant's transcendental ego and thus sees Hegel's philosophy as transcendental philosophy. This is a view, Williams argues, that overlooks Hegel's severe criticism of transcendental philosophy.[3] From the start, I want to make it clear that in my view, while Hegel is out to give us something very much like a transcendental deduction of the absolute, as I have outlined this in the introduction, I do not at all think that Hegel is out to give us a deduction of a transcendental ego, that is, of Kantian individual consciousness.

At any rate, the problem with claiming that Geist is a descendent of the transcendental ego, as Williams sees it, has to do with the ontological character of the transcendental ego. This ego requires a referent or carrier. If it is taken to be the human being, the result is a left Hegelian interpretation that will end up in a historical and cultural relativism that surrenders objectivity and universality. To avoid this sort of relativism, right Hegelians reject the identification of the transcendental subject with the human subject and work out a theological interpretation of Geist as God. This avoids historicism and relativism but it turns Hegel into a metaphysician like Aristotle or Plato and results in a dogmatism fundamentally at odds with the transcendental method, which even for Kant was designed to avoid the unprovable claims of traditional metaphysics.[4]

Williams argues that Hegel would reject both of these approaches, and I agree. There is a third possible interpretation of Geist—a social-intersubjective interpretation—which Williams wants to support. I would call this a cultural interpretation and, if I correctly understand Williams, I agree with him that this is Hegel's approach. The problem with this interpretation, Williams thinks, is that it tends to contradict Hegel's idealism, which, as Williams understands it, denies the ontological transcendence of the other and thus tends toward solipsism.[5] I think we can get around this problem if we can get beyond the individual subject. If so, then we can avoid solipsism while still accepting that the reality of the other is established through recognition, thus that it is not transcendent but immanent, and thus that it is perfectly compatible with idealism. In other words, if the other were taken to be merely mine, *merely* an object-of-my-individual-consciousness, we would be headed toward solipsism. If the other were taken to be radically or transcendently other, we would be headed back toward an unknown thing-in-itself. But if we get beyond the individual subject, if we come to see that the ego and the other are essentially parts of a cultural consciousness—and ultimately an absolute consciousness—then we would have an intersubjective community, a culture, that constructs its world, its members, its institutions, its religion, an absolute, and finds all of this to be real. The reality of the other is not transcendent. It is established immanently through cultural recognition in a way that is perfectly compatible with idealism yet has no tendency to slide toward the solipsism of individual consciousness.

This approach avoids all right Hegelian theology, dogmatism, or metaphysics. Yet it is not like ordinary left Hegelianism, which rejects the absolute and tends toward individual consciousness. It is true, however, that my approach will mean accepting cultural relativism—everything including the absolute is culturally constructed. My task, then, will be to show that cultural relativism is widely misunderstood and that it will not erode but strengthen Hegel's thought. But we are getting ahead of ourselves. At this point we must notice that in "Lordship and Bondage" Hegel begins to address the problem of the objectivity of otherness. To understand this we must attend to desire.

II. Lordship and Bondage

At first sight we want to ask, what have desire, a fight for recognition, and lordship and bondage got to do with the transcendental unity of self-consciousness? As I have argued, Hegel starts with simpler forms of consciousness and then moves on to more complex ones. At each stage, he takes up a suitable example. We cannot deny that various forms of desire exist—desire for food, desire for other human beings (say, in the form of love), desire for recognition. Such desires obviously exist. The question, then, is, how they are possible? We want to get at the presuppositions necessary for desire to be possible and then to continue on to ask the same sorts of questions of more complex forms of experience. It is Hegel's view that self-consciousness is necessary for desire to be possible.

Moreover, Hegel takes desire as his example because desire undeniably exists in an especially wide variety of forms. Hegel's chapter on self-consciousness begins with desire for things like food and ends with desire for a relationship with God. Even for Kant, the faculty of desire directs us toward the highest good (CPrR, 114–17/KGS, V, 110–13). An examination of desire, then, can lead us toward totality. This is so because we desire what we lack. If the doctrine of internal relations is correct and the reality of things involves the totality of their relations—the absolute—then to cut things off from the absolute will create in them an absence or lack, which in those things with consciousness will stimulate desire. In order to prove the absolute, I have been arguing, the *Phenomenology* proceeds by abstracting from it, bracketing it, ignoring the interrelations among things. It takes up simple forms of experience, forms of experience that attempt to explain themselves without and apart from all the rest, that think themselves self-sufficient. And when each of these attempts fails, consciousness will experience a lack, an absence, that will provoke a need or desire, and this desire will nudge us further along toward an awareness of the connectedness of things and thus toward the absolute.

At any rate, we must see that desire fundamentally implies self-consciousness. Unlike sense-certainty, perception, or understanding, in desiring something—at least in the sort of desire that Hegel wants to study—we are not wrapped up with, absorbed in, concerned with the object out there for *its* sake. As Kojève says, desire brings us back to ourselves out of absorption in the object. In desiring food, our focus is on our-desire-for the food, on our hunger. The subject only wants the sensuous object as a means. It really seeks itself. When I say, "I want that object," the emphasis is on the "I want," not on the object. My desire is what is important; the object is a means to its satisfaction. The object is subordinate, negative. The object is nothing but an object-of-my-desire, an object-of-my-self-consciousness (*PhS*, 105/GW, IX, 103–4).[6] Moreover, in satisfying desire, we often negate the object we desire. If we desire food, we want to consume it. We want to assimilate it. We transform otherness into oneness, difference into identity. Only in negating the object—its independent otherness or difference—do we affirm ourselves. In negating the object we feel assured of our selves, our identity. The self-and-its-desire is more important than the object. The object is nothing but an object-of-my-desire (*A*, I, 36/*SW*, XII, 64–5).

Strangely enough—and this is another reason why desire is such an excellent example for Hegel to take up—at the same time that desire affirms the self and negates the other, it also does the very opposite, it affirms the other and denies the self. Desire's attempt to negate the other will not easily succeed in superseding the other, eliminating its otherness, making it simply an object-for-my-consciousness. Objects resist desire (*PhS*, 112/*GW*, IX, 110). We might even say that desire itself sets off the resistance of the world to our desire—certainly it does so in sexual desire and in laboring on the world. Desire wishes to have the other, control the other, use the other, but in fact it illuminates the difficulty in having, the resistance and independence of the other—it illuminates the other's reality. Even further, if my sense of importance, significance, and reality—in short, what Hegel calls "self-certainty"—is achieved through negating the other, then that means that my self-certainty depends on this other. It means that this other must be there for me to negate. And so I cannot simply negate it and be done with it. I will desire it again and again, so as to be able to negate it again, so as to continue to shore up my self-certainty. Desire desires the existence of the other as much as its negation. Desire, then, shows self-consciousness that there is an other and that this other has an independence that cannot easily be eliminated.

If I cannot gain self-certainty by negating the other, if I cannot even succeed in negating the other, then, Hegel suggests, self-consciousness must take a different tack: the other must negate itself. It must submit, recognize me, and deny itself. One way to achieve this would be by defeating the other in combat. This is the example that Hegel takes up in the *Phenomenology*. Fighting involves an especially human form of desire. In fighting, we risk our natural, animal life and the regular satisfaction of natural desire. We make all this secondary and unimportant—we put ourselves above it. We risk death in order to gain something higher. We seek human recognition—respect, honor, prestige. We demand that the other person submit and recognize us. As Hegel puts it, self-consciousness attempts to prove that its essential being is not just submergence in the expanse of life, but rather pure being-for-self (*PhS*, 114/*GW*, IX, 111).[7] Self-consciousness would like to prove that what it is for-itself, its own estimation of itself, its own self-certainty, is simply and purely what it is—really, ontologically, at rock bottom. It wants to prove that it is not dependent on anything else. It wants to prove that its own doing, its honor and prestige, its own opinion of itself, are what it really is. I am simply what I say I am, I am not for-another, I am not dependent on another, I do not need another, I do not care about any other. Except, unfortunately, what such a self-consciousness out to prove itself overlooks is that it needs the other to recognize in it the fact that it does not at all need the other.

At any rate, two such self-consciousnesses begin to fight. These two must risk their lives; they must choose recognition, prestige, and honor over mere life. Each self-consciousness takes itself to be real and important, not the other, and demands this recognition from the other. Several tries may be necessary before we get the case that Hegel wants to explore. If the combatants die, nothing happens. Even if one dies, it does not work. I cannot get recognition from a corpse. Life, then, we come to see, is just as important as the risking of life (PhS, 115/GW, IX, 112; PM, 172/SW, X, 283).[8] Sooner or later, one must risk his[9] life and win the fight. The other must finally back away from the threat of death, prefer life, prefer natural desire, not care about prestige, like an animal, and submit to the winner. We then have a master and a slave, or a lord and a bondsman. This is the case that Hegel wants to study.

The master becomes an independent or self-dependent consciousness— a consciousness purely for-itself. The master risked his life and won. He has made himself what he is. He is the one who is real and important. He does not admit to a dependence upon anything. He has asserted himself, proven himself, wrested recognition from the other in battle. The master no longer even has to sacrifice his natural desires. They are satisfied for him without any work or effort on his part. The slave is put to work and satisfies the master's desires. We have a division of labor and a separation of work and enjoyment. The slave works and the master enjoys. And, of course, in winning, as well as continuously through the slave's work and subservience, the master gets the recognition he won. The master's self-certainty, importance, and truth are continually affirmed.

The slave, on the other hand, becomes a dependent consciousness. He gets no recognition. He refused to risk his life. He preferred mere life and the satisfaction of natural desire. But his desires do not get satisfied. He just toils for the master's satisfaction. In himself he is nothing, nothing but a thing-for-the-master. The slave finds his essence, his reality, his definition, outside himself in the other—the master.

But then we get the profound reversal that makes Hegel's master-slave dialectic so classic (PhS, 116–17/GW, IX, 113–14). This reversal is hinted at in Diderot's *Rameau's Nephew*, where the main character implies that a master dependent on a subordinate is really *lower* than the subordinate. Such a master is subservient to a nobody; whereas the subordinate at least is subservient to a somebody.[10] At any rate, Hegel's master is not the independent consciousness he thinks he is. He is dependent on the slave for recognition as well as for the work that now satisfies his every need and desire. The master does little for himself. He has given himself over to the slave. Moreover, what truth, confirmation, self-certainty, can the slave, this inessential reality, this nothing, this object, give the master? The master is not pure being-for-self.

The master is radically *for-another,* dependent on that other—and on an other who is nothing. The master's reality and importance, his essentiality, then, become hollow and inessential.

For the slave, on the other hand, it is the master who is taken to be real and important, while the slave, even for himself, is taken to be unimportant and inessential. Fear and work, however, transform the slave. In the earlier combat, the slave backed away in fear from the risk of death. Now the slave fears death daily at the hands of the master. This permeates the slave's entire being and, as Hegel tells us, "Fear of the lord is . . . the beginning of wisdom" (*PhS,* 117–18/*GW,* IX, 114). Fear forces the slave's consciousness back upon itself. The slave interiorizes, deepens, and becomes self-referent—far more so than does the master. Fear of death shows the slave his self-importance. It pushes him toward being-for-himself—in fact, Hegel says, toward *"pure being-for-self"* (*PhS,* 117/*GW,* IX, 114).

Second, the slave is transformed through work. The master originally won the combat, we might say, through his control of nature (natural implements, weapons, tools of war) and through his control of natural desires (controlling his fear of death). The slave did not as effectively control nature (weapons and tools of war) and remained subservient to natural desire (he feared to risk his life). Thus he ended up subordinate to the master. Labor, however, overcomes such subordination. Labor is not subservient to the natural—it works on it, transforms it, controls it. The slave transforms nature to suit his purposes and desires. Moreover, labor requires that desire be restrained, checked, that it wait till the end of the labor process (*PhS,* 118/*GW,* IX, 115). Lacking such discipline, we do not labor, we just grab. Thus the slave transcends the natural and natural desire. Both nature and desire are controlled and made subordinate to self-consciousness's own ends. In this way, the slave surpasses the master. For Hegel, the slave does not rise up and overthrow the master. He develops interiorly beyond the master. The slave—not unlike much of the modern feminist movement—develops beyond the master by changing perspectives, revaluing values, teaching us a different meaning of independence, self-determination, accomplishment, being-for-self through being-for-another.

Furthermore, through work the slave proves himself more than a nothing. The slave asserts himself, overcomes the resistance of obstacles; he objectifies his ideas, plans, and purposes in the world. He accomplishes things. And he can recognize himself in his product—see it as his own doing, his expression, his creation. The slave can start to become aware of himself, his powers, and his abilities. The master may ignore the slave's objectification, deny it recognition, may even claim the slave's doing as his own, may even persuade the slave of this, but despite all of this the slave's objectification leaves something permanent and objective there before us all.

Notice that there is a dual movement here. There is an externalization or objectification. An idea or purpose is actualized in the world. There is also an internalization. The master from outside defines the slave as one who toils. The slave internalizes this and becomes interiorly what he was defined as externally. Moreover, in this process of internalization the external force is transformed. The external force produces a turning inward, a discipline, a sublimation, which becomes an accomplishment, a creation. This transformation is even the beginning of a form of freedom. How can this be freedom when the slave is still a slave? Because the external repression is transformed into an internal discipline, and self-discipline is the beginning of self-determination. All we need to move on to a Kantian form of freedom is that this self-determination become a *rational* self-determination. This model is worth noting because we will see it again and again. It is Hegel's view—he states it explicitly in the *Philosophy of History*—that it is not so much *from* slavery as *through* slavery that human beings achieve freedom (PH, 407/PW, II, 875).

In all that we have seen so far, there are two crucially important concepts that we must be clear about: objectification and recognition. All individuals, even cultures, even God, Hegel thinks, have a drive to objectify themselves in whatever confronts them externally and to recognize themselves in the external object. In the *Aesthetics*, Hegel says that we can see this in something as simple as a child skipping stones across a pond. Children take joy in the fact that they alter things and see themselves, their own doing, in that alteration. This drive runs throughout our activities, right up to art. The same would also be true of labor as well as of cultural, political, and religious activity. We alter external things in order to strip them of their foreignness, their independence, their alienation. We seek to recognize ourselves, our own doing, in the external thing—and thus we humanize it (A, I, 31–2/SW, XII, 58–9). We lift the external world out of its foreign, independent naturality. We absorb it into the spiritual, the cultural. We recognize ourselves in it and are at home.

Also, it is only through this very same process that we bring what is within us (our powers, capacities, ideas, and values) to reality. An engineer who does not build bridges or an artist who does not paint pictures—but only imagines them—is no engineer or artist. They must objectify, express, realize, their powers, capacities, values, and ideas in an actual bridge or painting. We make explicit, we develop what is within us, only by objectifying it. We bring what is inner into sight, into our sight and the sight of others, where it can be recognized (or fail to be recognized). It is the same for cultures and religions.

The only way a thing becomes real is by being objectified and recognized. We might find this idealist notion a bit hard to accept, but if we think about it, we can at least find very persuasive examples. Nations, for example, do not seem to become real until their ideals become objectified in concrete institutions and widely recognized. Imagine a coup that establishes a new government while the members of the old government flee to France to set up a government in exile. Which is the real government? What makes a government real—if we think it is? It is its ability to do something significant (alter the world, objectify itself) and keep the recognition of enough people. Otherwise it is just not the real government any longer and no one will think it is.

If we draw all of this together, the following emerges from what we have seen so far in the section on self-consciousness. If we are to get beyond the self as a mere Humean flux, which is all that appears to us, if we are to get a solid, unified, independent self, then it must be constructed. But if it is constructed, how can we have any self-certainty; how can we believe in ourselves? The answer is: only if this self objectifies itself, accomplishes things, and gains the recognition of others. It is an illusion to think, as the master did, that one can have self-certainty by oneself alone. However, recognition is not without its own problems. We are, after all, constructed by the other. The slave is constructed by the master and the master is constructed by the slave. And so what is recognition by the other worth? The master did not think the slave's recognition was worth anything from the start and this ends up undermining the master himself. The slave, on the other hand, never expected any recognition from the master. Doing something of significance, accomplishing some great labor, objectifying ourselves, we have said, can objectively call for recognition, but we are going to need a recognizer other than the arrogant master who will not even glance our way. Hegel's task throughout the rest of the *Phenomenology* will be to seek out forms of objectification and recognition that have greater solidity and scope so as to shore up constructed reality—to keep it from imploding into the solipsistic illusoriness of subjective idealism.

III. Theory and the Object

It is the master, more than the slave, who exemplifies a Kantian transcendental unity of self-consciousness. The master takes himself to be a single, unified, independent, autonomous consciousness for whom all objects are objects-of-his-consciousness, objects that are constituted by and exist within the unity of his consciousness, objects that apart from his consciousness as they are in themselves are completely unknown—or, as Hegel would put it, are nothing.

Moreover, once the master is able to put the slave to work for him, the master need not deal with the gritty resistance of things; he need not exert himself against the independence of objects. The master's relationship to things can be theoretical, cognitive, conceptual. Reality, for Hegel, is established through both recognition and objectification. The master exemplifies recognition far more than objectification. So too for Kant, if we experience an object, it is our recognition or categorization that makes it real and objective. The third moment of the threefold synthesis, after all, is the synthesis of recognition in a concept (CPR, A103). Again, this is all very cognitive, theoretical, conceptual—this is a master's way of relating to things. Work, exertion, activity, objectification, on the other hand, are slavish ways of relating to things that the master does not deign to concern himself with.

The master, we might say, represents a principle of subjective idealism, which recognizes nothing outside itself, and if, as Hegel argues, we must reject Kant's unknown thing-in-itself, master consciousness will slowly implode into solipsism. Whereas the slave, we might say, introduces us to objective idealism. For objective idealism, all is just as much an object-for-consciousness, but the slave relates actively and practically to things that resist and show independence. The slave produces objects that remain solid and last. The praxis of the slave continually finds itself over against something real. The master denies the reality of whatever he might relate to and thus shrinks into himself.

It is the slave who teaches us how to understand objects. He does not take himself to be superior to them as the master did—after all he even sees himself as an object. The slave works on objects and transforms them to suit human need. And in doing so, he gets beyond a slavish dependence upon objects. Natural objects no longer dominate him. The object is no longer a force that willy-nilly causes him to need and desire the object. Work requires that desire be checked, restrained, and disciplined. Through work the slave controls the object, forms it in accordance with his own ideas and purposes—in short, he makes it an object-of-his-consciousness. And he does this not in a merely theoretical or contemplative fashion, but actively through labor that produces a solid and lasting result that is the objectification of the slave's ideas and purposes. It is practical consciousness that achieves what theoretical consciousness boasted only it could do.

Hegel is an idealist, and idealists have difficulty with the object. The object tends to collapse into subjectivity in a way that violates all the instincts of ordinary consciousness. Moreover, if, as I have suggested in the introduction, Hegel is going to end up holding that God is a cultural construction, then he would appear to be in even worse shape than Berkeley, who, inconsistent as it was, could at least try to appeal to a transcendent God to get some sort of solidity for the object.[11] Since Hegel has also rejected the Kantian unknown thing-in-itself, and thus lost any possibility for anchoring objects in some sort of external ground in this way,[12] Hegel would seem to be in a fix. For Hegel, there is no outside to appeal to. All reality is immanent. How then do we keep the bubble of consciousness from collapsing into the solipsism of our own subjectivity? If we are going to go beyond Kant, we have a problem with the object. We have got to ground this object—anchor it, shore it up—but this can only be done immanently from within consciousness.

It is the slave and his labor that ground the object. The slave shows us a concrete, solid, gritty, resistant object. There is no way to deny this. The slave works on it, sweats over it, wrestles with it, suffers with it, and transforms it to satisfy human needs and desires. Labor becomes a key epistemological category. It transforms, constructs, constitutes—and not mere Kantian appearance, but solid reality. And it does so not just in an abstract theoretical sense; it actively produces an object that is stable, lasting, fixed, and objective—both for the slave and for other people. It produces a solid object that satisfies needs and desires that would not otherwise be satisfied. The object the slave produces is a real object. Yet at the same time, the slave's object is his objectification, his creation, an object-for-his-consciousness—an object perfectly compatible with objective idealism.

IV. Theory and Power

Fanon says that under modern imperialism the master does not need recognition, only work.[13] The implication would seem to be that if masters are sufficiently powerful, then they need not depend on their slaves enough for a Hegelian reversal ever to occur. This, however, is to miss another most important implication of Hegel's master-slave dialectic, that concerning the relation of knowledge to power. The Kantian theoretical consciousness of the master claims to know, or to be on the way toward knowing, all that can be known. Everything else, certainly anything to do with the slave, would be irrelevant, unimportant, and inessential. The master marginalizes the slave, makes the slave a radical other, pushes the slave outside the bounds of significance. This marginalization of the other may itself turn on and undermine the master. The theoretical consciousness of the master makes radically totalizing claims—that all reality and significance belong to it, that it alone contains what is essential and true. It denies any reality, significance, or truth to the slave. But the master is wrong. Besides maintaining the master himself, the slave's labor even creates new reality. The master may try to deny this or take credit for it himself, but in the long run this becomes increasingly difficult because the practical consciousness of the slave constructs its truth in the form of an objectification that sits there and stares us in the face.

The Kantian consciousness of the master cannot avoid its negativity. If all objects are constructed by the transcendental unity of self-consciousness, then other *persons* will be also—and this inevitably implies power and domination. If this consciousness claims to contain all reality, it will inevitably marginalize others—deny them reality. The Kantian consciousness of the master claims to be innocent of all this; it claims to be merely theoretical, cognitive, contemplative. It is not an active and practical force like the lower form of consciousness belonging to the slave. But this simply is not the case. The Kantian consciousness of the master marginalizes and oppresses—it *is* a force. Furthermore, it is not only a force, but a negative force, whereas the lowly slave, as a force, is at least positive—the slave creates new reality.

Hegel's point here, I think, is that all theoretical knowledge, all understanding, inevitably marginalizes something or someone; and this sort of knowing is a power (L, 171–3/SW, VIII, 218–20). Moreover, it cannot be avoided. All we can do is become aware of it. Spinoza argued that all determination is negation.[14] To define is to set boundaries. To determine a thing is to cut it off from other spheres of being and to limit it. Anything finite must have such limits—only the absolute is total. To say what we are and what is valuable and significant about us is to say what we are not, what we leave outside, what we marginalize, what we take to be unimportant or less important, and this inevitably is to take a negative attitude to the other who is not like us.

In the *Philosophy of Mind,* Hegel claims:

> The principle of European mind is, therefore, self-conscious Reason which...opposes the world to itself, makes itself free of it, but in turn annuls this opposition, takes its Other...back into itself, into its unitary nature. In Europe, therefore, there prevails this infinite thirst for knowledge which is alien to other races. The European is interested in the world, he wants to know it, to make this Other confronting him his own...the European mind strives to make manifest the unity between itself and the outer world. It subdues the outer world to its ends with an energy which has ensured for it the mastery of the world (PM, 45/SW, X, 77–8; see also L, 88/SW, VIII, 129; PWHI, 78/PW, I, 92).

The Kantian consciousness of the master is a cultural product of Europe that first separates itself from the other, the object, the world, takes itself to be above it, and then seeks to claim that this other is its own, that it will know it, that it is master of it, that it is all and the other nothing. While this introduces the theme of ethnocentrism—the superiority of Europe to its others, something we will have to deal with in the proper place—notice at the same time that if imperial European reason cannot accept anything outside, anything unknown, anything not its own, then it will never be satisfied short of totality. We have a cultural drive that implies the absolute. Understanding this drive will be crucial to understanding our culture and will be key to the *Phenomenology*'s task of giving us a deduction of the absolute.

At the same time, though, just as the master creates a situation in which the slave undermines and subverts him, so I think we must be prepared to see that the imperial European absolute sets up a situation that invites its others to undermine and subvert it. The absolute, which is at the center of European identity, claims to be all of reality and it too will cover any short-comings with arrogance. It will deny that there is anything of significance outside itself; it will marginalize what it cannot accept, it will claim that what it does not understand does not amount to anything. If anything of significance does emerge outside Europe, it will claim that it already knew about it, or that it can come to know it better than the other can, or dismiss it in some other way.

At the same time, oddly enough, there is an enormous *humility* to the absolute—indeed, a humility that stems from its very arrogance. It must be everything, and if not, it can be nothing—certainly not the absolute. Thus, as soon as the other, which the absolute has cast as nothing, shows itself to be *something*, something other, something different, anything at all real that is not part of the absolute, well then the absolute is simply not absolute—not *all* of reality. This gives the other, the excluded and marginalized, an exceptional power to challenge the absolute, to undermine it, and to make itself central. If the absolute has been announcing far and wide its absoluteness, then the other, the excluded, when it steps out of the shadows to reveal its exclusion, gains center stage at the expense of the absolute. And a new absolute must be built that includes the other at its center.

Too many of Hegel's readers see only the arrogance of the absolute—its claim to be the totality of all reality systematically organized, fully realized, completely known, closed, finished, and sealed. That is to fail to understand Hegel. No system empowers the other, the outsider, the oppressed, the differ-ent, the marginalized, more than Hegel's.

However, as the other remakes the absolute with itself at the center, it too will leave an other or others outside, marginalized, inessential—any determination means negation. We must see that there is a tragic dimension to the absolute's humility. The other subverts the absolute and reconstructs the absolute with itself at the center. This new absolute, however, will also marginalize others who will in turn subvert this absolute. We can only make a place for the other, the slave, by going under ourselves, even if we ourselves began as slaves. The absolute is a cultural construction that sooner or later not only allows all others in, but demands their inclusion, demands it even despite itself. Moreover, we must see that the absolute, at least ultimately, demands this inclusion honestly and radically. It drives us to the inclusion of the other, not by forcing the other to assimilate to the absolute's standards (though it certainly tries this approach at first). It drives the other to objectify itself, create new reality, and gain recognition by the other's standards, at which point the other is included not in the existing absolute, which is transcended, but in a new, higher absolute. The absolute sacrifices itself to make the other absolute.

We have two opposed drives here. First, there is a drive for absolute totality, which claims to be all, which claims to master, comprehend, explain everything, and which negates as inessential all otherness. Second, we have the very opposite, a drive that denies this totality, subverts it, protests against its imperialism. It asserts a difference, an exception, an otherness that is not inessential; it thus subverts the absolute's absoluteness. Both of these drives are fundamental—one does not finally win out over the other. As soon as one drive triumphs, it incites the other—as if they were opposed poles of a magnet brought into range of each other.

But won't we finally achieve an absolute that is *absolute*—fixed, closed, final? Doesn't everybody know that this is what Hegel is about? I will argue against such an interpretation. However, it is certainly true that Hegel does not dwell on the tragedy and humility of the absolute. And why should he? After all, he cannot jump over Rhodes. Why should Hegel be in a hurry to leap past his own age (PR, 11–13/SW, VII, 35–7)? He wants to live in his age; he wants to enjoy it. The next age will come soon enough. And it can only be brought about by the other. It cannot be done for the other by a benevolent master.

Hegel knows the next age is on its way: "Philosophy in any case always comes on the scene too late.... As the thought of the world, it appears only when actuality is already there cut and dried after its process of formation has been completed.... When philosophy paints its grey in grey, then has a shape of life grown old. By philosophy's grey in grey it cannot be rejuvenated but only understood. The owl of Minerva spreads its wings only with the falling of the dusk" (PR, 12–13/SW, VII, 36–7). The implication here is that when we understand our age, it is about over. When we have achieved our world and become content with it, it is nearing its end. Just as we have established, say, that all are free, just as our world has finally realized this principle that it has been struggling toward for centuries, just as it has been fully embraced in our consciousness and embodied in our institutions, someone will ask, What about us? If all are free, what about us? What about us black slaves? What about us women? What about us outside Europe in Africa, Asia, and Latin America? We have been ignored, overlooked, excluded from this absolute.

Todorov suggests that we have a great deal of difficulty linking otherness and equality. If we really do treat people as our equals, our tendency will be to deny their otherness, treat them as identical to us, assimilate them, see ourselves in them, and negate their own different reality. On the other hand, if we do recognize their otherness, their difference from us, then it will be very difficult to see them as our equals. We will tend to rank them—and probably as inferior. What is most difficult is to let the other be other, different, and yet see the other as our equal.[15] We must notice that Hegel comes pretty close to this. The other, the slave, at least ultimately, does not have to assimilate to the absolute of the master. The slave was pushed to at first, as the master tried to negate and marginalize the slave's otherness, but the slave finally subverts the absolute of the master. And the slave does this by asserting a difference, an otherness, which then is no longer ranked as inferior and unimportant, but is constructed as the center of a new absolute—an absolute in which this other comes to have a central place.

We need a certain amount of otherness. We also need a certain amount of identity. Equality requires identity—it is impossible without it. If we are all to be equally human, equally citizens, or equally anything else, there is something about us that must be taken to be the same, identical, in unity. Otherness or difference pushed too far, made fundamental and absolute, would mean that we all could not be equally human, equally citizens, or equally anything else. Identity, then, is necessary. But difference is also necessary. Too little difference or otherness would not make us all equally human or equally citizens; rather it would tend to assimilate the less powerful to the particular conception of humanity or citizenship enforced by the more powerful. To be equally a citizen or a human, to be just as much so as anyone else, one cannot be coerced into conforming to the mainstream; one must be as free as anyone else to be oneself, to be different, other, not homogeneously the same. This identity in difference, otherness in unity, is precisely what the absolute as a concept is supposed to capture—and we will follow it to see if it finally succeeds.

V. Stoicism and the Flight from Heteronomy

As we move on in the chapter on self-consciousness, it becomes increasingly clear that the theoretical consciousness of the master and the practical consciousness of the slave—both of them—are necessary and important. We cannot have one without the other—we are not being asked to choose one over the other. Hegel split them in two, into the master and the slave, for purposes of analysis. He did this because Kant separates these two forms of consciousness. Hegel, for his part, wants to criticize and ultimately to undermine this split. In the following sections of chapter IV of the *Phenomenology*—"Stoicism," "Scepticism," and "Unhappy Consciousness"—these two forms of consciousness fall into one consciousness.

"Stoicism," for Hegel, involves both master consciousness and slave consciousness. As Hegel puts it, we have a consciousness that aims to be free "whether on the throne or in chains" (*PhS*, 121/*GW*, IX, 117), a reference to two of the most famous Stoic philosophers, Marcus Aurelius and Epictetus—one an emperor, the other a slave. In Stoicism, consciousness turns away from the external world. The citizen of imperial Rome had lost all opportunity to participate in a public assembly where citizens themselves could be in control of important civic matters. The citizen had become a small cog in a big, complex, and impersonal machine (PCR, 156–7/GW, I, 369–70). In an important sense, all are slaves in Rome. All must serve the abstract concerns of a huge and far-flung empire. And they serve much as a slave does—they must be ruthlessly disciplined to serve effectively and they must sacrifice all personal concerns.[16] In such externally oppressive circumstances, consciousness is driven inward. It seeks peace of mind—what the Roman world called *ataraxia.* Stoicism achieves ataraxia in a peculiar way. It participates fully in the world, it rigorously and unflinchingly fulfills every duty to Rome, yet the inner person disengages, withdraws, and turns inward. The Stoic cuts off concern, desire, entanglement with the world, becomes emotionally uninvolved, and seeks inner peace. It is here that master consciousness begins to emerge. It is Stoic withdrawal that gains us the independence of the master. As we withdraw into thought alone, we are free and independent in that we are no longer constrained by the otherness of the world, we are above it, superior to it, despite the fact that as external persons we must continue to do our slavish duty in the world. Stoicism is a form of freedom that is possible in a time of oppression and bondage, Hegel says, as long as there is also a universal culture raised to the level of thought (PhS, 121/GW, IX, 118).

We still have, then, the imperial Kantian master, who first came on the scene as a theoretical consciousness out to assert itself, who could not stand otherness, who put the slave to work as soon as he could so that he himself would not have to deal with the gritty resistance of the world or wrestle with its natural obstacles. And here we begin to see, just a bit, the masterly and imperial dimension of Kantian *practical* reason. Stoic consciousness stands above the world—it withdraws, turns within, and finds a freedom above it all. It denies the world, the other, as heteronomous and inessential (PhS, 120–1/GW, IX, 116–17). It seeks a different, higher world. We have here, as for Kant, a theory of two worlds. Stoicism cuts itself off from the slavish and heteronomous determinism of the external world so as to be free of it. It severs itself from the concrete world. It is free in thought, in inner disengagement. Stoic freedom, Hegel thinks, is abstract (PhS, 122/GW, IX, 118).[17] As we proceed, we will see that this is also very much the sort of criticism that Hegel will develop against Kantian ethics.

VI. Scepticism and the Attack on the Transcendental Self

"Scepticism" pushes Stoic consciousness even further. Stoic freedom of thought and negation of the other are even more thoroughgoing in scepticism.

We get a more complete rejection of the world and a clearer vision of its inessentiality. Scepticism, Hegel argues, completes in thought the negation of the other begun in the victory of the master, and scepticism's negation of the other also results in a more thorough affirmation of the self and its freedom, at least for a brief moment, and then we get a reversal worse even than that of the master.

The arguments of sceptical philosophers were calculated to systematically sever all concern, attachment, or engagement—to suspend all belief in the world and its truth. Scepticism thought that if we could not be certain of anything, then we could not be committed to anything, therefore we would not be emotionally involved, and thus not determined or coerced by anything. In this way scepticism emancipates the self, disengages, and achieves ataraxia.[18] Epicureans had already attacked all determinism as a threat to ataraxia.[19] The sceptics go even further. Even commitment to philosophical truth binds us, compels us, determines us, and thus threatens ataraxia. Sceptics sought to demolish all philosophical arguments—arguments that this is true or that false—and thus to eliminate all possibility of coercion. Ataraxia, peace of mind, inner freedom above it all, then, could be achieved.

As Hegel puts it, "Sceptical self-consciousness thus experiences in the flux of all that would stand secure before it its own freedom as given and preserved by itself" (PhS, 124/GW, IX, 120). Compare this to a passage from Kant's *Critique of Pure Reason*: "In what we entitle 'soul,' everything is in continual flux and there is nothing abiding except...the 'I,' which is simple solely because its representation has no content" (CPR, A381). In other words, scepticism achieves the free, self-identical consciousness of the master, much as for Kant, by separating itself in thought from the flux of experience, from all content, and from any commitment it might have to it, so that it can abide—alone and secure—above it all.

There is, however, only one problem. For scepticism, much as for Kant, we must distinguish two selves: the self-identical consciousness above it all, which Kant calls the transcendental self, on the one hand, and as Hegel puts it, "the confused medley, the dizziness of a perpetually self-engendered disorder" (PhS, 124–5/GW, IX, 120), that is, the flux of the empirical self, on the other hand. By now, it should be clear that a noumenal or transcendental self, as opposed to an empirical self, simply cannot be established. There are not two worlds. There is no unknown thing-in-itself. These are merely our constructions. And so we must admit that the free, self-identical self of scepticism, or the transcendental self of Kant, are also constructions. And if it is the case for scepticism that *all* is under sceptical attack, then this consciousness that stands alone above it all must also come under attack. Moreover, it collapses under this attack just as readily as anything else does, and all we are left with, then, is the flux of the empirical self.

The collapse of this self-identical consciousness, Hegel suggests, leaves us in deep bewilderment. After all, it was this very self-identical, masterly, Kantian consciousness with which we launched the attack. How can we accept that it collapses under sceptical attack when without it we could not have launched the sceptical attack? Sceptical consciousness thus ends up a very confused and bewildered consciousness that keeps jumping from one of its forms to the other and then flops back again. As Hegel puts it, we have a "thoughtless rambling which passes back and forth from the one extreme of self-identical self-consciousness to the other extreme of the contingent consciousness that is both bewildered and bewildering" (*PhS*, 125/*GW*, IX, 120–1).

VII. Unhappy Consciousness and the Highest Good

What we need, then, Hegel suggests, is a new form of consciousness that brings together the two sides of sceptical consciousness. We need one consciousness with two modes: a self-identical, unchangeable mode and, in its other mode, a changeable, self-bewildering flux (*PhS*, 126/*GW*, IX, 122). The unchangeable consciousness is taken as essential and will slowly come to be seen as—be projected as—God. The changeable consciousness is taken as inessential.

Consciousness, then, tries to shake loose, free itself, from the inessential, changeable consciousness and to get to the essential and unchangeable. Consciousness thinks it is freeing itself from itself to get to an other. This other, however, is just as much consciousness's own essence. We are talking about Christianity here. Both sides are parts of the self. Consciousness can escape neither side. If it seeks one, it loses itself by abandoning the other. We have a struggle against an enemy, Hegel says, but the enemy is the self. To win is at the same time to lose (*PhS*, 127/*GW*, IX, 122). Christianity conceives human nature as a dual and a split nature. We have a natural-physical nature and a spiritual-supernatural nature—Adam was first formed out of clay and then a spirit was breathed into him. Both natures are part of our essence, but they are in conflict. To seek our highest fulfillment is to seek to satisfy our spiritual-supernatural nature, but that requires abandoning our natural-physical nature and denying our fleshly desires. On the other hand, to seek to satisfy our natural-physical desires is to abandon our higher spiritual-supernatural quest. Think of Augustine in the *Confessions*, who wants to stop lusting after women and convert to Christianity—but not quite yet.[20] He is torn in two directions, where every gain is a loss and every joy a suffering— in short, what we have here is an unhappy consciousness.

"Unhappy Consciousness" is one of the most obscure and complex sections in the *Phenomenology*. Hegel obviously intends his treatment to allude to various moments of Christian history, and commentators spend a good deal of effort establishing those connections and explaining the details. I am not going to do that. I have no special disagreement with the commentaries on this section. I think the *Phenomenology* is intended, like a novel, to allude to a lot of different things. What I want to argue is simply that one of the things—not the only one, but one of the things—that "Unhappy Consciousness" alludes to (and to my knowledge nobody has pointed it out yet) is the section of Kant's *Critique of Practical Reason* that deals with the postulates of pure practical reason. That is what I want to focus on.

For Kant, we said earlier, the highest good requires the reconciliation of virtue and happiness. The virtuous person must be happy if we are to have the highest good for human beings. But virtue and happiness would seem to be irreconcilable. Happiness, Kant thinks, requires the regular satisfaction of our needs, interests, and desires. But to be virtuous, we certainly cannot be determined by needs, interests, or desires. We must be determined by the moral law. If we lived solely in one world, then, there would be no reason to expect virtue and happiness to be reconcilable. Only if there are two worlds can we imagine such reconciliation, and only if we postulate—that is, Hegel will insist, only if we construct—a God who will see to it that nature is ordered such that while we act virtuously our desires will at the same time be satisfied so that we can also be happy (CPrR, 111–19, 128–33/KGS, V, 107-15, 124–8).

In discussing the highest good in the *Critique of Practical Reason*, Kant compares his own approach to that of the Stoics and the Epicureans. This, I suggest, helps explain why Hegel discussed Stoicism as he led up to "Unhappy Consciousness." However, Kant does not mention scepticism and Hegel does not allude to Epicureanism—or at least Hegel has not done so quite yet. Kant argues that both the Stoics and the Epicureans mistakenly identified virtue and happiness. The Stoics held that virtue was itself the highest good and they understood happiness merely as a consciousness of the possession of virtue. Epicureanism, on the other hand, held that furthering one's own happiness was virtue. It held that happiness was the highest good and that virtue was simply the means to achieve it (CPrR, 115–16/KGS, V, 111–12). Kant will not accept either of these forms of identifying virtue and happiness. Virtue and happiness are different things. Each belongs to a separate world, and the postulate of a God is necessary to reconcile them.

Let us see if this will help us understand "Unhappy Consciousness," which for Hegel strives to attain oneness with the unchangeable and thereby overcome its unhappiness. In doing so, it successively adopts three different strategies.

The first strategy is described as pure devotion, the infinite yearning of a pure heart certain of being recognized. It attempts to become one with the unchangeable through purity of thought and devotion. But it never actually succeeds. The unchangeable always remains an unattainable beyond (*PhS*, 130–2/*GW*, IX, 124–6). What Hegel has in mind here, I suggest, is Kant's notion of holiness. The ideal of holiness, Kant claimed a bit earlier in the *Critique of Practical Reason*, implies complete agreement of the will with the moral law. One would not even be tempted to be untrue to morality. One would be inclined to morality and would not even desire anything else. Such perfection, Kant claims, is an ideal that we should strive for, but at the same time it is impossible for any creature to attain (*CPrR*, 84–7/*KGS*, V, 81–4).

We must recognize that such holiness—never being inclined to anything but virtue, desiring nothing but virtue—would mean that achieving virtue would necessarily satisfy our desires and thus make us happy. We must also see that, in effect, this is the Stoic position. Achieving virtue is itself what makes us happy for Stoicism. The Stoic sage, Kant even says, was like a god in the consciousness of his excellence, a hero subject to no temptation to transgress the moral law (*CPrR*, 131–2, 132 n/*KGS*, V, 127, 127 n). We must also notice that Kant's own position is only slightly different from the Stoic position. Basically, Kant accepts the Stoic view, but only as an ideal, an ideal that he thinks can never be achieved. For Kant, we must seek only virtue. Like the Stoic, we must seek the perfect agreement of our will and desires with the moral law. For Kant, such holiness in which virtue would amount to happiness, however, can only be imagined as involving an endless approach. We must even postulate the immortality of the soul as well as a God to see to it that in seeking only virtue our desires would also be satisfied and thus that besides being virtuous we could also be happy (*CPrR*, 126–33/*KGS*, V, 122–30).

This is the position, I suggest, that Hegel is trying to echo in unhappy consciousness's first attempt to reach the unchangeable and to overcome unhappiness. Consciousness seeks unity with the unchangeable through devotion, purity of heart, purity of thought, an attempt which as for Kant involves endless progress toward a beyond that always remains unattainable.

When unhappy consciousness finds that devotion is not enough, then, for Hegel, it adopts a second strategy, that of desire and work (*PhS*, 132–4/*GW*, IX, 126–8). This, I suggest, is intended to echo Kant's discussion of Epicureanism—though Hegel certainly does not help us out by mentioning Epicurus. In the *Critique of Practical Reason*, we have seen, Kant argues that Epicurus identified virtue with happiness. Furthering—that is, desiring and working for—one's own happiness, for Epicurus, is virtue. Happiness is the highest good, and virtue is the means to procure it. Kant completely rejects Epicureanism. Seeking happiness has nothing to do with virtue (*CPrR*, 115–17/*KGS*, V, 111–12). Virtue and happiness are different things. They belong to two different realms and require a God to reconcile them.

Here Hegel digs in. He fundamentally disagrees with Kant's conception of happiness and cannot accept the notion that it is incompatible with virtue. For Kant, happiness means the satisfaction of inclinations, desires, needs, and so forth (e.g., *CPrR*, 129/*KGS*, V, 124). Hegel, on the other hand, understands happiness quite differently. He understands it much as Aristotle did. Virtue is to be sought as an end in itself, but also it *is* a means to happiness. Happiness is understood as a satisfaction that arises out of activities, activities that are virtuous and that are excellently performed (*PhS*, 375/*GW*, IX, 333). Even in something as simple as playing the flute, if we are any good at it, we will find it satisfying. And such satisfaction will tend to make us even better at playing it. And the better we are at it, the more we work at it, the more excellent we become at carrying out the activity, the more satisfaction we will get. It is a self-reinforcing circle. Moreover, the higher the activity, the more it accords with our rational nature, the higher the satisfaction that we can get from it (*NE*, 1097a–1098a, 1100b, 1174b, 1175a, 1176b, 1177a).

Thus, Hegel thinks that Kantian unhappy consciousness is deluding itself. It does not see that desire and work themselves can be satisfying and enjoyable. It does not see that to reconcile virtue and happiness it need not work for and desire an alien beyond in the hope of receiving happiness as a gift—in other words, we do not need Kant's postulated God to reconcile virtue and happiness for us (*PhS*, 132–3/*GW*, IX, 126–7). Through activity, through desire and work, unhappy consciousness achieves happiness itself. It is just that it refuses to accept responsibility for its own happiness. It thinks only the beyond could be responsible for it (*PhS*, 134/*GW*, IX, 127–8).

If we understand happiness correctly, Hegel is suggesting, we just do not have Kant's problem. Kant misunderstands virtue and happiness. He assigns each to a different realm such that virtuous activity will not get us to happiness. Thus, we need to postulate a God, a supersensible beyond, to reconcile them. In Hegel's view, such a God is a construction to solve a problem we should not have caused in the first place.

The third strategy continues the second. Through work and desire, unhappy consciousness has gained satisfaction and enjoyment. It just denies its own responsibility in achieving this. It not only takes its own doing to be nothing, but in good Christian fashion it even takes its enjoyment to be a form of wretchedness. Through this self-denial, however, consciousness finally becomes aware of its unity with the unchangeable. What is required for this to occur, consciousness thinks, is a mediator. Consciousness denies that it has accomplished anything on its own. It makes the mediator responsible for everything. In this alienation, the nullification of its own doing, consciousness finally obtains relief from its misery—it achieves happiness (*PhS*, 135–8/*GW*, IX, 128–31). Most commentators take this mediator to be the church. I do not want to claim that this is incorrect, but it seems to me that

Hegel also wants to allude to Kant's mediator (CPrR, 119/KGS, V, 115), that is, the God that Kant postulates to reconcile virtue and happiness.

To see this, we must begin by recognizing that the mediator is our own construction (PhS, 136–8/GW, IX, 129–31). Consciousness denies that its own work and desire are what bring it satisfaction. It attributes everything to a mediator. Despite this self-denial, consciousness has accomplished a great deal here:

> [It has posited its] will as the will of an "other," and specifically of will, not as a particular, but as a universal will. This positive meaning...is taken by this consciousness to be the will of the other extreme, the will which, precisely because it is an "other" for consciousness, becomes actual for it, not through the Unhappy Consciousness itself, but through a Third, the mediator as counsellor. Hence, for consciousness, its will does indeed become universal and essential will, but consciousness itself does not take itself to be this essential will.... The universal will which thereby comes to be for it, is not regarded as its own doing.... [At this point,] there has arisen for consciousness the idea of Reason, of the certainty that...it has being absolutely in itself, or is all of reality (PhS, 138/GW, IX, 131; see also PRel, I, 295/VPRel, I, 199).

In this very obscure passage, Hegel is at least claiming that consciousness is all of reality and that the universal will is also our construction. Consciousness, we have seen, has brought about its own happiness, but it cannot accept the fact that this is its own doing. It projects it onto an other. Hegel has not finished unpacking all that this means yet, but it is clear that we have taken a big step toward an absolute self, a self that constructs all of reality—though still, like the Kantian self, it cannot see this yet.

One might object, however, that the mediator cannot be Kant's postulated God who reconciles virtue with happiness because Hegel's mediator is the middle term between individual consciousness and the universal unchangeable being. The mediator, it would seem, would have to be the church which mediates between individuals and God rather than God who mediates between virtue and happiness. I do not wish to deny that Hegel intends the mediator to be an allusion to the church. Nevertheless, Hegel also says, "This middle term is itself a conscious Being [the mediator]," which does make it sound like the mediator is God. At any rate, Hegel continues, saying that the mediator "is an action which mediates consciousness as such, the content of this action is the extinction of its particular individuality which consciousness is undertaking."[21] In other words, what the mediator mediates is consciousness. All three terms here—individual consciousness, the mediator, and the unchangeable—are constructions within self-consciousness. What self-consciousness has done from the start is to construct two worlds and to distance itself as an individual consciousness from the essential world which it casts as a beyond, a beyond which it seeks to be reconciled with through virtuous devotion, work, and desire in order to overcome its unhappiness. And it finally decides it needs a mediator to bridge this gap. The mediator, then, allows virtue to be reconciled with happiness and it also links individuals to God—it does *both*. There is no point, then, in insisting that it can only do one rather than the other. Virtuous action both achieves its happiness and links itself to God—and then believes a mediator was necessary to accomplish these things. The deeper point here is that self-consciousness *itself* plays all three parts—it is not only individual consciousness but the unchangeable as well as the mediator. It overcomes it own unhappiness as well as postulates (that is, constructs) its own God, a God that it then insists is responsible for mediating virtue with happiness and a God with which it insists it can be linked only by a mediator. The whole problem results from the fact that consciousness posited two worlds and now must bridge them. And it is self-consciousness itself that does the bridging. For Hegel this is to solve a false problem with an unnecessary solution. Except that, without seeing what it is doing (and if it saw what it was doing, it could not accept it), self-consciousness is constructing *itself* as absolute consciousness, which is to say that God or the absolute, *properly* understood (in Hegel's view), is beginning to emerge here. We will pay a good deal of attention to this issue as we proceed.

We must also notice that consciousness has adopted a new strategy here that ultimately will allow it to avoid the tendency toward reversal to which it has been prone since the master was first undermined by his dependence on the slave for recognition. Consciousness finally ceases to attack the other. It no longer seeks to negate or deny the other. That, we have discovered, will not get it reality and self-certainty. Instead, self-consciousness surrenders to the other. Only by this very opposite strategy can it gain self-certainty, objectivity, and reality.

Let me try to explain this. At the end of "Unhappy Consciousness," we are told that self-consciousness alienates itself (*sich entäussert*) (PhS, 137/GW, IX, 130). It abandons itself, surrenders, gives up what is essential to it, empties itself, and gives its essence over to another—to God. To alienate our own essence in this way is to construct the reality, power, and universality of the other. We attribute our own doing to the other and we recognize it as the other's doing. In this way we recognize God as real. This form of alienation, we might say, constitutes the highest form of objectification—because it is total. Self-consciousness says that it is nothing and that the other, God, is everything. It gives total reality to the other. And in this way we gain an absolute, solid, grounded other which we have been seeking and which we have not had all through "Consciousness" and "Self-Consciousness."

Having rejected an unknown thing-in-itself, as we have seen, Hegel must anchor the object from within consciousness. Here the other is within consciousness, constructed by consciousness, a projection of consciousness, but it is a solid, ultimately real other—in the view of the believer, and in Hegel's view, we cannot have anything more real than God.

Moreover, we have not only achieved a solid other, we are well on our way to establishing a solid self. From the beginning of "Self-Consciousness," our problem has been that self-consciousness only exists for-another (PhS, 111/GW, IX, 109). How can consciousness be what Kant claims it is, that is, single, unified, and independent, if it only exists for-another? If my self-consciousness is for-another, if the other is an essential part of my self-consciousness, that would seem to introduce heteronomy into self-consciousness. The only way to avoid this is to deny that the other is heteronomous. We must stop trying to handle difference or otherness by splitting, certainly by positing two worlds. We must treat difference as inner difference, as difference within unity (PhS, 99/GW, IX, 98). This has finally been accomplished here. God is other, but is also our very essence. To be for-another, for-God, Hegel thinks, involves no heteronomy. It is in fact to be in touch with one's essence in the highest way—to be most oneself.

At the same time, we must stop dealing with the other in the way the master dealt with the slave, that is, by negating the other, treating it as nothing, ranking it below us. If we do that, the other's recognition of us becomes worthless and we will have done nothing to solidify our own reality. Rather, we must do the very opposite. Like the slave we must deny ourselves. And we must deny ourselves totally so as to establish an ultimately real other. We need an other whose recognition is worth something. It is not by negating the other and asserting ourselves that we become solid and real, but by denying ourselves and affirming the other. The more important the recognizer, the more real the recognized. If we are to anchor idealism, if we are to achieve a solid other so as to stop the collapse of all reality into solipsism, if we are to have a subjectivity with solid self-certainty, then the other must be absolutely real. Recognition by this ultimately real other can eliminate solipsism and shore up individual self-consciousness without introducing heteronomy into this consciousness. This is something that will become clearer as we proceed.

Still, there is a problem here. We would seem to have a radical case of pulling ourselves up by our own metaphysical bootstraps. If it is self-consciousness that constructs and projects its own God, how is the recognition that self-consciousness can get from this God going to be enough to make it real and significant?

It would seem that Hegel's views here are rather like those of Nietzsche. For Nietzsche, in order to avoid the empty, meaningless void of nihilism, the Übermensch must create a myth, an illusion, a lie—the Übermensch must construct all value and meaning because none would exist otherwise.[22] For Hegel too, we have just seen, consciousness faces the empty void of scepticism without any objective reality. It must construct its own God if it is to have any reality. Is this to say, then, that for Hegel we end up with myth and illusion? Well, the consciousness there on the stage that has recently overcome its unhappiness does not have this worry because it does not see, will not see, that it has created its God. Nevertheless, *we* see it. Is all, then, to be reduced finally to human being, human construction, such that we are left with a left Hegelian historical and cultural relativism, unless we are willing to turn back to a traditional and dogmatic right Hegelian deity? Or can we work out a theory of culture that will allow us to avoid both a radical relativism or Nietzschean illusionism as well as a dogmatic theology? These are questions we must struggle with through the rest of the *Phenomenology*.

I have suggested that Hegel is out to undermine and subvert the Kantian difference between theoretical and practical reason. Let me try to say a bit more about this. The difference between these two forms of consciousness, and certainly the tension between them, stems from Kant's commitment to two worlds. Theoretical reason constructs the phenomenal world of experience. Practical reason, on the other hand, has a special relation to the noumenal sphere. For Kant, we cannot say that practical reason constructs the noumenal sphere. Practical reason is extremely modest. It denies that it constructs anything. The noumenal, the thing-in-itself, reality, are all unknown for it. Practical reason simply benefits from the noumenal. For practical reason, the noumenal is the source of freedom, morality, the categorical imperative, the highest good. Practical reason dutifully serves the noumenal—it does not construct it.

Theoretical reason is just as rash as practical reason is modest. In the "Transcendental Dialectic" of the *Critique of Pure Reason* we see that theoretical reason is something of a metaphysical imperialist. It desires to know, to construct, to grasp the totality of nature, to apply its categories to all of reality. Its thirst for completeness leads it into applying the categories beyond experience, leads it into transcendental illusion—leads it, it even seems, not to want to tolerate the thing-in-itself remaining unknown. (CPR, A296–B354, A644–B675).[23] The corrective is practical reason, which dutifully shrinks back from the thing-in-itself. It openly confesses that it cannot know or constitute.[24] It openly admits that freedom, morality, it itself would be impossible if the noumenal were known. Indeed, as for "Unhappy Consciousness," this self-denial is what actually wins practical reason the noumenal, lets it benefit from the noumenal, gains it freedom, morality, and happiness.

But for Hegel this will not work. There are not two worlds. The notion of two worlds is our construction and it will not hold up. And if there are not two worlds, if we must reject that notion, what then happens to theoretical and practical reason?

If our two worlds go, we are certainly not going to be able to sustain Kantian practical reason. There would be no second noumenal world out there that practical reason could draw upon, serve, and respect. In fact, practical reason's modesty has not been all that honest. Practical reason has constructed its sphere as much as theoretical reason did its. There is no other place for the noumenal to come from. Moreover, if there is no thing-in-itself that remains unknown, there can be no way to distinguish a transcendental self from the mere Humean flux of the empirical self. And if we cannot lift our selves above this empirical flux, we cannot claim to have the sort of self that would be capable of employing theoretical reason, constructing experience, and having a priori knowledge of it. As we can see, major problems lie ahead in the *Phenomenology*.

3

Reason in the World

Part A. Theoretical Reason

We began the *Phenomenology* with a consciousness whose object kept eluding it in "Sense-Certainty" and "Perception." Then we met a consciousness that posited itself as the inner world behind the elusive flux of appearance in "Understanding." Then in "Lordship and Bondage" individual consciousness attempted to assert itself as all of reality and sought to prove to itself that it was so, first, and rather unsuccessfully, as a master who simply negated all others and demanded recognition for himself, and then, more successfully but rather humbly, as a slave who controlled the object through work, made it serve human desires, and thus made it an object-of-his-consciousness. Then, in "Unhappy Consciousness," these two forms of consciousness merged into one and shifted their attention to the religious realm, where we found even God to be a construction and projection of human consciousness. Recognizing all of this will allow us to see how human consciousness, now more effectively than before, attempts to assert itself as all of reality—assert that all of reality is constituted by, and can be known within, self-consciousness. At this point, it is true, consciousness lacks the confidence to make this claim in its own name. It does so only surreptitiously. It claims that all of reality exists within and is constituted by consciousness—not, however, its own consciousness, but *God's*. Still, in taking this to be so, human consciousness, which, after all, is also consciousness—indeed, the very consciousness that constructed the divine consciousness, though it hides this fact from itself[1]—can proceed with the assumption that all of reality is constituted by and within consciousness. And thus it can set out on its quest to show that all of reality can be known by consciousness.

Hegel has in mind, I suggest, Kant's "Transcendental Dialectic" with its emphasis on regulative ideas and ideas of reason. For Kant, after all, we must treat the world as-if it were created and ordered by a divine mind, which means, we have seen, that we must assume that nature forms a connected, consistent, and unified system of rational laws. This, for Kant, is a presupposition necessary for the project of natural science to be possible. For Hegel, however, who rejects an unknown thing-in-itself, there are no as-ifs here. The rational unity of nature, therefore, must actually be known and it must be proven. If the world has been created and ordered by God, then science should be able to show that the natural world can be grasped and known as entirely lawlike and rational. If the world has been created and ordered by absolute reason, then nothing should be lost to reason. This fairly sums up, Hegel thinks, the attitude of theoretical reason as natural science—what it is, what it takes itself to be, and what it attempts to do—an attitude that culminated in Kant but which had been developing in the modern world since the Renaissance, when reason first discovered a "new real world" (*PhS*, 140/*GW*, IX, 133) and set out to study it. That attempt is what we follow in part A of chapter V of the *Phenomenology*.

At any rate, individual human consciousness sets out to prove to itself that all can be known. It sifts through all the phenomena of nature and seeks to understand them as constituted by a consciously ordering mind. This is what Hegel means by "reason." Reason is a synthesis of consciousness and self-consciousness. Consciousness confronted an object—an other-than-consciousness. Self-consciousness confronted itself—the object was merely an object-for-consciousness. In reason we have a solid and real natural object— one created, ordered, and maintained by God. We also have a self-consciousness, for which the object is not other than self-consciousness. It has been constituted by self-consciousness, it is an object-for-self-consciousness, it is within self-consciousness, but it is also a real, solid, God-created object. Reason, thus, "seeks to possess in thinghood the consciousness only of itself" (*PhS*, 145/*GW*, IX, 137). Individual consciousness must now set out to actually prove this truth through science.

Another way to put all of this is to say that reason seeks itself in the world. Just as for self-consciousness, reason expects to find nothing but itself, that is, nothing but rational order and law. Reason, nevertheless, does confront an other. There is a real natural world there before it. Moreover, theoretical reason no longer takes a negative attitude toward this other; it no longer seeks to cancel it (*PhS*, 139/*GW*, IX, 132). Instead, it seeks to know it. It believes that the world is rational and thus reason sets out to find *itself* in the world. There is a real other there before it, and reason recognizes it as such, but nevertheless believes it to be itself.

The first part of chapter V of the *Phenomenology* attempts to decide the place, importance, and scope of theoretical reason (*Vernunft*). Grand claims have traditionally been made on its behalf—that it is the highest form of knowledge and that it is capable of knowing everything that can be known. In the early modern period, this sort of commitment launched natural science's quest to demonstrate that reason is, as Hegel puts it, all of reality—that all can be rationally known (*PhS*, 140/*GW*, IX, 133). Even Kant would admit that reason, as long as it does not go beyond experience (in which case it produces transcendental illusion), as long as it confines its operation to the realm of observation and phenomena, can lead us toward solid empirical knowledge of everything that can be known in the world. There is nothing unusual here—these are the traditional sorts of claims made by theoretical reason.

But all of this overlooks a real problem—and Hegel zeroes right in on it. Theoretical reason, certainly as understood by Kant, cannot make good on its grand claims. Hegel thinks, in direct opposition to Kant (*CPR*, Bxiii–iv), that we cannot hold both that self-consciousness constructs all of reality within the transcendental unity of self-consciousness and that theoretical reason can give us knowledge of *all* things in the world. Scientific knowledge, empirical observational knowledge—theoretical reason as traditionally understood and as understood by Kant—will not even allow us to take the most basic step. It will not allow us to understand the transcendental self that for Kant constructs our world and does the knowing. Kant himself would admit this openly, though he would not seem to find it the embarrassment that Hegel suggests it is. But more than this, Hegel will argue, scientific reason will not even give us an adequate understanding of the empirical self—the sort of understanding promised by empirical psychology—and Kant certainly thought it could do that. Indeed, the very attempt to apply scientific reason to understand the self, Hegel will argue, will end up being grossly reductive of the self.

Thus, theoretical reason will fail miserably in its claim to know all of reality. Reason, as Lauer puts it, has been engaged in a "rational conquest of the world," it has "eliminated all other contenders—myth, faith, authority, tradition."[2] As Hegel puts it, reason "plants the symbol of its sovereignty on every height and in every depth... [It] digs into the very entrails of things and opens every vein in them so that it may gush forth to meet itself" (*PhS*, 146/*GW*, IX, 138). But reason's conquest will not succeed. Nevertheless, I will try to argue that its failure serves a very important function. Its failure, strangely enough, will shore up idealism. The fact that reason is unable to know everything, unable to pull every last bit of reality into the unity of self-consciousness, this failure permanently prevents a collapse into solipsism. Theoretical reason confronts a solid and irreducible other in its world that it cannot totally absorb.

I. Affirmation of Idealism

Hyppolite says that Hegel "rejects a purely mathematical conception of nature like Newton's.... But he also rejects Schelling's and Goethe's view of nature as a manifestation of genuine reason. Reason, which observes and which seeks itself, in part discovers itself in nature, *but only in part.*"[3] Another way to put this is to say that for Hegel nature is not radically other than consciousness—we certainly have no unknown thing-in-itself out there. Yet, on the other hand, nature is not simply and wholly within consciousness, certainly not as for Berkeley. For Hegel, we have an objective idealism. Nature is an object-of-consciousness, but it is not wholly comprehended by consciousness. It is not completely dissolved into consciousness. Within consciousness, it always remains an object over against consciousness. Reason finds itself in nature, but reason cannot be fully at home in nature. In the *Logic*, Hegel says, "The aim of knowledge is to divest the objective world that stands opposed to us of its strangeness, and, as the phrase is, to find ourselves at home in it: which means no more than to trace the objective world back to the notion,—to our innermost self" (L, 335/SW, VIII, 404–5; see also PR, 12/SW, VII, 35). The natural world has to be transformed. It must be worked on. It must be understood. As we have seen, we find this drive to alter, this drive to strip things of their foreignness, in something as simple as a child skipping stones across a pond as well as all the way up to art, religion, and philosophy (A, I, 31/SW, XII, 58). Natural science involves the same drive to remove the foreignness of things, and we will follow its attempt to allow us to see ourselves in the world and be at home in it, but it is not spirit and will not succeed to the extent that art, religion, and philosophy can and will.

Hegel's idealism is a robust, subtle, and very interesting idealism. It is quite different from other forms of idealism. All of reality, for Hegel, is an object-of-consciousness, as we have realized since "Self-Consciousness," but, as for "Consciousness," we have a real object there in the world. Moreover, the object is not just an object of perception, and thus we need not deny, as did Berkeley, that it is actually out there. Objects really are out there for Hegel.[4] How is he, then, an idealist? Hegel's view, we can say, is that their *esse est intelligi.* The essence of the thing, what it really is, is what reason *knows* about it. This in no way requires the rejection of actual objects or things. Take, for example, the concept of matter. Hegel is fully able to accept the existence of matter. It is just that in examining what we know about matter, what matter really is, Hegel is going to end up putting the emphasis on the *concept* of matter, where the materialist will put all the emphasis simply on the *matter* (PhS, 154/GW, IX, 144). Hegel does not need to deny that there is something out there. It is just that as soon as we try to get clear about what we know of the thing out there, what it is, we cannot avoid the idealist turn. We begin to conceptualize—that is, to idealize. And only thus do we really know the thing. All that we know about the thing, what it really is, its essence, is ideal. To be an idealist, it is not necessary to hold that there is nothing but mind. It is enough to hold that we cannot adequately understand or explain the real without recourse to mind.[5]

Is this a coherent position? Can Hegel consistently hold that things are really out there while holding that all is an object-of-our-consciousness? Well, Kant held the same thing. For Kant, the thing-in-itself is really out there.[6] And while it is true that the thing is unknown as it exists in itself out there, nevertheless, as it appears to us it is part of the transcendental unity of apperception and thus is very definitely an object-of-our-consciousness. The difference between Hegel and Kant, then, is really a subtle matter of emphasis. Hegel does not reject things-in-themselves. And he too thinks they are really out there. He just thinks that Kant has not thought the concept through. And if we do think it through, we will find that we are unable to avoid the idealist turn.

Hegel's rejection of an unknown thing-in-itself leads to a fundamental difference between his idealism and Kant's. For Hegel, reason grasps the essence of things, their very reality: "Self-consciousness and being are the same essence, the same, not through comparison, but in and for themselves" (PhS, 142/GW, IX, 134). Another way to put this is to say that reason is not merely a subjective phenomenon, a characteristic activity of minds; reason, for Hegel, is also objective. Reason expects to find itself in nature. The object embodies reason. Our subjective reason wants to meet reason in the object and be at one with it. This is a view that one can find in medieval and Renaissance thought and which Hegel wants to revive in modern form. For Aquinas, reason was embedded in the objective world by God in the form of natural law.[7] If we were to imagine this traditional conception of God replaced by an absolute transcendental unity of consciousness, then nature, we would say, would not lie outside this absolute consciousness, but would be constituted within it. The difference, then, between our individual consciousness and nature (both of which would be within this absolute consciousness) would not involve a radical difference between consciousness, on the one hand, and nature or matter, on the other. We would not have two worlds here. While there would be a difference between nature and our individual consciousness, while nature would always be an object outside our individual consciousness, nevertheless, this would still be a difference within one consciousness—within absolute consciousness. From the perspective of individual consciousness, then, nature would be outside it, an object over against it, but from the perspective of absolute consciousness, and of individual consciousness insofar as it raises itself to the perspective of absolute consciousness, nature would be inside consciousness. Moreover, to say that nature is rational, that it obeys rational laws, would not be to say only that our mind subjectively perceives it as rational—that the rationality is only in our individual minds. Rationality would permeate nature itself. Nature would be a part of an absolute rational consciousness—God's consciousness. It would be inseparable from rationality. So in science our subjective rationality should be able to grasp objective rationality in the natural object.

In Kant's *Critique of Pure Reason*, there is a section entitled, "Refutation of Idealism" (*CPR*, B274–9). It will be instructive to compare this section to Hegel's very firm *affirmation* of idealism. Kant distinguishes between the problematic idealism of Descartes, which holds that the existence of objects in space outside us is merely doubtful and indemonstrable, and the dogmatic idealism of Berkeley, which holds that space itself is false and impossible. Kant wants to deny that he is an idealist of either sort. He wants to refute idealism. And so he argues, against both Descartes and Berkeley, that inner experience is only possible on the assumption of outer experience. He does this by arguing that he is conscious of his own existence as determined in time. However, all determination of time (the flux of inner experience), Kant argues, presupposes something permanent. We are only able to perceive determination of time through change, and we can only perceive change against the background of something unchanging or permanent. Without a permanent, then, we would not be able to perceive change in any ordered way—as we obviously do perceive it. So, for example, prisoners kept in the dark for long periods of time have no permanent against which to order temporal change and thus lose all sense of time. Such experience can be extremely disorienting. Where, then, can we find this necessary permanent? Certainly not in inner sense—which is nothing but a continual Humean flux. A permanent is possible, then, Kant concludes, "only through a *thing* outside me and not through the mere *representation* of a thing outside me" (*CPR*, B274–6, A106–7).[8] Thus Kant is not an idealist of the Cartesian or Berkeleyan sort. He is an empirical realist. The empirical world really exists out there in outer sense.

All of this, however, will not clear Kant of the charge of idealism, certainly not as soon as we realize that for him the empirical world of outer sense is also our construction, a phenomenon, an appearance. For this appearance to be something more than a *mere representation*, there must be, it would certainly seem, an unknown thing-in-itself out there behind the appearance. After all, besides being an empirical realist, Kant is also a transcendental idealist (*CPR*, A368–70, A375, A385; see also *HP*, III, 442–3/*SW*, XIX, 571–2).

In Hegel's view, Kant has certainly not refuted idealism. Kant *is* an idealist. And the fact that Kant claims to be a transcendental idealist while remaining an empirical realist, in Hegel's opinion, just lands Kant in a spurious form of idealism (*PhS*, 142/*GW*, IX, 134). In this form of idealism, Hegel says, reason first claims that all reality is its own—that all is within the transcendental unity of apperception. But all this gives us, as Hegel puts it, is an empty "mine"—a sheer empty unity of self-consciousness. All we have is the claim that all objects are objects-of-my-self-consciousness, but this does not give us the actual objects. For this empty mine to get any filling, any content, it will at the same time have to be an absolute empiricism (where Kant argues that transcendental realism leads to empirical idealism [*CPR*, A369], Hegel argues that transcendental idealism leads to absolute empiricism). Any objects, any content, any filling, for the transcendental unity of apperception, the empty mine, will have to come from an extraneous source, from outside—an unknown thing-in-itself. Where else could the filling, the content, come from? It certainly cannot be generated by the transcendental unity of apperception itself. And thus all of reality, after all, is not really mine. Moreover, Hegel argues, in such empiricism, reason will only be able to achieve the kind of knowing that we met in sense-certainty, perception, and understanding, that is, the apprehending of an extraneous other through observation or experience. Such knowing, however, is not a true knowing—by the very standards of this idealism itself. True knowing is only possible as constituted within the unity of apperception—the mine (*PhS*, 144–5/GW, IX, 136–7).

This spurious idealism, then, ends up with a duality of opposed factors—the unity of apperception and an extraneous source or unknown thing-in-itself. And reason is fundamentally unable to bring these two sides together. The transcendental unity of apperception cannot give itself any filling; it cannot provide a world—the multiplicity and detail of sensation. And the kind of knowing that can perceive and understand the empirical world, we shall see, will be incapable of knowing the unity of apperception. To find itself in the world, to open up the new world of science, to succeed as natural science, then, reason will have to abandon its true self, reduce itself to the knowing of observation, perception, understanding, a form of knowing incapable of grasping the transcendental unity of apperception, and, moreover, a form of knowing which when directed toward the self will be radically reductive—ultimately, we shall see, it will reduce mind to a mere skull bone. Such knowing, then, fails to know *all* of reality—it fails to make all its own. It fails even to know itself. This is deeply ironic because it was, Hegel suggested, the commitment to the unity of apperception, the mine, the notion that all of reality exists within one consciousness and was created by that consciousness, thus that all of reality was consciousness's own and thus was knowable, that originally drove reason to the scientific project, to the attempt to systematically know all of reality. Yet in the end such scientific knowing fails to grasp, reduces, destroys, this very unity of self-consciousness that got it started in the first place.

Kant himself admits that understanding, the sort of knowing that employs the categories, cannot grasp the unity of apperception: "Apperception is itself the ground of the possibility of the categories... It does *not* know *itself through the categories*, but knows the categories, and through them all objects, in the absolute unity of apperception, and so *through itself*. Now it is, indeed, very evident that I cannot know as an object that which I must presuppose in order to know any object" (*CPR*, A401–2). Hegel thinks that the inability of this self (which makes all knowing possible) to know itself is an embarrassment. Indeed he thinks that such knowing— scientific knowing, observation, experience—does not know what knowing really is.

Thus, the thrust of Kant's thought, we have seen, is to flee idealism, to be embarrassed by it, to find an other, a permanent, an unknown thing-in-itself—as if he were afraid of being trapped within the transcendental unity of apperception. Hegel thinks we should move in precisely the opposite direction. He thinks we should affirm idealism. He even thinks that reason, ordinary reason, reason as understood by the scientific tradition as well as by Kant, if we watch it carefully, despite what it takes itself to be doing, really moves us in the right direction. Scientific reason "approaches things in the belief that it truly apprehends them as sensuous things opposite to the 'I'; but what it actually does, contradicts this belief, for it apprehends them *intellectually*, it transforms their sensuous being into [concepts], i.e. into just that kind of being which is at the same time 'I,' hence transforms thought into the form of being, or being into the form of thought; it maintains, in fact, that it is only as [concepts] that things have truth."[9]

Reason seeks laws—scientific laws, laws of nature—and that means, for Hegel, that it seeks conceptions, abstractions, which replace the independent, indifferent subsistence of sensuous reality. As Hegel puts it in the *Logic*, "The positive reality of the world must be as it were crushed and pounded, in other words, idealized" (*L*, 88/*SW*, VIII, 129; see also *PhS*, 146–7/*GW*, IX, 138). In the *Philosophy of Mind*, he says, "Every activity of mind is nothing but a distinct mode of reducing what is external to the inwardness which mind itself is, and it is only by this reduction, by this idealization or assimilation, of what is external that it becomes and is mind.... This material, in being seized by the 'I,' is at the same time poisoned and transfigured by the latter's universality; it loses its isolated, independent existence and receives a spiritual one" (*PM*, 11/*SW*, X, 24–5).

For example, by testing a law through experiment, one might think that the independent, external, and sensible would be established against the abstract and conceptual—that the conceptual law would be overwhelmed, lost, in the particularity and multiplicity of the sensible. One might think that we would come to the empirical and particular rather than to the conceptual.

But really, Hegel argues, exactly the opposite occurs. Sense existents are absorbed into the conceptual. The conceptual law is brought out in its abstract shape. Specific existence, specific cases, are established as cases-of-the-conceptual-law. The same abstract law is seen to have many particular instances and these are conceived as instances-of-the-abstract-law (PhS, 152–3/GW, IX, 143–4). Moreover, natural science even unifies particular laws under higher level and more general laws—for example, the law of planetary motion and the law of terrestrial motion under the law of gravity. The independent subsistence of the sensuous particular tends to vanish; it tends to become an instance of a higher level conceptual law.

Kant, then, wanted to refute idealism by showing us that inner sense required something really out there, a permanent, and not just the representation of a permanent, but, it would seem, an unknown thing-in-itself. Thus Kant is an empirical realist. The empirical world really is out there. But he is also a transcendental idealist because we cannot know things as they are in themselves. Hegel rejects this refutation of idealism. He rejects the notion that knowledge is ever going to hand us a permanent really out there—if "out there" means anything like independent of our knowing. Knowledge is not even going to steer us in that direction. Knowing does not direct us beyond itself. It does the very opposite—it appropriates, transfigures, crushes and pounds, in short, idealizes. Even scientific knowledge, which at first sight seems a paradigm case of knowing that confirms ordinary consciousness's belief in the objective, external, material world, Hegel shows us, really moves in the opposite direction. It idealizes. It affirms idealism—it does not refute it.

At this point, we again have to wonder whether Hegel's idealism can really avoid solipsism. Hegel eliminates all external anchors. He refuses to appeal to an outside, to a Kantian unknown thing-in-itself, or to a Berkeleyan transcendent God. For Hegel, the thing-in-itself is known and God is our construction (PhS, 138/GW, IX, 131; PRel, I, 295/VPRel, I, 199). Even matter gets idealized. There is nothing, then, but consciousness and its objects. How, then, do we avoid radical solipsism? It is clear that reality can only be shored up immanently. But how? What is left to make it solid and real?

It is true that scientific reason has an idealizing tendency, but not only will it never lead us into solipsism, it will permanently block such a consequence. In the following sections of chapter V, we begin to see something very much like the sort of reversal that we have gotten used to since the master-slave dialectic. Scientific reason idealizes, but it is incapable of fully and adequately idealizing what confronts it, and this is so because reason also objectifies. This is especially obvious when reason turns to itself, to mind. At this level, as we shall see, reason is a total failure. And because of this failure, we might say, scientific reason finally turns out to be the hero of ordinary consciousness. It gives us, guarantees us, a stable world of objects out there over against us. It prevents solipsism—as long as we stick with scientific reason and do not go on to a higher sort of reason. Let us follow this development.

II. Inner and Outer

Scientific reason, we have said, seeks itself in the world through observation, experience, and experiment. Two concepts that permeate this quest, and that scientific reason cannot do without, are the concepts of inner and outer.[10] In seeking itself in the world, reason cannot find itself directly—it cannot confront itself, as it were, face to face. Rather, it takes reason in the world to be a hidden inner that in some way gets expressed in the outer. It is only the outer that we can observe. We can study the outer consequences, the deeds, the effects, from which we hope to infer the inner, and then we can seek to grasp the relation of inner to outer as a law. Such an approach, in Hegel's opinion, is flawed. In employing it, reason will fail to find itself in the world in adequate fashion.

In chapter V of the *Phenomenology*, Hegel examines reason's attempt to study and to find itself first in inorganic nature and then in organic nature. In neither case does reason find itself adequately. Reason then turns directly to itself, and Hegel explores the science of empirical psychology and then the pseudosciences of physiognomy and phrenology.

Let us begin with psychology. As we have seen, for Kant, the self knows whatever it knows through the categories, but cannot know itself through the categories (*CPR*, A401–2, B422). As Kant puts it, "I cannot have any representation whatsoever of a thinking being, through any outer experience." The inner self cannot be known through outer experience, though we can for Kant develop an empirical psychology, we can make "use of observations concerning the play of our thoughts and the natural laws of the thinking self to be derived from these thoughts" and "there would arise an empirical psychology...capable perhaps of explaining the appearances of inner sense" (*CPR*, A347; see also A549=B577-A550=B578).

Hegel objects to all of this. In the first place, as we shall see, scientific reason cannot successfully separate inner from outer. In the second place, it is the very reliance on a form of knowing that can only observe outer objects, actions, and events, namely, scientific or observing reason, that will not only guarantee that we are unable to grasp directly a supposed inner self, as Kant admits, but will also keep us from inferring across the gap from outer to inner, and thus will not even give us the empirical psychology Kant thinks we can have.

Hegel argues that empirical psychology assumes, on the one hand, an already given world of circumstances, customs, and so forth, and, on the other hand, a mind simply given as separate and as containing all sorts of faculties, inclinations, passions, "a contingent medley of heterogeneous beings ... together in the mind like things in a bag" (*PhS*, 182/*GW*, IX, 169).[11] Empirical psychology, then, would attempt to establish the laws that determine the effect exerted on the individual mind by specific circumstances, customs, and so forth (e.g., *CPR*, A554=B582).

This simply will not work, Hegel argues, because individuals both conform to circumstances as well as set themselves in opposition to (and, indeed, even transform) circumstances. Therefore, exactly what circumstances are to affect the individual and what kind of effect they are to have depends to a significant extent on the individual. Of course, if these circumstances, customs, the general "state of the world, had not been, then of course the individual would not have become what he is," but the fact that this particular individual was particularized in this specific way implies that this individual must have had at least something to do with being particularized in that way (*PhS*, 183–4/*GW*, IX, 170–1).

If individuals were directly and simply formed by the world, then we would only have to study the world to understand the individual: "We should have a double gallery of pictures, one of which would be the reflection of the other: the one, the gallery of external circumstances [would] completely determine and circumscribe the individual, the other [would be] the same gallery translated into [the inner individual]" (*PhS*, 184/*GW*, IX, 170). This is obviously unacceptable. The same world does not form all individuals in the same way. Clearly, the world does have an effect on the individual, but the world that has this effect could either be the world understood as it is in and for itself or the world understood as affected and transformed by the individual, and the influence on the individual expected from the former could be absolutely the opposite of that actually brought about by the latter. "The result of this ... is that 'psychological necessity' becomes an empty phrase, so empty that there exists the absolute possibility that what is supposed to have had this influence could just as well not have had it" (*PhS*, 184–5/*GW*, IX, 171).

In Hegel's view, we are influenced by our world. But the world cannot be understood as something existing simply in and for itself outside and apart from the individual. We must see that the world is transformed by the individual. Nor can we understand the individual as separate from the world. The individual is formed by a world that the individual transforms. We do not have a situation that falls apart into a world as given and individuals existing on their own account. If we insist on separating world and individual, as scientific reason does, then we will find no necessity and no law that connects them (*PhS*, 184–5/*GW*, IX, 171). What Hegel wants is to get beyond this sort of distinction between inner and outer, between individual and world. We must get beyond a form of knowing that sets objects out there over against an inner self. In Hegel's view, everything is inner, that is, *within* absolute consciousness, and nothing is outer, that is, outside absolute consciousness. Getting beyond the concepts of inner and outer used as empirical psychology uses them, then, should move us toward the absolute. From this point forward in chapter V, Hegel launches an attack on such distinctions.

III. *Physiognomy and Phrenology*

Hegel next takes up physiognomy, the doctrine propounded by Lavater to the effect that the inner character of individuals is expressed outwardly in their bodily form and facial expressions. If we wonder why Hegel spends so much time attacking what to most people is a pseudoscience, part of the answer is that Hegel's attack hits at more than just physiognomy—it hits at Kant's ethics as well.[12] In physiognomy, observation regards the deed and its performance as inessential and irrelevant. It regards only inner intentions as essential and thinks it can discern these inner truths through, say, facial expressions (*PhS*, 191–2/*GW*, IX, 176–7). As Hegel puts it, "If anyone said, 'You certainly act like an honest man, but I see from your face that you are forcing yourself to do so and are a rogue at heart'; without a doubt, every honest fellow to the end of time, when thus addressed, will retort with a box on the ear" (*PhS*, 193/*GW*, IX, 178).

Kant is certainly not a physiognomist. He does not believe that facial expressions will allow us to discern inner intentions,[13] but very much like physiognomy he does hold that such difficult to discern inner intentions are central to understanding moral worth. In the *Foundations* he says, "When moral worth is in question, it is not a matter of actions which one sees but of their inner principles which one does not see" (*F*, 23/*KGS*, IV, 407). How is it, then, that we can be sure about these inner intentions? Well, that is a problem even for Kant. And it will require an assumption just as objectionable as, though different from, that of physiognomy. Kant writes:

> If we attend to our experience of the way men act, we meet frequent and, as we ourselves confess, justified complaints that we cannot cite a single sure example of the disposition to act from pure duty.... It is in fact absolutely impossible by experience to discern with complete certainty a single case in which the maxim of an action, however much it may conform to duty, rested solely on moral grounds and on the conception of one's duty. It sometimes happens that in the most searching self-examination we can find nothing except the moral ground of duty which could have been powerful enough to move us to this or that good action and to such great sacrifice. But from this we cannot by any means conclude with certainty that a secret impulse of self-love, falsely appearing as the idea of duty, was not actually the true determining cause of the

will. . . . Our concern is not whether this or that was done but that reason of itself and independently of all appearances commands what ought to be done. Our concern is with actions of which perhaps the world has never had an example, with actions whose feasibility might be seriously doubted by those who base everything on experience, and yet with actions inexorably commanded by reason. (F, 22–4/KGS, IV, 406–8)

We have long since rejected Kant's distinction between phenomena and noumena, and thus a possible home for the sort of transcendental self that would be necessary to ground such pure intentions, unsullied by self-love, of which the world has perhaps never seen an example, but which are inexorably commanded by reason anyway (F, 70–4/KGS, IV, 451–5; CPrR, 101/KGS, V, 97–8). We do not have a noumenal realm that can keep reason and its pure intentions apart in a beyond where they can be considered an inner essence behind the outer appearance of self-love. Just as it will do no good to think that facial expressions can give us knowledge of real inner intentions that otherwise would not appear to us, so it will do no good to imagine a transcendental self to ground inner intentions that otherwise we cannot be sure exist.

We must abandon this concern with such inner intentions. As we have seen in chapter 2 above, the reality of the self is dependent on others for recognition. And what can be recognized is the deed, the doing, the action. There simply is no inner self that escapes beyond the theoretical reason of others—that is not constituted by others. There is no second world to ground a practical reason that is outside, apart, above the supposed heteronomy of the phenomenal world.

For Hegel, there is no way to get hold of inner intentions—certainly not if that is intended to allow us to measure or critique or avoid the deed. The deed is not the mere outer expression of an inner intention. The deed is the fact itself (*die Sache selbst*). The deed is what it is: murder, theft, bravery. It is what can be said of it, which is not at all to say, as we shall see in later sections, that the deed is easily understood—it always risks "being altered and perverted." But it is to say, for Hegel, that the individual human being is what the deed is—murderer, thief, hero. We should not fancy that we are something else than what we have done. We should not explain away our deed by appeal to intentions—something "meant," something conjectured. What we are, our essence, is the work we have done (*PhS*, 194, 191/GW, IX, 178–9, 176–7). For Hegel we must focus on the deed, on action, and not on difficult to discern inner intentions that we cannot be sure exist. Thus we need neither Lavater's physiognomy nor Kant's transcendental self to allow us to discern these inner intentions. More will have to be said of this in later sections.

At this point, though, Hegel takes up phrenology, which is even more absurd than physiognomy. Phrenology, as propounded by Gall, contends that the individual's character, through the causal effect of mental processes and brain functions, produces various bumps on the individual's skull which can be interpreted by the phrenologist. Hegel writes:

> It must be regarded as a complete denial of Reason to pass off a bone as the *actual existence* of consciousness; and it is passed off as such when it is regarded as the outer being of Spirit....It is no use saying that the inner is only being inferred from the outer, and is *something different*, nor that the outer is not the inner itself, but only its expres-sion....When...a man is told "You (your inner being) are this kind of person because your skull-bone is constituted in such and such a way," this means nothing else than, "I regard a bone as *your reality*." To reply to such a judgement with a box on the ear, as in the case of a similar judgement in physiognomy mentioned above...the retort here would, strictly speaking, have to go the length of beating in the skull of anyone making such a judgement, in order to demonstrate in a manner just as palpable as his wisdom, that for a man, a bone is nothing *in itself*, much less his true reality. (*PhS*, 205/*GW*, IX, 188)

Scientific reason is a failure. It is reductive and positivistic. It cannot grasp itself in the world. It is inadequate to grasp mind, spirit, consciousness. If it tries, Hegel's point seems to be, it becomes a pseudoscience—it reduces mind to a bone. And so theoretical reason must "abandon itself and do a right-about turn" (*PhS*, 206/*GW*, IX, 188). Consciousness must cease to try to find itself as immediately given in the world. Instead it turns to practical reason and tries to "produce itself by its own activity" (*PhS*, 209/*GW*, IX, 191).

The sort of reason that Hegel focuses on in chapter V of the *Pheno-menology* is an as yet undeveloped, unconsummated, lower form of reason (*PhS*, 146/*GW*, IX, 138). In the introduction to the *Philosophy of History*, Hegel distinguishes between two forms of reason:

> The Greek Anaxagoras was the first to declare that the world is gov-erned by a "*nous*," i.e. by reason or understanding in general. This does not signify an intelligence in the sense of a self-conscious reason or a spirit as such, and the two must not be confused. The movement of the solar system is governed by unalterable laws; these laws are its inherent reason. But neither the sun nor the planets which revolve around it in accordance with these laws are conscious of them. (*PWHI*, 34/*PW*, I, 37)

Indeed, when Socrates read Anaxagoras, Hegel points out, Socrates was disappointed to discover that Anaxagoras dealt only with external causes such as air, ether, water, and so forth, not with a deeper sort of reason. Hegel goes on to suggest that to get at the deeper sort of reason that rules the world we might start by examining the concept of providence (*PWHI*, 34–5/*PW*, I, 37–8).

In chapter V of the *Phenomenology*, the sort of reason that is presented and examined is *nous*, but a higher sort of reason is there lurking behind the surface, and we can get a hint of it from the way nous behaves—a behavior that contradicts itself. Nous claims to study independent, external objects that remain there before it in the world, but, without realizing what it is doing or what it means, nous idealizes—it transforms sensuous objects into concepts (*PhS*, 147/*GW*, IX, 138).

The characteristics of nous are that it takes objects to be things that present themselves to observation as found, given—they merely are (*PhS*, 181/*GW*, IX, 167). They exist in the form of immediate being (*PhS*, 146/*GW*, IX, 138). They are outside, external, and they suffer passively whatever action the mind performs on them (*PM*, 13/*SW*, X, 27–8). Reason as nous fits things into fixed categories and denies them all opposite or opposed categories. Then it merely strings such predicates together (*L*, 62–3, 37/*SW*, VIII, 101–2, 73–4)—it connects them as external relations. It even sees the mind as made up of faculties, inclinations, heterogeneous beings, as if they were inert things in a bag (*PhS*, 182/*GW*, IX, 169). And, as Hegel puts it, "When being as such, or thingness, is predicated of the mind, the true and genuine expression for this is, therefore, that mind is such an entity as a bone is . . . we do not *mean* it . . . but that is what we *say*."[14]

Nous, scientific reason, Kantian theoretical reason, which claims to rule the world, and which sets out to find itself in the world, is doomed to failure. It limits itself to observation, experience, the phenomenal, and thus it will not even be able to understand itself—it will turn mind into a bone. If, on the other hand, this sort of reason tries to go beyond experience, it will be denounced as transcendental illusion. Hegel would suggest that the illusion lies instead in scientific reason's belief that it can rule the world when it cannot even see that it does not understand itself.

If nature is the realm of nous, of scientific reason, then history and culture are the realm of spirit—the realm of art, religion, and philosophy. Nous cannot finally overcome the otherness of the object, cannot completely idealize it, always meets a limit, and when it turns to mind, even reduces it to a bone. Spirit is different. Art, religion, and philosophy are able to overcome otherness and objectification. Reason in culture is able to see that it has constructed reality, is able to see itself in that reality, and is able to be fully at home with itself. In culture, all is the doing, the action, the construction of self-consciousness. What, for example, is a government? It is not a set of buildings or even persons. It is not a thing—like a bone. It is a set of beliefs, commitments, practices, procedures, ideas, laws, and so forth. It is our construction—all the way down.

It is true that nature, for Hegel, is constructed just as much as culture is. Nevertheless, in nature there is always something there that remains an other, over against us, an it, that we cannot dissolve. Nous fails in its attempt to find itself adequately in nature. Spirit does not have this problem in culture. Culture is the realm in which reason can find itself and be at home with itself in the world. If anything, we shall see in future chapters, spirit has the opposite problem. If we too quickly see that culture is our construction, it can lose its reality for us. If we too quickly see that we have constructed God, religion can collapse. If we too quickly see that government is nothing but the practices and beliefs of individual citizens—perhaps especially of certain classes of those citizens—government can collapse. In short, where we could not get around nature's objectivity and otherness, cultural institutions can be in need of a certain degree of objectivity and otherness. They will have to generate this objectivity—through the trappings of monarchy, clerical ritual, or something of the sort.

To better understand spirit, as opposed to nous, let us look at the *Philosophy of Mind*, where Hegel speaks of

> the mind or spirit that makes world-history. In this case, there no longer stands, on the one side, an activity external to the object, and on the other side, a merely passive object: but the spiritual activity is directed to an object which is active in itself, an object which has spontaneously worked itself up into the result to be brought about by that activity.... Thus, for example, the people and the time which were molded by the activity of Alexander and Caesar as *their* object, on their own part, qualified themselves for the deeds to be performed by these individuals; it is no less true that the time created these men as that it was created by them; they were as much the instrument of the mind or spirit of their time and their people, as conversely, their people served these heroes as an instrument for the accomplishment of their deeds. (PM, 13/SW, X, 28)

It will be instructive to compare this passage with our discussion a few pages back of empirical psychology. Empirical psychology, in Hegel's view, attempts to give us laws that would explain how circumstances determine mind. But it fails because individuals both conform to, as well as set themselves in opposition to, and even transform, circumstances. What happens, then, depends as much on the individuals as the circumstances. There is a complex interplay between the two that cannot be determined as a law. The people, the circumstances of their time, and leaders like Caesar or Alexander shape and influence each other in mutually determining ways that scientific reason cannot fix. Nous is at a loss in this realm. If it tries to move ahead anyway, it will move into pseudoscience. On the other hand, the historian, the artist, the theologian, the political theorist, the philosopher are quite at home with such cultural phenomena and can handle them without special problems. Indeed, their doing so even contributes to the further development and articulation of culture or spirit. They are a significant part of the process by which culture constructs itself, grasps itself, and comes to be at home with itself. Through such activity spirit constructs its world, fills it out, and roots us in it. We have a long way to go yet in explaining spirit, but we are at least beginning to see the difference between it and nous.

Reason's very failure to find itself in the object, to idealize the object completely, to win through to spirit, is its success for ordinary consciousness. The failure of reason to absorb all into consciousness cuts off and makes impossible an implosion into solipsism. Solipsism is impossible if the tendency of theoretical reason is to objectify—to take mind to be a bone. Thus, for Hegel, we end up with a subtle, nuanced, and solid idealism. Hegel does not and need not deny the external world or insist that only ideas exist, as for Berkeley. Reason faces a world of matter and material processes that it stud-ies scientifically. Such study transforms, idealizes, the world. The essence of the world is grasped in thought. *Esse est intelligi.* But theoretical reason cannot go all the way. Spirit will be able to do so, but for nous there always remains an it that we cannot dissolve. Reason cannot grasp itself in the world as if there were nothing but reason, spirit, mind, and no other, no object. Nevertheless, this it, this object, is not a Kantian unknown thing-in-itself. Though theoretical reason is unwilling to accept it, we know that we have constructed this world. We have constructed the object and the object is known. But because of the form of knowing involved—theoretical reason, nous—we are unable to fully comprehend, fully idealize, the object. Scientific reason, much like the slave's labor, works on the object and idealizes it, makes it an object-for-consciousness. But, at the same time, the more we work on the world, the more we objectify it, the more we bring to light resis-tance that must be wrestled with, transformed, struggled with. In short, the more we work on the world, the more we try to idealize it, the more nature will be stimulated to resist us and demonstrate its independence (*PhS*, 118/*GW*, IX, 115).

Idealism has been given a bad name by its enemies. And, at least, we must fight against silly stereotypes of it. Johnson thought he could refute ide-alism by kicking a stone and uttering, "I refute Berkeley thus." Hegel would seem to turn this very ploy against Johnson. It is the slave and the scientist who stub their toes against nature and wrestle with the resistance of the world. But far from refuting idealism, their work is the very thing that ideal-izes the world while giving us the experience of solid objects within it. In experiencing the resistance of Johnson's stone, the slave and the scientist might have said, "We refute *Johnson* thus."

Reason anchors idealism not only by giving us resistant objects, but also in a second way that we must begin to recognize. Hegel suggests in chapter V of the *Phenomenology* that reason is larger than the ego. Reason is "dimly aware of itself as a profounder essence than the pure 'I' *is*" (*PhS*, 146/*GW*, IX, 138). In seeking reason in the world, we have seen, subjective reason seeks to find objective reason embedded in nature. In this quest the ego will become aware that it is a part of a larger rational unity, a unity that includes all egos and all objects in the world. This begins to make clearer to us how reality can be constructed by consciousness yet be something that consciousness finds to be objective. The world is objective in the sense that it is an object, a thing, a natural resistance, but also in that the world is rational, organized, lawlike. This is to say that as subjective reason finds itself, finds objective reason, in the world, it finds an authority, something it must answer to, something that makes legitimate demands on it. Reason is both an activity of consciousness and its sovereign. Consciousness has constructed the world and reason is the action of consciousness, but it is not as if consciousness, certainly not individual consciousness, is arbitrarily in control here. To become aware of reason in the world is to become aware of reason as a regularity, a norm, an authority that is not other than me but which is greater than me.

At any rate, natural science is not sovereign and the spiritual sciences marginally important underlaborers. If the task of idealism is to construct the world, understand it, and be at home in it, science certainly has an important role to play in this process. Indeed, it is the hero of ordinary consciousness. But its role is a smaller one that should not blind us to the more fundamental role of the human and cultural sciences. If we want to understand how we construct the world and can be at home in it, as we shall see, we must look finally to art, religion, history, and philosophy.

Part B. Practical Reason

Theoretical reason, Kant claimed, must presuppose a transcendental self to make sense of its experience. But if theoretical reason fails in its attempt to know this self, perhaps we should turn to practical reason. Practical reason, it is true, cannot claim to know this self either. In fact, it even insists that such knowledge would eliminate its freedom. Nevertheless, practical reason, just as much as theoretical reason, must presuppose such a self—indeed, a noumenal self. If it cannot know it, perhaps it can at least demonstrate this self to us—show us this self through action (*CPrR*, 3, 92/*KGS*, V, 3, 89; *PhS*, 209/*GW*, IX, 191)—so as to justify the Kantian presupposition of it.

And so in the second section of chapter V of the *Phenomenology* we move on to practical reason. Reason still seeks to find itself in the world, but in turning to practical reason it no longer expects to find reason as something alien—merely a bone. Reason expects to succeed in finding other self-consciousnesses and to be recognized by them in return (*PhS*, 211/*GW*, IX, 193). Theoretical reason, we might say, was unable to be *for-itself*. It was unable to exist as knowledge for-itself—it could not grasp consciousness without reducing it to a bone. Practical reason, on the other hand, certainly for Kant, is very much for-itself. It exists for-itself as the source of its own universal and rational principles—as the source of all moral law. Moreover, this rational self forms itself in accordance with its own principles. It makes itself moral—it produces itself by its own activity and transforms the world (*PhS*, 209/*GW*, IX, 191). Practical reason has no trouble with the for-itself. Its trouble, rather, is with the in-itself. It fears the in-itself, backs away from it, insists that it is unknown. It thinks that such knowledge would eliminate its freedom, make morality impossible for it, and thus destroy its very essence. What we need, for Hegel, what spirit will try to get for us, is a synthesis of theoretical and practical reason, the in-itself and the for-itself (*PM*, 185–6/*SW*, X, 303–4).[15] We need a moral reality that exists on its own in-itself but is also consciousness's own doing, its own action, its construction for-itself.

The Kantian difference between theoretical and practical reason, and certainly the tension between them, we have seen, stems from Kant's commitment to two worlds. Theoretical reason constructs the phenomenal world of experience. Practical reason, while it hopes to produce a moral character and a moral world, would vehemently deny that it constructs anything—certainly not the noumenal thing-in-itself. Theoretical reason is capable of forgetting itself, lapsing into transcendental illusion, and trying to grasp the thing-in-itself. In fact, in Hegel's view, as we saw in the last section of chapter 1 above, it actually constructs the thing-in-itself without recognizing that it does so. Practical reason, for its part, shuns any such action as a threat to its very existence. The noumenal, it insists, is unknown and must remain so if it is to serve practical reason as the source of freedom, morality, the categorical imperative, and the highest good. Practical reason feels it would lose all this, lose itself, if the thing-in-itself were known.

For Hegel, however, we cannot accept a Kantian distinction between two worlds, and if this is so, then it will be impossible to preserve a practical reason apart, outside, or beyond the ordinary world of experience and heteronomy. If this is impossible, then Hegel will have two major problems to confront as he proceeds. First, he will need a different conception of freedom, one that does not require a noumenal world. Second, we will have to admit that Kantian practical reason constructs its sphere as much as theoretical reason does its. The transcendental self, morality, God, the highest good—they are all our constructions for Hegel. Where else could they come from, if we reject the notion of a noumenal realm? The second problem here, then, is simply a particular aspect of the more general problem that has continuously occupied us so far, namely, idealism's struggle to anchor itself immanently, to avoid being reduced to solipsism, and to shore itself up without appealing to anything outside. In part B of chapter V, Hegel takes up this same problem in its moral dimension. Even Kant admitted in the "Idea for a Universal History" that morality is brought about by cultural development (*IUH*, 21/*KGS*, VIII, 26). If, with Hegel, we reject any notion of a noumenal sphere, any transcendental ground for morality, then we must admit that morality is fundamentally a cultural phenomenon. And if, as Hegel does, we also hold that culture, society, and history are all our doing, our construction, then morality would seem to dissolve into a sort of social solipsism, that is, cultural relativism. How, then, do we gain objectivity for morality? Hegel's response to this problem is the same as his response to the closely connected first problem, the problem of how freedom is possible without a noumenal sphere. His response is to develop a concept of *Sittlichkeit*, or "ethical life." This Sittlichkeit, however, will be incompatible with Kantian morality. In the first place, Sittlichkeit is impossible at the level of individual consciousness. To realize Sittlichkeit, then, will require going beyond individual consciousness to cultural consciousness—to spirit. The strategy of this section, then, is to show us that Kantian freedom and morality will not hold up and that to account for our experience of freedom and morality we will have to move on to Sittlichkeit and to spirit.

In the section entitled "The Actualization of Rational Self-Consciousness Through Its Own Activity," Hegel begins to explain his concept of Sittlichkeit. We have seen throughout chapter V that reason seeks to find itself in the world. Scientific reason failed in this endeavor. Kantian practical reason, we shall see, will also fail. It is only in Sittlichkeit, which will require spirit, that reason will succeed. Reason, Hegel argues, can only be actualized in a free nation (*PhS*, 214/*GW*, IX, 195). Only there can it adequately find itself in the world. Only there can we find reason objectively realized in the customs, traditions, practices, laws, and institutions of a people. Such institutions, practices, and traditions are nothing but the actions of the citizens—actions that have taken on a substantial and objective form. Subjectivity finds itself in this world far more adequately than it did in theoretical reason's study of nature. Moreover, what we have is reason, not merely nous. We do not have planets that follow laws merely unconsciously; we find a reason that is self-conscious—citizens self-consciously making and following their own laws and recognizing each other doing so (*PhS*, 211–13/*GW*, IX, 193–4).

The citizens pursue their purposes, objectify themselves in their institutions, and see themselves in their world. They create a common public life that is the outcome of the activity of the individual citizens, yet is objective and substantial—it is a force that develops, sustains, and morally empowers its citizens. This common public life first appears in the Greek polis. The polis is the construction of its citizens. It exists through their work, recognition, and sacrifice. It establishes a common life that is objectively rooted in social and public institutions, public values, traditions, and laws, as well as its own philosophy, religion, and art. Citizens are willing to serve and to sacrifice for this objective reality, a reality that motivates them, becomes their mission and purpose, and forms and empowers them as a people. Moreover, this objective reality is not other, alien, or heteronomous. The citizens are not unfree. They see themselves in a world they have constructed, they find this world to be their own, they are motivated to act by it, and they are at one with it. They find reason in their world and are at home with it.

To understand Hegel's critique of Kantian morality, we must notice that Hegel distinguishes between *Moralität* and Sittlichkeit. Moralität begins with Socrates and reaches its high point in Kant. Moralität is rational and reflective morality. Individuals must themselves rationally decide what is moral and do it *because* reason tells them that it is the right thing to do. This rational and reflective component is relatively absent in traditional Sittlichkeit, which is best represented, for Hegel, in the Greek polis before the rise of Socratic Moralität. Sittlichkeit is ethical behavior grounded in custom and tradition and developed through habit and imitation in accordance with the laws and practices of the community. Personal reflection and analysis have little to do with traditional Sittlichkeit. Sittlichkeit is ethical life built into one's character, attitudes, and feelings.

Furthermore, Moralität involves an ought. It is morality that ought to be realized. This ought is also absent from Sittlichkeit. For Sittlichkeit, morality is not something we *ought* to realize or *ought* to be. Morality already exists—it *is*. It is embedded in our customs, traditions, practices, character, attitudes, and feelings. The objective ethical order already exists in, is continuously practiced by, is actualized in, the citizen. Even Kant admits that an ought would be out of place for a will in which volition of itself necessarily agreed with morality (F, 31/KGS, IV, 414).

The only sort of morality that Hegel discusses and critiques in the remainder of chapter V is Moralität—individual, rational, and reflective morality with individual consciousness as the source of moral determination. When we get to chapter VI, we will find that spirit will involve Sittlichkeit—ethical life built upon custom and habit—the morality of a people with moral content given in their traditions, institutions, and practices, not the abstract and formal Moralität of Kant.

In one sense Sittlichkeit is superior to Moralität. It has a rich content and it is objective, public, and lived, whereas Moralität is formal and abstract. But in another sense traditional Sittlichkeit is inferior to Moralität.

Traditional Sittlichkeit's laws are immediate; they are given as absolutes by tradition, the gods, custom. In contrast to Moralität, the role of subjectivity and reflection is minimal and individual freedom is undeveloped.

What Hegel wants for the modern world is neither traditional Sittlichkeit nor modern Moralität. He wants a synthesis of Sittlichkeit and Moralität, which, though at times confusing, he also calls Sittlichkeit. This higher Sittlichkeit, which Hegel lays out in detail only in the *Philosophy of Right*, combines the rational and reflective side of Moralität with the transcendence of the ought characteristic of Sittlichkeit. It is rational reflective morality that actually exists as concretely embedded in the customs, traditions, laws, character, practices, and feelings of a people. It is a reflective consciousness of the ethical substance (*PhS*, 216/*GW*, IX, 197).

In the *Phenomenology*, then, we get a development from Moralität (in chapter V) on to the traditional Sittlichkeit of the Greek polis (in chapter VI), and then a development on toward the higher modern Sittlichkeit that combines Moralität and traditional Sittlichkeit. This development is rather complex. It involves three movements: a phenomenological movement, a sociocultural movement, and finally a movement that combines the phenomenological and the sociocultural. The section entitled "The Actualization of Rational Self-Consciousness Through Its Own Activity" gives us a rather obscure but important sketch of these three movements, thus of how the *Phenomenology* is organized and how it develops. Let us try to understand this.

The first movement is the obvious one that we have been engaged in thus far in the *Phenomenology* and that we have discussed many times, beginning in the introduction. It can be described as a phenomenological movement from individual consciousness on to culture or spirit, and it includes the movement from Moralität on to the Sittlichkeit of the Greek polis. This movement began in the very first chapters of the text and will continue on into the first part of chapter VI. It began with the attempt to justify individual consciousness (from "Sense-Certainty" through "Reason"), an attempt that will finally fail, and that thus will force us to move beyond individual consciousness, force us to move on in the second part of the *Phenomenology* to spirit and Sittlichkeit, that is, to reason objectified in the ethical life, the customs, traditions, institutions, and practices of a people. Hegel says, however:

> The wisest men of antiquity have therefore declared that wisdom and virtue consist in living in accordance with the customs of one's nation.
>
> But from this happy state of having realized its essential character and of living in it, self-consciousness, which at first is Spirit only *immediately* and in *principle*, has withdrawn, or else has not yet realized it; for both may equally well be said. (*PhS*, 214/*GW*, IX, 195)

The ancient polis is part of our past. The Sittlichkeit that existed there collapsed and Moralität has developed as a higher form of individual consciousness. The phenomenological development that we have been tracing so far in the *Phenomenology*, in fact, would only be conceivable given the higher development that the modern mind has actually achieved since the Greek polis (*PhS*, 16/*GW*, IX, 24–5). Greek spirit was limited. Subjectivity was relatively undeveloped. The *Phenomenology* could not have been written if consciousness had not developed beyond Greek consciousness. So while the *Phenomenology* would be impossible without this higher development of subjectivity, a development that had not yet taken place in ancient Greece, nevertheless, the *Phenomenology* (in "Consciousness," "Self-Consciousness," and "Reason") began with just such a consciousness. It began with a consciousness that would not develop until after the collapse of the Greek world, despite the fact that the *Phenomenology* had not yet arrived at the Greek world—indeed, we have not yet arrived there even in chapter V. The *Phenomenology*, we have said, will move from individual consciousness on to Greek culture, spirit, and Sittlichkeit. It moves from the simple to the complex. Culture, then, must come later in the *Phenomenology* than individual consciousness. But historically it was the reverse. Culture, spirit, and Sittlichkeit in ancient Greece came before the development of subjectivity, individuality, or Moralität.

So we must also have a second movement that is the reverse of the first. The first, we have said, is a phenomenological movement that advances conceptually from individual consciousness to Greek Sittlichkeit. This movement, however, cannot be one that just goes forward conceptually from the simple to the complex; it must also be a movement that goes backward in time. The second movement, then, which will begin in chapter VI, will go back from modern individuality, subjectivity, and Moralität to Greek culture, spirit, and Sittlichkeit and trace the sociocultural development of consciousness from the breakdown of ancient Greek Sittlichkeit to the rise of modern Moralität. And so, for Hegel, it can equally well be said, as he put it in the passage just quoted above, that self-consciousness "has withdrawn, or else has not yet realized" Sittlichkeit. We have withdrawn from ancient Sittlichkeit, we have moved past it historically, but in chapter V we have not yet reached it in the phenomenological development that takes place in the *Phenomenology*.

Moreover, the *Phenomenology* is not ultimately after traditional Sittlichkeit as it existed in the Greek polis. It is after a higher Sittlichkeit—a synthesis of Moralität and traditional Sittlichkeit—and this Sittlichkeit has not yet been realized either. The *Phenomenology*, then, will go on further to describe how to achieve this higher Sittlichkeit:

> Reason *must* withdraw from this happy state; for the life of a free people is only in principle or immediately the *reality* of an ethical order. In

other words, the ethical order exists merely as something *given*...which only in the higher stage, viz. in Spirit's consciousness of its essence, sheds this limitation and in this knowledge alone has its absolute truth, not directly as it *immediately* is.... Self-consciousness has *not yet* attained this *happy state* of being the ethical substance, the Spirit of a people....it is established only as an *inner* essence or as an abstraction....It is the *practical* consciousness, which steps into its world which it finds already given, with the aim of duplicating itself.... [It] has only to become so *for it* through its own agency. (*PhS*, 214–15/GW, IX, 195–6).

Thus we must also have a third movement, one that is both phenomenological and sociocultural. It involves a sociocultural movement from Sittlichkeit to Sittlichkeit. It includes the sociocultural movement in chapter VI from traditional Greek Sittlichkeit to modern Moralität and then moves on toward the higher modern Sittlichkeit that we are after. To achieve this future Sittlichkeit, however, will also require a higher phenomenological-conceptual development of consciousness, certainly, than existed in the Greek polis, where there was little subjectivity, and also than exists in modern, individual Kantian Moralität, where there is plenty of subjectivity but not enough Sittlichkeit.

A higher development of consciousness than existed in the Greek polis was necessary even for the first part of the *Phenomenology*, which leads to and explains abstractly, conceptually, phenomenologically the lost Sittlichkeit of the ancient polis. Then a further phenomenological-conceptual development will have to take place in our sociocultural world if we are to go beyond Greek Sittlichkeit and modern Moralität to this higher Sittlichkeit.

So we have a sociocultural fall from ancient Sittlichkeit and the development of modern Moralität, a hoped-for future sociocultural movement to a higher Sittlichkeit, and a phenomenological-conceptual movement from individual consciousness to a cultural consciousness and on to this higher Sittlichkeit. We could not have the last movement without the fall from ancient Sittlichkeit and the development of modern individuality. We have not gone beyond modern individuality to achieve the development of the higher Sittlichkeit yet and will not be able to do so without the phenomenological-conceptual development that the *Phenomenology* lays out.

The *Phenomenology*, I have argued, begins by abstracting from the whole, the absolute, the entire cultural world of spirit and Sittlichkeit in order to show individual consciousness that to explain its experience it must return to the whole. Thus, we can say that we have lost Sittlichkeit in two senses: it was abstracted from at the beginning of the *Phenomenology* and it disappeared after the collapse of the ancient world. So also, we will reattain Sittlichkeit in two senses: at the end of the *Phenomenology* we will have worked our way back to the whole from which we abstracted at the beginning and also, hopefully, we will actually produce in our culture a Sittlichkeit similar to that which was lost after the fall of the ancient world. This suggests two things: that the future modern Sittlichkeit will be consciously constructed and thus better than the unreflective Sittlichkeit of the ancient world and also, it would seem, that Hegel's *Phenomenology* itself will be responsible for—or at least contribute to—constructing this new world.

At our present point in chapter V of the *Phenomenology*, we have worked our way from individual consciousness through self-consciousness into the middle of reason and are on our way toward culture or spirit. As we begin to understand culture and become convinced that we cannot explain our experience without it, we will also see that culture develops, and then we will realize that so far in the *Phenomenology* we have ignored this development or left it out. At that point, to explain our experience, it will be necessary to recapture this cultural development. We will have to return to the beginning of culture—which for Hegel in the *Phenomenology* means ancient Greece—and then come back to ourselves, our present, culturally. Similarly, at a later point in the *Phenomenology*, we will see that we have also left out religion and we will have to return to the past to retrieve it and then return to ourselves.

Our problem, as we begin to deal with practical reason in the middle of chapter V, is that we have not yet reached culture, Sittlichkeit, the whole. All we have is individual consciousness—all we have is Kantian Moralität. And thus we are in much the same position as the modern world, which has lost ancient Sittlichkeit, which has lost a sense of the whole, which has become buried in individual consciousness, and thus cannot have a proper sense of culture, a sense which Hegel must try to restore to it.

Without any explanation, I have suggested in the last few pages that Hegel's treatment of practical reason in chapter V deals with Kant. Everyone would admit that the last two sections of the chapter, "Reason as Lawgiver" and "Reason as Testing Laws," refer to Kant's categorical imperative, but I hope to show that Hegel's entire treatment of practical reason is intended as a critique of Kant. To my knowledge, no other commentators have recognized this.

Moreover, while many philosophers have found Hegel's critique of Kantian ethics to be interesting in certain respects, overall most tend to find it rather shallow and to think that Hegel either misunderstands Kant's thought or has a rather crude understanding of it. I hope to show that if we understand that Hegel examines and criticizes Kantian ethics throughout parts B and C of chapter V, that is, for more than half of the chapter, we will see that Hegel demonstrates a rather sophisticated understanding of, and gives a serious and thorough critique of, Kantian practical reason. Let me try to make the case.

IV. Pleasure and Necessity

The first consciousness we meet, in the section entitled "Pleasure and Necessity," is a hedonistic consciousness. It pursues pleasure. "It plunges...into life and indulges to the full....It does not so much make its own happiness as straightway take it and enjoy it....It takes hold of life much as a ripe fruit is plucked, which readily offers itself to the hand that takes it" (PhS, 218/GW, IX, 199). What, one might ask, has this to do with Kantian ethics? I have already suggested that in Hegel's view it is going to be impossible to separate practical reason from theoretical reason in Kantian fashion because, for Hegel, we cannot accept the Kantian distinction between two worlds nor the existence of an unknown thing-in-itself. It follows from this that we are not going to be able to maintain a neat Kantian distinction between a pure autonomous reason, on the one hand, and, on the other, pathological inclinations, interests, or desires. Hegel starts with pleasure because he is not about to let Kant banish it from the realm of reason and morality into some pathological and heteronomous outside.

It cannot be denied that Kant does at times present a crude picture of the relation of duty to inclination, as if they were necessarily opposed and such that moral action must be done, as he says in the Foundations, "only from duty and without any inclination" (F, 14; see also 46/KGS, IV, 398, 428). But it is not only such views that Hegel is attacking. Hegel is well aware that Kant's considered view is not that duty and inclination are mutually exclusive and need be opposed. He is quite well aware that for Kant the *agreement* of duty and inclination is an "ideal of holiness...which we should strive to approach...in an uninterrupted infinite progress" and that such holiness is even "the supreme condition of the highest good" (CPrR, 86, 126/KGS, V, 83–4, 122). Indeed, Hegel will discuss this very ideal at length not only in "The Moral View of the World" at the end of chapter VI, but, as I shall argue shortly, also in the section that immediately follows "Pleasure and Necessity," namely, in "The Law of the Heart." At any rate, Hegel does not find acceptable even Kant's considered view. Kant's considered view is that a moral act need not be free of inclination—indeed, it is even the case that it can never be (CPrR, 34–5/KGS, V, 34). But still a moral act must not be determined by inclination. Even when duty and inclination accord, the act must be done from duty, not from inclination (CPrR, 86/KGS, V, 83–4; MPV, 12/KGS, VI, 213–14).[16] In Hegel's view, Kant does not give enough place to inclination. A general theme of the remainder of chapter V, I shall argue, is that inclination, interest, love, or desire are far more able to produce morality, and that Kantian practical reason is far less able to produce morality, than Kant thinks is the case. This whole section is one of the most fascinating in the Phenomenology.

Thus, it seems to me that Lauer radically misunderstands "Pleasure and Necessity" in taking it to be a traditional attack on pleasure as self-defeating.[17] It is not that at all, but the very opposite, a defense. In "Pleasure and Necessity," we meet a self-consciousness that still (as scientific reason did) seeks to find itself in the world, but it seeks to find itself in another self-consciousness (*PhS*, 217/*GW*, IX, 198). And so it plunges into the world in a way that echoes another side of the Renaissance, one especially captured in the Faust story. Just as we turn in chapter V from theoretical reason to practical reason, so Faust abandoned science and theory in order to plunge into life and find pleasure. Moreover, the pleasure-seeking of this self-consciousness, Hegel tells us, is quite different from the desire we met in "Lordship and Bondage." This consciousness does not at all want to destroy the other, but only its otherness (*PhS*, 218/*GW*, IX, 199). Here, with Faust echoed in the background, Hegel is talking about love. In the *Philosophy of Right*, Hegel says:

> Love means in general terms the consciousness of my unity with another, so that I am not in selfish isolation but win my self-consciousness only as the renunciation of my independence and through knowing myself as the unity of myself with another and of the other with me.... The first moment in love is that I do not wish to be a self-subsistent and independent person and that, if I were, then I would feel defective and incomplete. The second moment is that I find myself in another person, that I count for something in the other, while the other in turn comes to count for something in me... love is unity of an ethical type. (*PR*, 261–2/*SW*, VII, 237–8)

As Robert Williams puts it, in love, "self and other are united without eliminating individuality or difference."[18] In "Pleasure and Necessity," Hegel contrasts the ethical unity involved in love to whatever it is that makes individuals separate. In a very obscure passage, he says, "But here this element which gives to both a separate actuality is rather the category, a being which is essentially in the form of *thought*. It is therefore the *consciousness* of independence—let it be natural consciousness, or consciousness developed into a system of laws—which preserves the individuals each for himself" (*PhS*, 218/*GW*, IX, 199). If this passage is not intended to refer explicitly to the Kantian categorical imperative, it is at least the case that the categorical imperative is one example of what Hegel is talking about. Kantian practical reason certainly grounds the separateness and independence of the individual. It roots the individual in a transcendental sphere apart and makes the individual the source of all law—even a system of laws. Each individual is taken to be a supreme lawgiver from which can arise a kingdom of ends. Kant says, "By a 'kingdom' I understand the union of different rational beings in a system by common laws. Now since it is by laws that ends are determined as regards their universal validity, hence, if we abstract from the personal differences of rational beings, and likewise from all the content of their private ends, we shall be able to conceive all ends combined in a systematic whole" (FP, 50/KGS, IV, 433).

For Kant, to achieve the universal, to produce a kingdom of ends, to live in ethical unity with others under a system of laws, we must withdraw into the individuality and apartness of practical reason to become our own supreme lawgiver, we must abstract from the personal interests and private ends of human beings, we must, at least in Hegel's view, seek an abstract beyond. Are we really going to find unity with others in this way? We would seem to be moving away from unity toward the separate, individual, abstract, and isolated.

Hegel is suggesting that Kantian practical reason is less likely to succeed in producing the ethical union it seeks and more likely to produce individuality and isolation than is love, which indeed, Hegel says, actually achieves the "*unity* of itself and the other self-consciousness"—it achieves the universal (PhS, 218/GW, X, 199). Love's unity with the other self-consciousness is certainly a movement away from individual isolation toward the universal, and if love expands to an even larger unity with others in a kingdom of ends (as we shortly shall see that it does in "The Law of the Heart"), it will move further toward the universal. What Hegel is trying to suggest here is that there is good reason to think that love might tend more effectively toward unity, the overcoming of separateness, the universal, the moral, than does Kantian practical reason.

When Kant discusses love in the *Foundations*, the *Critique of Practical Reason*, and the *Metaphysical Principles of Virtue*, he insists that love as an inclination cannot be commanded as a duty. We cannot have a duty to do something gladly. Thus, for example, when Scripture commands us to love our neighbor or our enemy, in Kant's view it cannot mean to command love as an inclination, but simply beneficence from duty—not pathological love, but practical love (F, 15–16/KGS, IV, 399; CPrR, 86/KGS, V, 83; MPV, 60–1, 70, 113–14/KGS, VI, 401–2, 410, 449–50).

It is quite clear to any sensible reader, however, that the ideal of the Gospels is not at all beneficence from duty, but precisely love as an inclination. In the *Spirit of Christianity*, Hegel attacks Kant's distortion of the Gospels and his reduction of love to moral duty (SCF, 205–24/HTJ, 261–75). In love, for Hegel, all thought of duty vanishes. Love is higher than law and makes obedience to law superfluous. Inclination is unified with the law and love fulfills the law such that law is annulled as law. Love transcends all cleavage between duty and inclination (SCF, 212–14/HTJ, 266–8).

Love so transcends the law, Hegel goes on to argue, that the Gospels even reject the concept of a purely moral duty. Such duty would mean the "intrusion of something alien, resulting in the impurity of the action" (*SCF*, 219; see also 220/*HTJ*, 272, 273). It is not, as for Kant, inclination that introduces impurity (*MPV*, 12/*KGS*, VI, 213). *Duty* introduces the impurity. A charitable action done out of love would be spoiled if one started to think of it as a mere duty. But Hegel goes even further than this. Since duty and inclination have been unified and all opposition overcome, he says, the law can "be taken up [*aufgenommen*] into love" (*SCF*, 225/*HTJ*, 277). Very interestingly, this can be seen as exactly the reverse of what Allison calls Kant's "incorporation thesis." In *Religion Within the Limits of Reason Alone*, Kant writes, "Freedom of the will [*Willkür*] is of a wholly unique nature in that an incentive can determine the will [*Willkür*] to an action *only so far as the individual has incorporated* [*aufgenommen*] *it into his maxim* (has made it the general rule in accordance with which he will conduct himself); only thus can an incentive, whatever it may be, co-exist with the absolute spontaneity of the will [*Willkür*] (*i.e., freedom*)" (*R*, 19/*KGS*, VI, 23–4; *KTF*, 39–40).

Thus, for Kant, love may determine our will in a moral act, but only insofar as it is incorporated into a maxim, that is, only insofar as it becomes beneficence from duty or practical love—whereas Hegel's view is the very opposite, that in the ideal case duty could determine our will, but only insofar as *it* had been incorporated, taken up, into love.

I find Hegel's view preferable to Kant's, but, whatever one decides on this matter, it is quite clear that Hegel is not, as Ameriks and Allison seem to suggest, merely attacking a crudely understood view of the opposition of duty to inclination.[19] Hegel is taking on Kant's subtlest and most considered views and attempting to show that, even so, duty involves an abstract and alien distance that falls short of the ethical union achievable by love.

At the same time, I do not want to suggest that in the *Phenomenology* Hegel is holding, as he may have been at moments in the *Spirit of Christianity*, that love is simply moral and that Kantian practical reason is not. After all, Hegel goes on to recognize (again with Faust, his love for Gretchen, and her death in mind) that the life of pleasure can be a life of necessity, fate, destiny—even of death and destruction. It can be a life with very bad consequences.

Neither is it the case that Hegel here has fallen back into the crude view according to which inclination and pleasure are simply and necessarily opposed to the moral—that is, that the fact that they lead to necessity, fate, and destiny means that they are simply heteronomous, determined, part of a realm of causal necessity. This is not what Hegel is suggesting. We must attend more closely to the way in which Hegel understands fate. He says, "Necessity, fate, and the like, is just that about which we cannot say *what* it does, what its specific laws and positive content are, because it is ... a *relation* that is simple and empty, but also irresistible and imperturbable, whose work is merely the nothingness of individuality" (*PhS*, 219/*GW*, IX, 200). Fate is not to be identified with ordinary causal determinism. Fate is more like chance. It is certainly nothing that a scientist can predict ahead of time—because we cannot say what the laws are. Yet a life at the mercy of chance can certainly be experienced as a cruel fate. Chance is not at all like the regular and predictable causal determinism to be expected in the Kantian realm of phenomenal appearance. Yet, Hegel is suggesting, the total absence of predictability and control is just as much, or more, a necessity, a fate, a heteronomy.

If this is conceded, then it will be interesting to notice that it raises problems for Kant. While it is true that Kant usually holds that freedom has its own laws, at least in some places he explains freedom as independence from the laws of nature (*CPR*, A447=B475; *KTF*, 20; *CPrR*, 100/*KGS*, V, 97). For Hegel, I suggest, freedom as absence of law can be seen as fate. We cannot say what it does—it is blind, imperturbable, and irresistible. To be cut off from the world is very likely to end up at the mercy of the world. In Hegel's view, to the extent that the Kantian transcendental self is separate from the concrete causal world, to the extent that it is cut off from the empirical, it risks subjecting itself to the mercy of fate. Fate occurs because we turn away from the world, leave it to itself, to chance, and thus end up at the mercy of chance, which appears as an uncontrollable necessity. If this is so, it raises problems for Kant. Fate, though it arises from freedom, subverts freedom. If we are subject to fate we are not self-determined. If the self has a destiny, if it is at the mercy of fate, if it is the plaything of chance, the self becomes alien to itself. Heteronomy emerges within the autonomous self. The Kantian and Stoic flight to the noumenal sphere, intended to preserve autonomy, creates fate.

I have argued that history will be very central to Hegel's theory of spirit. The sociocultural realm is the historical product of human activity, a product that in turn transforms and develops human beings themselves. It is also a realm which they can come to understand and in which they can come to be at home and thus free. At the same time, I have argued that there is no real history in the *Phenomenology* until the very end. Spirit is first beginning to emerge here at the end of chapter V, and fate is the first, simplest, thinnest view of history. We have nothing but purely individual consciousnesses, their drives, passions, desires, and the clashes between them—all understood as something completely uncontrolled, ununderstood, mere chaos, mere chance. Such a view of history emerges because we view the world only from the inadequate perspective of individual consciousness and are unable to see how consciousness can understand let alone produce or control its historical world—it merely suffers it. Two sections further on in the *Phenomenology*, in "Virtue and the Way of the World," we will already have moved, I shall argue, to a more complex view of history, the view Kant spells out in his "Idea for a Universal History," where fate will turn into providence. In other words, history for Kant will appear rationally directed. To speak of fate is to say there is no rationality—no order, direction, or control.

V. The Law of the Heart

In the next section of chapter V, "The Law of the Heart and the Frenzy of Self-Conceit," we move from Goethe's *Faust* to his *Werther*, and we get a more complex moral consciousness that still seeks pleasure, but does more than merely tend effectively toward the universal as did love in "Pleasure and Necessity." It actually and explicitly seeks to promote the welfare of *all* humanity as a universal end *and* it takes pleasure in doing so (*PhS*, 221–2/GW, IX, 202–3). This consciousness acts on a Kantian categorical imperative. Or, as Hegel puts it, this heart "has within it a law" (*PhS*, 221/GW, IX, 202). In other words, it takes up or incorporates the law. Hegel says that what this heart "realizes is itself the law, and its pleasure is therefore at the same time the universal pleasure of all hearts. To it the two are undivided; its pleasure is what conforms to the law, and the realization of the law of universal humanity procures for it its own particular pleasure" (*PhS*, 222/GW, IX, 203).

Compare this to Kant, who in the *Fundamental Principles* says:

> To be beneficent when we can is a duty; and besides this, there are many minds so sympathetically constituted that, without any other motive of vanity or self-interest, they find a pleasure in spreading joy around them, and can take delight in the satisfaction of others so far as it is their own work. But I maintain that in such a case an action of this kind, however proper, however amiable it may be, has nevertheless no true moral worth, but is on a level with other inclinations, for example, the inclination to honor, which...deserves praise and encouragement, but not esteem.[20]

Acting from inclination has no true moral worth. But, on the other hand, acting from duty and being inclined to do so, for Kant, is an ideal of holiness. Kant says, "To love one's neighbor means to like to practice all duties toward him. The command which makes this a rule cannot require that we have this disposition but only that we endeavor after it" (*CPrR*, 86/KGS, V, 83). The perfect agreement of duty and inclination is an "ideal of holiness...unattainable by any creature...yet an archetype which we should strive to approach...in an uninterrupted infinite progress. If a rational creature could ever reach the stage of thoroughly liking to do all moral laws, it would mean that there was no possibility of there being in him a desire which could tempt him to deviate from them.... To such a level of moral disposition no creature can ever attain" (CPrR, 86/KGS, V, 83).

Such holiness is "the supreme condition of the highest good" (CPrR, 126/KGS, V, 122). The highest good, for Kant, sets as its ideal a perfect agreement between the moral *law* and *inclination*—in other words, in Hegel's language, it is a *law* of the *heart*. Moreover, the regular satisfaction of our inclinations would amount to happiness, and the highest good also involves the reconciliation of virtue and happiness. If happiness did not accompany virtue, we certainly would not have the highest good for human beings. But virtue and happiness, we have already said, would seem to be irreconcilable. While happiness requires the regular satisfaction of our inclinations, interests, and desires, to be virtuous we certainly cannot be determined by inclination, interest, or desire. We must be determined by the moral law. And there is no reason to think that virtue will produce happiness. If we lived solely in the phenomenal world, Kant thinks, there would be no reason to expect virtue and happiness to accord. Only if there is also a noumenal world can we imagine such reconciliation as an ideal, and only, Kant thinks, if we postulate a God who will see to it that nature is ordered such that while we act virtuously our desires will at the same time be satisfied so that we can also be happy—and happy in proportion to our worthiness to be happy, that is, in proportion to our virtue (CPrR, 111–19, 128–33/KGS, V, 107–15, 124–8).

What we have here then, Hegel insists, and Kant fully admits, is a mere ideal. Inclination ideally ought to agree with the moral law—but this is not at all something actually achieved (CPrR, 86/KGS, V, 83; MPV, 151/KGS, VI, 482). Thus Hegel says that the law remains separate from the heart and exists on its own such that most of humanity, while accepting the law, will not actually find it in unity with the heart and so will have to dispense with actual enjoyment in obeying it. It follows from this that the law will start to become for the heart a mere show that will not seem to deserve the authority it is supposed to have (PhS, 222–3/GW, IX, 203–4). Hegel's point in all of this, I suggest, is that we have not transcended all cleavage between objective law and subjective feeling so as to annul the law as law—we have not achieved Sittlichkeit. We merely have a Kantian ideal of unity between law and inclination. And this ideal, Hegel wants to go on to argue, is not likely to work in any actual case.

From the start, the law of the heart has hated and opposed any imposition from outside (by authorities, the government, whatever) of laws that offend the heart. All law must agree with the heart—that is the only acceptable law. Kant would at least seem to be in agreement with this. In *Religion Within the Limits of Reason Alone*, he claims that we have a practical knowledge that rests "solely upon reason and ... lies as close to every man ... as though it were engraved upon his *heart*—*a law*, which we need but name to find ourselves at once in agreement with everyone else regarding its authority, and which carries with it in everyone's consciousness *unconditioned* binding force, to wit, the law of morality."[21] Where does this law—capable of producing such complete agreement as if engraved upon our very hearts—come from? In the *Foundations*, the third formulation of the categorical imperative tells us that each rational being is a supreme legislator, "subject only to his own, yet universal, legislation, and . . . only bound to act in accordance with his own will, which is, however, designed by nature to be a will giving universal laws" (F, 51/KGS, IV, 432).

Kant sees no trouble at all in claiming that we are subject to no law but our own, yet that we can end up with universal legislation—which might seem to mean legislation for *all*. Lacking Sittlichkeit, Hegel thinks there will be a great deal of trouble to be found here. In the *Metaphysical Principles of Virtue*, Kant admits that there is a distinction we must notice. In ethics, the "law is conceived as the law of one's *own* will and *not* of the will in general, which could also be the will of others; in the latter case such a law would give rise to a juridical duty."[22] This suggests that while a law one gives oneself can be one's own, others would not take it as *their own*. Indeed, Kant says that I can "be forced by others to actions which are directed as means to an end, but I can never be forced by others to have an end; I alone can make something an end for myself . . . for I can have no end except of my own making" (MPV, 38–9/KGS, VI, 381). Thus, while it is our duty, for Kant, to promote the happiness of others as our end (MPV, 46, 43/KGS, VI, 388, 385–6), the fact that I have adopted this as my end cannot cause others to accept it as their end. In fact, in *Religion Within the Limits of Reason Alone*, it seems that in an ethical commonwealth not only will it be the case that others will not accept my legislation as their own but that even "the people, as a people, cannot itself be regarded as the law-giver. For in such a commonwealth all the laws are expressly designed to promote the *morality* of actions (which is something *inner*, and hence cannot be subject to public human laws), whereas, in contrast, these public laws—and this would go to constitute a juridical commonwealth—are directed only toward the legality of actions, which meets the eye, and not towards (inner) morality" (R, 90/KGS, VI, 98–9). However, it would seem that Kant wants it both ways. The state cannot force an inner disposition to virtue, yet seems to count on it:

> It would be a contradiction . . . for the political commonwealth to compel its citizens to enter into an ethical commonwealth, since the very concept of the latter involves freedom from coercion. Every political commonwealth may indeed wish to be possessed of a sovereignty, according to laws of virtue, over the spirits [of its citizens]; for then, when its methods of compulsion do not avail . . . their dispositions to virtue would

bring about what was required. But woe to the legislator who wishes to establish through force a polity directed to ethical ends! For in so doing he would not merely achieve the very opposite of an ethical polity but also undermine his political state and make it insecure.[23]

The legislator wants everyone to take the legislator's law as their own, be disposed toward it, take it as a law of their heart, but woe to the legislator who tries to legislate such a law of the heart. We are certainly not very far along here toward the ideal of agreement between duty and inclination, virtue and happiness, the law and the heart. And so, as Hegel puts it, what will happen is that others will not find the law to be "the fulfillment of the law of *their* hearts, but rather that of someone else; and, precisely in accordance with the universal law that each shall find in what is law *his* own heart, they turn against the reality *he* set up, just as he turned against theirs. Thus, just as the individual at first finds only the rigid law, now he finds the hearts of men themselves, opposed to his excellent intentions and detestable" (*PhS*, 224/GW, IX, 204). Others cannot recognize themselves in the law of my heart. If my legislation were to stand as a universal ordinance, others would find it merely my imposition and would turn against it as the very law of the heart demands (*PhS*, 223–4/GW, IX, 203–4).

What Hegel is suggesting here (and it is something he will further develop in the section entitled "The Spiritual Animal Kingdom") is that Kant was quite correct in the view that the law must come from our own reason—though Kant was not fully aware of what this actually implied. It is not enough that laws just be rational. They must be our *own*. Human beings are motivated by what is their own—their desire to express themselves and recognize their own doing in the result. And if forced to choose between what is rational or universal and what is their own they will find such a situation oppressive. Lauer argues that the trouble with the law of the heart is that it does not act on the categorical imperative.[24] That is seriously mistaken. The law of the heart does involve a categorical imperative, and that is precisely what is wrong with it. Hegel is attacking the categorical imperative.

But worse is yet to come. Hegel thinks Kantian morality will always result in an alien situation, one that always establishes a law that is not our own—even if we ourselves instituted the law. In the *Spirit of Christianity*, he said, "The consciousness of having performed his duty enables the individual to claim universality for himself; he intuits himself as universal, as raised above himself *qua* particular and above the whole sphere of particularity, i.e., above the mass of individuals ... and this self-consciousness of his is as foreign to the action as men's applause" (*SCF*, 219-20/HTJ, 272). Hegel is suggesting that such a claim to universality—necessarily implied in acting on the

Kantian categorical imperative—itself involves heteronomy. In the "Law of the Heart," Hegel says that in carrying out "the law of his heart...the law has in fact escaped the individual; it directly becomes merely the relation which was supposed to be got rid of. The law of the heart, through its very realization, ceases to be a law of the *heart*. For in its realization it...is now a *universal* power for which this particular heart is a matter of indifference, so that the individual, by setting up his own ordinance, no longer finds it to be his own. Consequently, what the individual brings into being through the realization of his law, is not *his* law...but actually is for him an alien affair...a superior power which is [not] only alien to him, but one which is hostile" (*PhS*, 223/*GW*, IX, 203).

After all, if the legislation of public law, as we have seen Kant himself say in *Religion Within the Limits of Reason Alone*, cannot be taken to demand anything inner, if the legislator cannot expect to legislate disposition to virtue (without undermining the political state and making it insecure), then what difference does it make who the legislator is—we ourselves or someone else? As soon as a public law is established that must keep its distance in this way from the inner, from disposition, from our own, from the heart, such a law (Hegel is perfectly correct in claiming) will escape the individual and become an alien power—even for the very individual who established the law. We should notice that Hegel's critique here very much anticipates the postmodern attack on universalization and totalization as forms of domination.

The problem here, for Hegel, is that we do not have Sittlichkeit. We have instead a modern separation of universal law and the heart—a separation perfectly expressed in Kantian ethics. Moreover, Kantian ethics simply would not accept Sittlichkeit. The Kantian individual, as Hegel puts it, would certainly find the "divine and human ordinance[s]" of the ancient world, which were taken "as an accepted authority," to be instead "a dead authority in which not only its own self...but also those subject to that ordinance would have no consciousness of themselves." In short, Kantian ethics would find the objective laws of the ancient world to be an alien authority—it would find them to be heteronomous. It would see nothing of itself, its own, in those laws. Custom and tradition, laws based on religion or mythology, for Kant, are not and could not be forms of rational autonomy. They would be other, heteronomous, alien. What this completely misses, in Hegel's view, is that ancient law was "really animated by the consciousness of all," it was in fact "the law of every heart...for this means nothing else than that individuality becomes an object to itself in the form of universality in which, however, it does not recognize itself" (*PhS*, 224–5/*GW*, IX, 205). No doubt, Hegel ignores the disagreement and conflict that could be found in any given city-state. Nevertheless, the laws of the city-state in a meaningful way were constituted by the cultural and historical action of the citizens themselves and were embedded in their customs, traditions, practices, and feelings such that they *were* their *own* laws. They had an objective and universal form such that citizens did not see that they had constituted them, but in a meaningful sense they were the law of every heart. The universal and feelings were not separate here, their unity was not a far off ideal, it was actual.[25] As Hegel put it in an earlier text:

> As free men the Greeks and Romans obeyed laws laid down by themselves, obeyed men whom they had themselves appointed to office, waged wars on which they had themselves decided, gave their property, exhausted their passions, and sacrificed their lives by thousands for an end which was their own. They neither learned nor taught [a moral system] but evinced by their actions the moral maxims which they could call their very own. In public as in private and domestic life, every individual was a free man, one who lived by his own laws. The idea (*Idee*) of his country or of his state was the invisible and higher reality for which he strove, which impelled him to effort; it was the final end of *his* world or in his eyes the final end of *the* world, an end which he found manifested in the realities of daily life or which he himself co-operated in manifesting and maintaining. Confronted by this idea, his own individuality vanished; it was only this idea's maintenance, life and persistence he asked for, and these were things which he himself could make realities.[26]

The sociocultural construction of institutions and laws will be traced at length in chapter VI of the *Phenomenology*—from the ancient world through the French Revolution. And in chapter VI, the further we move into the modern and Kantian world, the more it will be the case that our laws are not seen as our own. In the ancient world, laws were our own—they were laws of the heart.

The failure of the law of the heart in the modern world leads to the frenzy of self-conceit. We blame the domination that arises not on ourselves—our heart is pure, all we want is the happiness of others. The fact that they do not accept our law, the fact that they see it as domination, is not due to us (*PhS*, 226/*GW*, IX, 206; cf. *R*, 25, 32–3/*KGS*, VI, 30, 37). The only trouble, however, is that everyone's attitude is the same:

> The consciousness which sets up the law of its heart therefore meets with resistance from others, because it contradicts the equally *individual* laws of their hearts; and these others in their resistance are doing nothing else but setting up and claiming validity for their own law. The universal that we have here is, then, only a universal resistance and struggle of all against one another, in which each claims validity for his own individuality, but at the same time does not succeed in his efforts, because

each meets with the same resistance from the others, and is nullified by their reciprocal resistance. What seems to be public *order*, then, is this universal state of war, in which each wrests what he can for himself, executes justice on the individuality of others and establishes his own, which is equally nullified through the action of the others. It is the "way of the world," the show of an unchanging course that is only meant to be a universality. (*PhS*, 227/GW, IX, 207)

The "way of the world" or the "course of the world" (in German, *der Weltlauf*)—is a term Hegel finds in Kant (CPR, A495, also A450=B478; see also MPV, 15/KGS, VI, 216).[27] Certainly, Hegel's description here of the "way of the world" is intended to refer to an arrangement central to Kant's political philosophy and philosophy of history. Compare the above passage from Hegel to the following passage from Kant's *Perpetual Peace*:

Many say a republic would have to be a nation of angels, because men with their selfish inclinations are not capable of a constitution of such sublime form. But precisely with these inclinations nature comes to the aid of the general will established on reason, which is revered even though impotent in practice. Thus it is only a question of a good organization of the state (which does lie in man's power), whereby the powers of each selfish inclination are so arranged in opposition that one moderates or destroys the ruinous effect of the other. The consequence for reason is the same as if none of them existed, and man is forced to be a good citizen even if not a morally good person.

The problem of organizing a state, however hard it may seem, can be solved even for a race of devils, if only they are intelligent. The problem is: "Given a multitude of rational beings requiring universal laws for their preservation, but each of whom is secretly inclined to exempt himself from them, to establish a constitution in such a way that, although their private intentions conflict, they check each other, with the result that their public conduct is the same as if they had no such intentions."

A problem like this must be capable of solution; it does not require that we know how to attain the moral improvement of men but only that we should know the mechanism of nature in order to use it on men, organizing the conflict of the hostile intentions present in a people in such a way that they must compel themselves to submit to coercive laws. Thus a state of peace is established in which laws have force. (PP, 112–13/KGS, VIII, 366–7)

The assumption of the ancient world was that in a good city the universal and the heart (law and morality, on the one hand, and inclination, interest, custom, and tradition, on the other) would agree—Sittlichkeit was the

norm. In the modern world, the assumption is the reverse, that the universal
and the heart are separate and will diverge, though the heart can be manipu-
lated so as to produce the universal. For Kant, the ideal of holiness is that the
universal and the heart, duty and inclination, agree. This ideal is the supreme
condition of the highest good. It is what Hegel calls the law of the heart. But
it is only an ideal and all we end up with is the frenzy of self-conceit, the
organization of a race of devils into the appearance of a nation of angels,
public order that is really a state of war, the reciprocal nullification of conflicting interests appearing as the universal. At any rate, we have already
arrived at the next section: "Virtue and the Way of the World."

VI. Virtue and the Way of the World

The law of the heart, then, dissolves merely into virtue. In other words, the
consciousness now before us no longer takes pleasure in acting on the universal; it no longer combines inclination and the moral law. It simply does its
duty. All we have is ordinary Kantian virtue, and it stands opposed to the
way of the world, the conflict of particular interests, which it intends to
manipulate in order to produce virtuous results. Like Lauer and Hyppolite,
many commentators seem to think that "Virtue and the Way of the World"
is about Don Quixote.[28] I think there is a passing reference to Quixote in one
passage (PhS, 231/GW, IX, 210), but that is not what the section is about. No
commentator that I am aware of sees what the section, at least in my opinion,
is so very clearly about, namely, Kant's philosophy of history.[29]

In the "Idea for a Universal History," Kant tells us that there are two
forces at work in history. The first is the conflict of particular interests; the
second is morality. And both, for Kant, lead to the very same end—peace,
justice, and a league of nations. Conflict and war, for Kant, will lead toward
morality (IUH, 18–19/KGS, VIII, 24–5; PP, 112–13/KGS, VIII, 366–7).[30]

Kant thinks that we find two propensities within human beings. He sums
these up as "unsocial sociability." Human beings have an unsocial propensity—
a propensity to isolation, selfishness, and lack of concern for the interests of
others. But they also have a social propensity, a propensity to associate with
others in society. They need others. They must cooperate with others to satisfy
their needs. These two propensities together—being near others, associating
with them, yet being selfish and unsocial—produce conflict, competition, and
even war. While there is an obvious negative side to this conflict, there is also a
positive side which is perhaps even more important. Conflict and selfishness
do, after all, awaken our human powers and stir us out of complacency.
Selfishness drives us to accomplish things; competition sharpens our abilities.
We develop our human potentialities. We are driven toward the fullest development of our powers, capacities, and talents (IUH, 15/KGS, VIII, 20–1).

So, for Kant, we are driven to society by sociability and the need for others. Once in society, antagonism, competition, and selfishness set in and our powers and capacities develop. This development, for Kant, will eventually lead to the society of morality, justice, and peace that he is after (*IUH*, 15/*KGS*, VIII, 20–1; *PP*, 106, 111/*KGS*, VIII, 360–1, 365). Selfishness and aggression will lead toward morality—that is Kant's argument.

The notion that conflicting self-interests lead toward what morality demands is quite similar to, and perhaps Kant even gets it from, Adam Smith. In a market economy, all pursue their own self-interest. Nevertheless, this self-seeking not only produces a common good, it does so, for Smith, more effectively than if individuals had consciously and cooperatively sought the common good. Aggressive self-seeking, given the interdependence of each upon all, produces a national capital, the wealth of the nation, that common good out of which all struggle to gain their particular share. Self-seeking produces this common good through an "invisible hand," that is, behind our backs and despite our intentions.[31]

For Kant, there is also an "unsocial sociability" at the international level. We find the assertion of national self-interest that drives nations toward aggression and war. Yet there is also an important form of sociability among nations, namely, their interest in commerce and trade. It is the dynamic interplay between these factors that will lead to a league of nations, peace, and international law.

As wars become more serious, destructive, and expensive, they become more uncertain. They come into conflict with ever-increasing economic interests. Wars, as they become more disruptive, interfere with trade. As world trade grows, as nations become more interdependent, as they rely more and more on each other commercially, war poses an ever-greater threat to the smooth functioning of the international market. At the first sign of war, other nations will intervene to arbitrate, to quash the war, in order to secure their own national commercial interests. This is the first step toward a league of nations (*IUH*, 23/*KGS*, VIII, 28; *PP*, 114/*KGS*, VIII, 368).

The second force at work in history is morality. We can easily see that morality, the categorical imperative, would demand fair laws, just constitutions, and an end to wars. We could not will that everyone be allowed to do the opposite. We could not will to universalize war, unjust constitutions, and unfair laws. Morality would also demand a league of nations (*PP*, 100/*KGS*, VIII, 356). And morality, for Kant, is one of the forces at work in history. Moreover, the other force, we have already seen, drives us toward the very same point that morality does. War among nations and commercial interest drive us toward peace, law, and a league of nations. Both morality and war converge toward the same end—one consciously, the other unconsciously (*IUH*, 18–19/*KGS*, VIII, 24–5; *PP*, 111–13/*KGS*, VIII, 365–7).

In the long passage quoted above from *Perpetual Peace*, we see a good example of these two forces at work. Kant argues that selfish inclinations must be arranged so that they cancel each other out and thus devils could end up with a society that might have seemed possible only for those with the morality of angels. Both of these forces are necessary for Kant. One without the other is not enough. Reason and morality alone, he says, would never achieve our end. Humans are too corrupt. Our reason alone is not powerful enough to produce a league of nations and just states (*IUH*, 17–18/*KGS*, VIII, 23). On the other hand, conflict alone will never actually make us moral. Conflict and war drive us toward peace, a league of nations, and legality. But this is only to say that our self-interest drives us toward peace and law, and self-interest is not moral for Kant.

If, for Kant, we are able to form an idea for a universal history, if we can see with Adam Smith that self-seeking combined with commercial interdependence lead to the common good, if we can see that in history the dynamic tension between war and commerce will lead us unconsciously toward the same point that reason and morality would consciously lead us, then Kant thinks that the second force at work in history, our own reason, our own morality, can begin to guide this historical development toward its goal (*IUH*, 22/*KGS*, VIII, 27). History can be rationally guided. We can have providence (*IUH*, 25/*KGS*, VIII, 30), not just fate.

Hegel clearly has Kantian morality and philosophy of history in mind as he plays out the interaction between the two consciousnesses that stand before us: virtue and the way of the world.[32] Virtue, he says, is the consciousness that universal law is essential and that individuality—which involves inclination and particular interest—must be sacrificed to the universal and thus brought under its discipline and control. Virtue wills to accomplish a good that is not yet actual; it is an ought that must be realized. And it can be realized only through virtue's nullifying of individuality (*PhS*, 228–30/*GW*, IX, 208–10). In the *Metaphysical Principles of Virtue*, Kant says that the "moral capacity of man would not be virtue if it were not actualized by the strength of one's resolution in conflict with powerful opposing inclinations. Virtue is the product of pure practical reason insofar as the latter, in the consciousness of its superiority (through freedom), gains mastery over the inclinations" (*MPV*, 145/*KGS*, VI, 477). He also says you must "dare to do battle against all the forces of nature within you and round about you, and to conquer them when they come into conflict with your moral principles" (*MPV*, 152, also 64–5, 67–8/*KGS*, VI, 483, 405, 408).

For the way of the world, on the other hand, individuality takes *itself* to be essential—which is to say that it pursues self-interest. It seeks its own pleasure and enjoyment, and in doing so subordinates the universal to itself. For Kant, we saw, both morality and the conflict of particular interests converge toward the same universal end. So also, Hegel says, the way of the world, through conflict of particular interests, achieves the universal—the very same universal that virtue seeks (*PhS*, 228–9, 235/*GW*, IX, 208–9, 213). For Kant, it was morality's task to guide the historical conflict of particular interests and hasten it toward its end. For Hegel too, virtue attempts to assist the way of the world to realize the universal.

At this point, however, Hegel's disagreement with Kant sets in. Hegel argues that, in fact, virtue's assistance is *unnecessary*. The way of the world is quite capable of realizing the universal on its own. It does not need virtue. Virtue's belief that only it can realize the universal—this Quixotic attitude on the part of this knight of virtue—is nothing but a sham (*PhS*, 230–2/*GW*, IX, 209–11). Virtue always wants to bring the good into existence by the sacrifice of individuality and particular interest. But it is individuality, the conflict of particular interests, that actually realizes the universal. Virtue denies the accomplishments of the way of the world and attempts to claim them for itself. Virtue always wants to treat the universal as something that does not yet exist, something that *ought to be*, something opposed to particular interests, something *it* will bring about, rather than as something that already *is*. Sittlichkeit is emerging here. Hegel says, "Virtue in the ancient world had its own definite sure meaning, for it had in the *spiritual substance* of the nation a foundation full of meaning, and for its purpose an actual good already in existence. Consequently, too, it was not directed against the actual world as against something *generally perverted*, and against a 'way of the world.' But the virtue we are considering has its being outside of the spiritual substance, it is an unreal virtue, a virtue in imagination and name only, which lacks that substantial content" (*PhS*, 234/*GW*, IX, 212–13).

For Hegel, we must drop the idea that virtue exists only as a principle, an ought, which as yet has no actual existence and which must be brought into existence through the sacrifice of individuality, particular interest, or passion. Hegel's objection to Kantian morality is that it is abstract, outside the world, an ought, and that it believes that only it is capable of realizing the universal (*PhS*, 235/*GW*, IX, 213; see also A, I, 56–61/*SW*, XII, 90–6). It has severed itself from the concrete actual world of interest and passion, and faces it as an other.[33] From this superior position it wants to direct the world. Instead, morality must be rooted in the world.

Or, to put this another way, Kant's philosophy of history and his ethics are written from the perspective of individual consciousness—the perspective that there are only individual consciousnesses. Morality, for Kant, is a matter of individual will abstracted from the concrete actual world. Certainly, for Kant, inclinations, interests, and passions are part of the world and are to be carefully distinguished from the individual moral will if the individual is to be self-determined and thus free. It is this separation that Hegel objects to. It involves the "creation of distinctions that are no distinctions" (*PhS*, 234/*GW*, IX, 212). Kant has no notion of spirit or Sittlichkeit, which Hegel is trying to push us toward here. Sittlichkeit is morality embedded in a concrete spiritual world. For Hegel, virtue and the way of the world, particular interest and the universal, morality and the concrete world, are not separate opposed realities externally related to each other. They are internally related as parts of a single spiritual reality that already exists; it is not something that merely ought to be realized.

On the one hand, Hegel is attacking all egoistical ethical systems here. The claim that all people are selfish (concerned only with particular interest) overlooks the universal result, the moral result, that arises out of the conflict of particular interests. At the same time, Hegel also is attacking all antiegotistical ethical systems here. Egoism, self-interest, is what realizes the universal. Selfishness has a most important place that cannot be overlooked or swept aside. Another way to put this is to notice that just as Hegel rejected physiognomy's attempt to explain the outer as the expression of the inner, or action as the expression of intention, so he rejects any attempt to explain history as simply the expression of either virtue or self-interest. This is to say that he rejects the attempt to explain history as the expression of inner individual consciousness.

We must abandon the perspective of individual consciousness and adopt a perspective in which the concrete world and individual consciousness are seen as two aspects of one spiritual unity. Individual consciousness is the internalization of the sociocultural world and the sociocultural world is the outcome and objectification of the actions of individual consciousnesses. Each develops in interaction with the other, and each transforms the other.

Hegel agrees with the Kantian and Smithian notion that a conflict of particular interests leads to the universal. What Hegel does not accept is that this can be adequately understood at the level of individual consciousness. For it to be correctly understood, we must move to the level of spirit. Spirit explains how individual interest—the concrete way of the world—is connected to virtue. This will become clearer as we proceed, but here we can at least say that interaction among particular interests gives rise to a set of institutions, a world, which develops a spiritual life of its own and which reacts back upon and molds those individual consciousnesses and leads them to virtue. Particular interest and virtue are not two externally related realms eternally distinguished from each other. They are internally related as two interacting parts within a single spiritual unity. Each produces and molds the other. Virtue is simply mistaken in thinking itself independent and outside this spiritual reality, superior to it, and thus able to manipulate and guide particular interests from above. Particular interests as they are formed by their spiritual world actually take an *interest* in virtue and virtue is something that develops out of and engages our passions, inclinations, and interests. Moreover, there is no ought that is above, outside, independent, and that the individual will must set out to realize. Morality already exists as the spiritual unity that encloses us, that is our very being, and that is embedded in our feelings, desires, and interests. Hegel's task is to reconcile us to what is by allowing us to correctly understand what is. His aim is not to transform reality in accordance with an abstract and independent ought. Virtue is not something as yet nonexistent that we ought to realize; it is something already existing that we must come to more deeply recognize and rationally grasp in our actual sociocultural practice. As Hegel puts it in the *Philosophy of Right*, "After all, the truth about Right, Ethics, and the state is as old as its public recognition and formulation in the law of the land, in the morality of everyday life, and in religion. What more does this truth require—since the thinking mind is not content to possess it in this ready fashion? It requires to be grasped in thought as well; the content which is already rational in principle must win the *form* of rationality" (PR, 3, 11–12/SW, VII, 22, 35–6).

Earlier in chapter V of the *Phenomenology*, we have seen, Kantian theoretical reason ended in failure. It was unable to grasp consciousness and ended up reducing it to a bone. We now see that Kantian practical reason also ends in failure. It thinks it can direct the course of the world, but it turns out that this is Quixotic self-delusion. In fact, the course of the world does better than does virtue. In Hegel's view, a fixed Kantian opposition between theoretical and practical reason cannot be sustained. The phenomena/noumena distinction that underlies this opposition, we have seen over and over again, is untenable, and neither theoretical nor practical reason accomplish what they claim to be able to accomplish. If kept separate from each other, theoretical reason cannot grasp consciousness and practical reason cannot produce a moral world. This separation must be abandoned. Theoretical and practical reason must "reciprocally integrate themselves" (PM, 185/SW, X, 303), and we must move on toward spirit.

Part C. Individuality that Takes Itself to Be Real In and For Itself

Reason seeks to find itself, assert itself, gain a place, be at home in the world. But at the same time, as we have seen since we first met the slave, the world resists. And it is the world, the object, the in-itself, that triumphs, that resists the reasoning individual, the for-itself—the course of the world even succeeds in realizing virtue better than this reasoning individual. Try as we might, this is a fact we are unable to get around. At the same time, for Hegel, strange as it may be, it is we who have constructed this world. Our world is our construction, but it resists us and triumphs over us. What we must do, Hegel thinks, is cease setting up reality as an in-itself over against a for-itself, an object opposed to a subject; we must abandon the opposition between theoretical and practical reason.

And so in part C of chapter V of the *Phenomenology*, we get a consciousness that no longer takes the world to be given, there, outside the self. Rather, Hegel says, it takes the world to be transparently developed within the self. Both material and action lie within self-consciousness (*PhS*, 237/*GW*, IX, 215). Consciousness no longer seeks to realize itself in antithesis to reality. Being-in-itself and being-for-itself are interfused (*PhS*, 236/*GW*, IX, 214). We no longer have a virtue opposed to the way of the world. The only problem, though, is that we have not yet gotten beyond individual consciousness. If we see that we have constructed all reality, but take this "we" to be made up merely of individual consciousnesses, what will happen? Won't reality be constructed separately by each individual consciousness? Won't that be chaos? What can others be expected to think of my reality? Let us move on and see.

VII. The Spiritual Animal Kingdom and Deceit, or the Fact Itself

The way of the world realized a universal result that was brought about by the action of conflicting particular interests. What this shows us, Hegel suggests, is that action can only be judged by what it achieves. As we saw earlier in our discussion of physiognomy, Hegel rejects the notion that we can understand actions on the basis of inner intentions. Only the action achieved is a reality, not the idea that is supposed to guide the action from above or outside. We cannot determine the reality of the action until it takes place— we cannot see the universal moral result in the particular interests until the conflicting interests have actually realized the universal. The reality of any potentiality, capacity, or talent is its realization, not what we hope or desire or intend, but what becomes, what is actually realized in action. The talent of engineers or artists is seen in the bridges they build or the paintings they paint, not merely in their hopes, dreams, or intentions concerning possible bridges or paintings (*PhS*, 239–40/*GW*, IX, 217–18).

We can say, then, that self-expression occurs only through action— action expresses a capacity or talent. Moreover, this is the only way to understand individuality. The self or the individual is simply what is expressed, what is realized, in action or work. The self is not some mysterious entity behind or beyond its action. We cannot appeal to an inner self to measure the deed. It will even follow from this that there is no room for lamentation or repentance over the work. That would be to presuppose a self-in-itself that might have been, but failed to be, realized. There is no such self-in-itself. The original nature or potential of the individual can be nothing but what eventually gets carried out, expressed, realized in the world. We cannot lament that our work does not live up to our potential. Our potential is what we are finally able to realize in our work. Individuals are what they actually do, not what they merely hope, dream, or intend (*PhS*, 241–2/*GW*, IX, 219–20). This is a view that academics are not likely to find congenial. We are all convinced that we are capable of far more and much greater work than we ever actually turn out. Such is our self-delusion. There is no room for a Kantian self-in-itself behind or beyond or distinguished from what is actually realized.

At the same time, for Hegel, work is inescapably for-others. It produces a public result. However, if everyone takes work to be individual self-expression, then others will find our work to be alien, external, and unimportant to *them*. They will be concerned only with their own work—their own expression (*PhS*, 243/*GW*, IX, 221). All works, then, will be important as the self-expression of one person. And for others these works will be unimportant. They will not be recognized by others. And, for Hegel, if something is not recognized, it is not real.

In one of the examples that Kant gives of a moral act in the *Foundations*, he discusses talents. Hegel is suggesting that Kant's treatment of talents is seriously flawed. Kant asks if the moral law will allow us to leave a useful talent undeveloped, and concludes that it will not allow us to do so. We cannot universalize not developing a useful talent. The categorical imperative demands that we develop such talents (*F*, 40–1/*KGS*, IV, 422–3).[34] In the *Metaphysical Principles of Virtue*, Kant says that we have a duty to cultivate our natural powers, capacities, and endowments (*MPV*, 44, 108/*KGS*, VI, 386–7, 444).

The moral law, then, commands us to take as our end the realization of such talents. But for Hegel this is simply incoherent. It is impossible to determine what this end might be before it has actually been realized. What talent I might have, what my potential might be, can only be discovered in what I am finally able to make real through action. Do I have the potential to write a book that is truly a masterpiece and thus would have a moral obligation to keep at it until I actually produce that book? Or do I merely have the potential to write a few valuable and interesting things and when I have done so would best be advised to move on to another topic? Or is it the case that my talent really lies in a completely different field altogether and that I am wasting my time in writing? We cannot know what our end is, what our talent is, what potential we have, until we have actually realized it.

Bernard Williams tells a story of a Gauguin-like figure who, while concerned with the definite and pressing human claims made upon him by others and what would be involved in their being neglected, nevertheless turns away from them in order to realize his gift as a painter and to pursue his art. This involves a good deal of risk. Whether or not he succeeds in developing this gift, whether he actually has a significant gift, he cannot tell for sure ahead of time. Thus, whether his action can be justified depends, certainly in part, on whether he is finally able to develop this gift. Any justification, then, will at least in part have to be retrospective.[35] But for Kant the categorical imperative would certainly seem to require that we know and will our end ahead of time. We must act on a maxim—a maxim that we formulate, analyze, and find to be universalizable ahead of time. If we do not have such a rational principle to act upon, our act will be heteronomous, at the whim of the way of the world—not free or moral. However, Allison argues:

> Since maxims are self-imposed rules, one cannot make something one's maxim without in some sense being aware of it as such, or at least without the capacity to become aware of it.... This does not entail, however, either that we possess a "Cartesian certainty" regarding our motivation (which Kant, of course, denies) or that we must explicitly formulate our maxims to ourselves before acting. The point is rather a conceptual one: namely, that I cannot act on a principle (according to the *conception* of law) without an awareness of that principle, although I need not be explicitly aware of myself *as* acting on that principle. Moreover, it must be possible in subsequent reflection to discover and articulate (albeit not in an indefeasible way) the maxims on which one acts. (*KTF*, 90)

But where we cannot know ahead of time what our potential, our talent, and thus our end might be, it does not make sense to say that in subsequent reflection we could discover and articulate the maxim upon which we acted. If it was not possible to formulate a specific maxim in the first place, it would not be possible to discover and articulate one in retrospect. Instead of specific maxims, then, Kant would seem to have in mind all-purpose maxims to the effect that we should realize *whatever* useful talents we might have: "No principle of reason prescribes exactly how far one must go in this effort.... Besides, the variety of circumstances which men may encounter makes quite optional the choice of the kind of occupation for which one should cultivate his talent. There is here, therefore, no law of reason for actions but only for the maxim of actions, viz., 'Cultivate your powers of mind and body so as to be able to fulfill all the ends which may arise for you, uncertain as you may be which ends might become your own'" (*MPV*, 50–1/*KGS*, VI, 392).

However, such all-purpose maxims tell us nothing whatsoever about what it is moral to do in any specific case because we cannot know ahead of time where our talent lies or how much talent we have in any specific area. The categorical imperative cannot tell me whether I should keep working toward a masterpiece, switch topics often, or give up writing altogether.

Furthermore, all of this also presents problems for the second formulation of the categorical imperative. If it is a duty to "treat humanity, whether in your own person or in that of another, always as an end and never as a means only" (F, 47/KGS, IV, 429), and if as a consequence of this we have a duty to develop powers, capacities, and talents (MPV, 50–1/KGS, VI, 392), then we are in trouble. If we cannot know what our talents are ahead of time, and if to treat humanity as an end requires that we develop our talents and those of others, then we will not know how to act in these cases. Again, we cannot give in to Kantian virtue's claim that it must be put in charge, that it can survey the whole terrain, that it will foresee what must be done, either to direct the way of the world or even to develop our talents. Virtue must instead take a very different stance. It must deal with what is, with actuality, with what has already been actualized. As Williams suggests, it must largely be retrospective. We cannot simply and easily look ahead to what Kantian virtue claims ought to be realized.

What do we do then? Well, Hegel thinks real people just act. And he thinks Kant well knows they do. Indeed, in the "Idea for a Universal History," Kant takes a very different approach to the development of talents. There he holds that it is self-interest that leads to the realization of talent. As in Adam Smith's model of a market society, competing particular interests drive individuals to action, and it is out of such action that there arises the development of their powers, capacities, and talents. Selfishness awakens our powers and stirs us out of complacency. It moves us to action, drives us to accomplish things, and thus we realize our potential (IUH, 15–16/KGS, VIII, 20–1). It is the way of the world and not virtue that develops our talents.

Hegel, I suggest, thinks that Kant's approach in the Foundations is senseless and that the view Kant presents in the "Idea for a Universal History" is correct. Within a set of circumstances, our interests are formed, they lead us to action, and we realize a potential (PhS, 240/GW, IX, 218). At the same time, Hegel is trying to develop his own view, namely, that acting, the development of talents, is an objectification of the self. Only the public product, only the result, is the realization of the talent. So also the objectified talent or product (the bridge or painting) must be recognized by others. An unrecognized product means a nonobjective, nonreal talent—merely our own subjective opinion that we have a talent. A talent that will never be recognized is not a real talent.[36]

We are headed toward a crisis here. There is nothing to sustain a Kantian self-in-itself. We must give up the notion of a transcendental self grounded in a beyond; we must abandon the notion of a self that is supposed to have powers and talents that it should, but may or may not, realize. There is no such self. It is only in and through the actual realization of powers, capacities, and talents that a self emerges. The self emerges in its objectifications. A self becomes real insofar as it objectifies itself and is recognized. Our problem here is that at the level of individual consciousness—without spirit—the objectifications of the self cannot gain adequate recognition.

What we have in the "Spiritual Animal Kingdom," then, are works in which individuals have objectified their powers, capacities, and talents, but which are ephemeral and unreal because other individuals find them unimportant (not their expression, realization, or objectification) and thus do not recognize them. The attitude of this consciousness, then, is that its own certainty is the only thing that is important to it. Like any good member of an Adam Smithian market economy, only its own action counts for it—not the works of others or the total national product in which it cannot recognize itself. Reality then is taken as something for-consciousness. Its only importance is as my expression (*PhS*, 245–6/*GW*, IX, 223).

At this point, Hegel begins to take up the notion of *"die Sache selbst"*—the fact itself.[37] Hyppolite suggests that Hegel is distinguishing between a thing of perception (*Ding*) and a thing of spirit or culture, a human thing (*Sache*).[38] The point that Hegel wants to move toward, I believe, is that facts are sociocultural constructions. Individuals act, express, and objectify themselves (their powers and capacities) in a work. This is what constitutes facts. Facts are constructs, creations, interpretations. Individual activity creates them through work, scholarship, research, experiment, production, and so on. Reality is a spiritual-cultural substance formed by individual action or work.

Take the fact that "Augustus was an emperor of Rome." This might seem to be just a simple independently given fact. But Rome, its political institutions, and its emperors were all historical realities constructed by Romans. Without this historical construction, there would be no Rome, no Roman emperors, and no Augustus. For the statement "Augustus was an emperor of Rome" to have anything beyond the most trivial meaning, we must understand what Rome was, what its political institutions were, and what an emperor was (things that might not even exist in other cultures). And to gain this understanding would require interpretation—interpretation we could argue about and disagree over. At a certain point, our interpretations may crystallize into what looks like a simple independently given fact—the fact itself—but that is because our differences have paled and we have come to take these interpretations and constructions for granted (*PhS*, 16/*GW*, IX, 24–5).

At this point in chapter V, then, actuality—all that is actual—is now identified with the action or expression of individuals. The actual world is the outcome of all individuals expressing their talents and objectifying their powers in works or acts. Since we long ago rejected an unknown thing-in-itself, we cannot hold here that consciousness constitutes mere appearance as for Kant. What consciousness constitutes is reality. We noticed, beginning with the slave, that work actually transformed and constituted an object into an object-for-consciousness. We saw that for scientific reason even matter was a concept. Consciousness (at least for us) now knows that it constitutes its world. In working on reality, in forming it as a product, in expressing and objectifying its powers and talents, through research, experiment, work, and so forth, consciousness constitutes reality.

The problem remaining here is that we are still at the level of individual consciousness and thus each individual only recognizes itself in the object and only takes its own object to be significant. Others do not recognize our object nor we theirs. What Hegel calls "honest consciousness" responds to this by holding that even if it has not brought a purpose to reality, has not built a bridge or painted a painting, has not accomplished anything that others would recognize, but tried, "at least *willed* it"—well, that is good enough. Honest consciousness is consoled. Even failure was an attempt (*PhS*, 247–8/GW, IX, 224–5). As for Kant, this consciousness claims that it is not motivated by results, consequences, or the actual realization of purposes, and certainly not with recognition. Its concern is with its attempt, its intention, and the fact itself.

But this leads to deceit. Honest Kantian consciousness is not as honest as it claims. If honest consciousness were ever actually to achieve something, it would still claim not to be concerned with its own accomplishment or with recognition but simply with the fact itself and with trying hard—and, indeed, this too is the way others regard it. They assume that the real issue is the work, the fact itself, regardless of who accomplishes it. As long as we all really try, it does not matter who actually makes the scientific discovery or who gets the recognition. Only the fact itself really matters. Only the advance of science matters to honest consciousness—not its *own* accomplishment or recognition. Or so it would seem, until anyone tries to question honest consciousness's accomplishment. Just see what happens if we were to claim that *we* had already made this scientific discovery earlier, or even if we were simply to claim credit for significantly assisting in the discovery—and thus that we deserve a share in the Nobel Prize. We will quickly see that honest consciousness has left the position where it claimed to be and we all thought it was. It is really honest consciousness's *own* doing that concerns it—not merely the fact itself. Honest consciousness wants the credit for making the discovery itself. And when others come to see that this is honest consciousness's real concern, they will feel they have been deceived by honest consciousness. However, their own claim to have assisted demonstrated just as much that their real concern was not merely the fact itself either, but their own desire to be in on the discovery of the fact itself *themselves*. They are out to deceive in just the way they complain of being deceived.[39] Consciousness is not interested in the fact itself regardless of who expresses it.

We might compare this to Kant, who, in explaining the third formulation of the categorical imperative in the *Foundations*, argues that if we were only *subject* to moral laws, it would be possible to attach ourselves to them out of self-interest—we could be motivated to obey or disobey the law out of self-interest. But if we act as a supreme legislator, as we must, this becomes impossible. If we were to let our interest predominate, we would be subordinating the law (and our legislation of the law) to this interest. As legislators, then, we would not be supreme. The law would not be supreme. Our interest would be. If we are to act as a supreme legislator, then interest must go (*F*, 50–1/KGS, IV, 432–3).

Hegel, we must conclude, thinks this is deceptive. Whether or not the supreme legislator is motivated by self-interest in the sense that Kant seems to have in mind is not the real issue because what the supreme legislator is very definitely interested in is being the supreme legislator, the one who issues the moral law. The supreme legislator is as much or more interested in its supremacy as it is in the categorical imperative itself. What consciousness is interested in is its *own* doing. Honest consciousness is not interested solely in the fact itself apart from the fact that it came up with the fact itself. Others are the same way. If they seek to assist, they do so to get their own piece of the action. There is a deception here. They are not simply assisting us, but trying to manifest their own action and trying to take some credit for ours. And we behave in the same way toward them.

However, it would be a mistake to think that there is something perverse about honest consciousness. If consciousness confronts any sort of truth, work, fact, or object that is other, it has a drive to deny its otherness and claim it as its own. As early as the "Positivity of the Christian Religion," Hegel said that we take an interest in a thing only if we can be active in its behalf (PCR, 164/GW, I, 376). Isn't this what consciousness has been doing throughout the *Phenomenology*? Idealism claims reality as its own. Consciousness even claims that God is its construction. Hegel's point, I believe, is that it is a mistake to think that consciousness can or should be concerned only with objectivity, truth, the fact itself. Consciousness, just as much, and rightfully so, is concerned with its own doing, its involvement, its expression, its interest. Kantian practical reason neglects this important and real side of consciousness. Practical reason, for Kant, cannot legitimately attach itself to the moral law out of self-interest. Practical reason must attend to the fact itself—the moral law—as an abstract universal. Kantian practical reason is unable to give interest and the desire for recognition a significant place. We cannot act morally without subordinating our interest; we cannot act morally *from* interest. Kantian morality is unable to satisfy this other legitimate side of consciousness. Hegel's point is that spirit will be able to do so.

And so what we have as long as we remain at the level of individual consciousness is chaos. We cannot deny that the facts of the social world are constructed, but yet we will not really admit that they are. This means that individuals both want credit for their construction, discovery, or work, yet pretend only to be concerned with the fact itself and not their own doing, until others, as they naturally will, begin to point out their role in the work or try to take a role by assisting, at which point the fact itself becomes much less important than the fact that it is our own work. Moreover, remaining at the level of individual consciousness obscures the recognition that facts just are not constructed by lone individuals in the first place. They are socioculturally constructed. No one individual, then, can legitimately take all the credit for them. At the same time, remaining at the level of individual consciousness makes it impossible to reconcile concern for the objective fact itself with a legitimate concern for subjective action, work, expression—our own doing and interest.

Well, what if honest consciousness decides that it does not care about the fact itself, what if it finally admits that the only thing that interests it is its own action, its own contribution, its own work—and nothing else? Well, this will not succeed either. Our own expression, effort, or work simply becomes meaningless, becomes nothing, unless the fact itself is of some significance—of some *public* significance. As early as "Lordship and Bondage," we saw that recognition was necessary for reality. If our work is incapable of gaining any recognition, then it will do no good for honest consciousness to insist that all it cares about is its own work. If this work, if the fact itself, is insignificant and meaningless, then honest consciousness has made no contribution and done no real work. Both sides—our own work and the public significance of the fact itself—are essential.[40]

So the fact itself will eventually have to be seen as a cultural reality that is the outcome of individual talent, action, and interest, on the one hand, and that involves a permanent, public actuality with recognized significance, on the other. It must involve the action of the individual and of others. It must be a substance permeated by individuality. Spirit is emerging here. We have a "reality whose existence means the action of the single individual and of all individuals, and whose action is immediately for others, or is a 'fact,' and is only 'fact' in the sense of an action of each and all . . . It is substance permeated by individuality."[41]

We cannot explain the outer by the inner, action by intention, or historical action by either virtue or interest. To retreat too far into the inner life is not only to try to elude responsibility for consequences, as Pippin puts it, but it is also to strip action of any meaning. Kenneth Westphal makes a point that is worth noting in this context. Practical reason is inseparable from social practice. It is true that actions are carried out by individuals, but such actions are possible and only have meaning insofar as they participate in sociocultural practices. There are two important questions here, Westphal suggests: (1) Are individuals the only bearers of psychological states? and (2) Can psychological states be understood in individual terms? Individualists answer both questions in the affirmative, and most holists answer both questions in the negative. Hegel, however, answers the first question affirmatively and the second negatively.[42] In other words, it is only individuals who act, have purposes, construct facts, and so forth. Nevertheless, such acts, purposes, and facts cannot be understood apart from sociocultural practices—their meaning can only be understood as interpreted in a sociocultural context.

If that is the case, then as soon as we turn to the self and attempt to understand the individual subject, we will find that it too cannot be understood apart from sociocultural practices. It too can only be understood as interpreted within a sociocultural context. While we do have individual subjects, for Hegel, we will find that we will not be able to hold onto the notion of a subject that is radically distinct from other subjects, that can stand outside the world, that thus could be the source of a virtue that could guide the way of the world, that could be a supreme legislator, or that could be committed purely to the fact itself. In short, we do not have a Kantian subject, a subject that could alone be the source of a categorical imperative. Instead, we will have to develop a different conception of a subject—one embedded in a context of cultural practices and meanings, within which it objectifies itself and gains recognition.

VIII. Reason as Lawgiver

At this point, in order to finally push us over to spirit, Hegel focuses on the problems involved for Kantian Moralität in not having a public, given, recognized cultural world. What we have before us are only the facts themselves—facts produced by us as our objectifications. And individual consciousness refuses to recognize anyone else's facts. Indeed, doesn't Kantian morality fall into this category? It does not accept the facts of others—it cannot accept anyone else's claim as to what constitutes a moral law or a moral fact. It can accept only what its own reason tells it is moral—what its own rational analysis tells it is universalizable. Only it is a supreme lawgiver for itself. And so, in the final two sections of chapter V, "Reason as Lawgiver" and "Reason as Testing Laws," we take up an analysis of Kant's categorical imperative that is direct and explicit enough to be clear to all readers. Here we have a Kantian consciousness, a supreme lawgiver, that takes itself to be absolute, universal, and authoritative (PhS, 252–3/GW, IX, 228–9). It would claim to be the true and absolute ethical authority, but Hegel will try to show us that it is not, that this is only possible if we move to Sittlichkeit and spirit, and that all Kant can give us is the same old honest consciousness who really tries but usually fails (PhS, 259/GW, IX, 234).

At any rate, for Kant, practical reason claims to know immediately what is right and good and to be able to issue determinate laws accordingly. As Kant puts it in the Metaphysical Principles of Virtue, "An imperative is a practical rule by which an action, in itself contingent, is made necessary...a rule whose representation makes a subjectively contingent action necessary and therefore represents the subject as one who must be constrained (necessitated) to conform to this rule. The categorical (unconditional) imperative is one that does not command mediately...but immediately, through the mere representation of this action itself (its form), which is thought through the categorical imperative as objectively necessary" (MPV, 21-2/KGS, VI, 222).

Let us see if Kantian practical reason can, as it claims, give us laws that make subjectively contingent actions objective, immediate, unconditional, and necessary. Let us take an example of such a law: "'Everyone ought to speak the truth'" (PhS, 254/GW, IX, 229). Well, as Hegel points out, the condition will at once have to be admitted: if you know the truth. What is meant, then, is that everyone ought to speak the truth in so far as they know it. But:

> With this admission, it in fact admits that already, in the very act of saying the commandment, it really violates it. It said: everyone ought to speak the truth; but it meant: he ought to speak it according to his knowledge and conviction; that is to say, what it said was different from what it meant; and to speak otherwise than one means, means not speaking the truth. The untruth or inapt expression in its improved form now runs: everyone ought to speak the truth according to his knowledge and conviction at the time. But with this correction, what the proposition wanted to enunciate as universally necessary and intrinsically valid, has really turned round into something completely contingent. For speaking the truth is made contingent on whether I can know it, and can convince myself of it; and the proposition says nothing more than that a confused muddle of truth and falsehood ought to be spoken just as anyone happens to know, mean, and understand it. (PhS, 254/GW, IX, 230)

We do not have anything unconditional, necessary, or objective here, but merely good old honest consciousness still trying its subjective best. We might further change the proposition by adding that the truth ought to be known, but then we would contradict our original assumption that practical reason knows the truth. We would be admitting that it does not actually know what is true—it merely ought to know it. This is not unconditional and objective morality; it is merely subjective and intended.

Take the commandment "Love thy neighbor as thyself" (*PhS*, 55/GW, IX, 230). Such love would at least require, Hegel suggests, that we work to remove evil and do good for our neighbor. And that would mean that to love my neighbor intelligently I would have to know what is good and bad. Unintelligent love might well do my neighbor harm. We are slipping toward the subjectivity of honest consciousness again. At any rate, Hegel argues that the agency most capable of avoiding evil and accomplishing intelligent good for my neighbor would be the state, in comparison to which what any single individual is likely to accomplish would be minimal. Furthermore, the action of the state is so pervasive that if I as an individual in trying to benefit my neighbor were to oppose the state in a way that was intended to be criminal or if I (perhaps like the friends of honest consciousness) simply attempted to cheat the state of its due credit in order to claim it for myself, such actions would most likely be frustrated and rendered useless. While there is room for individual beneficence in single, isolated, contingent situations, generally speaking, the social, cultural, and political world is such a pervasive power that doing good of the sort that Kant envisions, that is, the doing good of an autonomous individual consciousness, cannot realistically be demanded necessarily and unconditionally. Such action is too easily swept aside or rendered meaningless—certainly if we have yet to get beyond the way of the world, that race of devils that only appears as a nation of angels. Whether the act will be a work that benefits the neighbor as intended, or be immediately undone, or twisted and perverted by circumstance into harm is a matter of chance. It cannot meaningfully be demanded necessarily and unconditionally that we act for the good of others if it will always be contingent whether any act, depending on how it fits with the way of the world, will be erased or reinforced, distorted or maintained, turned into its opposite or left as it is. It is as likely to be possible as not. We have not moved very far beyond fate to rationally ordered providence—we have chance here, not universality and necessity. If one objects that Kantian morality should not be motivated by concern for such consequences or contexts, the answer must be that it cannot then do good to its neighbor in any morally significant way. In the *Foundations*, Kant argues:

> An action performed from duty does not have its moral worth in the purpose which is to be achieved through it but in the maxim by which it is determined. Its moral value, therefore, does not depend on the realization of the object of the action but merely on the principle of volition by which the action is done, without any regard to the objects of the faculty of desire.... Wherein, then, can this worth lie if it is not in the will in relation to its hoped-for effect? It can lie nowhere else than in the principle of the will, irrespective of the ends which can be realized by such action. (*F*, 16 /KGS, V, 399–400; see also *MPV*, 119/KGS, VI, 455)

We are back to good old honest consciousness who has at least tried, or, as Hegel puts it, if "this consciousness does not convert its purpose into a reality, it has at least *willed* it, i.e. it makes the purpose *qua* purpose, the mere doing which does nothing…and can therefore explain and console itself with the fact that all the same something was taken in hand and done" (*PhS*, 247/GW, IX, 224).

We do not have a consciousness capable of giving us an objective, unconditional, immediate, and necessary law here. Its law "does not express, as an absolute ethical law should, something that is valid in and for itself"; its laws "stop at Ought, they have no actuality" (*PhS*, 256/GW, IX, 231). Kantian practical reason does not give us laws; it merely issues commandments.

What does it mean to say that we do not have a law, but merely a commandment? In the *Foundations*, Kant claims that we can derive the fourth formulation of the categorical imperative, namely, a kingdom of ends, from the fact that we must consider each individual to be a supreme lawgiver. A kingdom of ends is a union of different rational beings in a system through common laws (*F*, 51/KGS, IV, 433). In short, Kant is claiming that individual practical reason gives us all we need from which to derive a system of common laws. Hegel denies that individual consciousness can give us the sorts of laws we have or need in a state.

The sorts of laws that Hegel thinks we need are not grounded in the will of particular individuals. Laws must have their own intrinsic being—they must exist in and for themselves. This is not to say that laws are not constructed. Even God is constructed for Hegel. And the fact that laws are constructed will be essential if we are to be free. But the law is not constructed by *individual* consciousness. It does not have its source in individual Kantian practical reason. It is the work of all, of a community, a culture. Laws are rooted in and grow out of the customs, traditions, and practices of a people and are tied to their social and public institutions, their public values, their philosophy, religion, and art.[43] Such laws are not subjective and contingent; they are objective, unconditional, and necessary—they are true and absolute.

Let us see if we can understand and make at least a reasonably plausible case for the sorts of laws that Hegel is after. Consider the example of a state and its educational system. In Hegel's view, the state would expect that its professors teach the truth. We need not conclude that this will necessarily threaten academic freedom. Even if the state were a paradigm of respect for academic freedom, it would still assume, at least, that its professors did not knowingly and systematically teach falsehood. Even further, Hegel would hold, it will also expect these professors to know the truth, at the very least, in the sense that it would be fraudulent for the university to hire professors who have not undergone the proper training and engaged in serious study, whose only credentials were that they were enthusiastic about their opinions and sincere in their intentions. So when the university hires professors of engineering or art it does not expect them like honest consciousness merely to try their best. It expects them to actually be able to build real bridges and paint real paintings and to teach others how to do so. We hold professors responsible for actually doing these things, not just for trying. So also we expect the university to give its students an education that will (assuming a just society) fit them for life in the state, prepare them for a vocation, and give them the moral and scientific knowledge needed for these purposes. We expect this at least in the sense that were the university systematically to fail to do so we would conclude that it was not functioning properly. The law has a right to require more than that the university try. It is expected to succeed.

What we need and have in culture, Hegel thinks, is far richer and more powerful than mere subjective Kantian oughts. Sittlichkeit does not merely tell us that we ought to educate our children or do good to our neighbor, it gives us an understanding of what things like good to our neighbor and proper education actually are and it embeds them in our customs, traditions, practices, and institutions so that we are able to act in the world and actually do act accordingly. It enables us not just to try, but to succeed, and to pass this knowledge and ability on to others. It gives us much more than an ought—it gives us actuality.

So far I have only given the thinnest sketch of this Sittlichkeit. It will be spelled out at greater length as we proceed in the *Phenomenology*. But the point here is that it is missing in Kant and we need it to account for our experience. A true law must grow up and be rooted in a community, in its customs, traditions, and practices. It must be a force that morally empowers its citizens. It is just not enough (which is to say, for Hegel, it is not *ethically* enough) that it merely oblige them morally—that it be a mere maxim that can be universalized, that it merely be willed, that it merely be acted upon. But that *is* enough to establish its "moral value" for Kant, as he himself says (F, 16/KGS, IV, 399). And so Kantian reason is not a lawgiver. At best it is a test of laws.

IX. Reason as Testing Laws

But even as a test of laws, Kant's ethics fail. In taking up a given content to test it, to see if it is universalizable, we find, at least in some important cases, that one content will work as well as its opposite. If we ask, for example, whether there should be private property, we will find private property to be perfectly self-consistent—we can universalize it without contradiction. But we can just as well universalize the absence of private property—a community of goods or communism. That involves no contradiction either (*PhS*, 257–8/GW, IX, 233–4; *PR*, 89–90/SW, VII, 193–4).

M. G. Singer, in his by now classic criticism, claims that Hegel is "almost incredibly simple-minded" here. It seems to me, however, that Singer misses Hegel's point entirely. According to Singer, Hegel should be able to see that

> if everyone stole, whenever and whatever he pleased, there would be no such thing as property and hence the purpose of stealing would be made impossible....Yet [Hegel] seems utterly confused as to why it would therefore be wrong to steal....Kant's point...is a relatively simple one, which is perhaps why the profundities of Hegel are so far from the mark. It could not be willed to be a universal law that everyone could steal whenever he wished to, for if everyone stole whenever he wished to, or took for his own anything he happened to want, there would be no property and hence nothing to steal—there would be nothing he could call his own. Stealing presupposes that there is such a thing as property—something to be stolen.[44]

Singer so little understands Hegel's criticism of Kant that the last line of this passage, intended to undermine Hegel, in fact concedes Hegel's point against Kant. Hegel thinks that in formulating a maxim the Kantian *presupposes* a certain form of property as given and that only with this presupposition will the principle of universalization work. Unless we know what sort of property is right in a given culture—and universalization alone will not tell us—we cannot know what would constitute an act of theft and what would not. For example, suppose I enter a store, pocket an article of consumption that I need, and walk off without putting down any money. Was that theft or not? Was it immoral or not? Asking whether the maxim can be universalized will not tell me. If I live in a market economy with private property, the act was theft. If I live in a communist society based upon the principle "to each according to need," the act was not theft. Both private property and communism are equally universalizable. Universalizability will not decide the issue. We must have a cultural world with cultural content given to us. Either private property or communism must be given as right before we can go on to decide what constitutes an act of theft. We need Sittlichkeit, that is, settled and given customs, traditions, and practices—we need culture—for morality to be possible.

Singer basically has Hegel's argument backward. He makes the common but mistaken claim that in Hegel's view the categorical imperative is empty and contentless: "Hegel assumes that the categorical imperative is supposed to be applied in a vacuum...that Kant's ethics is an 'empty formalism.'" Hegel, in Singer's view, does not see that if "someone proposes to adopt a certain maxim, or to act in a certain way in certain circumstances in order to achieve a certain purpose, then we...'already possess a content,' to which the categorical imperative can be applied."[45] Singer completely misunderstands

Hegel here. Hegel is not denying that the categorical imperative has a content in Singer's sense; Hegel fully accepts that in formulating a maxim we take up a content. He says explicitly in the *Phenomenology* that what we have is a "standard for deciding whether a content is capable of being a law or not," and he goes on to talk about content at least three times on the following page (*PhS*, 256/*GW*, IX, 232).[46] Moreover, Hegel well knows that adopting a maxim commits the person to an act or an end. After all, as we have seen, one of Hegel's criticisms of the categorical imperative is that it gives us an *ought*—for Hegel it is a *mere* ought rather than an *is*—but nevertheless it does give us an ought (it gives us a commandment, though not a law).

The problem here stems, I think, from misinterpreting the following passage from Hegel's *Philosophy of Right*: "The Proposition: 'Act as if the maxim of thine action could be laid down as a universal principle,' would be admirable if we already had determinate principles of conduct. That is to say, to demand of a principle that it shall be able to serve in addition as a determinant of universal legislation is to presuppose that it already possesses a content. Given the content, then of course the application of the principle would be a simple matter" (*PR*, 254/*SW*, VII, 195).

Singer takes the implication of this passage to be that we do not have a content—that the categorical imperative is contentless. But that is not the point the passage is making at all. The point is that for the categorical imperative to work we must be given a content—in the sense of a determinate principle of conduct. In other words, our culture has to tell us, for example, that private property is right. Once we have this, Hegel is saying, then the categorical imperative will have no difficulty in telling us that walking off with the article from the store was theft. Hegel is not claiming that the categorical imperative has no content. He is claiming that it will not work without content. Where does the content come from? It is certainly not generated out of the categorical imperative itself. It is taken up from culture. Private property must be given as right before we can see that what we did in the store was theft. Hegel makes this point very clearly elsewhere in the *Philosophy of Right*: "The absence of property contains in itself just as little contradiction as the non-existence of this or that nation, family, &c., or the death of the whole human race. But if it is already established on other grounds and presupposed that property and human life are to exist and be respected, then indeed it is a contradiction to commit theft or murder; a contradiction must be a contradiction of something, i.e. of some content presupposed from the start as a fixed principle" (*PR*, 90/*SW*, VII, 194).

The argument against Kant, then, is not that the categorical imperative is contentless. The argument is that the categorical imperative *presupposes* its content; it takes up its content *uncritically*. The Kantian formulating a maxim concerning theft assumes that private property is given. As Hegel puts it in the *Phenomenology*, "Laws are . . . *tested*; and for the consciousness which tests them they are *already* given. It takes up their *content* simply as it is, without concerning itself . . . with the particularity and contingency inherent in its reality. . . . Its attitude towards it is just as uncomplicated as is its being a criterion for testing it" (*PhS*, 257/*GW*, IX, 232-3).[47]

Perhaps the point that a content must be given to us is made most clearly in the *Natural Law* essay, though Hegel overstates his case in that early text. He says:

> If this formalism is to be able to promulgate a law, some matter, something specific, must be posited to constitute the content of the law. And the form given to this specific matter is unity or universality. "That a maxim of thy will shall count at the same time as a principle of universal legislation"—this basic law of pure practical reason expresses the fact that something specific, constituting the content of the maxim of the particular will, shall be posited as concept, as universal. But every specific matter is capable of being clothed with the form of the concept. . . . There is nothing whatever which cannot in this way be made into a moral law. (*NL*, 76-7/*GW*, IV, 436)

While Hegel is overstating his case in holding that *any* content can be made into a moral law, nevertheless, he is suggesting that very different contents can be and have been established as moral laws by different cultures— very different forms of property, for example. And it is obvious that quite consistent social organizations can be built around such different laws. The principle of universalization is not going to show us that all but one of these forms of property and social organization are contradictory; there will at least be many different forms of property and social organization that it will not show to be contradictory. The categorical imperative, then, will not tell us which of these forms of property is right. Only after we are given one of these forms of property as right can the categorical imperative begin to tell us what would be an act of theft and what would not.

Hegel is not out to junk the categorical imperative. He is simply claiming that a certain content must be given for it to work, a content which in his view Kant naively presupposes. This content is given by culture and thus morality needs a theory of culture. Hegel is trying to drive us toward spirit and Sittlichkeit. Furthermore, Hegel is not out to junk universalizability. In Hegel's view, universalizability is necessary for morality; it is just that it does not *amount* to morality. Acting on a categorical imperative—insofar as that means acting merely on what reason tells us is universalizable—is not enough to be moral. As Hegel puts it, something is not right because it is noncontradictory, "it is right because it is what is right" (*PhS*, 262/*GW*, IX, 236).

Let us see if we can even better explain the sort of law that Hegel is after. For Hegel, we can fail in two ways. If we have a real law, the sort that Hegel wants, an absolute, not a mere commandment or an ought, then this law could not be established or imposed by a single person or an individual consciousness. That would turn the law into something tyrannical and it would turn obedience to such a law into something slavish. On the other hand, while Kantian testing of laws certainly frees us from such objectionable laws, which are rejected as alien and heteronomous, nevertheless it leaves us merely with individual consciousness and thus the loss of an absolute grounding (PhS, 260/GW, IX, 234–5). Hegel wants to avoid both of these alternatives.

What Hegel wants in a law is that it be valid in and for itself—it must be absolute. Thus, it must not be grounded in the will of particular individuals. In obeying such laws, self-consciousness must not be subordinating itself to another individual—to a master whose commands would be alien and arbitrary. Rather, self-consciousness must find these laws to be "the thoughts of its own absolute consciousness, thoughts which are immediately its *own*" (PhS, 261/GW, IX, 235). These absolute laws are our *own* laws. After all, we construct them, we issue them—it is just that we do not do so as individual consciousnesses. Rather, we construct these laws as participating in a cultural consciousness—the consciousness of a people or nation. These laws are not arbitrary, tyrannical, or alien. They are not heteronomous. They are our *own* laws. We constructed them and thus are free in obeying them. But they are also absolute laws. They are universal, objective, the will of all, the will of my people, my nation, my gods.

Self-consciousness should not even *believe* in its laws. Belief in something, Hegel thinks, suggests that the believer is an individual consciousness and that what it believes in is alien to it. For Hegel we should be immediately one with our laws (PhS, 261/GW, IX, 235). It is not enough to merely believe in them. Laws must be so rooted in the customs and practices of my culture that I simply know them. They are facts. They are true. They are absolute. Is this really so strange? I suggest that we do not merely believe, for example, that murder is wrong. We certainly do not need, in order to know that it is wrong, to engage in a subjective process of analysis, a deduction, like asking whether murder can be universalized without contradiction.[48] To suggest that we must is to miss something fundamental about morality. It is to subjectivize something that is absolute. Hegel's concept of Sittlichkeit will attempt to avoid heteronomy and give us freedom, but without losing the absolute.

We must move on, then, to spirit—to the substantial reality that is already before us as the fact itself. Ethical content can only be found in culture, where it has an objective being of its own, where it is socially constructed as our customs, traditions, practices, and public institutions—a given ethical world. In spirit it is not just subjective rationality that decides, that establishes what is moral, as for Kant. Things are not moral simply because my rationality finds them to be moral. They are also objectively moral—moral in-themselves. This is what we will find in the Greek polis. Yet this objective moral content is not something other, alien to consciousness, heteronomous, as Kant would insist. Think of the Athenian assembly creating its own laws—laws which are wrought up with its own customs and traditions, its myths and gods, and thus are objective, absolute, ethical in-themselves for the people they form. Only Sittlichkeit is capable of bringing together *all* the elements of the ethical: (1) subjective inclination, interest, engagement, involvement; (2) all located in a cultural context in which we are at home, which we find to be our own, because it was constructed by us, and thus where we are free; which (3) at the same time grows out of and is reinforced by age old custom and tradition, our institutions and our gods, our religion and our philosophy, and thus is objective and absolute; and (4) within this context we reflect rationally and establish universal laws. In such a context, citizens know and accomplish—they live in and are a part of—the ethical. Ethical life exists, it empowers its citizens, it pervades and is actually played out in their lives and practices. It is not a mere Kantian ought.

Defenders of Kant often want to claim that Hegel has not understood Kant or that Hegel attacks a crudely understood Kant. I hope I have shown that Hegel understands Kant in a rather sophisticated way, thinks Kant is wrong, and does a reasonable job of arguing against him. Moreover, it seems to me that many Kantians can be accused of misunderstanding Hegel, and once they begin to understand him, they will find arguments against Kant that, whether they can finally be answered or not, certainly cannot simply be dismissed as shallow misunderstandings of Kant.

4

Culture and Reality

I. The Transcendental Deduction and Culture

We have now completed the first part of the *Phenomenology*, which was devoted to an examination of individual consciousness, and are ready to move on to chapter VI, which makes up the second part of the *Phenomenology* and deals with cultural consciousness. Chapter VI is an extremely important chapter. Its length alone suggests that. It is the longest chapter in the *Phenomenology*. In fact, its 146 pages (in Miller's edition) make it not much shorter than all the previous five chapters lumped together (which come to 204 pages in Miller's edition). Yet chapter VI often is not treated by commentators in accordance with its importance.

For example, Taylor and Pippin, who agree that the *Phenomenology* is attempting to give us a transcendental deduction, do not seem to think that chapter VI plays any role in that deduction. Taylor suggests that we find transcendental arguments only in the first three chapters of the *Phenomenology*. Pippin does not even discuss chapter VI. As soon as he finishes his treatment of "Self-Consciousness," he moves on to a discussion of the logic.[1]

Connected with this, there are some scholars who subscribe to a "patchwork thesis." As Merold Westphal puts it, Haering was the first to argue that Hegel's original intention was to break off the *Phenomenology* somewhere in chapter V and to go from there directly to the logic. The rest of the *Phenomenology*, chapters VI to VIII, in which Hegel develops his concept of spirit, was added in the process of writing. The first part of the *Phenomenology* fits with the epistemological orientation of the introduction and was intended as a reply to Kant. The last three chapters venture off in new directions and so Hegel had to add a preface oriented to them. Thus, having lost sight of his original purpose, Hegel in the last three chapters turns to social and religious concerns.[2]

Westphal does not accept this traditional interpretation and neither do I. I do not want to argue one way or the other about the claim that Hegel had a change of mind as he wrote the *Phenomenology*. And I certainly do not want to have to defend the claim that in every respect chapter VI is perfectly consistent with all that was said in the first five chapters. What I do want to argue is that from the very start Hegel was out to give us a Kantian-style deduction of the absolute. Second, I want to hold that there is no way chapter V, which does not get beyond individual consciousness, was ever going to complete that deduction. Third, I hope to show that chapters VI through VIII, which deal with cultural, religious, and absolute consciousness, are essential to that deduction. In short, my claim is that, in fact, Hegel could not have completed the deduction he set out to give without chapters VI through VIII. In this sense the two halves of the *Phenomenology* are consistent. Exactly when Hegel became aware that he would have to move beyond individual consciousness and whether other inconsistencies might exist, I leave open.

At any rate, chapter VI is crucially important to Hegel's deduction. His approach, we have seen, is to take up different forms of consciousness and to see if they are adequate to account for our experience. In chapter V, we found individual consciousness to be inadequate to account for our experience of morality, history, and society. In chapter VI, we continue to take up experiences we cannot deny that we have—the experience of being a family member, a legal person, the subject of a monarch, a religious believer, an enlightened rationalist, a revolutionary, and so forth—and we will find that to explain the possibility of our experience we will be forced to presuppose a form of consciousness that goes beyond individual consciousness. We will be forced to develop the notion of a cultural consciousness—and thus we will be pushed further along toward absolute consciousness.

A big part of the problem in chapter VI is to understand exactly what Hegel is attempting to move us toward. Many commentators have difficulty here because they do not seem to be able to think themselves beyond individual consciousness. For example, I think this problem is at the core of Robert Williams's claim that Hegel's commitment to intersubjective recognition is incompatible with idealism. Hegel's exploration of intersubjectivity, which began as early as the master-slave dialectic, is greatly expanded in his treatment of culture in chapter VI. Intersubjectivity requires the actual existence of other subjects capable of recognizing us, whereas idealism, at least as Williams understands it, eliminates the other, or cannot take the other seriously, and therefore excludes intersubjectivity.[3] It seems to me that intersubjectivity is only at odds with idealism if we mean by idealism, subjective idealism—that is, the idealism of individual consciousness. But Hegel is out to reject that sort of idealism. He wants to get beyond individual consciousness and to establish objective idealism.

. If, to make sense of our experience, we are forced to understand our consciousness as a cultural consciousness, as I shall argue that we are, then we need find no incompatibility between idealism and intersubjectivity. Certainly there are subjects out there in culture, and each is dependent on others for recognition. But if we admit that there are many subjects, how, then, can we have idealism? We have idealism because cultural consciousness, not individual consciousness, is what constructs reality. What is real for us is what cultural consciousness will allow to be real and what it makes real. Reality for us is what can make sense within the horizon of our cultural possibilities. A thing can only exist as real for us insofar as our cultural awareness makes it possible for it to exist as real for us.

This is certainly not, as some would have it, to posit a superhuman consciousness. We do not somehow tap into a single and unified cultural mind that exists on some metaphysical plane. We are not talking about anything but ordinary human consciousness here. All we have are individual subjects. Nevertheless, we find significant unity among these subjects. One culture is identifiably different from another. Ancient Greece was significantly different from eighteenth-century revolutionary France. A culture has an underlying unity that can be seen clearly in contrasting it with another culture. It is made up of a lot of different individual subjects who have a common history and to a significant degree share values, meanings, and knowledge, though at the same time there is room for a good deal of difference and even conflict among individuals and groups within a culture.

This shared cultural consciousness exists in varied and complicated ways; it is stored in memories, texts, libraries, bureaucracies, and so forth. To become aware of something, I may have to learn from people in other departments of the university or government, other spheres of business, science, or everyday life. Cultural development, upbringing, and education are necessary to make possible access to this huge and complexly dispersed cultural wealth—to a deposit of cultural consciousness, awareness, or knowledge that is much larger than me but nevertheless is mine. This cultural consciousness allows for the construction of a cultural world which then molds, shapes, and constructs the individuals who share that consciousness.

But why insist on calling this "idealism" rather than "intersubjectivity?" The reason is that idealism, for Hegel, does not (and never did) mean that nothing exists outside my (individual) consciousness; rather idealism means that *esse est intelligi*—it means that what is real is what consciousness grasps. And so it is very important that we come to see that consciousness is not to be understood as *individual* consciousness such that reality would be limited to what individual consciousness can grasp—we must see that this will not account for our experience. Reality is what *cultural consciousness* constructs and grasps and thus is much more complex. If we let go of this and slide back to intersubjectivity, we are going to end up with individual subjects and individual consciousness and thus with an inadequate grasp of reality. We must see that while there clearly are individual subjects, they are each formed by and possess a larger, richer, and more complex cultural consciousness. Moreover, it is only such consciousness that could have constructed our cultural world and only that world could have formed our individual consciousness. Thus we must understand the deduction of this more complex consciousness.

To have both intersubjectivity and idealism, Hegel must show two things. First, that all reality is an object-of-consciousness—or that the reality of things is what consciousness grasps. To show this he tries to show, as we have seen, that there is no sense that can be made of unknown things-in-themselves independent of consciousness. And second, he must show that consciousness is not merely individual consciousness, that we cannot explain our actual experience of ethical life, citizenship, membership in a culture, and so forth by assuming that consciousness is merely individual. We are only able to know all that we do know by participating in a cultural consciousness and things are only real—they only exist—for consciousness insofar as they are constructed by a cultural consciousness. That is idealism and it makes room for intersubjectivity.

There is a further reason why there is a problem with intersubjectivity alone—certainly if this means only the subjectivity of individual consciousnesses. In chapter V, we rejected the Kantian notion of a transcendental self. All we have are deeds, works, or objectifications, on the one hand, and potentialities or talents, on the other. And for this indeterminate bundle to hold up as an individual subject, it requires recognition—recognition we found that we are not likely to get from other individual consciousnesses. We should be able to see at this point that intersubjectivity is not what we need—not if that means merely mutual recognition between individual consciousnesses. That is not enough. If we have to rely on other such consciousnesses for recognition, we are not likely to get it. What we need instead is recognition that is much more solid and reliable, much larger in scale and scope, and with much more authority and power. What we need, Hegel suggests in chapter VI, is the recognition of institutions—the family, social classes, law, the state, religion. If the state recognizes us as citizens, applies laws to us, respects our rights, forms and cultures us, then, perhaps, we can get enough recognition to be solidly real.

Fine, but then where do these institutions come from? Where else? We construct them (*PhS*, 294/*GW*, IX, 264). In the *Aesthetics*, Hegel says, "Man draws out of himself and puts *before himself* what he is and whatever else is.... Man as spirit *duplicates* himself... and only on the strength of this active placing himself before himself is he spirit" (A, I, 31/SW, XII, 58). Our institutions are nothing but our objectifications—our doings, beliefs, practices, interactions. This makes things easy in some senses. Certainly, it is all perfectly compatible with idealism. Moreover, we do not need to drag in any difficult to prove ontotheological entities. Spirit is social, not metaphysical.[4] We construct our own recognizer and our own recognition. We do not have to appeal to anything outside.

This virtue, however, is at the very same time a serious problem. If we recognize that we have constructed these institutions, what then will happen to all that powerful, solid, objective recognition that they are supposed to give us? Won't it collapse? Won't we quickly see through it? Won't we be right back where we started? What we will need, then, in chapter VI, odd as it may sound, is a bit of estrangement. We must not recognize that it is our alienation and objectification that produce the state, the law, and God. We must be estranged from these constructions if we are to take them to be real enough so that they in turn will be able to recognize and establish our reality. At the same time, of course, a world of estrangement will be a world of oppression and unfreedom—a world in which we cannot be at home. That is a problem that will eventually have to be handled and overcome. But right now our problem is whether or not this complex process of pulling ourselves up by our own bootstraps has any chance of succeeding. Can we succeed in making ourselves real by constructing our own recognizer just so long as we do not notice that we construct our own recognizer? That is our problem in chapter VI and we will either collapse back into a chaotic sceptical emptiness or we will find a way to push forward, shore up this culturally constructed reality, and move on toward absolute consciousness.

Where we are headed, clearly, is toward an absolute understood as a cultural construction—certainly not toward an absolute understood as the ontotheological, metaphysical entity of the right Hegelians. For many, this should make the absolute easier to accept. On the other hand, we must struggle to avoid the implication that the absolute in being a cultural construction is a realityless illusion. As we saw in the introduction, the fact that God is constructed in no way suggests that God does not exist. Nevertheless, this will be taken by some to mean merely that God exists despite our construction—independently of it. In other words, our construction cannot construct the *reality* of God, but merely God's appearance. We must get beyond this prejudice against construction. Our government is nothing but a construction—all the way down. It is nothing whatsoever but a constellation of our beliefs, values, ideals, practices, institutions, and so forth. Yet it is perfectly real. We can even compare it to other governments and think it better than they. And though I personally find right-wing jingoistic patriotism repulsive, there are many who find our government in the United States the truest—the best—that has ever existed. In short, constructions, at least in theory, can be perfectly real, good, and true.

At the same time, though, while rejecting the assumption that a cultural construction is necessarily a realityless illusion, we must not conclude that it is thereby necessarily true. We must also be prepared to admit the possibility that cultural constructions can contain falsity and illusion. Atheists think that God is a cultural construction—*and* one that is a complete illusion. While the illusoriness of God does not follow from the fact that God is constructed, it is certainly possible that God is constructed and is an illusion. Political leftists tend to think that governments, certainly the government of the United States, contain more than a little falsity and illusion—and I must count myself one of these. So also, to think that one's culture as opposed to other cultures is absolute, or that the absolute and one's culture are somehow to be identified, suggests the sort of illusion we have come to call "ethnocentrism." To claim that the absolute is a cultural phenomenon would seem, at least, to open the door to these possibilities and thus to raise a question about the absoluteness of the absolute. That might be a desirable consequence in that it prevents us from taking the absolute to be an ontotheological entity, but, nevertheless, it still raises a problem that will have to be addressed and handled if we are to get a deduction of the absolute. Can the absolute be absolute if it is our construction?

What we must keep clearly in mind here, then, is that while construction certainly does not guarantee the truth of anything, neither does it necessarily undermine the truth of anything. Constructions, most likely, will contain a complex mixture of truth and falsity. If we are to begin to understand how Hegel is going to shore up the cultural constructions we will meet in chapter VI, as well as, finally, the absolute, then we must notice two things. First, we must see that we can often discover more wisdom and truth in our constructions than we ever expected would be there. Any cultural construction may well have a depth, richness, and rationality that is worth unpacking. Cultural constructions are not our constructions in the sense that there can be nothing in them but what we thought we put into them. They can contain a far deeper truth than we would have been able to imagine ahead of time. Moreover, the fact that they are our constructions means that they express us, realize us, they can invigorate and empower us, and they are something we can be at home with.

Second, there is something we must notice about cultural constructions that we think are false. Even if we are atheists who think God is an illusion, or leftists who think the government problematic, or cultural relativists who think the absolute is just the absolute of a specific culture, we must see that these constructions have existed for us for a long time—they have shaped us, they have formed us, they have actually been cultural realities. Even if we think that God does not exist, or that our government is objectionable, or that our absolute is relative, nevertheless, our cultural reality, what we have actually become, is inseparable from God's existence, our government, and our absolute. There is a fundamental sense—a cultural sense—in which it is impossible to deny the existence of God or the absolute even if there is no God or absolute.

Another way to put this—the way Hegel chooses to put it—is that our cultural construction produces a substance. This rich, complex, dispersed, sometimes chaotic and conflicting cultural reality, which Hegel calls "spirit," he also understands as a substance. He says, "Spirit, being the *substance* and the universal, self-identical, and abiding essence, is the unmoved solid *ground* and *starting-point* for the action of all.... This substance is equally the universal *work* produced by the action of all and each as their unity and identity" (*PhS*, 264/GW, IX, 239). What does it mean to call culture, or spirit, a "substance?"

Hegel does not have in mind, I do not think, any sort of metaphysical substance. Substance is social, not metaphysical. What then is a social substance? In the first place, it is a unity. Substances hold things together over time, through change, or despite differences. Substances provide identity. To identify a group of people as a single culture requires some sort of unity that underlies all the differences that can be found among those people. If we reject the notion that this sort of unity is provided by some superhuman collective mind or metaphysical entity, where then does this substantial unity come from?

In rejecting the notion that race can serve to give us this sort of identity or unity, Appiah argues that to recognize two different events as parts of the history of a particular group or culture, we first have to have a criterion of identity for that group or culture—a criterion independent of their participation in the two events. In other words, simply being involved in the same series of historical events cannot be the criterion for being members of the same culture because we first have to have a culture and be able to identify it in order to identify *its* history. For example, we obviously cannot say that all who suffer oppression at the hands of the British are Irish. And to say that the Irish historically have suffered oppression at the hands of the British requires identifying who the Irish are and distinguishing them from others who have also suffered oppression (even perhaps suffered through the same oppressive policies, practices, and events) at the hands of the British. What is it then that gives the members of a culture the sort of identity that allows them to share a common history? Appiah's view is that such identities are constructed. This construction may appeal to invented and fictitious biologies or affinities that are seen as natural or essential, but they are simply constructed—invented, chosen, identified with—by the group in question.[5] This too, I think we shall see, is Hegel's view, except that, for Hegel, we must also add two important qualifications. Given the presence of estrangement, the members of a culture are not consciously aware that they construct or choose their identity. To them, it simply appears given and objective. And second, we must not think that *individual* consciousnesses do this choosing or constructing. It is not the case that what we have are really and fundamentally individuals who secondarily identify or link themselves up with a culture. These are fundamentally *cultural* consciousnesses. Culture is their being and *substance*—which at the same time they construct.

Furthermore, to refer to society or culture as substantial or a substance is to say that it appears to be a thing. In fact, our sociocultural world is nothing but a complex set of ideas, beliefs, values, practices, commitments, and so forth. But like any government it appears to be a solid thing—a powerful influence, a real force, something that works on us, directs us, leads us into action, and so forth. It is no illusion. It is a real and actual thing.

Culture is also a substance in a third sense: it is that in which, or the material in which, our entire spiritual life occurs. The sociocultural world is that in which we are born, live, act, think, value, develop, mature, and die. Our entire history, action, and government take place within it. It is also the form which activates us, gives us a purpose, a mission, ideals (*PWHI*, 27/*PW*, I, 28).

Finally, and most importantly, culture is also a substance in that it is our very essence—and thus it is where we can be at home. It is not alien or other. We are at one with it—it is our own. Our laws and institutions are the very substance of our being (*PR*, 106/*SW*, VII, 228–9). Culture thus forms a crucial element of our freedom. In culture we construct and identify with what we take to be most truly ourselves. We transform what otherwise would be alien, other, or heteronomous into a form of self-expression and self-determination. Consider, for example, the practice of bowing. Some cultures might find such a practice subservient, demeaning, an expression of unfreedom. But if bowing is a central practice of our culture, if we identify with it, it need not necessarily imply any subservience at all. We can take pride in the way we bow. It can be a form of self-expression—showing respect for the person to whom we bow and commanding respect for the elegance, grace, and dignity with which we bow. Proper deference to a worthy superior can also be an expression of personal self-esteem. We all know graduate students whose devotion to their famous thesis director is a way in which they construct their own identity and affirm themselves. On the other hand, even if the outer form is supposed to indicate deference to superiors, a bow that is not quite deep enough can transform this deference into a subtle expression of contempt. Or a bow that is a bit too deep can ironically subvert the superiority of the other. If anyone thinks that the bow of a samurai, for example, the moment before he pulls his sword on you, implies any subservience, one simply does not understand the complex reality of culture.

At any rate, identification with the institutions of one's culture is a crucial and necessary dimension of freedom. On the other hand, it is clearly not sufficient to make us free. After all, slaves, dominated women, or real subordinates of other sorts can be found in all cultures and may well identify with their allotted role as fully as anyone else in that culture. Such forms of oppression must also be overcome. But if they are, then culture can contribute to making real freedom possible. It can make us feel at home, eliminate all sense of strangeness, otherness, domination, or oppression. Culture, after all, is our product—it is created by the action of each and all. Moreover, it gives us meaning. It gives us purposes and goals. Only in it is our work accomplished and only through it do we share in the results of that work (PhS, 263–4/GW, IX, 238–9). It is a complex and mediated form of self-determination which at the same time is objective, solid, and substantial.

Human beings take in the values, aspirations, knowledge, beliefs, and practices of their sociocultural world. After they internalize these things, they of course work on them, transform them, perhaps develop them, and then deposit them back in their world for others to take in and repeat the process. Individuals are produced by culture. Individuals in different cultures or at different historical periods of a single culture will be individualized differently. At the same time that culture produces individuals, however, individuals also produce their culture. Culture is nothing but the outcome of individual action—nothing but the sum total of beliefs, values, practices, knowledges, actions, and so forth of the individuals of that culture. Culture produces individuals who then transform culture. Changed individuals change their culture and a changed culture produces changed individuals.

At any rate, our cultural world is to be understood as a substance, and Hegel will tell us, in a famous phrase, that we must come to understand this substance as subject (PhS, 10/GW, IX, 18). This is not to say, in my view, that the cultural substance is to be understood as an individual subject—and certainly not as a superhuman metaphysical subject. It is to say, rather, that cultural substance is cultural subjectivity. Culture is constructed as a substantial unity out of the actions, beliefs, ideas, values, practices, and commitments of subjects, who thereby develop a cultural identity. They produce a cultural substance which forms them as cultural subjects, is their cultural identity, and allows them to become free. This substance is a cultural formation of their subjectivity.

What we must see from the start as we begin the chapter on spirit is that spirit is a substantial unity. We must remember this because despite the fact that spirit or culture will divide itself—into human and divine law, citizen and government, noble and bourgeois, Enlightenment rationalist and religious believer, and so forth—and despite the fact that this may lead to the most intense conflict and estrangement, nevertheless, all this opposition is in a certain sense superficial. It takes place within a deeper spiritual unity (*PhS*, 267/*GW*, IX, 241–2). Indeed, as we shall see, to recognize this spiritual unity after estrangement and opposition have been overcome will be to regain the unity.

As we begin chapter VI we must also recall, as we started to see in the second part of chapter V, that Hegel is deeply enamored of the Sittlichkeit of the ancient world. This was a Sittlichkeit, however, that was lacking in individual, reflective Moralität. Greek Sittlichkeit broke down, then, as Moralität began to arise. In Hegel's view this Moralität reaches its peek, politically, in the French Revolution, economically, in Adam Smithian capitalism, and philosophically, in Kantian ethics. This is the development we trace in chapter VI, the development of individuality from the Greek polis to the modern state. This sociocultural development comes after an earlier development in the *Phenomenology*, a conceptual or phenomenological development from "Sense-Certainty" through various forms of individual consciousness, a development that finally shows us the inadequacy of individual consciousness and forces us to move beyond it to cultural consciousness, which we finally reach in chapter VI. So also, the second development—the sociocultural development in chapter VI—will come to be seen as inadequate. After all, it only takes us to the Moralität of Kant, Adam Smith, and the French Revolution. And, for Hegel, we are not after modern Moralität—we want to go beyond it. What chapter VI wants to show us is that even the simplest Sittlichkeit, the undeveloped Sittlichkeit of the ancient polis, in important ways was preferable to modern Moralität. At the same time, Hegel also wants to show us that the Sittlichkeit of the ancient polis is inadequate to the modern world. It breaks down in the face of rising individuality. Individuality and Moralität are good things, for Hegel, they must have a place, but they go too far in the French Revolution, Adam Smithian economics, and Kantian ethics. We need a higher Sittlichkeit that overcomes the destructiveness of modern Moralität by combining the undeveloped Sittlichkeit of the ancient world with the rational reflection and individuality of modern Moralität. To achieve this higher Sittlichkeit will require a third movement, a movement that will take us beyond the sociocultural development of the modern world to a higher conceptual-phenomenological level. We will have to move from culture to religion and the absolute. To do this will require combining a sociocultural development with a conceptual-phenomenological one. We will only be able to understand this movement as we move beyond chapter VI to religion and absolute consciousness, but we must begin to anticipate it now if we are to understand what is going on in chapter VI and where it is headed.

At the beginning of chapter VI we are told that all the previous forms of consciousness that we have met in the course of the *Phenomenology* were abstractions from spirit (*PhS*, 264/*GW*, IX, 239). None of those stages of individual consciousness—from "Sense-Certainty" through "Reason"—could actually exist on their own apart from spirit or culture. They were abstracted out for purposes of analysis, and that analysis has driven us back to spirit or culture. How then are we to understand the relation of culture to what will follow it at the next stage of the *Phenomenology*—religion and the absolute? In the introduction, I argued that just as individual consciousness was abstracted from culture, so culture is abstracted from religion. However, at this point we must begin to see that in going beyond chapter VI to chapter VII, in moving from culture on to religion, we will not go beyond culture in the sense of leaving it behind. Religion is not outside or above culture—it is a part of culture and within it. *Geist*, the German word for "spirit," after all, refers both to culture and to religion.

This can also be seen in the way Hegel structures the sections of the *Phenomenology*. For Hegel there are three major sections to the text: "(A) Consciousness," "(B) Self-Consciousness," and "(C)," which does not have a title of its own, or shares a title with its first subsection. Its subsections are: "(AA) Reason," "(BB) Spirit," "(CC) Religion," and "(DD) Absolute Knowing." "Reason," "Spirit," "Religion," and "Absolute Knowing" are all part of the same section. If "Reason" is the high point of individual consciousness, there is a sense, then, in which we do not, as we move on to cultural consciousness, go beyond individual consciousness, that is, we do not get a superhuman consciousness, a metaphysical entity, or a transcendent deity. Instead, we dig deeper, we only go beyond individual consciousness *within* individual consciousness. We find a deepening and broadening of individual consciousness. We find that it must be understood as a cultural consciousness. And so also, we will have to dig within cultural consciousness. To move beyond it to religious consciousness, we will need a deepening and broadening of cultural consciousness. Religion is a cultural phenomenon— nothing but a cultural phenomenon—but, in Hegel's opinion, it is the part of cultural consciousness that (next to philosophy) is deepest, broadest in scope, and most profound.

II. The Ethical Order, Women, and Oppression

As anyone who has read Hegel's early writings would expect, Hegel's treatment of culture or spirit begins with ancient Greece. In Hegel's view, this was an age of ideal beauty that produced a social community and an ethical life in which citizens were free and at home. What is a bit surprising, however, is that in the *Phenomenology* Hegel does not begin his treatment of the ancient world with the heroes of Homer, the philosophers of Athens, or even with the general cultural perspective of men. He starts, in the section entitled the "Ethical Order," with Antigone and the perspective of women. It is quite true that the perspective of Antigone and of Greek women is constructed from the perspective of men, the perspective of Sophocles and of Hegel himself, nevertheless, it is still rather surprising that Hegel begins with Antigone.[6]

What does this mean? Could it mean that when we arrive at Greece, quintessentially the land of the master, Hegel insists on beginning with the slave? Is it fair to see Antigone as like the Hegelian slave? Many scholars reject such a notion.[7] Nevertheless, Antigone is subordinate to Creon and does end up subverting him—much as the slave does the master. If we admit that women are like the slave, this would tend to suggest that while dominated and oppressed, they will ultimately subvert the master, emerge as an equally significant principle, and move us toward a higher development of culture. Could Hegel really be suggesting this sort of thing about women? We will be pushed toward such a conclusion if we decide that Antigone is like the slave.

But the question as to why we begin with Antigone is even more complicated than this. Oliver argues that after the "Ethical Order," women are simply left behind in the *Phenomenology*—they are never resuscitated and are not preserved in later stages of the dialectical movement.[8] I think that women are not preserved or resuscitated adequately in the later stages of the *Phenomenology*, or in Hegel's thought in general, but I do not think that they are simply and completely left behind. To see this, recall that Hegel contrasts the Sittlichkeit of the ancient polis with the inadequate Kantian Moralität that develops in the modern world. Ancient Sittlichkeit left little room for individuality and, as individuality began to arise, it caused the collapse of the ancient community and its ethical life. However, the individuality connected with Moralität, as it develops unchecked in the modern world, goes too far, causes the French Revolution, and becomes radically destructive. Hegel wants to overcome this extreme form of individualism, but not simply by returning to ancient, undeveloped Sittlichkeit. He wants for the modern world, as I have said, a synthesis of ancient Sittlichkeit and modern Moralität—of community and individuality. At any rate, it is quite clear that Antigone represents the principle of individuality which in Hegel's view subverted the ancient community and led to its collapse. Insofar as Antigone is associated with this principle of subversion and the development of individualism, then, it will be difficult to deny her contribution to cultural development. Nevertheless, Hegel is not after a destructive form of individualism for the modern world, certainly not of the sort that caused the French Revolution. He is after an individualism that is compatible, and can be synthesized, with Sittlichkeit. While Antigone does represent the sort of individualism that subverted the inadequate Sittlichkeit of the ancient world, nevertheless, her individualism is not like the destructive individualism that Hegel wants to overcome in the modern world. Her individualism, I suggest, at least prefigures, and would be resuscitated in, the sort of individualism that would make possible a modern synthesis of Sittlichkeit and Moralität—and *that* is why Antigone is so important for Hegel.

We must notice from the start that Hegel's conception of individualism is quite different from the individualism of the liberal tradition. Individuals, for Hegel, are not natural, they are not just given, they do not come ready-made. We do not just find them there in a state of nature as for Hobbes or Locke. Individuals are constructed by their sociocultural world. Nevertheless, this construction may involve conflict—individualism may even cause the collapse of culture as it did in the ancient world and again in the French Revolution. Hegel's goal is to get beyond this destructive form of individualism to an individualism formed by, in harmony with, and reinforcing the institutions of our sociocultural world.

Thus we must distinguish between two important forms of individualism. Moreover, I would like to suggest that both of these forms of individualism are at least prefigured in the "Ethical Order;" they are prefigured by the two principles that are the foundation of the ancient world: the human law and the divine law. The first has to do with citizens, males, and their public activity in society for the community and its government. This individualism centers around warfare, wealth, property, economic interests, and so forth. Hegel says, "The acquisition and maintenance of power and wealth" that is involved here "belongs to the sphere of appetite" (*PhS*, 269/*GW*, IX, 243). This is the form of individualism that Antigone's brothers possess. I do not want to suggest that this is already liberal individualism. It is not; it is still embedded in Sittlichkeit and thus quite the opposite of liberal individualism. Nevertheless, it involves an appetite for and an interest in power and wealth, and, as the ancient Sittlichkeit of which it is part collapses and as it develops in the modern world, it will come to be centered in civil society and thus develop as a part of liberal individualism. Moreover, there is a certain tension between this form of individualism and the family, both in modern civil society (*PR*, 148/*SW*, VII, 314) and, we shall see, here already in the ancient polis. Hegel does not want to eliminate this form of individualism. He wants to allow it a place; but it must be contained so as not to be destructive.

The second form of individualism is prefigured in the divine law and it is quite clear that Antigone represents this form of individualism. It does not involve a radical standing alone, apart, in a state of nature. It is true that the individualism of her brothers, still embedded in Sittlichkeit, does not involve such standing alone either. But Antigone's individualism does not even involve individual appetite for power, wealth, or personal glory in warfare. Her individualism, rather, is manifested in and through acting in perfect solidarity with the family, religion, and tradition. This is the key, I think, to why Hegel is so interested in Antigone and why Antigone is so important.

Just a few pages back I argued that Hegel's concern was to show that culture must lead us on to religion. We will therefore need an individualism that will not be hostile to religion. I have also just said that Hegel wants a form of individualism that is compatible with modern Sittlichkeit. Antigone's individualism would seem to fit the bill. Her individualism is the sort that allows a self embedded in a context of cultural relations, institutions, and common customs, traditions, and practices to develop an individual identity. Since we are all formed and shaped by our culture, if we are to become individuals and at the same time avoid the sorts of vagaries associated with what we have come to call cultural relativism, we need a solid identity, in Hegel's view, an absolute identity. Individuals must have the sense that they are right, that while they act within a particular community, tradition, or culture they do more than simply act in accord with personal appetites, private interests, or with whatever their particular community, tradition, or culture happens to value. They must be able to think (as all Europeans certainly have been able to think) that they as individuals are contributing to something objectively important, that the divine or the absolute is acting through them, or at least that they are acting in accord with the divine or the absolute, that it is their destiny to realize some objective truth or good, or something of the sort. This is the form of identity that Antigone has and represents. It is an identity embedded in the local and particular, within which, however, the individual is able to find an absolute reality, importance, and truth. It is a form of individualism that is not only compatible with religion, culture, and Sittlichkeit, but derives from them. More will have to be said to explain this second form of individualism in both this chapter and the next; my only point here is to begin to indicate the importance of Antigone.

At any rate, Hegel wants a balance here. Too much liberal individualism in the modern world gives us the French Revolution, chaos, destruction, and the loss of an absolute identity. Not enough liberal individualism in the ancient world gave us the closed world of immediacy found in the Greek polis. Hegel wants a balance and harmony between ancient Sittlichkeit and modern Moralität, a balance that was at least prefigured in the balance between divine law and human law, and, we must also see, in the balance between male and female.

For Hegel, the latter are two essences. And the authentication of one occurs through the other (*PhS*, 78/*GW*, IX, 250). This is to say that neither "of the two is by itself absolutely valid.)... This equilibrium can, it is true, only be a living one by inequality arising in it, and being brought back to equilib-

rium by Justice" (*PhS*, 276–7/*GW*, IX, 248–9). What are we to make
rather obscure statement? I think it does indicate that at least in this ~~section~~
of the *Phenomenology* Hegel is not engaged, as O'Brien suggests, in history's
most ambitious attempt to define humanity as simply masculine.[9] But, on the
other hand, it does not seem to me either that Hegel is simply arguing for
equality between the sexes, as Ravven suggests.[10] Let us begin to examine
this section in detail.

The two main institutions of ancient Greece were the family and the
community (or polis)—and they were intimately related in a self-reinforcing
circle. The family provides men to the community. They serve in the political
and governmental sphere and most importantly in war. The family raises children who as young men go off to war. Reciprocally, the community, for its
part, must protect and preserve the family. In war it protects individuals and
their families from the enemy, and in peacetime it organizes and fosters property which makes possible the substance and subsistence of families.[11] Each
institution serves the other and each would be impossible without the other.
The community owes its very existence to families and its fundamental purpose is to defend and make the good life possible for members of families.
And families, for their part, could not defend themselves or prosper without
the community, which they must in turn serve.

However, warfare is not engaged in solely as a means to protection. For
young men it is also an escape from the confines of the family and an arena in
which to achieve virtue and gain public honor. And from its perspective the
city must see to it that citizens do not get too deeply rooted and isolated in
their concerns for property. From time to time the citizens must be shaken to
their roots by war. They must be made to serve the highest concerns of the
community. As Hegel puts it, they must be "made to feel in the task laid on
them their lord and master, death" (*PhS*, 272–3/*GW*, IX, 246). On the one
hand, the family is protected by warfare; on the other hand, it loses its members to the community and they die in war—the family is both preserved by
the community and destroyed by it. Even this death, however, links the
family and the community. Death is the highest service the individual under-
takes for the community, and the individual's burial is the highest duty of the
family (*PhS*, 271/*GW*, IX, 245). Individuals die for the community and are
buried by the family—they are honored by the community and mourned by
the family.

Proper burial is most important in Greek culture. In book 11 of the
Odyssey, we see that Odysseus had to return to bury one of his men who otherwise could not have entered the underworld and found peace. Moreover,
the individual cannot simply be abandoned to the natural and to decay. The
burial ceremony is caught up with the need to preserve, remember, and recognize heroic virtue—Patroclos's burial ceremony lasts for twelve days in

book 23 of the *Iliad*. The individual must be made to live on in the memory of the family and the community.

In this ideal Sittlichkeit, then, these two fundamental institutions, the family and the community, each preserve and produce the other—each confirms and substantiates the other.[12] The spiritual or cultural world is a product created by the action of each and it constitutes their unity. Only in this cultural world are things accomplished and only through it do individuals share in the results (*PhS*, 264/GW, IX, 239). Human law and divine law, in this ideal, are supposed to reinforce each other harmoniously.

However, these two laws soon come into disequilibrium—a disequilibrium that needs to be restored by justice (*PhS*, 276–7/GW, IX, 248–9). Hegel takes up two classic examples that he finds in Sophocles. The first is Oedipus, who saves the city of Thebes, becomes its ruler, and rules well. His actions are in perfect accord with the human law. However, he violates the law of the family, the divine law, in the worst possible way, by murdering his father and marrying his mother. He does this in ignorance, but he does it nevertheless (*PhS*, 283/GW, IX, 255). Divine law takes its vengeance on human law by producing a plague in the city.

The second case is that of Antigone. This time we get a conflict between the two laws that is intentional. Antigone has two brothers—Eteocles and Polyneices. As would be typical, at a certain age they leave the home for the community, for politics and government, while their sister remains in the home. Eteocles, it turns out, becomes ruler of the city and Polyneices attacks it. Both die. The city recognizes Eteocles, its ruler, and condemns Polyneices, who attacked the city, as an enemy and a traitor—which seems to be in perfect agreement with human law. Creon, the new ruler, accords burial honors to Eteocles and refuses them to Polyneices. This is not acceptable, however, to divine law. It will not recognize such distinctions; both brothers are equally members of the family and Antigone must bury both—even the one who attacked the city (*PhS*, 285–6/GW, IX, 257).

Here, the community and the family are no longer in harmony. Why does this occur? From the beginning there has been a basic tension between the community and the family. The community, after all, draws the family member out to war and to death, thus destroying the family and breaking its happiness (see *PR*, 209–11/SW, VII, 433–7). This is bad enough, but for Creon to refuse to bury Polyneices is to go too far. For Antigone, Creon's action on behalf of the city is not justice, it is not the restoration of equilibrium, it certainly cannot represent a universal moral principle, it is an outrage. It can only be, in her view, the perverse decision of this particular individual (her uncle Creon) against another particular individual (her beloved brother Polyneices). So Antigone attacks, derides, ridicules Creon's action, and asserts that the commitment to her brother demanded by divine law is more important than the human law of the community, all of which seems in perfect agreement with divine law. The community, for its part, naturally tries to suppress Antigone and what it sees as her individualism, but in doing so only feeds it and creates an eternal enemy in women (*PhS*, 288/*GW*, IX, 259). Antigone's action fractures the substantial unity of ethical life and turns adherence to ethical law into mere sentiment or disposition—mere individual and subjective commitment (*PhS*, 284/*GW*, IX, 256).

What, then, can we say about Hegel's attitude toward Antigone, women, and their equality with men? It is certainly the case that women are excluded from political life in the polis. Moreover, the role of women certainly seems to be established by nature or as part of a fixed essence. And furthermore, the possibility that women might have interests other than the family never even arises.[13] At the same time, though, it is just not the case that Antigone is locked away out of the real order of things. She is excluded from the realm of human law, but the divine law is every bit as real, significant, and important. In fact it is more primordial and ultimately more powerful—indeed, it finally triumphs (*PhS*, 273/*GW*, IX, 246).

While there is no way that Hegel is going to cut a figure as an acceptable modern feminist, nevertheless, we would be wrong, I think, to assume that he simply sides with Creon, the community, the government, and human law against Antigone. Furthermore, we cannot let our reading of the *Philosophy of Right*, written fifteen years after the *Phenomenology*, lead us to project things back into the *Phenomenology* that are not there. I do not wish to argue that in all respects the two texts differ, but the texts clearly do differ on some issues. For example, Hegel has been called the official philosopher of the Prussian state for his supposed glorification of the state in the *Philosophy of Right*.[14] While I think this is an incorrect reading even of that text, nevertheless, we should notice that the *Phenomenology* is notably free from anything resembling such glorification of the state.[15] There is certainly no glorification of the Greek state. If anything, I would say that Hegel sides with the subversive Antigone against Creon. Moreover, we find that this same negative or critical attitude toward the state will continue throughout the rest of chapter VI of the *Phenomenology*. We see this in the way that Hegel treats state power, noble and base consciousness, and the heroism of flattery, all of which lead up to the French Revolution's overthrow of state power, a process with which Hegel has a certain sympathy despite his opposition to the destructive individualism involved. If it is impossible in the *Phenomenology* to saddle Hegel with the view of the state that he will supposedly hold in the *Philosophy of Right*, if Hegel is more critical of the state than he will be in the *Philosophy of Right*, there should be nothing wrong with being very careful before we attribute to him the negative views of women that we will find in the *Philosophy of Right*.

Quite clearly, the *Philosophy of Right* holds a more conservative view of women than does the *Phenomenology*. In the *Philosophy of Right*, the family must have as its head the husband (*PR*, 116/*SW*, VII, 249). Moreover, Hegel holds that while women are capable of education they are not made for the advanced sciences that demand a universal faculty. Also when women hold the helm of government, the state is in jeopardy, since women are not regulated by the demands of universality but by arbitrary inclinations and opinions (*PR*, 263–4/*SW*, VII, 247). In the *Phenomenology*, on the other hand, it is explicitly the case that the man is *not* the head of the household: "The wife remains...the head of the household and the guardian of the divine law" (*PhS*, 275/*GW*, IX, 248). Moreover, in the *Phenomenology*, men and women, at least as brother and sister, are equal (*PhS*, 288/*GW*, IX, 259). It is true, though, that husband and wife are not equal. From this fact, however, we cannot conclude—as Tuana does—that the community and the human law, to which the husband belongs, are superior to the divine law and the family, of which the wife is guardian and head.[16] That is not Hegel's view. For Hegel, neither has any advantage over the other—they are equally essential (*PhS*, 285/*GW*, IX, 256). While it is true that women are confined to the family, it is also true that the Greek family, unlike the modern family, was the fundamental economic unit of society—it was the basic unit of production and produced for itself most of what it needed. To be the head of such an institution could not be, and was not considered, insignificant.

The view of women found in the *Phenomenology* is not as objectionable as that found in the *Philosophy of Right*. Nevertheless, I do not want to suggest that the *Phenomenology* treats women as sufficiently equal. In fact, I want to argue against an interpretation of Hegel that would tend in that direction. Some commentators seem to think that Hegel's conception of love implies equality between men and women. I think that is mistaken. I do not think Hegel believes in the equality of men and women. On the other hand, one cannot deny that love and certainly recognition are central and important categories of Hegel's thought. So if it can be shown that love requires, necessitates, or even pushes toward equality, as some argue, then the claim that Hegel does not believe in the equality of men and women would not at all be as clear. However, love does not require, necessitate, or imply equality.

In trying to understand Hegel's conception of love, we must notice that it is capable of overcoming the lack of recognition that plagued the self in chapter V. There we found that it was impossible to sustain a Kantian transcendental self. The self turned out to be nothing but a bundle of talents or potentials objectified in actions or deeds. The only trouble was that each self was so involved with its own actions and objectifications that it would not recognize the works of others, and thus selves seemed to float in a realm of unreality. Love overcomes this problem. In chapter VI, Hegel says, "The relationship of husband and wife is...the primary and immediate form in which one consciousness recognizes itself in another, and in which each knows that reciprocal recognition."[17] In love I am real and significant insofar as I exist for-another. In an earlier text, Hegel said that individuals intuit themselves in the being of the other consciousness and thus have a communal existence with the other (FPS, 232/GW, VI, 302; see also PWHI, 100/PW, I, 119). Indeed, Baillie suggests that in chapter VI of the Phenomenology Hegel is following Aristotle's treatment of friendship in books 8 and 9 of the Nicomachean Ethics (PhM, 465). It is clearly Aristotle's view that friendship or love is what holds the polis together. In fact, friendship is more important than justice in this respect—since friends treat each other better than justice would demand and it would be far worse to harm a friend than someone else (NE, 1155a).

I want to be quite clear, then, that I do not ignore love or dismiss it. In fact, I agree with commentators like Robert Williams and Merold Westphal about the importance and centrality of love for Hegel's thought. On the other hand, though, love simply will not give us the equality that these commentators seem to think it will. According to Williams, "Love seeks a union with its other, in which domination and subordination are out of place. Love allows the other to be, i.e., it seeks the freedom of the other."[18]

While love is compatible with equality, as between brother and sister, love certainly does not require equality. Love is perfectly compatible with inequality. Let me be as clear about this as possible so as not to be misunderstood. I certainly think that in a relationship between a man and a woman equality is desirable. I also think that the relationship will be a better relationship if it is one of equality. And I think that love is a valuable and desirable thing. But I do not think that there is anything about love which requires equality in a relationship. I just do not think that love and equality are necessarily related. I think it desirable that a loving relationship also be one of equality, but just as a relationship of equality need not involve love, so we can perfectly well have love without having equality. To think that love and equality necessarily or normally go together is to romanticize love—to expect something of it which it is not. We can easily love someone we consider our inferior or our superior—God, our dog, the king, the queen, our children, our parents. For centuries, men have been loving their wives while thinking them their inferiors—and I have no reason to believe that many of these men did not really love their wives—certainly not because there is any incompatibility between love and inequality. Certainly those relationships would have been improved by equality, but I see no reason to think that the love as love would necessarily have been deepened or made truer. Love and equality are just different things. There is nothing about loving someone whom one considers an inferior that necessarily distorts the love. Love can be perfectly true love when it is love of an equal, a superior, or an inferior. Certainly, Aristotle did not think that love implied equality when he claimed it was what held the city together.

The question, then, is whether Hegel recognizes that love does not require equality. I think he clearly does recognize this. It is only the relationship of brother and sister that is a relationship of equality. The relationship of husband to wife is not one of equality. In an earlier text, the *System of Ethical Life,* Hegel explicitly held that the husband was the master (*SEL,* 127/*SS,* 36). Hegel does not actually make this claim in the *Phenomenology.* He does say, however, that the son is "lord and master of the mother who bore him" (*PhS,* 288/*GW,* IX, 258–9). If that is so, it would be hard to imagine that Hegel would not also take the husband to be lord and master of his wife. In the *System of Ethical Life,* Hegel makes a much more direct and explicit connection between the relationship of lordship and bondage and the relationship between the sexes in love, marriage, and property. They are all treated within a span of thirty pages or less as part of a developmental sequence (*SEL,* 103–29/*SS,* 9–38). Indeed, Hegel says outright, "The lordship and bondage relation . . . is the [patriarchal] family."[19] In the *Phenomenology,* on the other hand, the master-slave dialectic is separated by more than two hundred pages from the "Ethical Order," where relations between the sexes, love, family, and property are discussed. Nevertheless, we must notice the connection. We must see that in the *Phenomenology* too, woman, like the slave, is dominated and man is the master. Hegel is explicit in holding that the community, the sphere of males, suppresses the family and women: "Since the community only gets an existence through its interference with the happiness of the Family . . . it creates for itself in what it suppresses and what is at the same time essential to it an internal enemy—womankind in general. . . . The community, however, can only maintain itself by suppressing this spirit of individualism, and, because it is an essential moment, all the same creates it and, moreover, creates it by its repressive attitude towards it as a hostile principle" (*PhS,* 288/*GW,* IX, 258–9).

The claim that the two principles—the human law and the divine law, the sphere of the masculine and the sphere of the feminine—are equally essential is not at all incompatible with the claim that women are dominated and oppressed by men. After all, even the master dominates and oppresses the slave while the slave is just as essential to human development as the master. Like the master-slave dialectic, then, the male community dominates women; this creates in women an enemy and it feeds the development of, the progress to, a new reality—in this case individualism. Moreover, again like the slave, the woman subverts the master. She sees the universal end of government as a mere private end and sees its universal activity as the work of a particular individual. She ridicules its wisdom—the fact that it cares only for the universal. She makes the state the laughingstock of youth and unworthy of their support. The state's continued suppression only feeds her hostility and spreads her message (*PhS*, 288/*GW*, IX, 258–9).

It seems to me that we must admit that we do have a situation here that is similar to the master-slave dialectic.[20] The question is whether Hegel himself would agree. We have seen above that in the *System of Ethical Life* he himself connects lordship and bondage with the patriarchal family, but what about in the *Phenomenology*? The upshot of Antigone's action is that the ancient community dissolves and we are left, as we see in the next section ("Legal Status"), with individuals facing a powerful and estranged governmental force that stands over and dominates them—Hegel calls this force the "lord and master of the world" (*PhS*, 290–2/*GW*, IX, 260–2). On the other hand, individuality develops, Hegel says, as the divine law emerges from an inward state into actuality—personality steps out of the life of the ethical substance. Hegel parallels this to his treatment of Stoicism earlier in the *Phenomenology* and says that just as Stoicism "proceeded from lordship and bondage, as the immediate existence of self-consciousness, so personality has proceeded from the immediate life of Spirit, which is the universal dominating will of all, and equally their service of obedience" (*PhS*, 290/*GW*, IX, 261). Even in the *Phenomenology* we have an explicit statement of a parallel between "Lordship and Bondage" and the "Ethical Order."[21]

Where are we to stand when we read the section on Antigone? How are we to react to it? Are we to side with Antigone or against her? Benhabib seems to think that Hegel has written an apologia for Creon.[22] If we were to decide that Hegel is a simple sexist and the philosopher of the Prussian state, then we would probably conclude that he expects us to dismiss Antigone and side with Creon. But how can we do that? Antigone represents an *equally essential* principle. What she does is *right*—it is in full accord with divine law. It is the state that in repressing her brings about its own collapse. And the master must be subverted—that is the only way we move to a higher principle. Antigone, after all, develops an important form of individualism.

Clearly the Antigone story is a tragedy. And tragedy for Hegel means the conflict of two principles, both of which are right (*A*, II, 1196, 1212/*SW*, XIV, 529, 550). It means that both sides are justified—not just Creon, not just the state, not just men. Tragedy means the collapse of the great, the master, the whole ethical world. It also means the emergence of a higher moral principle. If the Antigone story is to be a tragedy, and it is, we cannot side with the state and dismiss Antigone in sexist fashion. If we do, we destroy the tragic element.

However, there is also something besides tragedy going on in the last part of Hegel's treatment of Antigone. In the *Aesthetics*, Hegel explains comedy, especially Greek comedy, as a situation in which subjectivity (or individuality) has the upper hand. Comedy occurs in a world in which man is master, a world that destroys itself by its own folly, and that thus dissolves in laughter (A, II, 1199/SW, XIV, 533–4; see also PhS, 279/GW, IX, 251–2). In the *Phenomenology*, Hegel's view is that woman is the "everlasting irony in the life of the community" and she brings it down by making it a "laughing-stock."[23] We might say that from the perspective of the male master, the col-lapse of the community is tragic. But from an equally important perspective, the perspective of woman—the slave—the collapse of the community is comic.[24] And it seems to me that both of these perspectives are important for Hegel.

Certainly women are being treated seriously here. Women are sup-pressed and like the slave subvert the master. And this is positive, desir-able—it allows individualism to emerge. Subversion allows us to move to a higher principle. Moreover, if we decide that woman as the enemy of the state is to be taken seriously, positively, then we may even wonder whether we should read in a somewhat different way Hegel's claim in the *Philosophy of Right* that the state is in jeopardy when led by a woman. Perhaps—at least at times and even for Hegel—that is a good thing. Likewise, when we recog-nize Antigone's hostility to the universal ends of government and her com-mitment to the particular and individual, we may also want to read in a different way the claim in the *Philosophy of Right* that women lack a univer-sal faculty and are not regulated by the demands of universality. Perhaps—at least at times and even for Hegel—that too is a good thing (PR, 263–4/SW, VII, 247).

Does this mean that we can rehabilitate Hegel as an acceptable modern feminist? No, that is not possible. Hegel does not argue for the full equality of women and he holds too many objectionable views. Despite this, some femi-nists find that he has positive contributions to make.[25] I think that despite Hegel's intentions there is a valuable conceptual possibility present in his thought—one that he does not or will not develop for women, but which nevertheless is there for our appropriation. As we have seen above, no system empowers the oppressed and marginalized as does Hegel's. The absolute, like the master and like the worldview of Western culture, claims to be all of real-ity. It denies anything of significance outside itself and marginalizes what it cannot accept. It must be everything. If not, it is not the absolute. And so, as soon as the other can show itself to be something, something real, something significant, then the absolute is no longer absolute—it is not all of reality. This gives the other considerable power to subvert the absolute and to build a new absolute with itself at the center. Whether Hegel likes it or not, whether he would approve or not, he has shown us how the oppression of women places them where they can subvert the absolute and construct a new absolute that includes women at the center. And that certainly seems to be what is happening in the contemporary feminist movement.

Isn't it problematic, though, to say nothing of ironic, to be arguing that because Antigone is like the slave, therefore Hegel, despite himself, is treating her positively? Traditionally, women and slaves have been thought of as mere appendages to their masters. They are expected not to show independence or self-determination. In so far as they assert individuality, self-determination, or autonomy, they act improperly. The virtuous woman serves a man, accents him, assists him. Women cannot assert independence and be thought virtuous. Their virtue is defined by their subordination to men.

To give Hegel credit, I think we must see to what extent he is breaking from this traditional view. It is true that for Hegel a woman's virtue is still confined to the family and the service of men. It is true that the slave does not overthrow the master. Both remain in their allotted role. But both accomplish something, both subvert the master, and do so without abandoning their place. Antigone's commitment to the divine law never wavers. To achieve individuality she does not slacken her commitment to the family. To achieve self-determination she does not abandon tradition. She does the very opposite. She fulfills her role to the utmost. She satisfies her obligation to the family, to divine law, to tradition—all with a vengeance. And thereby she subverts the government and gives rise to a new individualism.

The slave, like the woman, develops individuality and independence through the unfolding of inner potentialities, through empowerment, not, like the master, through the domination of others. Slavery and service are the true models for virtue—the unfolding and development of a real inner capacity. After all, in Hegel's view, it is "not so much *from* slavery as *through* slavery that humanity [is] emancipated" (*PH*, 407/*PW*, II, 875).

Antigone's individualism, then, is not at all like liberal individualism; it does not involve the sort of freedom that one finds in a state of nature, the liberty to act on any desire that happens to catch one. It is an individualism compatible with family, religion, and tradition. It is human law, society, and men that are out of line and that eventually are subverted. If they could finally be brought into harmony with this different sort of individualism, then it would be Antigone who had given Hegel the sort of principle that he needs, a principle of harmony between individuality, self-determination, and autonomy, on the one hand, and community, tradition, and embeddedness in relations, that is, with Sittlichkeit, on the other hand. And some would say that this principle is a feminine principle. It is Antigone, then, who prefigures what Hegel is ultimately after, an individualism that is compatible with and finds its identity in the family, tradition, and religion, which, together with a compatible political community, could hopefully temper the destructive individualism of civil society and allow a modern Sittlichkeit to emerge, a Sittlichkeit, moreover, that while embedded in concrete and particular customs, traditions, and practices, nevertheless affords the individual an ultimate sense of being right.

At any rate, Antigone's action split the Greek community and produced an individualism that dissolved its ethical life in laughter.

III. Legal Status and the Emperor

Because of this individualism, the community, as Hegel puts it, ceases to be the substance of individuals. The ancient community breaks up into a multiplicity of atomic units, each of which counts equally as a person. Each is a self and a substance that possesses being-for-self (*PhS*, 290/*GW*, IX, 260–1). Direct involvement in the ethical life of the community is lost. At the same time, the government becomes merely a distant, formal, universal power. We are in Rome and have reached what Hegel calls "Legal Status." We must understand the transition to Rome as a split occurring within a spiritual whole. The life of the community breaks up into a distant estranged governmental power (the Roman state and the Roman emperor), on one side, and the crystallization of isolated individuals into persons, on the other side.

In Rome, as Hegel put it in an earlier text:

> The picture of the state as a product of his own energies disappeared from the citizen's soul. The care and oversight of the whole rested on the soul of one man or a few. Each individual had his own allotted place, a place more or less restricted and different from his neighbor's. The administration of the state machine was intrusted to a small number of citizens, and these served only as cogs deriving their worth solely from their connection with others. Each man's allotted part in the congeries which formed the whole was so inconsiderable in relation to the whole that the individual did not need to realize this relation or to keep it in view.... All activity and every purpose now had a bearing on something individual; activity was no longer for the sake of a whole or an ideal. Either everyone worked for himself or else he was compelled to work for some other individual. Freedom to obey self-given laws, to follow self-chosen leaders in peacetime and self-chosen generals in war, to carry out plans in whose formulation one had had one's share—all this vanished. All political freedom vanished also; the citizen's right gave him only a right to the security of that property which now filled his entire world. (*PCR*, 156–7/*GW*, I, 369–70)

The Roman person is like the Stoic self-consciousness we met earlier in chapter IV of the *Phenomenology*; in fact, Hegel says that Stoic self-consciousness merely reduces to its abstract form the principle of "Legal Status." The

Roman person has a distance from, and an independence of, actuality. The person exists solely for-itself (*PhS*, 290-1/*GW*, IX, 261). It has no communal or public attachment. We have an abstract person (recognized and thus made real by Roman law), and we have a detached and disconnected content before this person. The content is merely at hand, external, a fact of possession—it is the person's property. Persons have a right or title to property recognized by the Roman state (*PhS*, 291-2/*GW*, IX, 262).

The relation of the person to property is a relation that makes for a chaotic, unchecked, and destructive conflict—one which recalls the way of the world. Thus the government here must be different from that of the polis. It must control persons and property with force. This control is gathered into a single center that is the essential element. As Hegel puts it, it is the lord and master of the world—the Roman emperor who is a universal power. This lord and master gains its power through individual self-consciousness alienating itself and giving up its control over the public community. The lord and master, like a Hobbesian absolute sovereign, has all power and reality. Persons with property and property interests clash chaotically and are organized through force by this distant power. It dominates in hostile and destructive fashion. Like the master over the slave, Hegel says, it becomes conscious of what it is—of its supremacy—through this destruction (*PhS*, 292-3/*GW*, IX, 263).

Alienation first appeared in the *Phenomenology* at the end of "Unhappy Consciousness" (*PhS*, 293/*GW*, IX, 263). There we met an individual consciousness confronting a beyond—a deity. Here we have persons confronting an emperor. In both cases the reality that confronts individuals is their own alienation—their own construction. Here, however, it is much clearer that such construction is a cultural construction. Both of the alienated elements— emperor as well as persons—exist within the spiritual unity of a cultural world and each constructs the other. Individuals alienate themselves and abandon their power. It is lost to them and crystallizes into a power outside and over against them—the state and its emperor. They are left as isolated units—persons formed, recognized, and dominated by the state and its laws.[26]

Antigone was not able to gain recognition from her state, certainly not as an individual. Insofar as she was an individual, she was an irritant and was condemned rather than accepted. In Rome, we have solidly accepted persons recognized by the full weight of Roman law and invested with rights in property. We might say, then, that Antigone was unable to overcome the problem that arose in chapter V—that of the self's inability to gain the recognition of others. Antigone was able to gain recognition as a family member, as a representative of divine law, but not as an individual.

It is as if consciousness has started wondering whether the forceful assertion of individuality is the way to gain recognition for itself. Here the opposite seems to work better. To withdraw, to concern oneself only with one's property, to give reality over to the emperor, seems a better way to gain stably recognized individuality. The self has not succeeded in becoming real by demanding recognition for its work. So instead it serves another, recognizes the emperor, gives it power and scope, makes it real, and thus creates a force from which it can in turn gain the recognition it needs to make it real. At any rate, this is the strategy that consciousness will pursue for some time through the course of chapter VI—up until the French Revolution when it will radically reverse itself. This Stoic or Roman withdrawal, however, means the loss of community and Sittlichkeit, and so what we will need to reachieve before we are done is the harmony and compatibility of individuality and Sittlichkeit that was suggested in Antigone.

IV. Culture and Estrangement

The sort of domination that develops under the lord and master of the world, and which reminds us of "Lordship and Bondage," will continue throughout much of chapter VI. At the same time, like the slave, the citizens will gain in depth, scope, and reality through their domination by and service to the state. Moreover, like the reversal in "Lordship and Bondage," we will come to see that the state does not simply dominate its citizens, the state is also dependent on them for its own recognition and reality—the state is constructed by its citizens. When we see this, it will begin to spell the end of the state as master. Citizens will no longer subject themselves to such authority, but only to their own reason embodied in their laws and institutions. Rational self-mastery, rational self-determination—that is, freedom—will begin to emerge finally in the French Revolution.

    The state's domination will not so much be overcome as transformed and reunderstood. The state's discipline will transform the citizen and citizens will transform the state. Each will constitute the other such that what begins as external coercion becomes internal discipline and finally rational self-discipline. Hegel says, "The state is mind knowing and willing itself after passing through the forming process of culture (*Bildung*)."[27] This is the process that Hegel traces in chapter VI. To understand it, we might compare it to Aristotle's model of moral development. The child must learn to take pleasure in what is virtuous. The child's early upbringing is dominated by external authority and discipline, but if it works correctly, a character and disposition will be formed that finally, on its own, will find the good to be pleasant (*NE*, 1104[b]). In Hegel's view, it is quite possible for citizens to become free under such a master. It has to be *our* master—a master we identify with as our own. It also has to be a legitimate master—a master who acts in accordance with rational principles. It has to be a master with whom we rationally identify.

Absolutely key to this freedom is the fact that the state is our own construction. If it were not our construction, if it were simply an external and arbitrary authority, if it were simply heteronomous, we could never become free. In obeying the state we must in the deepest way be obeying ourselves—our rational selves. But at the same time, if we had seen this from the start, if we had seen that the state was nothing but our own construction, that the emperor or the monarch was just one of us, or that the parent was simply an equal and a friend to the child, we would not have granted them the authority and reality they needed to discipline us to the point where we come to take pleasure in the good or wish to be guided by rational laws. The state is our construction, and that is absolutely necessary if we are to be free, but we must not see that the state is our construction, if we are actually to become free.

Alienation is necessary. We must subordinate ourselves and sacrifice ourselves; we must serve the state. Only thus will the state be made real and powerful. The greater the power and scope of the state, the more it will then be able to lift citizens to its level, discipline them, broaden them. The more we give up to the state, the more real it becomes, and then the more it can culture us. But we must not recognize that we have constructed this state if it is to have the reality and authority it needs to transform us. The state must be estranged.

Let us engage in a very un-Hegelian procedure.[28] Let us try to start with a simple definition of the terms "alienation" and "estrangement" and then work out from there. The German word *Entäusserung*, which is usually translated as "alienation" or "externalization," refers to a subjective process on the part of individuals, a process of giving up, sacrificing, renouncing, or divesting themselves of something that is basic or essential to them. The German word *Entfremdung*, which is often translated as "estrangement," refers to the outcome of this subjective process of *Entäusserung*, an outcome that is an objectified result, usually a sociocultural process or institution that comes to have a life of its own, which turns upon, and which dominates and oppresses those individuals. Commentators and translators are by no means consistent in the way they translate these terms. I shall always use "alienate" and "alienation" as the translations of *entäussern* and *Entäusserung*, and I shall always use "estrange" and "estrangement" as the translations of *entfremden* and *Entfremdung*.

Estrangement, then, involves the existence of an objective power that seems to have an independent and autonomous life of its own. It dominates, reacts hostilely against, and oppresses individuals. It is the result of their own alienation, but it is not recognized as being so. Alienation, on the other hand, means a surrender, a giving up, of some basic or essential reality. Alienation, however, can take several forms.

In the first place, as we have just seen, alienation can *lead to* estrangement. Individuals alienate themselves and it takes on the objectified form of an independent thing or institution—like an emperor, monarch, state, or God—which comes to have a life of its own and is not recognized as the result of the alienation of individuals. This leads to domination, oppression, and thus estrangement. This is the process that we find described in chapter VI of the *Phenomenology* and that we will discuss in the present chapter.

Second, in chapters VII and VIII of the *Phenomenology* we will see that alienation can *overcome* estrangement. Because alienation is an objectification—because the alienation of individuals constructs the monarch, the state, or God—this very same alienation can also allow us eventually to recognize the estranged reality as our own creation, our own selves objectified, our own alienation, and thus alienation can allow us to see through, and thus overcome, the estrangement. Finally, we will also find a form of alienation that neither leads to estrangement nor works to overcome it. It simply allows us to recognize our difference from the other as well as our unity with it. These two forms of alienation will be discussed in the next chapter.

At this point, we want to focus on alienation that leads to estrangement. While such alienation and estrangement, very clearly, are negative, oppressive, and something we ultimately want to overcome, nevertheless, it is crucial to understand that there is also a positive and desirable side to them. The objectified reality—the monarch, state, or God—only becomes real through the process of alienation leading to estrangement. The reality of such entities can only come from the recognition, service, obedience, and sacrifice their subjects grant them. And for the state to really become the state, a significant power and authority, it requires real recognition—service to the point of death on the part of its subjects. This powerful state, once it exists, will then be able to mold and discipline individuals. It will culture them. Individuals will be forced to conform to the state—its laws, customs, demands, and expectations. The more the subjects conform, alienate themselves, serve this master, the more reality the state gains—the more universal, recognized, and accepted the state becomes. And, thus, the more power this state will have to mold its subjects and make them conform to the universal—the state and its laws. It lifts its subjects to universality.

At the same time, the more powerful the state becomes, the more the state is served and obeyed by its subjects, the more they sacrifice for it, then the easier it becomes for us to see that the state is just an entity whose reality consists in being recognized by its subjects. What ordinary consciousness assumes to be an external, substantial, worldly institution, we see more and more as something which is ideal, a construction of consciousness, an object-for-consciousness.

This state in turn recognizes its subjects and thus substantializes them. At the end of chapter V, the subject we had before us was a mere bundle of deeds and potentials that lacked any transcendental center and was unable even to gain recognition for its objectifications. In chapter VI, such selves or subjects begin to objectify themselves in an estranged form. They construct a state that all must serve and to which all must sacrifice themselves, a state that thus becomes highly recognized, a powerful state which, though it dominates and coerces them, yet cultures them, forces them to realize their potentials, and has the scope and power to give them the recognition necessary to make them solid, real, and substantial subjects. Indeed, these selves become so solid, real, and substantial that in the French Revolution they finally turn upon the state and overthrow it.

So the subject is becoming more solid, real, and substantial. And the state while becoming more powerful is nevertheless becoming more ideal—more an object-of-consciousness. The state gains in reality by embodying and institutionalizing (in an estranged way), the reality, action, and service of the subjects. The subjects gain in reality by being molded, related to, and recognized by the universal reality of the state (which is the subjects' own reality—their own selves—alienated). So the more powerful one becomes, the more powerful and real the other becomes. At the same time, the objective and substantial state is idealized—subjectified. And the subject is objectified—substantialized.

Throughout the section on culture, the historical period echoed in the background, but abstracted from, is that of the rise of the modern state in France. The rise of absolute monarchy required suppressing the independence of the feudal nobility. Nobles had to be made to recognize, serve, and subordinate themselves to an absolute monarch. The loss of their independence had the effect of making the nobility dependent on the whim of the monarch, and finally in the court of Louis XIV produced a completely subordinate, flattering, debased nobility and an all-powerful monarch. But for Hegel, a monarch so dependent on the recognition of debased subjects is headed for collapse. The French Revolution is not far off. That is the background to this section and it is a perfect case study for the exploration of alienation and estrangement.

At the end of "Legal Status," we had, on the one hand, a multitude of persons with property interests and, on the other, a Roman emperor. Basically, these are the two realities that stand before us now. Hegel calls them wealth and state power. State power is the good and wealth is bad. Wealth is bad because it is the realm of particular and selfish interests. It brings personal enjoyment and develops the individual's sense of being separate and particular rather than a member of the state attending to universal matters. The realm of the state, on the other hand, is good because it is the realm of universal concerns and of self-sacrifice for those concerns. It is the universal work of all in which the subjects' sense of their particular action has vanished—after all, the state is estranged and thus the subjects do not see it as the result of their own doing (PhS, 301/GW, IX, 270).

Wealth, however, is really more complex than this. It is not simply bad, because individuals, in seeking their own interest and enjoyment, serve the interest and enjoyment of all. Adam Smith, we have seen, argued that aggressive self-seeking produces a national wealth from which all have a chance to gain their own share. The self-interested pursuit of wealth thus leads to the universal—it produces a common good that benefits all (PhS, 301–2/GW, IX, 270).

The good and the bad, then, must also be viewed in a different way. We can hold that to be good in which we find ourselves affirmed and reflected and that to be bad in which we do not. From this perspective, wealth is good. It allows to each the satisfaction of particular self-interests. It thus affirms and reflects each—indeed, it contributes to the general enjoyment of all. It produces a common good that benefits everyone (PhS, 302–3/GW, IX, 271–2). On the other hand, state power, from this perspective, is bad. It is estranged and thus we cannot see ourselves reflected in it. It does not appear as our doing. Moreover, far from affirming us, it demands sacrifice, requires obedience, and is hostile and oppressive.

In one sense, then, state power is good and wealth bad, but in another sense, it is wealth that is good and state power that is bad. We need a more complex consciousness, then, that can combine the two senses of good as opposed to the two senses of bad. What Hegel calls "noble consciousness" takes a positive attitude toward both state power and wealth. It serves and respects the universality of state power and it also recognizes that wealth secures self-existence or being-for-self. Noble consciousness brings the two sides of the good together. It can do this, Hegel thinks, because property and political position—wealth and state power—are one and the same for it. In other words, noble consciousness is the consciousness of the feudal nobility, for whom political position is inseparable from landed estate. To be the Duke of Burgundy means to hold the title of Duke (and thus have political position and state power), as well as to hold landed wealth, specifically, the estate of Burgundy. Both are given by the monarch and thus we would expect the noble to respect the universal state power and appreciate the wealth through which it achieves its self-existence (PhS, 305/GW, IX, 273). At this stage, then, we must not identify wealth with civil society as Hinchman does. Feudal landed wealth must be distinguished from the capitalist wealth of civil society. The latter, however, does emerge within feudal society and will develop rapidly. Indeed, what we will get, as Lukács puts it, is the "gradual bourgeoisification of absolute monarchy."[29]

Besides noble consciousness, we also have what Hegel calls "ignoble" or "base" consciousness. It takes a negative attitude toward both state power and wealth. It sees state power as bad, as a fetter, as domination, as repressing particular interests. It hates the ruler and is rebellious. Furthermore, while base consciousness does in fact seek wealth and enjoyment, at the same time it despises it. It loves wealth but also hates it because, Hegel says, it only gives base consciousness a sense of being an isolated individual. Wealth does not link base consciousness to the state and to state power as it does for noble consciousness (PhS, 305/GW, IX, 273). In other words, base consciousness is the consciousness of the rising bourgeoisie under feudalism—not the proletariat, as Merold Westphal has it.[30] If we are bourgeois, wealth gives us enjoyment but does not gain us recognition—certainly it will not gain us nobility, title, or political status. It will not connect us to universality and state power as it does for the nobility.

Hegel next focuses on noble consciousness and the heroism of service. For state power to become more than a vague principle that nobles may or may not obey as they feel like it, which was the case under feudalism, for state power to become real, it must become a monarch that the nobles really submit to and obey. The centralization of state power and the rise of the modern state require total subordination and an end to the independence of the nobles. The acceptance of such subordination is the heroism of service. Noble consciousness, like virtue in chapter V, sacrifices the individual to the universal. It takes a positive attitude toward state power and a negative attitude toward its own self-interest (PhS, 306/GW, IX, 274). And like virtue, noble consciousness and the heroism of service will finally lose out to base consciousness and the way of the world.

At any rate, the heroism of service establishes the state as an actual, universal power. It also wins the noble self-respect and the respect of others. We do not yet have, however, an absolute monarch. Unless there is a total alienation of self, the noble remains a haughty vassal, active in the interests of state power only so long as the state is not a real monarch. The haughty vassal is only willing to serve state power in order to maintain its own honor and self-importance. It is only willing to give council and advice for the general good. It only sacrifices its outer existence, not its intrinsic being. It must alienate itself completely. State power needs service to the point of death (PhS, 306–8/GW, IX, 274–5). The problem of the haughty vassal, in Hegel's opinion, was not merely a problem faced in the rise of absolute monarchy in France. As we see in one of Hegel's earlier writings, The German Constitution, the haughty vassal was especially a problem in Germany and stood in the way of its development as a modern state.[31]

But it is not just service to the point of death that is needed by state power. An even deeper and more complete alienation of the self is required. The heroism of silent service must become the heroism of flattery (*PhS*, 310/*GW*, IX, 277–8). Hegel is thinking of the court of Louis XIV. The reality of an absolute monarch depends on the recognition, the homage, the flattery of the nobles. In flattery, the noble alienates the "pure *intrinsic being of its thinking*" and establishes individuality in the monarch, which, as Hegel said in chapter V, "otherwise is only a presumed existence"—in other words, there is no transcendental self, the self must be constructed (*PhS*, 311/*GW*, IX, 278). It is constructed as the nobles (and the imagery here is Hegel at his very best) "group themselves round the throne as an *ornamental setting*... continually *telling* him who sits on it what he *is*." Louis "thereby knows himself, *this* individual, to be the universal power" (*PhS*, 311/*GW*, IX, 278). Thus, as Hyppolite puts it, Louis "can say 'L'Etat c'est moi.'"[32] The total alienation of self—through risk of death, flattery, and humility—produces the state as a self. The alienation of many selves, renouncing their own inner certainty, is fused into one (*PhS*, 311/*GW*, IX, 278). The nobles have alienated, given up, abased their selves, which have been ceded to, transformed into, the monarch as the only independent self.

If, as we saw in chapter V, the self is a mere bundle of deeds and potentialities, if there is no transcendental self, if, as Hinchman puts it, the self has no determinate core,[33] then the only way to construct a solid self is through alienation. Hegel says, "Self-consciousness is only something definite, it only has real existence, so far as it alienates itself from itself. By doing so, it puts itself in the position of something universal."[34] We give up our inner reality, project it onto a monarch, whom we recognize and serve to the point where the monarch becomes a solid, real, universal power. Thus we establish for the first time a solid self. We create this self as alienated, as a loss to us, as an other self, but we create it nevertheless. To overcome this alienation, to get a solid self back for ourselves, comes later. But such a self has to be constructed in the first place.

An absolute monarch, then, is different from the master, the emperor, or the sort of head of state served by the haughty vassal. The absolute monarch is a self and for the monarch to be a self requires a great deal more alienation and a deeper, more internal sort of alienation than the haughty vassal was willing to give or than existed for the master or the emperor.

At any rate, absolute monarchy is made effective through alienation, service, and flattery, but what the noble really wants out of this is to get back its own reality through the recognition (status, titles, political position) and the wealth (estates) that it gets from the monarch. State power is supposed to exist as a pure spiritual principle for the nobles; the nobles should recognize, honor, and give homage to the state rather than seek wealth and status from it. But more and more this spiritual principle is ignored and the state appears only as a source of wealth and status to the nobles—the state buys the nobles' recognition, service, and flattery. The nobles only seem to stand in accord with the universal. On the one hand, the nobles alienate their will, their inner reality, to state power, and render it service and flattery, but, on the other hand, the nobles retain their own will in the honor and wealth they receive from the state. In part, the nobles establish the universal reality of the state, but in part they subordinate the universal power of the state to their own particular interest. The distinction between noble and base consciousness is disappearing. We can no longer say that the nobles choose the universal over their own self-interest (*PhS*, 312–14/*GW*, IX, 279–81).

The nobles, moreover, are dependent on and must be grateful to the monarch for the wealth they receive. Wealth at first meant independence—independent landed estates where state power was only a vague principle. Now wealth means dependence—the nobles depend on the monarch for favors and must flatter, grovel, and humiliate themselves. The recognition that the nobles receive—thus the very reality of their selves—becomes highly unstable. It all depends, Hegel says, on the contingent personality of the monarch, on the accident of the moment, on caprice, certainly not on the universality and uniformity of law. For the noble, gratitude alternates with dejection and rebelliousness. All law, good, and right seem rent asunder. "All identity dissolves away." The noble feels humiliated, wants to revolt, and thus is now completely like base consciousness (*PhS*, 313–14/*GW*, IX, 280).

We can see this sort of decadence in Molière's *Le Bourgeois Gentilhomme*. The nobility have title, prestige, and privilege, but are wretched, dependent flatterers, often in poverty. The bourgeoisie, on the other hand, have wealth but no status. The nobility often prey upon, borrow from, even defraud, the bourgeoisie, who are impressed by their titles. Flattery gives way to base flattery, and base flattery gives reality to wealth (*PhS*, 315/*GW*, IX, 282).

The first thing to go here is the repute of the benefactor—including that of the monarch. Nobles flatter to get wealth and we begin to realize that the benefactor is at the mercy of the flatterers. Benefactors only dole out wealth in order to establish themselves and gain recognition. We begin to despise the benefactor. It is wealth that is real—not title, status, or nobility. Moreover, what kind of master is it who needs such slaves, such base flatterers? And what kind of reality can be gained from the recognition of such grovelers? We have a strong echo of the master-slave dialectic and of Diderot's *Rameau's Nephew*.[35]

The world is collapsing and the base flatterers see that it is. They flatter in front of their benefactors, but insult them behind their backs. We have the inversion and perversion of all conceptions—universal deception. It is so bad that shamelessness—the open admission of this deceit and contradiction—is the only and the greatest possible truth here. Again, this is a point made in *Rameau's Nephew*,[36] which Hegel is following here (*PhS*, 317/GW, IX, 283). The plain, simple, and honest mind that believes in the true and the good is hopelessly out of place and appears completely foolish before the sophisticated, cultured, and shameless mind for whom everything is inverted. Everything changes into its opposite—good into bad, noble into base. We have the relativism of *"pure culture"* (*PhS*, 316–19/GW, IX, 282-5).

At any rate, once the chaos, decadence, and perversion in the world of culture is recognized, consciousness turns away from the world (much as consciousness after the master-slave dialectic turned to "Stoicism," "Scepticism," and "Unhappy Consciousness"). Consciousness now turns inward, toward a beyond, a heaven, toward faith. It sees the vanity of the world. It sees state power as hollow and vain, and we move on to belief and its clash with the Enlightenment (*PhS*, 319–20/GW, IX, 285).

The important point here is that alienation on the part of the subjects—their service, risk of death, and flattery—is what establishes the objectivity, independence, and reality of the monarch. The monarch, for its part, transforms, molds, and cultures its subjects. It recognizes them and links them to the universal. The more the subjects alienate themselves, the more real and powerful the monarch becomes. And the more reality and power the monarch gets, the more it is able to mold and transform its subjects.

This is a good example, then, of why, as we saw in chapter V of the *Phenomenology*, empirical psychology cannot get away with holding simply that external circumstances are what determine individuals. Individuals determine their circumstances as much as they are determined by them. The subjects construct their monarch as much as they are constructed by it.

It might seem to some, now that we have arrived at culture and have come to understand the reciprocal recognition that is fundamental to it, that we will have to reverse ourselves and admit with Robert Williams that what we find in Hegel is a social intersubjectivism—not idealism. Social intersubjectivism means that we have many interacting subjects. Idealism, at least for Williams, in rejecting the ontological transcendence of the other, collapses into solipsism.[37] We must see, however, that there is nothing in culture that is incompatible with idealism—as Hegel understands idealism. What we are getting in the course of the *Phenomenology* is the construction of subjects, subjects that we hope will be able to hold up as subjects capable of recognizing each other intersubjectively. Such subjects are not given to us ready-made from the start. They do not exist on their own in some sort of a state of nature. They must be constructed. Such subjects have no ontological transcendence. On the other hand, we have seen that Hegel's idealism is not committed to the notion that there is nothing out there—no others, no subjects, outside my consciousness. Rather, his idealism holds that *esse est intelligi.* What is real is what is grasped by consciousness. Individual selves only develop, are only grasped, are only made real through a cultural process of recognition.

What we must see, then, is that in perfectly idealist fashion we construct the self that will in turn construct our selves. We construct the monarch through recognition and service and the monarch recognizes us in turn. There is no ontological transcendence here. The monarch is not a transcendental self; it does not exists on its own independently of its subjects. We have said that government is nothing but a set of practices, beliefs, values, commitments, and ideals. And that is all the monarch is. That is all the monarch is as person, as individual, as *self*—which, as Hegel says, otherwise would only be a "presumed existence" (*PhS*, 311/*GW*, IX, 278).

The subject that gets constructed here is not an individual subject in the way that liberal individualists tend to understand individual subjects. The monarch is an individual, but at the same time he is constructed by us as *our* monarch—as the state. He is the state. The monarch is an office. And we are constructed as subjects through the recognition the monarch grants us in turn. Each constructs the other as part of a nation, a culture—a spiritual whole. There are no individual subjects or selves sitting around at the start. There is no state of nature. Individuals, subjects, selves, are crystallizations of culture—they are realized potentials. They are molded by social, political, and cultural institutions, institutions that are the result of the recognition of those subjects. Cultural institutions are the result of the externalization of individuals and individuals are the result of their internalization of culture. Liberal individuals of the sort that populate a state of nature are the imaginary creations of a certain sort of culture.

But how can this monarch, one may want to object, be constructed unless we start with individuals, selves, or subjects to do the constructing? Don't individuals have to come first in order to construct their institutions? In one sense this is not a problem for Hegel here because the course of development played out in the *Phenomenology* simply is not intended to be temporal or historical. Hegel is not taking up the question of whether individuals precede culture or culture individuals. Instead, he is asking what we must presuppose in order to explain the experience we actually have. And he is claiming that culture is necessary for us to exist as selves and experience ourselves as individuals. Whatever we were before culture, we were not what we mean in our culture by individuals, selves, or subjects. What we do mean by individuals, selves, or subjects, as well as their existence has involved a construction—a reciprocal construction in which we form our culture and are formed by it.

The reason that we come closer to successfully constructing a solid and stable self with the monarch is at least in part that we do not have a relationship between equal individual consciousnesses. We construct the monarch as much more important, universal, and powerful than we are. This means that only collectively do we have the ability to construct such a powerful institution and it means that the recognition that we can get back from such an important and powerful institution can make us more real. If we had nothing but isolated, equal, individual subjects, we would have no individual subjects. And, indeed, as soon as we cease to construct the monarch as superior to us, as soon as with Rameau's nephew we hold it in contempt, see it as no better than us, it collapses and we head toward the French Revolution.

There is a fundamental problem here. To establish ourselves as solid selves, we must construct a powerful, alienated, monarchical self who will then give us the recognition we need to be solid and real. But as soon as we recognize that this is all our own construction, it collapses. Hegel says, "As the self that *apprehends* itself, completes [the stage of] culture; it apprehends nothing but self and everything as self, i.e. it *comprehends* everything, wipes out the objectivity of things and converts all *intrinsic* being into a being for *itself*."[38] And again later, "Just by the fact that it gets the mastery over them it knows them to be not real by themselves, knows rather itself to be the power within them, and them to be vain and empty."[39]

If there is no transcendental self, if the self has no determinate core, if the only thing it can do is to construct cultural institutions to shore itself up, then as soon as it comes to see that all of this is nothing but its own construction, it all collapses and we end up with a self like that of Rameau's nephew—a fragmented, shifting, chaotic, confused whirl of different poses, personas, and theatrical constructions.[40]

This is why alienation and estrangement are necessary. We must not see that we construct our social, political, and cultural institutions. They must take on an autonomous life of their own. They must be a power and a force that dominates us. In chapter V of the *Phenomenology*, we saw that while scientific reason constructed its world, nevertheless, as it confronted nature it always confronted an object, a limit, an it. It could not dissolve all of nature into itself. It was simply unable to. It failed to idealize everything—and thus it prevented a collapse into solipsism. In the cultural sphere, art, religion, and philosophy are different. As we shall see, they are quite able to see through otherness and grasp the self in the other. This can be quite dangerous—it can produce collapse. The cultural realm, then, stands in need of a certain amount of otherness, estrangement, solidity. The sociopolitical realm stands, as it were, somewhere between science and nature, on the one hand, and art, religion, and philosophy, on the other. It will not give us a natural object incapable of collapsing into the self, but it cannot see through the other as easily as can art, religion, and philosophy. Furthermore, we can say that the greater our alienation, the greater in power, scope, and complexity the social, cultural, and political institutions we construct over against us, the more solid, stable, and objective our cultural world will be (*PhS*, 206/*GW*, IX, 189). Though, of course, we can come to see through our sociopolitical institutions—revolutions do occur. And the more powerful and estranged our institutions, the worse the final collapse.

On the other hand, we do not want only otherness, solidity, and stability in the world of culture; we also want to be at home and to be free. We can be at home and free in culture because we construct it—and we could come to construct it so that we fit, so that we unfold our potentialities and realize our aims, purposes, and values. The problem we face, then, is complicated. Because we construct culture, we can come to be free in it. However, it is necessary that we not see that we construct our culture if it is not to collapse on us. Alienation and estrangement, then, are necessary. But this means otherness, domination, and heteronomy, which eliminates our freedom. Alienation and estrangement, then, must be overcome. But that then will mean the collapse of culture. This is the agonizing process we will have to go through as we head toward the French Revolution. What we must find is a way to overcome estrangement and realize freedom without producing collapse.

Hegel's view that we construct our social world and that we can come to be free and at home in it would seem to fit naturally with democratic theory. Nevertheless, here as well as later in the *Philosophy of Right* Hegel resists full-fledged democracy and he does so because of the side of his theory of culture that we have just seen, namely, that if we recognize that our social institutions are nothing but our own construction, our own doing, they are likely to collapse on us.[41] Hegel was very deeply influenced by the French Revolution. To avoid such collapse, he thinks, we must come to see that we do not construct our world as the liberal democrat thinks we do, that is, as *individual* consciousnesses. We construct our world as *cultural* consciousnesses, as part of a spiritual whole that is much larger and more powerful than we are and that shapes us as much as we shape it.[42] Moreover, there must be forces in this world that are more powerful than we are and that lift us above ourselves. Only thus will the institutions we construct have the authority, objectivity, and reality to withstand collapse.[43]

This process has started here in Hegel's treatment of culture, but it has also failed. It is true that we have come to see that individuals are not mere givens that exist in a state of nature. They are instead the outcome, the crystallization, of culture. Nevertheless, these individuals that have been constructed by culture have been cultured so as to *see* themselves as isolated individuals—*as if* they existed in a state of nature. We have on the one hand a capricious personal monarch and on the other nobles interested only in seeking personal wealth and status through self-interested flattery. All are becoming more and more like the bourgeoisie for whom the self-interested pursuit of wealth is at odds with and isolated from the larger political and cultural sphere.

One of the other things we must do to avoid collapse is come to see that while we do construct our cultural institutions, it is not the case that anything goes. Our institutions actually exist in and for themselves—they are not mere illusions. They establish limits and necessities that shape and form us. Moreover, in constructing these institutions we embed a potential in them that has not yet been realized. Reality, even when constructed by us, is always richer and more complex than we think it is. Only through interaction with these institutions can we see what they are capable of and what we can make of ourselves by serving them. Only by interacting with other human beings in and through social, cultural, and political institutions can we realize our potential and theirs. So it is not just that we construct our cultural institutions. They in turn construct us. There is a reality here that cannot be dismissed as just our construction—certainly not as some form of illusion. We objectify ourselves, alienate ourselves, in our cultural institutions, and these institutions end up with the power, scope, and universality to form us as sociocultural beings, beings who then have an increased potential to objectify ourselves in even more powerful institutions, which can then further transform us—on and on in a self-developing cycle. Culture, of course, can be seen as a hollow and vain illusion—self-criticism, after all, is a real cultural possibility. Nevertheless, it is only through culture that we have a chance to become what we can become. The fact that culture is constructed does not mean that it is empty illusion, though self-consciousness must discover that this is one possibility before it proceeds on to find itself at home in culture.

The development of the subject that occurs in this section is finally a debasement that ends in collapse. Culture and sophistication often mean decadence. Hegel would seem to have Rousseau as well as Diderot in mind. The final result of this culturing of the subject, which is a debasement, is that the state power loses its reality and prestige. But with the monarch's loss of reality and recognition, which was nothing but the alienated reality of its subjects, this will all shift back to the subjects. But there would not have been a developed, cultured reality to shift back to if we had not passed through this development involving alienation and estrangement.

One last point before we conclude this section. As we have seen, despite similarities between the master-slave dialectic and the dialectic of culture, there was no alienation leading to estrangement in "Lordship and Bondage." Many people think we find the paradigm of alienation and estrangement there. That is a mistake. The German words *Entäusserung* and *Entfremdung* never even appear in that section of the *Phenomenology*.[44] The relation of the master to the slave is not estranged. There is direct and visible domination of the slave by the master, and the very fact that this domination is direct and visible implies that no estrangement is present. For alienation to lead to estrangement, the activity of individuals must give rise to a dynamic that takes on an independent and autonomous life of its own. And the individuals must not be able to see, not understand, that they have created this power that turns upon them and dominates them. This power cannot be simply the power of another individual consciousness. It is true that the slave's recognition and service establish the master as master, that the slave's work feeds and supports the master, but this is all perfectly visible and completely understood. The master-slave relationship is only transformed into an estranged relationship in culture, where we no longer have a clear, direct, and visible relationship between two individual consciousnesses, but a whole cultural world, with a socioeconomic and a political realm, where the activities of individuals give rise to classes and state power, which are the outcomes of individual activity, but which do not appear to be so. They take on a life and dynamic of their own and domination is not the direct and visible domination of one individual consciousness over another. Even the sort of domination which might appear to be domination by an individual, for example, domination by a personal monarch, would be impossible except that the monarch is an institution, not just a person. The monarch is the outcome of the recognition and service of individual citizens that has taken on an abstract, autonomous, institutional form, and does not appear to be the outcome of the activity of those individuals. In short, to have estrangement, the dominated and whatever dominates must be cultural constructions, institutions, that have an abstract, independent, autonomous dynamic of their own which makes this domination possible, which is nothing but the outcome of the activity of those dominated, but which is not seen to be so.[45]

V. Enlightenment's Attack on Belief

Once consciousness recognizes the chaos, decadence, and thus the vanity of culture, it turns away from the world, and much like consciousness, as it passed through "Stoicism" and "Scepticism" toward "Unhappy Consciousness," it turns inward, toward a beyond, a heaven.

Here we are dealing with religious consciousness as we did in "Unhappy Consciousness" and as we will in chapter VII, entitled "Religion," but at this point Hegel uses the term "belief" or, in Miller's translation, "faith"—not the term "religion." "Unhappy Consciousness" involved the relation of an individual consciousness to an alienated beyond that lacked any content. It involved a yearning for this beyond together with a feeling of loss and emptiness. Belief, on the other hand, involves the relation of a cultural consciousness to an absolute that is full of content. Where did the content come from?

From culture. Just as cultural consciousness alienated its reality to the monarch, so in belief it alienates its reality to the absolute being. When it recognizes the decadence and vanity of culture, consciousness turns to belief and projects its reality to the absolute—to God. The absolute takes up and embodies culture's content (PhS, 296, 321–5/GW, IX, 266, 286–90).

Belief is not yet religion. Belief is still estranged consciousness. As we saw in the last section of chapter 3 above, belief suggests that the believer is an individual and that what it believes in is alien to it. For Hegel we should be immediately one with our laws or our God. It is not enough to merely believe in them. Religion, in Hegel's view, will involve the overcoming of this estrangement. Consciousness will see itself as the absolute—without any estrangement present.

Belief as well as religion are cultural realities. Religion, as opposed to belief, while it does not exist outside or beyond culture, nevertheless, in Hegel's view, gives us reality in and for itself (PhS, 322/GW, IX, 287). Religion gives us the truth of culture. As we shall see, culture will ground itself and derive its reality (a higher reality) from that part of itself that is religion.

Earlier, in "The Tübingen Essay" of 1793, Hegel wrote:

> Human understanding is nonetheless rather flattered when it contemplates its work: a grand and lofty edifice of knowledge divine, moral, and natural. And true enough, it has provided out of its own resources the building materials for this edifice which it is making ever more elaborate. But as this building, which engages the efforts of humanity as a whole, becomes gradually more extensive and complex, it becomes less and less the property of any one individual. Anybody who simply copies this universal structure or appropriates it piecemeal—anybody who does not build within (and indeed from inside) himself a little residence of his own, roofed and framed so that he feels at home in it, with every stone if not hewn then at least laid by his own hands—anybody who neglects to do this becomes a person who can only rigidly adhere to the letter, who has never really lived.
>
> And were the individual to have the great house rebuilt for him as a palace, and inhabit it as Louis XIV did Versailles, he would have only the barest acquaintance with its many chambers and would actually occupy a mere cubical. By contrast, a family man is far more familiar with the details of his ancestral home, and can give an account of every bolt and every little cabinet.[46]

In the Phenomenology, it is still Hegel's view that we construct our reality—divine, moral, cultural, and natural. What is different in the Phenomenology is that we are not yet able to be at home in our construction. We are still lost somewhere in the corridors of Versailles being pursued by

Enlightenment critics. It will not be until we get to religion in chapter VII of the *Phenomenology* that we will settle into the ancestral home that we construct for ourselves.

At any rate, here in chapter VI, belief turns away from the edifice of culture and rejects it. Consciousness is forced back upon itself, it seeks to escape the world of vanity, flattery, deception, and perversion. It unfolds a realm of thought. The content of this thought comes from the cultural world in which that thought has been embedded. It is alienated from the cultural world and projected as a belief—lifted, elevated, to an abstraction. Belief in absolute being is consciousness in estrangement (*PhS*, 321, 323–5/GW, IX, 286–7, 288–90).

Actually, as consciousness is forced away from the world, Hegel says, it falls apart into a dual consciousness. One moment emphasizes the negation of the world, the other emphasizes the holding and projection of the content. The first Hegel calls "pure insight." It is a continuation of the Rameauean consciousness. It criticizes, judges, denounces. It negates the objective world before it and in doing so it realizes its own self-identity—its being-for-self. Pure insight appears to have no content or to be independent of all content. We have something very much like Kantian pure subjectivity—a transcendental unity of consciousness within which any content must exist to be my content. But then that content is negated. We only attend to, only affirm, the self—and we affirm it by negating everything over against it, all objective content (*PhS*, 323–4, 328/GW, IX, 288–9, 292).

Belief, on the other hand, is the opposite of pure insight. Belief emphasizes the content, which it holds in thought and projects onto an absolute being. It is nothing else but the actual world raised to the universality of pure consciousness (*PhS*, 324–5/GW, IX, 289–90). Moreover, in serving this absolute being, belief renounces its own independence and being-for-self (*PhS*, 331/GW, IX, 295). Where belief emphasizes content and renounces itself, pure insight affirms itself and negates content. These two are really a unity—we cannot have thought without content or content without thought. But they do not see this—they are alienated from each other.

Belief seeks absolute being through service, praise, and worship. Belief is a perpetual process of coming into unity with the absolute—a process that is never completed, at least in culture. Insight, on the other hand, holds that self-conscious reason is the entire truth and it seeks to realize pure insight universally throughout society (*PhS*, 326–7/GW, IX, 290–1). It thus "calls to *every* consciousness: *be for yourselves* what you all are *in yourselves—rational*."[47]

The historical background here is the French Enlightenment's rationalistic attack on religion. We hear echoes of the *philosophes* of the *Encyclopedia*. Pure insight will resolve the confusion of the world through reason (*PhS*, 328/GW, IX, 292–3). It knows that belief is opposed to reason and it considers belief a tissue of superstition, prejudice, and error. Moreover, while the naive masses might really believe these superstitions, insight knows that the priests certainly do not. They know the truth. But they deceive the masses and conspire with oppressive despots out of self-interest (*PhS*, 329–30/*GW*, IX, 293–4).

Insight thinks that belief and insight really are the same. Belief really has insight. Behind belief's deception, it really knows the truth. So the admission of this truth (or insight) must be forced out of belief. Insight's attack spreads throughout society like an infection and finally carries the day (*PhS*, 331/*GW*, IX, 295).

But there is a problem here. Insight thinks it is attacking an other. But what it attacks is really no different from what it itself asserts. Insight is the same as what it attacks (*PhS*, 333/*GW*, IX, 296–7; see also *F&K*, 55–6/*GW*, IV, 315–16). When insight grasps a content, the content is one with consciousness—part of a Kantian transcendental unity of consciousness. Consciousness does not go outside itself. All content is within consciousness. But what is insight's accusation against belief? That the absolute being is something that belief dreams up. That this being comes from belief's own thought; that it is something created by consciousness and only exists within consciousness. But what is wrong with that? Insight is no different—what it declares to be an error and a fiction is the very same thing that it itself holds (*PhS*, 334/*GW*, IX, 297).

Furthermore, belief trusts in its God. It feels in unity with absolute being. It takes it to be the pure essence of its own consciousness, so that, in confronting the absolute, it does not feel lost or negated. This too is just like insight. Consciousness "apprehends an object in such a way that…consciousness preserves itself, abides with itself, and remains present to itself" (*PhS*, 334/*GW*, IX, 297). However, Enlightenment insight would try to say that priests foist what they know to be a lie, an alien reality (namely, God), upon the masses. Yet at the same time, insight cannot deny that belief trusts this reality. This, however, is impossible. Belief could not trust this reality if it knew it to be a lie. Insight's claim that it does know it to be a lie can only be seen by belief as itself a malicious lie. Besides, how can Enlightenment insight claim that belief foists an *alien* reality upon us when it knows that consciousness preserves and abides with itself in all its contents (*PhS*, 335/*GW*, IX, 298)?

Nevertheless, insight's arguments against belief do employ principles implicit in belief itself. Insight merely brings together what belief lets fall apart. Insight sees the whole and thus has an absolute right in attacking belief (*PhS*, 344–5/*GW*, IX, 306–7). Belief really does produce its object. Just as service created the monarch, so obedience, worship, and action produce the certainty that absolute being exists. This does not appear to be the case to belief, but absolute being does not exist beyond the consciousness of the believer (*PhS*, 334–5/*GW*, IX, 297–8). Absolute being is the spirit of the community and is only produced by its consciousness. Belief itself, in trusting in the absolute being, even feels it to be the essence of its consciousness. Insight correctly reminds belief of all this whenever belief forgets it and tries to assert that the absolute being exists in and for itself beyond the activity of consciousness (PhS, 345/GW, IX, 307).

On the other hand, Enlightenment insight does not bring its own thoughts together either. It is true that absolute being is the spirit of the community "only by being produced by consciousness," that is, "it does not exist as the Spirit of the community without having been produced by consciousness." Nevertheless, this is only one side of things, "Absolute Being is at the same time in and for itself" (PhS, 335/GW, IX, 298). Despite being produced by consciousness, the absolute exists in and for itself. For us to understand this fully, we will have to wait until we get to "Religion." Right now, however, we can notice that Enlightenment does not understand it at all. Enlightenment insight isolates the action of consciousness and asserts that the in-itself of belief is nothing but a product of consciousness. In doing so it takes the action of consciousness to be a picture thinking, a creating of fictions, the creation of a thing that does not exist in-itself, or which in-itself is nothing but a product of consciousness. But the next moment, insight turns around and claims the reverse, that the absolute being for belief is beyond consciousness, an alien and unknown entity in-itself. In fact, belief itself also does the same thing. One moment it puts its trust in absolute being and sees it as one with itself, but the next moment it claims the absolute is unsearchable and unattainable (PhS, 345–6/GW, IX, 307–8). For Hegel, these two sides must come together if we are to get to the absolute. We must see both that the absolute is constructed by consciousness and that it is true in and for itself. Both of these sides are present here but they are separated, opposed, and in conflict. We have yet to eradicate a two worlds doctrine. Belief is not able to bring these two worlds together (PhS, 346/GW, IX, 308).

Thus, Enlightenment's attack on belief "seems to rend asunder the beautiful unity of trust and immediate certainty, to pollute its spiritual consciousness. . . . But as a matter of fact, the result of Enlightenment is rather to do away with the thoughtless, or rather non-notional, separation which is present in faith. The believing consciousness weighs and measures by a twofold standard; it has two sorts of eyes, two sorts of ears, speaks with two voices. . . . In other words, faith lives in two sorts of non-notional perceptions . . . and in each of them it has its own separate housekeeping" (PhS, 348/GW, IX, 310).

At any rate, belief collapses under Enlightenment's attack. It is expelled from its kingdom and its kingdom is ransacked (PhS, 349/GW, IX, 310). And finally, "heaven is transplanted to earth below" (PhS, 355/GW, IX, 316).

One thing that is perfectly clear here in chapter VI is that in religion, or in religion appearing as belief, we are still engaged in a phenomenology. We have not moved on, as Hyppolite thinks Hegel will, to a noumenology. The absolute being is in essence a cultural phenomenon. It is the spirit of the community and is only produced by the consciousness of that community (*PhS*, 335, 345/*GW*, IX, 298, 307; see also *PRel*, I, 186–7/*VPRel*, I, 96). Moreover, in Hegel's view, religion involves picture thinking (*PhS*, 321/*GW*, IX, 286). It involves representation, images, imagination. And where does imagination get these images, pictures, content? From culture. And then it projects this content into another realm. I shall argue as we proceed that the *Phenomenology* remains a phenomenology. In my view, Hyppolite is wrong. The *Phenomenology* never tries to become a noumenology.[48]

On the other hand, I do not agree with Kojève either. The fact that God is constructed, for Hegel, in no way amounts to a denial of God's existence.[49] For God to have any meaning for a culture, God must be constructed by and for that culture. And that would be the case whether or not God exists. The fact that God is constructed tells us nothing one way or the other about God's actual existence. Atheists will of course think religion is constructed, but believers too must accept that it is if it is to have any meaning for them in their cultural world. On the other hand, atheists, for their part, must admit that God has a powerful affect on any culture—whether or not God exists. Any culture in a very significant way is the product of its God. It is shaped and formed by its religious conceptions. If recognition and objectification make something real, then a culture's recognition of its God is going to mean that that conception will be objectified in that culture—that it will be a real force in that culture. God may well not exist in the way that the atheist understands God's existence at the same time that God certainly may exist in the way that Hegel understands God's existence. God exists for Hegel as the spirit of a community. God is constructed by the consciousness of that community, but, for that community, God exists in and for itself (*PhS*, 335/*GW*, IX, 298). God is as real and powerful a force as anything else in that culture. Certainly it is as real and powerful as its government—and government is normally thought to be perfectly real. Hegel is not ever going to argue that the absolute exists in the way that the atheist understands existence, that is, independently of consciousness, culture, spirit, and so forth. But in Hegel's view, nothing exists in that way. In his view, to exist for-a-consciousness or for-a-culture, is not some less real form of existence. And so when pushed, Hegel will answer the atheist "No, the absolute does not exist in the sense that you understand existence." And as the atheist turns away with a self-satisfied smirk, Hegel will get back to a discussion of the absolute's *real* existence for us within culture.

The believer who accepts Hegel's argument that God must be constructed if God is to have any meaning for us is likely, however, to think that God's existence is not dependent on this construction—that God exists despite our construction, independently of it, and beyond it. This is not Hegel's view either. Our recognition of God, our particular conception of God, objectifies that God as a real force in our cultural world. God's reality for a culture is dependent on that culture. On the other hand, this is not to shift to the side of the atheist, because a culture's God is also going to have a religious depth that its constructors were unaware of in their construction. It will contain a truth that they can unpack, study, and explore, a truth that will take them beyond themselves. It will contain greater depth than they ever thought they were capable of producing (A, I, 310–11/SW, XII, 417). Religion is a culture finding its highest values and its greatest depths to be true—absolute.

It may well be that Hegel has a theory of religion that—at least to a certain degree—is capable of reconciling atheists and believers. I am not a believer, but neither am I a fanatical Enlightenment atheist who thinks that religion is the root of all social evil. I do not think that religion is guilty of greater evil than, say, the modern state. Both have been guilty of a good deal of evil as well as a considerable amount of good. I think that some of the values of religion are among the most impressive that we possess. Atheists, it seems to me, could learn a great deal from Hegel and should come to take religion far more seriously than they do. Religion is just as important a cultural reality as politics, art, or philosophy. At the very least, we should come to see the silliness of Enlightenment atheism—the view that religion is completely false, worthless, evil, a deception fostered by priests. We should at least become Feuerbachian atheists who see that atheism is perfectly compatible with admitting that religion contains a great deal that is valuable and true.

Feuerbach was deeply influenced by Hegel's treatment of religion in chapter VI of the Phenomenology. Indeed, Feuerbach follows Hegel very closely. Religion is a projection of the contents of this world into a beyond. Religion does give us insight and truth; it is just that it attributes it to another world. Thus, heaven ought to be brought down to earth and religious truth realized in this world. Feuerbach agrees with Hegel, develops him, but then suggests, as do Marx and Hyppolite, that Hegel finally moves beyond culture, moves beyond the view that religion is fundamentally a cultural phenomenon, that Hegel attempts to give us a deduction of an absolute that exists in and for itself in another world.[50] I think this is a misunderstanding of the Phenomenology. We have seen that belief's kingdom has been ransacked by Enlightenment and that "heaven is transplanted to earth below." I think it remains there for Hegel. Hegel is more Feuerbachian than Feuerbach admits. Or so I hope to show as we proceed.

Religion also plays an important role in Hegel's deduction of the absolute. Hegel's tactic is to seek out the presuppositions necessary for our experience to be possible and to show us that ultimately the absolute is a necessary presupposition. As long as we can point to something we must count as experience, we can ask what makes that experience possible. We must account for all experience that can be brought up and ultimately we need a set of presuppositions that will hold all of our experience together in a unified and consistent fashion. Nothing short of God or the absolute will do this, Hegel thinks—or, to put it another way, the concept of all experience holding together in a consistent and total unity *is* the concept of the absolute.

The absolute will have to account for all of reality—nothing can remain outside. We must notice that cultures and their religions often make this very claim—the claim that they possess all truth and are the source of all meaning and value. Whatever is found in other cultures or religions is either not worth having or is included in equal or better form in our culture or religion. While this is obviously ethnocentric, and we will have to deal with this ethnocentrism in the proper place, nevertheless, the fact that culture and religion claim to be total, claim to possess all truth and value, is a part of our experience and thus must be accounted for.

At this point our atheist has become irate: But God does not exist! Yes, we patiently reply, but still our religion and conception of God have fundamentally shaped our culture, our selves, our experience. And we must give the necessary presuppositions for the possibility of our experience. God or the absolute is a necessary presupposition. Without it we would not be what we obviously are. But, the atheist screams, God does not exist! Fine, we reply. Quite possible. Still, the concept of God is a necessary presupposition of what we are. But, the atheist responds, God is a mere illusion! No. God is a reality, a force, that has formed us culturally. God may not exist in the sense in which you mean existence, but God is a real force. Exasperated, the atheist claims that this will not get us to the absolute, but only to a *conception* of the absolute. *Exactly,* we reply. Fine. What else do we need besides the conception, the necessary presupposition, that allows us to be what we are?

We must see that Hegel is not trying to give us, nor does he need, a proof for the existence of God in the traditional sense. God does not exist in the traditional sense for Hegel. We must, at least to start, think of God or the absolute as like any other social, cultural, or religious institution—say, like government. Such institutions are our cultural constructions, and without them we would not be what we have actually become. Without them we would not be the culture we are, know what we know, value what we value, believe what we believe, accomplish what we accomplish, and so forth. And it will be impossible to explain what we have become without these necessary presuppositions. That, at least, is the first step. We must then notice that religion claims to grasp the absolute in and for itself. And we must realize that this is an experience that also must be explained. Hegel says that beyond the world of culture, there stands, for belief, the unreal world of *pure consciousness*, or of *thought*. . . . Since, however, thought is in the first instance [only] the *element* of this world, consciousness only *has* these thoughts, but as yet it does not *think* them, or is unaware that they are thoughts; they exist for consciousness in the form of *picture-thoughts*. For it steps out of its actual world into pure consciousness, yet is itself generally still in the sphere of the actual world and its determinateness. . . . Consequently, the essence of its thought has for it the value of *essence*, not merely in the form of the abstract *in-itself*, but in the form of a *common actuality*, of an actuality that has merely been raised into another element without having lost therein the specific character of an actuality that does not exist merely in thought.[51]

What is it that is unreal here? Hegel is claiming, I think, that the religiously real *is* a thought, a product of our consciousness, our construction. What is *unreal* is that we do not *think* these thoughts—we only *picture* them. We use nous or understanding—not reason in the highest sense. If we really think, then God or the absolute will still be thought, still our construction, but will nevertheless be absolutely real. Thought gives us reality. Real thought allows us to see what is true in and for itself—not as a picture, not as a common actuality raised to a beyond, not as an existence understood in the way the atheist understands existence. Real thinking can take us beyond all this to the absolute in and for itself. Reality is what is grasped by the highest thought. The absolute is the highest reality because it is the highest thought.

Lest our atheist rise from irritated confusion and begin grumbling again that such an absolute is only a thought and not a reality, let us put off until we deal with chapter VII on religion the question of whether religion actually grasps the absolute in and for itself or whether this is merely so for-religion— or whether, as I doubt, it is ultimately possible to distinguish between these two or significant to try to do so.

However, we have fallen unacceptably under the sway of Enlightenment insight here. It seems to have convinced us that all problems are with religion. Religion is what is suspect. It must prove to us that its God really exists, or exists in some complex, subtle, and meaningful Hegelian sense, or whatever. The whole burden has fallen upon religion. Enlightenment has deflected our attention toward religion and away from itself—away from *reason*. What trouble could there be with reason? It is our rock solid foundation. It is our ultimate and most legitimate authority.

In Enlightenment's attack on belief, we have, for the very first time in the *Phenomenology*, an admission by the consciousness there on the stage (we, of course, have known it for a long time) that consciousness constructs its reality. We also have an admission that consciousness is a cultural consciousness and that its construction is fundamentally shaped by culture. Or, to be more precise, we have a partial admission of all this. Enlightenment reason does not admit this about itself—it accuses belief of it. But clearly it is Hegel's view that reason—certainly nous, understanding, picture thinking—is no less culture bound than belief. Indeed, the whole point that we should take away from the battle between Enlightenment and belief is that there is no significant difference between the two. Everything Enlightenment accuses belief of, Enlightenment is guilty of itself. If anything, Enlightenment reason is more blind to itself than is belief. It is certainly not less so—and it is more arrogant about it. Enlightenment reason is itself unable to conceive of anything but common actuality—ordinary cultural entities. Its accusation against belief is that belief does nothing but project such common actualities into a beyond. But while Enlightenment reason is very good at deflecting our attention from itself, we must notice that again it is no better than belief. It too is incapable of conceiving that belief might do anything but illegitimately project such common actualities into a beyond. It too is incapable of getting beyond picture thinking. It too is incapable of really *thinking*. It certainly cannot see that thought and reality might be one. It keeps asking for a proof that God exists and cannot conceive that the absolute as a thought, as a construction, can be real. But then we ourselves still have to show that it is.

This blindness, however, serves a purpose. As we have seen, if we admit that cultural objects are the result of our construction, we cease to believe in them and they collapse. Monarchy, our whole cultural world, and now belief have collapsed as we realize we have constructed them—and of course we are still headed for the grand collapse of the French Revolution. But Enlightenment reason will not admit to itself that it constructs its object— though, of course, it does so. Enlightenment reason is an especially positivistic reason, that is, it distances itself from its object, takes it to be simply out there, separate from us, independent of us—something that has not been culturally constructed by us. Just as belief confronts an absolute being that it takes to be an in-itself over against it and not constructed by it, so reason confronts existents that it takes to exist in-themselves over against it—givens which are not constructed by it (*PhS*, 333, 340–1/*GW*, IX, 296–7, 303–4). For Hegel, we must eventually find a way to overcome such positivism without causing the collapse of our whole reality, but, in the meantime, just as scientific reason in the realm of nature prevents a collapse into solipsism, so does positivistic reason in the realm of culture—it is a form of estrangement that makes it more difficult for us to get around the otherness, the givenness, the fixity of the object. It refuses to see its own role in construction and thus remains smugly confident in its possession of a stable and secure world—at least for a while.

VI. Reason, Revolution, and Terror

After Enlightenment's clash with belief and its attempt to rid the world of superstition, all that remains for positivistic reason, Hegel says, is: (1) an absolute being as a mere vacuum; in other words, deism (a God with no characteristics, no determinations, no qualities), and (2) over against this vacuum, the singleness of all being outside the absolute being. We have sense-existents that confront consciousness immediately and indifferently (*PhS*, 340–1/*GW*, IX, 303–4). The absolute being and sense-particulars are realities external to each other. Sense-particulars can be taken as they are in-themselves or they can be related to the absolute as having being-for-another—for the absolute. Everything, then, is something in-itself as well as something for-another, that is, everything is *useful* (*PhS*, 341–2/*GW*, X, 304). As Hegel puts it:

> Everything is at the mercy of everything else, now lets itself be used by others and is *for them*, and now, so to speak, stands again on its hind legs, is stand-offish towards the other, is for itself, and uses the other in its turn.... Man is *good*, as an individual he is *absolute* and all else exists for him; and moreover... *everything* exists for his pleasure and delight and, as one who has come from the hand of God, he walks the earth as in a garden planted for him.... Just as everything is useful to man, so man is useful too, and his vocation is to make himself a member of the group, of use for the common good and serviceable to all. The extent to which he looks after his own interests must also be matched by the extent to which he serves others.... One hand washes the other.... He makes use of others and is himself made use of. (*PhS*, 342-3/*GW*, IX, 304-5)

We have gained a great deal here. We have a solid relationship between subject and object. The object is for-the-subject—it is useful to the subject. At the same time, we have solid objects, objects that are objective in-themselves, objects that have being-for-the-absolute, objects thus that are absolute. The process of laboring upon the world that began with the slave, the attempt to constitute real objects that will not implode back into solipsism, has now been achieved in utility. The object in-itself is absolute, but it is also for-consciousness—it is useful. This is a world in which consciousness is at home with its objects; it is a world that fits consciousness. It is a world that is useful to consciousness.

On the other hand, belief finds this world to be deeply objectionable (*PhS*, 343, 353/*GW*, IX, 305, 314), and, indeed, we have every reason to worry about the fact that persons view each other as essentially useful. We have to wonder whether there is anything to prevent them from using each other as mere means—even chopping each other up like cabbages. And as soon as utilitarian consciousness begins to act we will get exactly that in the French Revolution and the Terror.

But to start with, we must notice that the world of utility is a world of absolute freedom. The will cannot meet anything essentially an obstacle to it. Everything in-itself is for-another. Things are essentially useful—essentially means ready to be used. The world is thus a universal arena for the will. Consciousness has constituted the world of utility, knows that this is its world to act in, and that this is so for all individuals. Thus "absolute freedom ascends the throne of the world without any power being able to resist it" (PhS, 357/GW, IX, 317).

Hegel's attitude toward the French Revolution was always, at least in part, positive. After all, reason finally put itself in charge of the world. Even as late as the *Philosophy of History*, Hegel wrote: "It has been said that the *French Revolution* resulted from Philosophy.... Never since the sun had stood in the firmament and the planets revolved around him had it been perceived that man's existence centres in his head, *i.e.* in Thought, inspired by which he builds up the world of reality. Anaxagoras had been the first to say that *nous* governs the World; but not until now had man advanced to the recognition that the principle of Thought ought to govern spiritual reality. This was accordingly a glorious mental dawn" (PH, 446–7/PW, II, 924–6).

Moreover, throughout chapter VI of the *Phenomenology*, Hegel is much more willing than in other texts to identify with those who stand against the state: with Antigone against Creon, with Rameauean critics against Louis XIV, as well as with the French revolutionaries. With the revolution, consciousness no longer subordinates itself to a master, an emperor, or a monarch. Each individual raises itself out of its particular concerns and attends to the universal, the general interest, the common good. All social classes are abolished. Consciousness's "purpose is the general purpose, its language universal law, its work the universal work" (PhS, 357/GW, IX, 318). Hegel uses Rousseau's *Social Contract* as the vehicle through which to understand the French Revolution. Rousseau wanted a sovereign assembly in which all citizens would sit and vote. Each would attend exclusively to the general interest and would establish rational and just laws that would express the general will.

For Rousseau, the general will never errs, always seeks the common good, and is perfectly just (SC, 59, 61, 63, 66–7). It gives us universal and rational laws. It is, basically, a political version of Kant's categorical imperative. To realize the general will, for Rousseau, four things are necessary. First, all citizens must vote as individuals on all laws. There can be no representatives and no factions (SC, 59 n, 61, 79–80, 102, 118). Second, only general and abstract questions can be put to the citizens—questions that do not name particular persons or facts (SC, 62–3, 66). Third, the questions put must always and only have the form, "What is the general will?" or "What is the common good?" The citizens must not be addressed so as to elicit their particular interests (SC, 110–11; see also 109). Fourth, laws must be rigorously and equally enforced, and all must realize when they are voting that this will be the case (SC, 63, 104).

The point here is that citizens are made to consider their interest in the abstract case. Even if one were to decide to steal in a particular case where it served one's self-interest, one would nevertheless vote against theft in general. Certainly the majority would vote against a rigorously and equally enforced law that allowed theft for all—even a thief would vote against such a law. Otherwise one could end up the victim of an act of theft oneself. Rousseau gives us a mechanism intended to insure that laws would be universal, rational, and just. To use Kant's language, they would be laws that would accord with a categorical imperative.[52]

Private or particular will is replaced by the will of the citizen. Each citizen leaves behind all that is particular and rises to the universal. Classes, representatives, branches of government are all eliminated because anyone involved in these particular spheres would be cut off from the universal (PhS, 358–9/GW, IX, 318–19). They would be confined to the particular, would develop particular interests, and these would undermine the universal.

Despite Hegel's admiration for certain aspects of the French Revolution, he also has serious criticisms to make of it. He argues that the general will cannot achieve anything positive. This is a variation on his earlier criticism of Kant's categorical imperative. In "Reason as Testing Laws," Hegel argued that simple universalizability will not tell us what the right thing to do is—private property as well as communal property are equally universalizable (PhS, 257–8/GW, IX, 233–4; PR, 90/SW, VII, 194–5). Here in chapter VI, he goes much further.

The general will directs itself exclusively to the universal and abstract—and thinks it must do so to be right and just. It must avoid the particular. But in Hegel's view, for government to be able to function, for it to act at all, it must involve the particular. No governmental work or deed, then, has any chance of being found acceptable in this revolutionary Rousseauean world that demands only universality and abstraction. The government cannot but involve particular branches, offices, persons, and actions. Any law, to be executed, has to be executed by a particular governmental agency rather than another and it has to be executed against particular individuals rather than others. These will involve, and will be viewed as involving, particular policies, concerns, and interests. Indeed, Rousseau virtually concedes this himself. The sovereign body, if it is not to err, must ask only abstract and general questions, must ask only, "What is the general will?" Nevertheless, each time this body meets it must begin by asking itself whether it should continue the present government in office (SC, 107; see also 105). There is nothing whatsoever universal or abstract about this question. It asks about, and implies the evaluation of, particulars—particular persons, particular offices, particular actions. Party interest, factional interest, particular interest will come alive each time such a question is raised. Any decision will benefit some individuals and their interests as opposed to other individuals and their interests.

We get an echo of the "Law of the Heart" here. Any governmental action will inevitably involve at least an element that will not be a law of our heart. It will not be our *own*; it will not be the direct outcome of our participation in voting for the abstract and universal. We will be excluded. Other particular persons, offices, or actions will be responsible. And so, as the law of the heart passed over to the frenzy of self-conceit, we pass over to the rage and fury of destruction.

No positive action by government can be acceptable. No positive action can avoid particularity. The only sort of action that could possibly be acceptable, then, would be *negative* action. The government can and must be attacked whenever it undermines the universal by falling to the particular— that is, however, virtually anytime it does anything at all. All particular factions and offices must be rooted out. All institutions, groups, or factions that are particular, limited, not universal, must be destroyed. But that means destroying just about everything. This gives us the Terror, where ultimately the only action is the meting out of death and destruction. And given the expectation that all make themselves of use for the common good and the willingness to use others ruthlessly when they do not, death comes to have no more significance, as Hegel puts it, than the cutting off of a head of cabbage (*PhS*, 359–60/*GW*, IX, 319–20).

Hegel's view is that a morality of abstraction like that of Rousseau or Kant, a morality that makes the universal and universalization its central principle, is headed for trouble. But where Kantian morality gave us merely the arrogance of a virtue that thought itself superior to the way of the world, if such morality is also coupled with utility, then, Hegel is suggesting, we risk actual terror. And thus Rousseau's morality in which society considers its interest in the abstract case is more threatening than Kantian morality which shuns interest altogether. Indeed, at the end of "Absolute Freedom and Terror" we "pass over into another land of self-conscious Spirit" (*PhS*, 363/*GW*, IX, 323)—from France to Germany, from Rousseau to Kant—and, as we shall see, we arrive at an ethics of reconciliation.

At any rate, Hegel is aligning himself with the tradition of Schiller in seeing abstract moral reason as a principle of domination—a tradition continued by many contemporary postmodernists. Schiller associated the French Revolution with an ethical or rational state in which duty opposes the citizen with the majesty of law, fetters the citizen's will, and subjects the citizen to the general will. Schiller contrasts this rational state to an aesthetic state, a state in which duty and inclination, reason and nature, feeling and the moral law spontaneously agree, reinforce each other, and produce social *character*—that is, we could say, he contrasts Moralität with Sittlichkeit.[53]

Freedom, as Hegel understands it, involves four moments. First, it involves the ability of consciousness to abstract from everything external, withdraw from the world, and turn into itself. This is something we first find in Stoicism. Thought is alone with itself. It faces no obstacles or obstructions—nothing other (*PR*, 20–2/*SW*, VII, 50–6).

Second, freedom requires reason. We must be rationally self-directed toward the universal—our actions must be universalizable. Such subjective Kantian reason by itself, however, is not enough. The universal must also be objectified in our cultural world—reason must be concretized in our laws, institutions, and practices. Social reality must be constructed in accordance with reason. Thus consciousness would be free not only when withdrawn into abstraction, but also in the world—a world which would no longer be external, heteronomous, or other, but our own. It would be a world essentially at one with reason. Reason could find itself in its world. Reason would no longer find the world an obstacle to reason, but an arena laid out for its operation.

In "Absolute Freedom and Terror," we stand between these first and second moments. Consciousness is emerging from abstraction and beginning to remake its world in accordance with reason. In Hegel's view, if freedom is thought to consist in this alone, then in politics we are likely to have the "fanaticism of destruction" (*PR*, 22/*SW*, VII, 54).

Third, to get beyond the fanaticism of destruction, we must be rooted in our world in an even deeper sense. We must be embedded in a cultural web of institutions, practices, customs, and traditions. This Sittlichkeit must also accord with the rational and the universal, but it is not abstract. It involves concrete feelings, inclinations, passions, family ties, social relations, political connections, and so forth. Yet, at the same time, it is not other or heteronomous—it is our own. This third moment bonds us together into a community and makes it impossible for us to stand outside and above either with the arrogance of a virtue opposed to the way of the world or the fury of a reason responsible for revolutionizing society. Participation in a Rousseauean sovereign body is not enough—it does not involve sufficient community. All we have for Rousseau are individual wills involved in the abstract and general process of making laws—a process abstracted from all relationships built upon bonds of custom, tradition, feeling, and particularity.

At this point, we are able to appreciate the desirability of this third moment, though we have yet to explain sufficiently how embeddedness in a cultural web makes for freedom rather than heteronomy. We will do some of that in the present chapter, but some of it will have to wait until our discussion of religion. Only then will we be able to take up the fourth moment of freedom. It is only in religion, Hegel thinks, that unity with our world and with others can be understood as so much a part of our spiritual essence that it cannot in any way be thought to involve heteronomy. Furthermore, the absolute will be necessary, in Hegel's opinion, if our freedom is to be grounded as real and true freedom—as opposed to mere whim, arbitrariness, something culturally relative, or some other form of caprice.

Moreover, the absoluteness we can gain from religion will certainly be necessary if we are ever to work ourselves out of the general dilemma that has been plaguing us and which now has reached crisis proportions. We know that we must construct our own reality—there is no other place for it to come from. And only if we construct our own reality can we be free. But at the same time, as soon as we recognize that we have constructed this reality, it collapses on us. As soon as we saw that we were responsible for constructing the monarch, it collapsed in a Rameauean whirl. As soon as Enlightenment insight convinced us that belief had constructed its own beyond, belief collapsed on us. In the French Revolution, we get a new and more complex variant on this same theme. Reason has become aware that consciousness has been constructing its world, it realizes what a miserable job it has been doing, and so sets out with a fury to tear it all down—at which task it succeeds admirably. But then reason seems to think that it will be able to construct its own world with greater success than previous consciousness. Of course it succeeds no better. In fact, due to its arrogance and fury, it causes far greater destruction.

This raises an important issue—an issue that has become all the more significant in being taken up by postmodernists. Can reason be oppressive? And for Hegel, what we must be concerned with here is whether *true* reason—reason that gives us truth—can be oppressive. If we think there is no such thing as truth, then there would be no difficulty at all in finding oppressive an aggressive reason out to ruthlessly remake the world. Even if we merely *think* reason has given us the truth, when in fact it has not, then clearly reason could be oppressive. But Hegel believes in truth. The question then is whether truth can be oppressive. If we think there is no truth, then we cannot really say truth is oppressive. We can claim that what people *think* is true is oppressive, but not truth—if it does not exist. Many of those who hold that truth is oppressive really think there is no truth, and so their view is really that what is taken to be truth can be oppressive. Our question, however, must be, If there *is* truth, can it be oppressive?

Most Western philosophers have thought that the true, the good, and the just tend toward agreement. I take oppression to be something that is not at all good or just. The question, then, is whether something can be true but not good or just. It will not help us here to concern ourselves with what only looks like oppression but really is not—with what really is for the good of society and thus just. The question is whether truth can really be oppressive—thus not good or just.

. As we saw earlier, Hegel does think we have a tendency to mastery and that it is even impossible to speak or think except in universals. We have a tendency to miss the specificity and particularity of others and thus a tendency to marginalize them. This would be especially problematic for Enlightenment reason given its explicit and aggressive concern for universality and universalization. It would seem, then, that Enlightenment reason would at least have a strong tendency toward mastery and the marginalization of the other—that it would have a tendency toward oppression. If this is the case, the question remains whether such reason is true reason.

We have also seen that attempts at mastery tend to stimulate the other to undermine the master. It incites those excluded and oppressed. If we have been announcing far and wide our claim to possess the universal, to be total, to be absolute, then all the marginalized need do is step out of the shadows and reveal its exclusion to gain center stage at our expense. The absolute implies total openness. Any exception subverts it. Reason which has to marginalize, exclude, or hide the other in order to claim its own absoluteness is obviously not true reason. And the fact that it will incite the other to subvert its mastery will tend sooner or later to show us that it is not true reason. It will also tend to move reason toward greater inclusion and thus toward truth.

We must also notice that Hegel distinguishes between two notions of truth. For ordinary consciousness, truth means a correspondence between the object and our conception of it. Hegel would prefer to call this "correctness" (L, 51–2, 305/SW, VIII, 89–90, 372–3). This is what we find in Enlightenment reason. It claims that it possesses the right concept—the concept that corresponds to the object. From there it goes on to claim that all objects that somehow fail to correspond to this correct concept have to be remade and transformed—the social world must be made rational so that it does correspond to the concept. Well, there is no denying that for Enlightenment reason there will be a certain amount of correspondence between object and concept—Enlightenment reason may well be correct a good part of the time. But also, given Enlightenment reason's tendency to marginalize, there is no denying that there will also be a good deal of failure of object and concept to correspond, and thus, given Enlightenment reason's aggressiveness and ruthlessness, there is room for a good deal of oppression here. Enlightenment reason, then, *can* be oppressive.

However, we must also see that this concept of truth is not an adequate one. Hegel goes back to an older conception of truth where truth means living up to the ideal. A true friend or a true state are ones that accord with the notion of, live up to the ideal of, realize the essence of, friendship or the state (*L*, 51–2, 305/*SW*, VIII, 89-90, 372–3). Here it can make no sense to ask whether the true state is good or just. It cannot be a true state and be unjust. It cannot be a true state and not be a good state. The same sort of thing must be said about the true friend.

Enlightenment reason, then, is not true reason in this second, higher sense. True reason does not in Rousseauean, or even Kantian, fashion simply proclaim its general truths, its universal laws, its abstract concepts, and expect the world to conform or be ruthlessly remade. True reason is reason that lives up to the ideal. It *is* the case that there is an Enlightenment side to true reason. It has sought to be universal, it has tried to issue general laws, it has certainly formed general concepts. It would not be reason otherwise. But there is also another side to true reason, a side more likely perhaps to be captured by the religious consciousness that Enlightenment reason so viciously attacks. True reason has also experienced failure, it has been subverted, it has seen its false exclusion of the other, it has come to be embarrassed by its false attempts to marginalize the other, it has come to recognize its own arrogance in claiming to be absolute. And after repeated experience, it comes to see that reason is a long process of failure, a "pathway of doubt," a "way of despair" (*PhS*, 49–50/*GW*, IX, 56). It finally becomes humble. It seeks to open itself, to become more inclusive. *Enlightenment* reason has a long, long way to go yet.

Conceptions of truth that reject the notion of living up to an essence, that instead simply concern themselves with the correspondence of object to concept, that insist that we accept this correspondence or be mistaken, lesser, in need of guidance—such conceptions of truth *can* be oppressive. But can real truth? If it is oppressive, doesn't it still come up short of truth? More must be said to establish the notion of real truth and whether or not it can be oppressive. We will take this matter up in the next chapter.

We must also notice that chapter VI of the *Phenomenology* deals with the development of individuality. Individualism, as Hegel understands it, must be distinguished from individual consciousness, found in the first part of the *Phenomenology*, which was the result of abstracting from culture, and it must as well be distinguished from individualism as understood by traditional liberalism. Quite like individual consciousness, liberal individualism, at least for traditional liberals like Hobbes and Locke, takes the individual to exist independently of or prior to culture. The individual is just there, given, to be assumed—in a state of nature. For Hegel, on the other hand, individuality is produced—it arises out of culture. From the beginning human beings are rooted within a cultural world. At first, in the Greek polis, they are not distinguished from their cultural roles. What they become later in history is due to a development of culture and to a crystallization within them of this cultural reality. Human beings create, serve, and work within their cultural institutions, and their cultural institutions mold, shape, and form them as individuals. Individuals take in their culture, work it over, and deposit it back in the common cultural world for others to take in and repeat the process. A changed culture produces changed individuals and changed individuals change their culture. Individuals are rich, culturally filled, complex beings, not isolated, empty, atomic units. They are constructed, educated, cultured—that is, individualized—in and by culture.

To exist, individuals need to be recognized. And the more real, powerful, and significant the recognizer, the more real and significant the individuals recognized. The liberal tradition makes a real error, as far as the construction of individuals is concerned, in thinking that individuals originally exist and thereafter can or should be left alone. The action of real individuals in history belies this principle. They themselves get together and set about constructing powerful institutions that they can collectively serve. Not, as liberals are likely to think, just to make others subordinate, inferior, or oppressed, but to create a reality important enough that the recognition they can get from it will make them significant. I doubt that Hegel could have chosen a better example to show all of this than the construction of the French monarchy and its collapse under Louis XIV. Those who construct and serve the monarch become real and important by doing so. And when they finally come to see that the core of the whole process has been self-interest and base flattery, the whole thing collapses.

I think we can gain a bit more insight into this process by considering the liberal notion that the right ought to take precedence over the good. In the *Philosophy of Right*, Hegel, I think, would accept this as a legitimate principle for civil society. Nevertheless, he thinks that there is a deeper sense, largely lost upon the liberal tradition, in which we must see that the reverse is also the case—that the good must take precedence over the right. To hold, as liberals do, that right should take precedence over the good is to hold that individuals should have the right to freely choose their own conceptions of the good. Hegel, however, does not think that individuals really and ultimately do choose their own goods—at least not as liberals tend to understand the process. It is not that Hegel wishes to deny individuals their subjective choice; it is rather that he thinks that a good chosen in the liberal fashion would not amount to a good. For Hegel, goods, like anything else, must be constructed. Liberals tend to think that goods, like individuals, just lie around ready-made. Ready-made individuals freely choose whatever ready-made goods they wish. It is much more complicated once we come to see that goods must be constructed—because they can only be constructed by us.

How do we construct a good? At least one of the things we must do, Hegel thinks, is raise the good above ourselves—make it something worth choosing. It has to be important, sacred, divine, absolute—or in some way come to have objective value. The good must have enough scope, depth, and meaning to be experienced as good and be able to actually do for us some good. (The fact that something is constructed, we have seen, in no way implies that it is an illusion, is untrue, that it does not exist, or anything of the sort.) At any rate, after such goods have been constructed, there is no trouble in letting right take precedence over the good—in leaving us to freely choose our goods. But if we do this before the good has been constructed, and recognize that we are doing so, it is not likely that the good will be constructed. We must serve the good, subordinate ourselves to it, be absorbed by it, be lifted above ourselves by it. It must take precedence, *for us*, over our free and individual choosing of it. Furthermore, such goods are not constructed by single individuals; they are constructed by cultures—peoples. Nevertheless, we cannot say that, in itself, this process eliminates individuality, freedom, or choice. After all, *we* are constructing our own goods. It is just that if we recognize this our good is likely to collapse.

Indeed, despite the fact that it no longer has value for our era, the rise of absolute monarchy is a perfect example of such a constructed good. The fact that it finally underwent collapse meant a serious loss. Individuals lost a power that could culture them and lift them above themselves. As Rameau's nephew comes to see his patron as contemptible, he also finds himself contemptible in having served such a patron.[54] On the other hand, there is also a gain here in that it is no longer the case that individuals must subordinate themselves to the state in the sense that they find their essential reality separated from themselves, outside and above themselves, alienated from themselves. The state collapses and the individual regains that essential reality. Nevertheless, that essential reality only developed to the point it did because of the universal, powerful, and absolute state. Moreover, when the state collapses and individuals regain their more highly developed essential reality, what do they do? They begin the same process over again now at a higher level. They construct an even higher good, a purer reality, a greater power in whose service they will be lifted further above themselves. They turn to belief and create an absolute being. With the collapse of culture all is not lost. Individuals have been cultured, their horizons have been expanded, their powers have been developed, they have been raised to the universal, they have gained greater scope and depth. When the absolute monarch collapses, they set about creating something even greater—an absolute being.

We must also see that this servitude is closer to freedom than most liberals would like to admit. After all, the principle one serves—the monarch or the absolute being—can no longer be seen as simply heteronomous. *We construct it.* It is the objectification and projection of our essence. There is a great deal of self-determination going on here. Moreover, this principle becomes increasingly universal. And as we get to the French Revolution, the laws that the state promulgates will more and more be rational laws—laws that will conform to the general will or the categorical imperative. What at one point appeared simply as heteronomy and coercion we must now admit is also the construction and discipline of citizens who are self-determined in accordance with universal and rational laws. The element of full self-consciousness or awareness is still absent. But if we gain that self-consciousness, if we see that we have constructed our higher goods, they will collapse and we will have nothing to raise us above ourselves.

We get a good bit closer to such self-consciousness with the Enlightenment rationalist's attack on belief. All of the power, authority, reality, and universality that belief projects into an absolute being in the beyond, the Enlightenment rationalist, we could say, projects into absolute being as its own ego—its own reason. Indeed, here we have absolute freedom—a consciousness that takes itself to be the highest rational authority, an absolute authority, the source of all rational and universal laws. It has nothing but itself, nothing above itself. Thus too it has nothing to lift itself above itself and perhaps for this reason it looks for something below itself to attack and destroy. Much as for "Scepticism," as well as for the lord and master of the Roman world, this attack upon others shores up its sense of self (PhS, 123–4, 293/GW, IX, 119–20, 263). The destructiveness that the rational, and then the revolutionary, ego exerts against the world establishes its power, authority, reality, and stability. It puts it on the throne of the world. Enlightenment rationality, we have seen, can be oppressive.

Despite the fact that we are essentially cultural beings, beings who form and are formed by our culture, we have let our culture form us as isolated individuals. We each find given within ourselves reason as an autonomous authority and over against ourselves an independent world given for us to order usefully. We have also constructed a morality based on individual autonomy and rational reflection—an extreme Moralität. We are far removed from the Sittlichkeit of the Greek polis—and in Hegel's opinion we have gone too far.

Without losing the individuality gained in the modern world, Hegel wants to recapture Sittlichkeit. He does not want to return to the ethical order of Antigone and Creon where the individual was the expression of a social role. He wants to preserve the rational autonomy, authority, and universality gained in the French Revolution—even, I expect, something of the idiosyncratic and eccentric personality of a Rameau's nephew. But Hegel wants individuals to come to understand their individuality, to become aware of its cultural origins, its complex connections to the world, and its embeddedness in an intricate web of relations with others. He wants us to see that there is something much larger than us that is the source of, that forms and shapes, that is expressed through, and that is crystallized into, our individuality.

Individuals, for Hegel, are cultural beings that are constructed by and construct their world. Until they see this, Hegel thinks, they will be doomed to continually repeat a cycle of necessity (PhS, 361/GW, IX, 321). We construct a monarch, then tear it down. We construct a heaven, then attack it. We construct a revolutionary rational state, and we destroy ourselves in the process. We have cultural consciousnesses at work here, but these cultural consciousnesses are limited by an ideology of individualism. They think they have a mere individual monarch served by individual citizens, individual believers duped by individual priests, individual members of a sovereign body voting on and imposing abstract laws on individual citizens. It is this ideology that continually causes the collapse.

Given what this ideology understands an individual to be, who is going to believe in a monarchy constructed by individuals or in a monarch who is an individual? Who is going to believe in a heaven constructed by individual believers? And Hegel is trying to persuade us that we have no better cause to believe in an individual reason that claims that religion is constructed through the duplicity and self-interest of priests or that claims to issue abstract and universal laws. Reason that takes itself to be located only in individuals, that can manifest itself only as individuals seek the pure, abstract, and general, reason that cannot admit to itself that it is the outcome and expression of a larger cultural reality—such reason is going to be destructive. It denies its cultural origins, refuses to accept its embeddedness in an intricate web of relations, and when it cannot get away with denying this turns around and denounces it all as factionalism—as fallen from the pure, abstract, and general into particularity. Obviously (it holds), factions do not reason, only individuals do. Factions do not seek the abstract and universal, only individuals reflecting alone do. Factions are driven by interests—particular interests that must be rooted out and brought down if reason is to prevail.

We have a reason that claims to be individual but yet at the same time universal. Reason is something that takes place in the minds of individuals and must not be influenced by anything heteronomous from outside. Yet this reasoning, if carried out correctly, is supposed to give us universal laws to which all must agree. The problem here is that the more we demand that our laws be universal and general, then the more we tend toward sameness and homogeneity. Yet at the same time, the more we insist that individuals are individual, the more we move in the opposite direction, resist sameness, and encourage difference and particularity. To insist on both universality and individuality will sooner or later mean that the universal will have to be *imposed* on individuals. They will have to abandon all particular interests, all local concerns, all differences—all individuality. If we try to avoid imposing the universal, if instead we try to seek spontaneous unities, groups with similar concerns, communities of interest based on families, clans, classes, or something of the sort, we will not find sufficient scope of agreement—certainly not universality. If we *insist* on universality, then we are going to have to *impose* it.

Among postmodernists, Foucault's historical studies, in their own way and with much greater detail than Hegel, cover much of the same ground as chapter VI of the *Phenomenology*. Foucault studies different institutions—asylums, prisons, clinics, punishment, and sexuality—nevertheless, like Hegel, he focuses on early modern France and at times goes back to the ancient world. Moreover, both seek to understand the construction of modern cultural institutions and their construction of the individual. Furthermore, while Foucault refuses to focus only or primarily on law, sovereignty, and the state,[55] nevertheless both Hegel and Foucault do focus on power, discipline, and domination, and for both, the construction of morality, knowledge, and individuality is inseparable from power, domination, and alienation. Hegel would agree with Foucault that power is not just negative, juridical, and repressive but productive, disciplinary, and positive.[56]

For Hegel, however, what begins as external domination gets internalized and becomes a discipline. Then as the state becomes more universal and rational, this discipline is transformed into rational self-determination. This is not something Foucault would be able to accept. Nevertheless, it is not at all clear that individuals do not gain something from the institutions they construct—recognition, discipline, reality—that they would choose despite the domination and oppression that accompany these gains. Or what we should say is that to the extent that this is so, Hegel has done an impressive job of illuminating it. Indeed, I would say that Hegel has done a better job of explaining this dimension of things than Foucault, who in many other respects is without a doubt more complex and sophisticated than Hegel.

On the other hand, we must not paint an overly conservative picture of Hegel as if his goal were always to favor reconciliation with powerful institutions. In chapter VI of the *Phenomenology*, Hegel also spends a lot of time depicting the hollowness of institutions. Moreover, it is quite clear that the course of the development of institutions is not always a steady march toward the realization of the highest good. The monarch, belief, and the French Revolution all collapse, and, at least to some extent, would seem to deserve that collapse.

VII. Phenomenology or History?

We must assess where we are in the *Phenomenology* and try to understand the sort of development we have been going through so far in chapter VI. Many Hegel scholars think it obvious that the development of chapter VI is historical—that we have moved historically from the Greek polis through the French Revolution. This is the view of Hyppolite, Lukács, Taylor (*H*, 171, 365), Merold Westphal, Norman, Harris (*HL*, I, 10–11; II, 278, 306n), Forster, Stewart, and others.[57] On the other hand, there are some—Lauer, Kelly, and Kenneth Westphal, for example—who are quite correct in seeing that chapter VI is not historical.[58] However, they do not do much to explain this view.

Taking chapter VI to be historical can give rise to problems. For example, Taylor and Hyppolite wrestle with an issue first raised by Rosenzwieg. Rosenzwieg argued that in the *Phenomenology* Hegel abandoned the philosophy of the state that he held both before and after. Moreover, he argued that Hegel was never further from an absolutism of the state than in the *Phenomenology*. Hyppolite thinks this mistaken. In chapter VI of the *Phenomenology*, as we shall see, the development of spirit does not culminate in an ideal modern state, but in religion. After the French Revolution, chapter VI will move on to Kant's postulates and chapter VII will move on to religion—with no mention at all of an ideal state. Taylor (*H*, 172) agrees that chapter VI is historical, but holds that Hegel does not go on to discuss the modern state simply because he has different concerns in the *Phenomenology*—a rather vague response.[59]

I think that the *Phenomenology* does not go on from the French Revolution to talk about the historical development of the ideal modern state because the sort of development we find in the *Phenomenology* is just not a historical development at all—and thus to expect chapter VI to conclude with the historical development of the ideal state would be completely out of place. On the other hand, Hegel may well be as far from the absolutism of the state as he ever gets. He is certainly critical of the ancient city-state as well as of the modern absolutist state overthrown by the French Revolution. But this is quite possible without assuming that Hegel has given up on a philosophy of the state. If chapter VI is not historical, all we can reasonably conclude from this is that that aspect of a philosophy of the state that deals with its historical development would have no place in such a chapter—not that Hegel has given up on a philosophy of the state. At any rate, Hegel's views on history must be sorted out and explained clearly.

As we have seen, in the *Philosophy of History*, from the very start of the text, we find three elements present: individuals, nations, and the absolute (or God). In Hegel's view, historical reality involves an interaction between all three of these elements. Hegel thinks that without the whole—the absolute—we cannot have history (*L*, 26/*SW*, VIII, 62; *PWHI*, 67/*PW*, I, 77–8). History is the temporal unfolding and actualization of the whole of reality—the absolute.

The *Philosophy of History* starts with the absolute practically on the first page. The *Phenomenology* arrives at the absolute barely before the last page.

The *Phenomenology* is out to prove the absolute—give a deduction of it. Hegel tries to show us that without the absolute we cannot explain our experience. He tries to show this by abstracting from the absolute a long series of experiences in order to show us that on their own these experiences cannot hold up and explain themselves. He lays out these forms of experience from the simplest to the most complex. In the introduction, I divided the *Phenomenology* into three parts. Part 1 includes the first five chapters and deals with forms of experience connected with individual consciousness. Part 2 includes only chapter VI and deals with forms of experience connected with cultural consciousness. Part 3, which is made up of chapters VII and VIII, will deal with religious and absolute consciousness. Individual consciousness, cultural consciousness, and religious or absolute consciousness in the *Phenomenology*, correspond, at least roughly, to individuals, nations, and God in the *Philosophy of History*. What is together and present from the start in the latter text has been separated and set out in sequence in the former text. The *Philosophy of History* simply starts with the whole and examines its historical development. The *Phenomenology* wants to prove to us that we must finally accept the whole as the absolute.

If the *Phenomenology* engages in this complex process of abstracting from the whole, then it follows that it is only at the end of part 3 that we arrive at, or return to, the whole—that is, to the full, real, and actual historical world. If this is so, then the development that occurs earlier in the *Phenomenology* cannot be historical. There may be historical allusions, but not historical development proper. The movement from simple to complex, from abstracted moment to abstracted moment, until it reaches the absolute, Hegel tells us plainly in chapter VII, does not even occur in time. "Only the totality of spirit is in time." Only the whole has true actuality (*PhS*, 413/GW, IX, 365).[60]

In the *Phenomenology*, and especially in chapter VI, we can often sense a historical period in the background. On my view, this should not be surprising. We have abstracted from full historical reality, less so in part 2 than in part 1, and so we ought to be able to sense that historical background, more easily in part 2 than in part 1—and this is certainly the case.

If chapter VI is taken to be historical, then it would seem necessary to explain why Hegel takes up the particular historical cases he does take up. Some scholars seem perplexed as to why Hegel takes up Louis XIV—the reasons seem arbitrary.[61] Other scholars worry about breaks in the historical narrative.[62] We find allusions to the ancient world and the Roman emperor, but nothing about early Christianity as we move toward feudalism and then Louis XIV. On my view, none of these "historical" problems exist because we do not have history in chapter VI. Hegel is free to take his examples from wherever he wishes. What determines his selection of examples has nothing to do with historical completeness or historical accuracy, but rather with what he thinks will most effectively move us forward in the deduction of the absolute.

We should also notice that historical themes do not come up for the first time only in chapter VI. I argued earlier that "Virtue and Way of World" in chapter V was about Kant's "Idea for a Universal History." Once we recognized this it did not make us want to say that chapter V of the *Phenomenology* was historical. So also, I would say much the same thing about chapter VI. The development that occurs in chapter VI is not itself a historical development, but, nevertheless, chapter VI is *about* history. It reflects on historico-cultural themes and issues. It concerns itself with philosophy of history—especially in its treatment of alienation and estrangement, which give us an explanatory model for how we historically construct our cultural institutions yet are oppressed by them. It is also an attempt to drive us past individualism and Moralität toward a future Sittlichkeit. Chapter VI is a reflection on history and philosophy of history in culture as "Virtue and the Way of the World" was a reflection on history and philosophy of history at the level of individual consciousness. Neither is itself history.

Not all texts that refer to history are histories. Take the *Philosophy of Right*. It is a text filled with direct and explicit historical references, not merely veiled allusions like the *Phenomenology*. Nevertheless, Hegel is quite clear that the *Philosophy of Right* is not a historical text. Its concern is with the "*Idea* of the state"—it deals "exclusively with the philosophic science of the state" (*PR*, 156/SW, VII, 330). There are even further similarities between the *Philosophy of Right* and the *Phenomenology*. Indeed, I think that the *Phenomenology* is more like the *Philosophy of Right* than it is like the *Philosophy of History*. I would suggest that the relationship of chapter VI on culture to the absolute at which the *Phenomenology* finally arrives is like the relationship in the *Philosophy of Right* of civil society to the political state. Hegel's discussion of civil society in the latter text is filled with actual historical references, but the transition from civil society to the political state has nothing to do with history and is not a temporal development. Civil society did not develop in history prior to the political state. Political states, certainly governments, existed long before civil society, which is a relatively modern development that begins with the rise of capitalism. In the *Philosophy of Right*, the transition from civil society to the political state is a conceptual transition from a particular aspect of the whole to the whole—a transition which lifts a lower moment and grounds it in its proper place within a higher totality. So also in chapter VI of the *Phenomenology*, Hegel is trying to show us that we cannot remain at the level of culture; we must move on to religion and the absolute. Culture and its individualism are a moment that has been abstracted from the whole. We must be driven to see the reality of the higher totality and culture's proper place within that higher reality.

The transition from one stage to the next in the *Phenomenology*—even in chapter VI—is not a historical or temporal development. As I have argued, what determines these transitions is Hegel's strategic decision concerning what is necessary for a successful deduction of the absolute. It turns out that Hegel's strategic decision in chapter VI is to select a series of examples that roughly parallel cultural development in Europe. We get examples taken from the ancient Greek polis, the Roman empire, the development of feudalism, the rise of absolute monarchy in France, the French Enlightenment, and the French Revolution. What we have here are examples abstracted from their real historical context and used strategically to move us toward the absolute. This is quite different from what goes on in the *Philosophy of History*, which also moves from the ancient world to the French Revolution. That text attempts to give us an essence or principle which shapes and is shaped by each period, which explains the rise and fall of each period, and which brings about a transition to the next period. Nothing like this is going on in the *Phenomenology*. Even if I have not convinced the reader that nothing like this is going on in chapter VI, it is quite clear that this sort of thing is not going on in the *Phenomenology* as a whole, which moves from "Sense-Certainty" to "Absolute Knowing." Certainly the development between the three parts of the *Phenomenology*—part 1 (Individual Consciousness), part 2 (Cultural Consciousness), and part 3 (Absolute Consciousness)—is not the unfolding of a historical essence.

In the *Philosophy of History*, we also trace the development of individual consciousness and cultural institutions. The *Philosophy of History* treats this development as a development *within* history. The *Phenomenology* is the reverse. It views the development of consciousness from a phenomenological perspective—and it treats history and culture as moments *within* a phenomenology of consciousness. The *Philosophy of History* is a development, an unfolding, of the absolute in history. The *Phenomenology* is the development of consciousness to the absolute, which reflects on history (takes up historical examples within consciousness) on its way to the absolute. In the *Phenomenology*, we only get to the absolute at the end—after the French Revolution and modern culture. In the *Philosophy of History*, the absolute or God was present on the first page. It was a less developed absolute, but it was certainly there in the Orient, Greece, and Rome—not just after the French Revolution.

Hegel's *Philosophy of History* could have been written only in the modern world. It is an attempt to explain how the modern world was produced historically. But to write such a philosophy of history, it was not enough simply to live in the modern world. It was necessary to have achieved a certain level of consciousness. It was necessary to have grasped an absolute that had developed a long way past Greece and Rome—the absolute which formed and expressed the modern world. It is the *Phenomenology*'s goal to conceptually grasp this absolute. However, this last statement is not quite accurate.

At the beginning of the second part of chapter 3 above, I argued that in the *Phenomenology* we find three movements. The first is a conceptual or phenomenological movement in part 1 of the *Phenomenology* from individual consciousness toward culture. The second movement is the one we have been discussing in chapter VI. It is a cultural movement from ancient Sittlichkeit to the destructive extreme of modern Moralität. Hegel's attempt here is to push us toward a modern Sittlichkeit. At the end of chapter VI we have not yet achieved this higher Sittlichkeit. At this point, then, the *Phenomenology* is in the same position as the modern world—which has not achieved this higher Sittlichkeit either. And so we need a third movement—a conceptual-phenomenological as well as a cultural movement toward the realization of this higher Sittlichkeit in the modern world. What this will require, I think we can begin to see, is a higher development of consciousness than exists in the modern world. We must construct this Sittlichkeit ourselves. The task of the *Phenomenology* is to contribute to the *construction* of a higher absolute—a higher idea, vision, or purpose that will begin to mold us so as to realize this higher Sittlichkeit. Simple history, simply looking to the past or simply continuing forward as we are, will not accomplish this. In Hegel's view we must move higher—or deeper—we must move to religion and philosophy.

Quite clearly, my interpretation of the *Phenomenology* flies in the face of the doctrine of the "end of history," which Hegel has somehow come to be saddled with. Some scholars—like Kojève, Bloom, and Fukuyama—push this doctrine to extremes.[63] Bloom's interpretation of Kojève, with whom he seems to agree, is that for Hegel, "history is completed...nothing really new can again happen in the world."[64] This rather silly interpretation of Hegel arises from misinterpretations of things that Hegel says in the introduction to the *Philosophy of History* and the preface to the *Philosophy of Right*. In the former text, Hegel distinguishes stages of history: "firstly, that of the Orientals, who knew only that One is free, then that of the Greek and Roman world, which knew that Some are free, and finally, our own knowledge that All men as such are free, and that man is by nature free" (*PWHI*, 54–5/*PW*, I, 63). It might seem that our era is the final and ultimate stage. At times, Hegel even identifies this stage with the realization of God or the absolute (*PWHI*, 65–7, 77–8, 42/*PW*, I, 75–8, 91, 48). In the preface to the *Philosophy of Right*, Hegel also seems to suggest that philosophy cannot improve the world: "One more word about giving instruction as to what the world ought to be. Philosophy in any case always comes on the scene too late to give it. As the thought of the world, it appears only when actuality is already there cut and dried after its process of formation has been completed.... When philosophy paints its grey in grey, then has a shape of life grown old. By philosophy's grey in grey it cannot be rejuvenated but only understood. The owl of Minerva spreads its wings only with the falling of dusk" (PR, 12–13/SW, VII, 36–7).

As I have already suggested, I think it is incorrect to think that one can legitimately interpret these passages as holding that history has come to an end and that no significant change is possible in the future. Such an interpretation certainly did not occur to Hegel. Later in the introduction to the *Philosophy of History* he himself speaks of future history: "America is ... the country of the future, and its world-historical importance has yet to be revealed in the ages which lie ahead—perhaps in a conflict between North and South America.... It is up to America to abandon the ground on which world history has hitherto been enacted" (PWHI, 170–1/PW, I, 209–10). Moreover, after the preface, the *Philosophy of Right* goes on to give us a society which certainly did not actually exist yet in the Germany of Hegel's era, not in the ideal form given to it in that text.

Furthermore, a bit earlier in the preface to the *Philosophy of Right*, Hegel gives us an example of what philosophy's capabilities are vis-à-vis the present and the future, an example that further subverts the view I am opposing. Hegel claims that "philosophy is the exploration of the rational, it is for that very reason the apprehension of the present and the actual, not the erection of a beyond, supposed to exist, God knows where, or rather which exists, and we can perfectly well say where, namely in the error of a one-sided, empty, ratiocination" (PR, 10/SW, VII, 32). Hegel then gives us an example of a classical text that does what he wants, that expresses the actual and does not try to erect a beyond for the future, and his choice of text is quite surprising. Hegel picks one of the great utopias. He writes:

> Plato's *Republic*, which passes proverbially as an empty ideal, is in essence nothing but an interpretation of the nature of Greek ethical life [*Sittlichkeit*]. Plato was conscious that there was breaking into that life in his own time a deeper principle which could appear in it directly only as a longing still unsatisfied, and so only as something corruptive. To combat it, he needs must have sought aid from that very longing itself.... His genius is proved by the fact that the principle on which the distinctive character of his Idea of the state turns is precisely the pivot on which the impending world revolution turned at that time. (PR, 10/SW, VII, 33)

If Plato's *Republic* is not an illegitimate attempt to imagine a future ideal, what would be? Hegel's warnings that philosophy cannot issue oughts or erect a beyond do not mean that no change in future history is possible. Hegel is saying that philosophy is incapable of, and should refrain from, spinning subjective opinions or expressing subjective hopes and wishes concerning the future. What it should do is interpret the nature of the age, apprehend reason in the actual world, and in doing so it can accord with the "impending world revolution" of its time. Hegel clearly thinks that philosophy is capable of interpreting the rational movement of spirit, and that if it does this, if it attends to what is *real*, as opposed to subjective opinion, it can anticipate the future—of America, or of Greek ethical life, or of the modern German state.

In this respect, even Lukács, I think, sees too much of an opposition between the passages in the *Philosophy of Right* that we have just been discussing and a passage from the *Phenomenology* that I will quote. I think there is little difference between the two texts on these matters. But even if the reader is not convinced by my interpretation of the *Philosophy of Right*, it is certainly the case that Lukács is correct in holding that there is no end of history doctrine to be found in the *Phenomenology*. In the *Phenomenology*, Hegel writes:

> It is not difficult to see that ours is a birth-time and a period of transition to a new era. Spirit has broken with the world it has hitherto inhabited and imagined, and is of a mind to submerge it in the past, and in the labour of its own transformation. Spirit is indeed never at rest but always engaged in moving forward.... Spirit in its formation matures slowly and quietly into its new shape, dissolving bit by bit the structure of its previous world, whose tottering state is only hinted at by isolated symptoms.... But this new world is no more a complete actuality than is a new-born child; it is essential to bear this in mind. It comes on the scene for the first time in its immediacy or its Notion [Begriff]. (PhS, 6–7/GW, IX, 14–15)

And it is precisely philosophy that is capable of grasping this *Begriff*. Lukács quotes Hegel's 1806 concluding lecture on phenomenology: "This, Gentlemen, is speculative philosophy as far as I have been able to construct it. Look upon it as the beginnings of the philosophy which you will carry forward. We find ourselves in an important epoch in world history, in a ferment, when spirit has taken a leap forward, where it has sloughed off its old form and is acquiring a new one.... The chief task of philosophy is to welcome it and grant it recognition."[65]

Not only is there no end of history doctrine here, there is even a suggestion, as there is also in the passage on Plato's *Republic* quoted above from the *Philosophy of Right*, that philosophy itself, in *recognizing* emerging spirit, helps make it real. Philosophy helps actualize the new era—it helps construct it. It will certainly be Hegel's view that our recognition of God is what actualizes God (PM, 298/SW, X, 454; PRel, I, 186–7, 347–8/VPRel, I, 96, 248; DFS, 94, 98/GW, IV, 16, 19; PhS, 11–12/GW, IX, 19–20). In my view, then, the

Phenomenology wants to take us past the French Revolution by apprehending the essence of a new age that is dawning. It wants to interpret the nature of its world and to grasp conceptually and phenomenologically a new Sittlichkeit. It wants to be in accord with an impending world revolution and to help realize it by recognizing it.

VIII. Morality and the Final Purpose

In the destruction wrought by the French Revolution, individuals feel "the fear of death, of their absolute master" (*PhS*, 361/GW, IX, 321), and so "absolute freedom leave[s] its self-destroying reality and pass[es] over into another land of self-conscious Spirit" (*PhS*, 363/GW, IX, 323). We move from France to Germany, from Rousseau's general will and the French Revolution to Kant's categorical imperative and the postulates of practical reason. We move from a destructive reason terrorizing the world to reason constructing a God whose job is to reconcile virtue with happiness and thus realize the highest good as our final purpose.

What sort of shift is this? Lukács, who thinks that all of chapter VI is historical, sees its last section on morality as the transition to a new historical era. He thinks it is supposed to represent Hegel's vision of a Germany liberated and unified by Napoleon. But then Lukács is disappointed at how lacking in content the section is.[66] I think he simply expects the wrong thing. Hegel is not discussing a new historical period. We have not even gotten to history yet, and will not until the very end of the *Phenomenology*.

On the other hand, Hyppolite thinks that in "Morality" and in chapter VII, entitled "Religion," Hegel begins to shift beyond phenomenology to noumenology.[67] I do not agree with this view either. Neither "Morality" nor "Religion" leave, go outside, or go beyond culture. For Hegel, art, religion, and philosophy (including moral philosophy) are a part of culture—they are cultural phenomena. If there is anything to worry about here, it is cultural relativism, not the emergence of a metaphysical ontotheological domain. The shift to "Morality" and "Religion" is not, in my view, an attempt to transcend culture, but to turn back within it, to move to greater cultural depths, and there to find a profounder truth.

It was often said, at least in Germany, that the French Revolution was the practical application of Kant's categorical imperative. All laws and institutions were rationally assessed and where they were found wanting they were simply destroyed. Through this destructiveness, consciousness has become certain of is power, authority, and reality.

This consciousness now wants to move from an extreme of individualism, Moralität, and destruction to a Moralität that is internalized and thus no longer destructive. It turns away from society, and begins to seek happiness, God, and religion—it wants to achieve the highest good of Kant's postulates of practical reason. To do this it must reconcile virtue and happiness as well as duty and inclination. This is also to say that it seeks to reaccomplish the ethical order of the ancient Greek polis, the harmonious unity of substance and subjectivity, but not as a mere given and immediate unity. It wants to achieve this harmony as a unity realized within self-consciousness. We want all of reality within self-consciousness—a self-consciousness, therefore, on its way to becoming an absolute consciousness (*PhS*, 364–5/*GW*, IX, 324–5).

We still have a self-consciousness, however, that has not gotten beyond its Kantian commitment to two worlds—nature and morality. We have what Hegel calls the "Moral View of the World." Self-consciousness, from the beginning, for Hegel, has always implied mediation and negativity, and thus its very conception involves relation to some otherness. But since moral duty, for Kant, without lapsing into heteronomy, cannot have anything to do with otherness, we must have independence and indifference between these two worlds—between nature and morality. They are two self-subsistent wholes. Nature is unconcerned with moral self-consciousness, just as the latter is indifferent to it (*PhS*, 365–6/*GW*, IX, 325–6).

However, there is a problem here. Moral consciousness finds that happiness depends on nature. Happiness, for Kant, means the satisfaction of natural desires, interests, or needs. And nature may or may not satisfy our desires; it may or may not make us happy, since it is independent of us (*CPrR*, 129/*KGS*, V, 124; *PhS*, 366/*GW*, IX, 325–6).

Moral consciousness, for its part, then, must adhere to duty and ignore happiness. For Kant, we must act from duty; we must not be determined by inclination, happiness, or nature. Nature must be subordinate to morality (*CPrR*, 121–3, 129/*KGS*, V, 117–18, 124). But, Hegel says, moral consciousness cannot renounce its claims to happiness totally (*PhS*, 366/*GW*, IX, 326). Kant held in the *Foundations* that if we are miserable we might be tempted to give up on morality (*F*, 15 /*KGS*, IV, 399). Happiness, then, is necessary. Moreover, morality without happiness could not be counted as human fulfillment; it certainly would not be the highest good for human beings. Morality plus happiness would be higher—even for Kant (*CPrR*, 114–15/*KGS*, V, 110).

So this Kantian moral consciousness must *postulate* the harmony of morality and nature. It postulates that morality should lead to happiness. It holds this not as an actual reality, something that can be proven to be the case, but merely as a demand of practical reason, an as-if, a postulate (*CPrR*, 129–30/*KGS*, V, 124–6; *PhS*, 367/*GW*, IX, 326).

This also implies that the opposition of thought and sensibility, reason and nature, duty and inclination must be resolved and harmonized, if morality and happiness are to be reconciled (*CPrR*, 126/*KGS*, V, 122; *PhS*,

367/GW, IX, 326-7). If duty and inclination do not agree, either we will not do our duty and thus not be moral, or our inclination will not be satisfied and thus we will not be happy. Both nature and morality exist within one consciousness for Hegel, but more than this, they must not be opposed within that consciousness.

In the *Metaphysical Principles of Virtue*, Kant says, much as he did in the *Foundations*, "Adversity, pain, and want are great temptations to transgress one's duty. Thus it would seem that affluence, strength, health, and welfare in general, which are opposed to those influences, can also be regarded as ends that are at the same time duties; that is to say, it is a duty to promote one's own happiness." Surely this is the ideal. Surely this is what it means to reconcile morality and happiness, duty and inclination. But no. Kant insists that "the end is not happiness, but the morality of the subject; and happiness is merely the means of removing the hindrances to morality" (MPV, 46/KGS, VI, 388). In fact, one's own happiness can never be a duty. Why? Because "one's own happiness is an end which, to be sure, all men do have (by virtue of the impulse of their nature), but this end can never without contradiction be regarded as a duty. What everyone of himself already inevitably wants does not belong under the concept of duty, because a duty is a constraint to an end that is not gladly adopted" (MPV, 43/KGS, VI, 385–6).

So also, in the *Critique of Practical Reason*, Kant says, "To love God means in this sense to like to do His commandments, and to love one's neighbor means to like to practice all duties toward him. The command which makes this a rule cannot require that we have this disposition but only that we endeavor after it. To command that one do something gladly is self-contradictory" (CPrR, 86/KGS, V, 83).

Thus, for Kant, the reconciliation of duty and inclination, morality and happiness, can only be a postulate, an infinite task, pushed away into the remote future. It is something we always hope to achieve, ever strive for, but can never actually accomplish. In fact, Hegel suggests, for Kant we *must* never accomplish it. It is fine, as Kant says, to endeavor after it, but to actually achieve it, to actually reconcile duty and inclination, would land us in contradiction. If we did actually reconcile duty and inclination, morality and nature, then, morality would be done away with (CPrR, 126–9, 86-7/KGS, V, 122-5, 83–4; PhS, 367–8/GW, IX, 326-7). This is especially so if we reject a two worlds interpretation of Kant. If we reject an ontological distinction between two worlds, if with Hegel we think there is no legitimate distinction between phenomena and noumena that can be sustained, if there is only, as Allison puts it, a distinction between two perspectives, then, for Hegel, the distinction between morality and nature is nothing but a distinction made by moral consciousness. It follows from this, then, that moral consciousness will be in contradiction—it is saying both that morality and nature must be kept apart and that they must be reconciled. For morality to be possible there must be a clear distinction between reason, duty, the noumenal, on the one hand, and nature, inclination, the phenomenal, on the other—we cannot be moral if we act from inclination. Yet at the same time that consciousness makes this distinction and insists that the two sides be kept apart it also wants to bring the two sides together. It wants to reconcile duty and inclination, morality and happiness to achieve the highest good. But to reconcile the two sides of a conceptual distinction would be to give up the distinction. After all, we do not have two realities but merely two sides of a distinction made within consciousness. If their reconciliation enters consciousness as an actual fact, there would then be no distinction between nature and morality—duty and inclination. There could be no distinction, then, between acting from duty and acting from inclination—and thus morality would be impossible (PhS, 368/GW, IX, 327).

So to prevent the collapse of this distinction, Hegel suggests, we postulate two consciousnesses: first, a human consciousness that attends only to duties, not to inclination or happiness, and thus is unable by itself to reconcile morality and happiness, and second, a divine consciousness that from outside aligns nature with duty such that inclination and duty, happiness and morality, can be reconciled without collapsing the distinction between them. God must control nature so that it will satisfy our desires and thus make us happy, yet do this such that we can always at the same time act morally, that is, from duty and independently of our inclinations and desires. Furthermore, God is necessary to see to it that our happiness is in proportion to our worthiness to be happy (CPrR, 114–16, 127–30/KGS, V, 110–12, 122–6; R, 3–5/KGS, VI, 3-5; PhS, 370–1/GW, IX, 329–30).

This means that we have involved another consciousness—God's consciousness. Human consciousness, then, it would seem, is contingent and imperfect; it cannot look upon its happiness as necessary or guaranteed. Human consciousness is unworthy; it must look upon its happiness as dependent on a divine consciousness—it can only hope for happiness as a gift of grace (PhS, 371/GW, IX, 330). However, it is supposed to be human consciousness that is essential here. God is only a postulate, a thought product, a construction. That is all God has been all along in the Phenomenology, and essentially that is all God is for Kant (MPV, 157-8/KGS, VI, 487–8).

At any rate, for the first time in the Phenomenology, the consciousness there on the stage recognizes that it constructs its God. Nevertheless, consciousness still places its God outside—in a beyond. It cannot yet give up its doctrine of two worlds. This will give us a whole nest of thoughtless contradictions which Hegel takes up in the next subsection, entitled "Dissemblance" (PhS, 372–4/GW, IX, 330–2).

Here Hegel introduces, as he did in "Unhappy Consciousness,"[68] his own more Aristotelian conception of happiness rather than Kant's. Moral consciousness, in accomplishing a deed, actualizes a moral purpose. In doing so, moral consciousness sees existence transformed and the self objectified, expressed, and reflected in existence. It sees existence as it own doing and is at home with it. This objectification is a satisfaction, enjoyment, or happiness. And so we find that moral consciousness was not in earnest in postulating a God to reconcile virtue and happiness. Moral action—action in which we realize ourselves—achieves its own happiness. Consciousness fulfills the postulate itself. We have no need of a second Kantian world—a noumenal beyond. Happiness is achieved in moral action itself (PhS, 375/GW, IX, 333).

Still, we are not talking about the realization of a single purpose by a single moral consciousness. We are talking about a whole moral view of the world, the reconciliation of morality and happiness, reason and nature—the realization of the highest good as a final moral purpose in the world. We have, then, two wholes, two totalities, two realms here—the laws of nature and the laws of morality. To realize the highest good we need a harmony between these two worlds—between nature and morality. For the highest good, then, nature should not have a law different from and opposed to that of morality. But if this is so, morality will be impossible. Morality requires negation—it must separate itself from and reject the natural. As Kant says, "The moral capacity of man would not be virtue if it were not actualized by the strength of one's resolution in conflict with powerful opposing inclinations" (MPV, 145/KGS, VI, 477). But on the other hand, the negation of the natural, if nature is indeed in conformity with the moral law, would be immoral (PhS, 376/GW, IX, 334).

Moreover, to hold that moral action is necessarily opposed to nature, thus that we must brush nature aside and dismiss inclinations and impulses—which are also natural—cannot be held in earnest. To act at all, the natural is necessary as a mediating element. Nature and inclination, in fact, are the instruments by which moral consciousness actualizes itself (PhS, 377/GW, IX, 335)—as we saw in Kant's "Idea for a Universal History" and in Hegel's discussion of the way of the world. Natural conflicts, competing particular interests, conflicting inclinations, realize virtue. The harmony of morality and nature, then, would undermine what drives us to morality—it would be to give up morality.

So morality must reject an immediate harmony and push its goal off to infinity. The goal is ever sought, but never achieved. As Kant puts it in the *Metaphysical Principles of Virtue:*

> Virtue is always in progress and yet always begins at the beginning.... Virtue is an ideal and unattainable; but yet constantly to

approximate it is nevertheless a duty.... Virtue, with its maxims adopted once for all, can never settle into a state of rest and inactivity; if it is not rising, it inevitably declines. This is so because moral maxims...cannot be based on habit (for basing a maxim on habit belongs to the physical nature of the determination of the will). But even if the *exercise* of moral maxims were to become a habit, the subject would thereby lose the freedom of adopting his maxims; this freedom, however, is the character of an action done from duty. (MPV, 69/KGS, VI, 409)

We must always seek virtue, but never achieve it. This suggests that the middle state of incompleteness is the only thing that can be of value. The important thing is progress toward completion, the seeking, not the completion itself. But this will not work either. Real progress toward the harmony of morality and nature would be progress toward morality's disappearance. To progress would be to progress toward ceasing to be moral (PhS, 378/GW, IX, 336).

Moreover, if we avoid actually getting there and stick only to this middle state of striving, then we certainly could not achieve moral perfection, we would not even really be seeking it, and thus, it would seem, we would not even be *worthy* of happiness. If this is so, then we could only hope for happiness as a *sheer* gift of grace, and thus it could come to us only by chance or caprice. Furthermore, if we give up on the seeking of moral perfection and depend entirely upon God's grace, this would even suggest, then, that we are less concerned about morality than about happiness (PhS, 379/GW, IX, 337; see also R, 48–9/KGS, VI, 53). Moral consciousness indeed would be imperfect. This would further suggest that we must depend on God not just to reconcile virtue and happiness but to make up for our defective morality itself (PhS, 380/GW, IX, 337; MPV, 27, 102, 157/KGS, IV, 227, 440, 487; MEJ, 20/KGS, VI, 219; CPR, A812=B840–A813=B841). As Kant puts it in *Religion Within the Limits of Reason Alone,*

> [Our] continual and endless advance from a deficient to a better good, ever remains defective. We must consequently regard the good as it appears in us, that is, in the guise of *an act*, as being *always* inadequate to a holy law. But we may also think of this endless progress of our goodness towards conformity to the law...as being judged by Him who knows the heart, through a purely intellectual intuition, as a completed whole, because of the *disposition*, supersensible in its nature, from which this progress is derived. Thus may man, notwithstanding his permanent deficiency, yet expect to be *essentially* well-pleasing to God. (R, 60–1/KGS, VI, 67)[69]

Without God, then, our goodness would remain radically imperfect and defective. Only through God's grace, God's acceptance, can these otherwise defective acts be counted as good. At this point, Kant would seem to have moved a very great distance from his view in the *Foundations*: "Nothing in the world—indeed nothing even beyond the world—can possibly be conceived which could be called good without qualification except a *good will*" (F, 9/KGS, IV, 392–3). Only the will itself, for Kant, can be the source of morality. Anything else introduces heteronomy. Our reason itself must be the source of whatever is moral or sacred (CPrR, 113, 130, 133–4/KGS, V, 109, 125–6, 129).[70] What is God doing here then? Relying on God would introduce heteronomy.

What Hegel has done here is to twist Kant's postulates of practical reason into a series of contradictions, all of which has been possible because of Kant's doctrine of two worlds. From the start, for Kant, reason was opposed to nature, duty was opposed to inclination, morality was opposed to happiness, individual consciousness was opposed to God. So the whole moral view of the world must collapse, because the distinction on which it rests collapses—the distinction between what must necessarily be postulated (namely, God), yet which turns out not at all to be necessary (namely, not necessary to establish our duty, make us happy, or reconcile virtue with happiness). If it is not necessary, why postulate it (PhS, 382/GW, IX, 339)? And so, finally, consciousness gives up its two worlds doctrine and this gives us what Hegel calls "Conscience."

The section that we have just gone through recalls "Unhappy Consciousness" (PhS, 399/GW, IX, 354)—here seeking happiness. The problem in "Unhappy Consciousness" was that human nature had two opposed sides held in unity—a dual nature with each side being essential. It had a spiritual-supernatural side and a natural-physical side. As consciousness sought one side it lost the other. Every gain was a loss and every joy a suffering. To seek to fulfill one's natural desires was to abandon one's supernatural and spiritual quest. To seek to satisfy one's supernatural and spiritual aspirations was to ignore and suppress one's natural desires. For Christianity, the natural and the supernatural are opposed, much as the phenomenal and the noumenal are for Kant.

The "Moral View of the World" gives rise to much the same sort of opposition, except that self-consciousness is aware that the two sides—the supernatural and the natural—are within it. Consciousness is aware that it constructs nature and that God is its own postulate. Still, in seeking one side it loses the other. If it seeks happiness, it gives up virtue; yet seeking virtue will not make it happy. Even to depend on God for happiness as a free gift of grace is to end up seeking happiness rather than morality. But finally, for Hegel, since consciousness knows that these two sides are within it, it abandons the opposition, abandons the doctrine of two worlds—as it sees it must because of the contradictions that keep arising.

The only way out of "Unhappy Consciousness," this continual shifting where every gain is a loss and every joy a suffering, is to see that both sides of this split essence fall within a single spiritual unity. We must erase the line that divides the phenomenal and the noumenal, spirit and nature, individual and God. That is where all of this is headed. We are heading for "Conscience" and the transition to "Religion." We are not, however, headed for the sort of religion rejected by Enlightenment, that is, belief in an external beyond. Religion is not beyond but within—within culture and within consciousness. God is a postulate—our own cultural construction.

So conscience renounces the contradictions of the moral view of the world (PhS, 386/GW, IX, 343) and gives up its two worlds doctrine. It erases the line between the phenomenal and the noumenal, between a transcendental self and an empirical self, between duty and inclination, reason and nature, the individual and God (PhS, 385/GW, IX, 342). After all, God is nothing but a postulate, a pure thought, consciousness's own self, which it distinguished from itself and projected into a beyond. As Hegel puts it, conscience knows that it is this absolute self and that its inner voice is divine (PhS, 397/GW, IX, 352).

For conscience, then, duty is no longer a universal that stands over against and separated from the self. Conscience no longer confronts laws that are independent of it. Conscience acts, it produces a reality in the world, and doing so fulfills its duty without any contradictions or problems. Private individual conviction, one's own individuality and inclination, is one's duty. The validation of duty no longer lies beyond consciousness. Conscience has gotten beyond such divisions. Conscience knows and does what is concretely right (PhS, 385–8/GW, IX, 342–5). Or as Kant puts it, "Conscience needs no guide.... Conscience is a state of consciousness which in itself is duty" (R, 173/KGS, VI, 185). Moreover, "when a man is aware of having acted according to his conscience, then as far as guilt or innocence is concerned, nothing more can be demanded" (MPV, 60/KGS, VI, 401).

All conscience now needs is to secure its reality through others. Its conviction concerning its duty must be recognized. Conscience's own conviction is essential (the in-itself), but it must be recognized (for-others) to be fully actual, real, and objective (PhS, 388/GW, IX, 344–5).

This is where conscience runs into trouble. It is relatively easy for conscience to erase the line between the self and a postulated God, but this self still takes itself to be a cultural individual, thus separate from and over against other cultural individuals. If this is still the way we understand selves, if we still understand them as individuals, then how could other individuals be expected to agree with my individual conscience? And, as we shall see, they will not. Hegel wants to drive us beyond this final stand of Moralität. If we erase the line between phenomena and noumena, if we give up the notion of a transcendental self, then there is nothing left to hold the individual *essentially* apart from other individuals—from community and Sittlichkeit. I should come to see that others are essentially a part of my self. That will take us over to "Religion" and that is what Hegel wants to accomplish in this section (*PhS*, 397–8/*GW*, IX, 352–3).

So we hear echoes of good old honest consciousness and the problem we left unsolved in chapter V (*PhS*, 389/*GW*, IX, 345)—the fact that an individual's work was not recognized by anyone else. Conscience faces only a slightly different problem. It was honest consciousness's work or product that went unrecognized; it is conscience's inner conviction and honesty that go unrecognized.

In "Culture," consciousness realized that its entire cultural world was its construction. All of cultural reality is within consciousness. To be conscientious, then, conscience must exhaust reality, know all of the circumstances in which it acts, know the total situation in all its bearings. But it cannot. Reality is too complex. Conscience faces a bewildering multiplicity of details, facets of the situation, differing perspectives. But duty lies in conviction, so it must just act (*PhS*, 389–90/*GW*, IX, 346).

But just as the work of honest consciousness was not recognized by others, so here in "Conscience" others will see the situation differently than conscience does. They will hold by other facets of the situation. Even Kant, in his discussion of conscience in *Religion Within the Limits of Reason Alone*, admits that this is possible (*R*, 174–5/*KGS*, VI, 186–7). He says, "A change of heart is a departure from evil and an entrance into goodness, the laying off of the old man and the putting on of the new.... Although the man (regarded from the point of view of his empirical nature as a sentient being) is *physically* the self-same guilty person as before and must be judged as such before a moral tribunal and hence by himself; yet, because of his new disposition, he is (regarded as an intelligible being) *morally* another in the eyes of a divine judge for whom this disposition takes the place of action" (*R*, 68/*KGS*, VI, 74).

Is it any surprise that what conscience takes to be morality and duty in the eyes of a divine judge may well appear to others as wrong doing and evil? Duty can even appear to others as cowardice, dishonesty, or violence. After all, each conscience has this right of interpretation and each interpretation stands on the same level as the interpretation of others. There are very strong echoes of relativism here. Conscience is not bound by an external law (*PhS*, 391–2/*GW*, IX, 347–8). It is absolute in itself—and all consciences are equal in this way. But there is a disparity—they cannot agree with each other. Your act is not recognized or accepted by others. According to my conscience, your act is not right and thus you must be evil (*PhS*, 394/*GW*, IX, 350).

At this point, language becomes very important: "Language is self-consciousness existing *for-others*." It is the self's way of explaining itself, manifesting itself, and becoming objective for itself as well as for the consciousness of others. Through language conscience expresses its conviction and sincerity. It seeks the validation of its act in the recognition that it was sincere (*PhS*, 395–6/*GW*, IX, 351).

Hegel is giving us a very Lutheran notion of an absolutely inviolable conscience. Faith cannot be forced or demanded from outside. Individuals cannot be expected to accept or believe anything they are not convinced of in conscience. There is an immediate relation between conscience and God. The inner voice is a divine voice. Conscience is absolute (*PhS*, 397/*GW*, IX, 352; see also *PH*, 416, 423/*PW*, II, 880, 889).

Religion is beginning to emerge here. Self-consciousness has withdrawn into its innermost being, which includes the whole of existence, and for which all externality has vanished. God is immediately present in the mind and heart of consciences. Religion *is* this knowledge of a community concerning its own inner spirit (*PhS*, 398/*GW*, IX, 353), but it cannot be achieved as long as each conscience acts alone as an individual. These individual consciences cannot agree with each other. They disrupt the community. They do not recognize each other. When one expresses its sincerity in language, this appears to others as evil. Since each judges the actions of others differently than they do, each will judge the relation of the other's behavior to their expression of sincerity as hypocrisy—and hypocrisy must be unmasked (*PhS*, 401/*GW*, IX, 356).

But to judge others as hypocrites is to judge them by our own law. This, as in the "Law of the Heart," is to set up our own law as something to be acknowledged and recognized. But it is not acknowledged or recognized. As this continues, the judging consciousness—not just the judged—itself becomes a hypocrite. It begins to avoid action. It backs away from action—because it is always seen as evil by others whenever it acts. Instead, it simply judges others, it utters fine sentiments, it wishes its judgment to be taken as an expression and evidence of its purity and uprightness. After all, Kant thinks that since good acts always remain deficient, God judges our disposition (supersensible in its nature) as the act itself (*R*, 60–1/*KGS*, VI, 67). This is a real danger for Protestantism, Hegel seems to be suggesting, insofar as it puts faith ahead of works (*PhS*, 402–3/*GW*, IX, 356–7).

Judging consciousness can even go further. It can explain all acts of others as deriving not from conscience but from selfishness. No act can escape being judged in this way. But what we begin to see here is that judgment reflects not so much upon the judged as upon the judge. The one who judges in this way is base, mean, and hypocritical (*PhS*, 404/*GW*, IX, 358).

At any rate, we have a bunch of beautiful souls here. Each "lives in dread of besmirching the splendor of its inner being by action...and in order to preserve the purity of its heart, it flees from contact with the actual world, and...is reduced to the extreme of ultimate abstraction" (*PhS*, 400/*GW*, IX, 354).[71] We have the height of interiorized Moralität—a soul so abstracted into itself, a soul that so shuns external action that, far from wreaking the sort of destruction that resulted when abstract consciousness turned to action in the French Revolution, this consciousness cannot act in the world at all.

But no matter how hypocritical or judgmental this consciousness has become, it still has a *conscience*. And so, it finally sees itself to be just as bad as the hypocrite it has been judging. It sees itself to be a hypocrite too. So it confesses and repents. It sees and admits that it is sinful and hypocritical. And, of course, it naturally expects others to do the same. When, however, they do not do the same, well, that merely confirms the suspicion that they were sinful all along (*PhS*, 405/*GW*, IX, 359)! Hegel does an absolutely marvelous job here of capturing the dynamics of a certain kind of religious infighting.

So the repentant soul sees itself as a beautiful soul and the others as wicked—which is what it was after from the beginning anyway. The repentant consciousness wallows in its own penitence and condemns the stiff-neckedness of others. We lose all communication with others (*PhS*, 405–6/*GW*, IX, 359–60). Particularity, isolation, and abstraction have not been overcome but intensified.

Cultural individuals as individuals cannot make it to the absolute. Instead they must draw back, forgive, and cease to judge others. Individuals must renounce themselves totally. In abandoning themselves totally, in alienating themselves completely, in giving themselves up to God, God appears as a self—much as the alienation of the self earlier produced the monarch as a self. Hegel says, "The reconciling *Yea*, in which the two 'I's let go their antithetical *existence*, is the *existence* of the 'I' which has expanded into a duality, and therein remains identical with itself, and, in its complete externalization and opposite, possesses the certainty of itself: it is God manifested in the midst of those who know themselves in the form of pure knowledge" (*PhS*, 409/*GW*, IX, 362).

We have not jumped from phenomenology to noumenology here. A transcendent ontotheological entity has not miraculously appeared before us. God began this section as a postulate and ends as "manifested...in the form of pure knowledge." God is a construction of the self that will finally start to hold up when that self has given up its individualism, its antagonistic opposition to other individuals, when the individual sees that it is essentially a part of a community with others. All of this requires finally erasing the false line between phenomena and noumena.

What has happened in chapter VI is that noble consciousness first constructed (by alienating itself) an absolute monarchical self embedded in a rich cultural world. As consciousness became aware that it had constructed this cultural world, it turned against it, became critical, and this world dissolved in a Rameauean whirl. Culture, however, did not disappear; it remained embodied within the individual, though in a chaotic and confused state. From this point on, the self contained all of culture—not in a very orderly way, but it was there. Then Enlightenment insight came along and took up where Rameau's nephew left off. It especially continued the critical and negative attack on culture. However Enlightenment insight was rational and thus began to put things in order. It swept things clean and threw a great deal out—all superstition, deceit, error, especially belief and the supposed self-interested duplicity of priests. Indeed, reason did such a thorough job that by the time of the French Revolution it has become outright terroristic.

Despite the destructiveness involved here, we must see that the self has established itself as a powerful and real force. It has assumed the throne of the world—and not as a single emperor or monarch (the result of the alienation of its subjects). Rather, we *all* are selves and we all assume the throne of the world. Reason takes itself to be a universal and absolute authority and it sets out to remake the world in accordance with reason. And after having trashed the superstitious God of belief, it decides to construct, to rationally postulate, its own God—a God which is no longer a beyond but is one with conscience. We have a solid self here well on its way toward becoming an absolute self. It is just that it still takes itself to be a cultural individual and thus cannot get sufficient recognition from other individuals. After all, if all are individuals, how can they be expected to agree?

What we find in chapter VI is that by erasing the line between phenomena and noumena, between the transcendental self and the empirical self, we need not necessarily drop into a Humean flux, as Kant seemed to think we would, because in erasing the line between these two worlds we also erase the line between the individual and the absolute—and, indeed, conscience knows that its inner voice is a divine voice. But the self is not yet able to gain the recognition it needs from others to shore up its absoluteness and so it does at this point risk falling back into a confused Humean flux. But this, I suggest, is not because consciousness dared to erase the line between phenomena and noumena. It is because it has not yet erased that line completely.

We must notice that from the beginning of the *Phenomenology*, Hegel has been arguing that things cannot be understood except as relations. In chapter VI, Hegel is arguing that things cannot be understood except as sociocultural relations. Thus we cannot understand the self either except as such a relation. There is no noumenal realm that can give us a fixed and solid transcendental self apart from cultural relations. If we cannot sustain a transcendental self apart, if the self is *essentially* part of the sociocultural world, if its very being is constituted by its relations to others, then consciousness needs to see that its individuality is merely its own cultural construction. The self is not an individual over against other individuals in essence. It could construct a community—it could produce Sittlichkeit. And if the individual is a cultural construction, if the individual is constructed by others, then *others* are a part of our *essence*. If we erase the line between phenomena and noumena, if there is no transcendental self, then there is nothing to keep us essentially apart from others as individuals over against other individuals. Nothing individualizes us except culture. There is nothing, then, to prevent us from seeing that we are essentially cultural beings that could construct a community. And, indeed, this is what has been known for centuries—in religion. It is just that we have abstracted from religion up to this point in the *Phenomenology* and now must turn to it.

What the individual must do is give itself up, abandon itself, sacrifice its separateness, so as to realize its absolute self. A larger self has been present in the background throughout culture. The self was constructed by culture and the self transformed its culture. Individuals hide this cultural self from themselves, hide the fact that they are formed by culture, hide the fact that there is something larger than themselves within themselves, by asserting themselves aggressively and critically as cultural individuals against their culture—by criticizing monarchy, attacking belief, fomenting revolution, postulating God, and so forth. To give up this self is not to lose it. It is to see its connection to a larger totality, to an absolute self, and to see the individual as an individuation of this whole. The individual is an individual, and individuals do construct monarchy, tear down belief, and foment revolution, but they have failed to see that also something larger operates through them—something Antigone *was* able to see. Thus, we must move on—or return—to religion.

5

Culture, Religion, and Absolute Knowing

❦

We have completed the first and second parts of the *Phenomenology*, which dealt, respectively, with individual consciousness and with cultural consciousness. We now move on to the third part, chapters VII and VIII, dealing with absolute spirit, that is, with religion and absolute knowing.

I. Religion

Absolute spirit is a culture's consciousness of itself—its self-consciousness. It is the spirit of a people reflecting upon itself, understanding itself, and gaining self-awareness in and through its religion. Religion is a culture's vision of itself, its depiction to itself of its importance, its ultimate values, its mission and destiny, its meaning and significance—in short, its truth.

It is Hyppolite's view, we have seen, that chapters VII and VIII move beyond phenomenology to noumenology. Hyppolite concedes that a culture's portrayal of absolute spirit is phenomenology, but he thinks that insofar as Hegel also claims that religion is the self-consciousness of absolute spirit—the self-consciousness of God—Hegel moves beyond phenomenology to noumenology.[1] I do not agree with this interpretation. Hegel said in chapter VI that spirit "does *not* exist as the Spirit of the community *without* having been produced by consciousness." He did add that nevertheless it exists "at the same time in and for itself" (*PhS*, 335/GW, IX, 298). What this means, I think, is that the portrayal of absolute spirit by a people or culture *is* phenomenology, though, of course, any culture takes its deity to exist absolutely in and for itself. But this is something, we cannot forget, that is the case *for-this-culture*. In short, it does not get us beyond phenomenology. Even in chapter VIII Hegel writes, concerning the object of absolute spirit, "Self-consciousness *knows* the nothingness of the object, on the one hand, because it alienates its own self—for in this alienation it posits *itself* as object, or the object as itself, in virtue of the indivisible unity of *being-for-self*. On the other hand, this positing at the same time contains the other moment, viz. that self-consciousness has equally superseded this alienation and objectivity too, and taken it back into itself so that it is in communion with itself in *its* otherness as such."[2]

In other words, the object of absolute spirit—namely, God or the absolute—is a product of our alienation. It is ourselves alienated.

A culture certainly may concern itself with things in and for themselves, with things from the viewpoint of the absolute, from a God's-eye perspective, or from the perspective of God's self-consciousness, but nevertheless this is something that is the culture's own construction and thus remains the perspective-of-this-culture. We do not get a reality beyond culture—except *for-this-culture*. We must recall Meister Eckhart's phrase, which, even Hyppolite admits, Hegel liked so much: "The eye with which God sees me is the eye with which I see him; my eye and his eye are one and the same.... If God did not exist nor would I; if I did not exist nor would he" (*PRel*, I, 347–8/*VPRel*, I, 248).[3] The last phrase certainly makes God's existence dependent on culture, and the previous phrases need not be read as claiming anything fundamentally opposed to that. For Hegel, spirit exists "only insofar as it is *for* itself," that is, God exists "essentially in his community.... He is objective to himself, and is such truly only in self-consciousness" (*PRel*, I, 142, 186–7/*VPRel*, I, 56, 96; see also *PM*, 298/*SW*, X, 454). It is the self-consciousness of the community that gives God objective existence—and that is phenomenology.

Lukács, on the other hand, claims that for materialists there is always a "clear and unambiguous causality: it is man who creates his God (or idea of God)." Lukács admits that we do find this view in Hegel, but at the same time, for Lukács, we find "a strange and confused interaction." We also find God as a real actor in world history.[4] There is no confusion here except for materialists. For Hegel, God is a cultural construction, but that is not in any way inconsistent with God being a cultural *force*. A culture's constructions can and will have an extremely powerful influence on that culture. Moreover, the fact that God is a cultural construction, or the fact that a culture's portrayal of God is phenomenology, we have seen in the introduction and in the first section of chapter 4, does not mean that God is an illusion.

I want to steer my way carefully between left and right Hegelian interpretations here. We must hold with left Hegelians like Lukács and Hyppolite that God is constructed, but it does not follow from this that God is nothing but a construction. We must also concede to right Hegelians that for Hegel

God exists in and for itself. Nevertheless, we must remind the right Hegelian that God cannot for-us exist in and for itself without being constructed. At the same time, we must remind the left Hegelian that despite the fact that we have constructed our God, nevertheless, as a culture we have been fundamentally formed, molded, perhaps even created, by this construction.

At any rate, we must recognize that in chapters VII and VIII it remains Hegel's view that God is our construction. This is a theme that is developed throughout the final two chapters and which Hegel does not take back or go beyond. In natural religion, for example, Hegel argues that consciousness projects itself into a natural object. Spirit is constructed by an artificer—a producer of pyramids or obelisks. Human spirit produces itself as an object, but, Hegel thinks, without yet grasping the thought of itself. The significance, meaning, or thought of the work is not yet found in the work itself, but is related to the work as alien and external; either a dead and departed spirit is thought to take up its abode in the lifeless work or the work points externally and hieroglyphically toward spirit outside itself (*PhS*, 421, 423/*GW*, IX, 373, 374–5).

In what Hegel calls "religion in the form of art," by which he has in mind the religion of the ancient Greek polis, spirit's construction of itself becomes more conscious. Spirit "has raised the shape in which it is present to its own consciousness into the form of consciousness itself and it produces such a shape for itself." What it creates "is known by the individuals as their own essence and their own work.... This Spirit is the free nation in which hallowed custom constitutes the substance of all, whose actuality and existence each and everyone knows to be his own will and deed" (*PhS*, 424–5, also 435–6/*GW*, IX, 376, 385).

Even in revealed religion, that is, Christianity, consciousness constructs its deity: "Self-consciousness surrenders itself consciously, it is preserved in its alienation and remains the Subject of substance, but since it is likewise *self*-alienated, it still has the consciousness of the substance; or, since self-consciousness through its sacrifice *brings forth* substance as Subject, the substance remains self-consciousness's own Self"(*PhS*, 453–4/*GW*, IX, 400).

Nevertheless, Hegel claims, self-consciousness must get beyond focusing in a one-sided way only on its own self-alienation—its own construction. Even if "it knows all existence to be spiritual in nature, yet true spirit has not become thereby objective for it.... All existence is spiritual reality merely from the standpoint of consciousness, not inherently in itself. Spirit in this way has merely a fictitious or imaginary existence. This imagination is fantastic extravagance of mind, which introduces into nature as well as history, the world and the mythical ideas of early religions."[5] To get beyond this fantasy and imagination, we must stop focusing only on our own construction, we must see that substance, from its side, must also empty itself and become self-consciousness, which is the belief that Christianity introduces into the world with its imagery of incarnation (*PhS*, 457–8/*GW*, IX, 404–5).

We might be tempted to wonder whether Hegel is slipping toward noumenology here after all. We might be tempted to take the argument of chapter VII to be that, yes, religions construct their spirits or their deities, they are phenomenological, even Christianity does this, but for religion to get beyond the imaginary, the fictitious, the merely phenomenological, we must move, as Christianity does, to the noumenological and see that substance, God, the absolute, from its side must empty itself, create the world, incarnate itself, and become self-consciousness (in the form of Christ). Does religion begin as phenomenological construction but end up as noumenology? Is Hyppolite right after all? I do not think so. We must see that construction is inescapably present in any Christian imagery, including that which makes noumenological claims. The noumenological claim does not get us beyond construction. For example, in Genesis God is said to have created the world, and that is certainly a noumenological claim. But in reading Genesis it is impossible to avoid the fact that God's creation of the world is being con-structed by a culture—a culture that constructs a narrative in a certain lan-guage with specific imagery that makes sense to a certain people in a certain historical era. The story of God's creation of the world is the Jewish and Christian way of constructing their worlds. The fact that God created the world—even if it actually happened—does not mean that this creation was not constructed by us. We can no more say that because God created it it was not constructed by us than we can say that because it was constructed by us it was not created by God. Indeed, Hegel's very claim that religion is pic-ture thinking (*Vorstellung*) implies that religion is constructed—that it requires language and imagery that makes sense to a particular culture in a particular era (*PhS*, 475/*GW*, IX, 418–19).

Construction is at the very center of the last two chapters of the *Phenomenology*. Furthermore, as we move through the various forms of reli-gion taken up in chapter VII, Hegel wants us to see a development and a pro-gression. Absolute reality is always constructed, but it is increasingly constructed at higher and higher levels such that at the same time it is less and less other. We are increasingly able to see ourselves in the absolute, actu-ally see it as our construction, and thus be at home with it. Indeed, only if the absolute is constructed by us can we achieve the goal of the *Phenomenology*, which is to overcome alienation and estrangement, achieve freedom, and be at home. As Hegel says, "For what is *thought of*, ceases to be something [merely] thought of, something alien to the self's knowledge, only when the self has produced it, and therefore beholds the determination of the object as its *own*, consequently beholds *itself* in the object."[6] In the *Logic*, Hegel says that "freedom means that the other thing with which you deal is a second

self—so that you never leave your own ground but give the law to yourself....For freedom it is necessary that we should feel no presence of something which is not ourselves" (L, 49/SW, VIII, 87; see also ILHP, 56–7,
80/EGP, 83–4, 110–11).

II. Alienation and Estrangement Overcome

At this point, we must take up our discussion of alienation and estrangement where we left off in chapter 4. In particular we must explain how, in
the last two chapters of the Phenomenology, alienation and estrangement are
finally overcome.

In chapter VI of the Phenomenology, we saw how alienation led to
estrangement. Individual subjects alienated their essence, served the state,
surrendered themselves to an objective power, and this power reacted back
against them and dominated them. This hostile reaction and domination was
estrangement. Nevertheless, these individual subjects developed to universality through this alienation that led to estrangement. The state power became
real and universal due to the recognition and service granted it by its subjects, and this powerful state was then able to mold its subjects, culture them,
and lift them to universality.

In this process of alienation leading to estrangement, it was necessary
that each side not recognize itself in the other if each was to be effectively
acknowledged, constituted, and molded by the other. If the individual subjects had seen that they constructed the state, that they were the essence of
the state, then they would not have taken the state seriously, would not have
served it, and the state could not have developed. So also if the state had
seen that it had been constructed by its subjects, that its essence was its subjects, it would not have taken itself seriously, could not have developed, and
would not have been able to mold its subjects and lift them to universality.

Here in absolute spirit we now meet a second and a third form of alienation—alienation that overcomes estrangement and what we might call
"neutral" alienation. Both are very closely related to each other and to
revealed religion.

In Hegel's discussion of revealed religion, we find two important movements—one the reverse of the other. In the first, substance alienates itself,
goes outside itself, and becomes subjectivity. In the second, subjectivity alienates itself, becomes universal, and is reconciled with the substantial. In the
first movement we have neutral alienation. In the second we have alienation
as the overcoming of estrangement (PhS, 457, 459/GW, IX, 403–4, 405).

The first movement refers to the incarnation. The substance alienates
itself and becomes subjectivity; the Christian God alienates itself, goes outside

itself, and takes on a human form—that of Christ. This is neutral alienation. In itself, it neither produces nor overcomes estrangement. The two (the Father and the Son) are not hostile or opposed. Both are one—one God. Here spirit knows itself in its alienation—each side sees its unity with the other (*PhS*, 459/*GW*, IX, 405). In alienating itself, spirit remains within itself and at home with itself. We merely have a distinction within a unity—a distinction that does not cause the unity to go unrecognized. This is a general characteristic of neutral alienation as opposed to alienation that led to estrangement. In the latter, it was always the case that the estranged hostile power was not recognized as the outcome of our alienation.

Parallel to the incarnation, the creation of the world also involves neutral alienation. God creates the world (*PhS*, 467–8/*GW*, IX, 412–13)—God or spirit externalizes itself, goes outside itself, and posits itself as nature. This is alienation as neutral alienation. The distinction between God and nature does not obscure the unity of the two, certainly not for Adam and Eve, who, in their innocence, chat with God each day, name the animals with God's assistance, and are at one with nature. However, thought, self-consciousness, or (in pictorial language) Adam and Eve eating of the tree of the knowledge of good and evil, bring a separation and estrangement between spirit and nature—they bring sin. The world, nature, and human beings are estranged from God. Innocence, the immediate recognized unity, is lost (*PhS*, 468/*GW*, IX, 412–13).

On the other hand, the second movement to be found in revealed religion is the reverse of the first. Subjectivity alienates itself, becomes universal, and is reconciled with God. Here alienation overcomes estrangement. Christ takes on the sins of the world, he takes estrangement onto himself, he sacrifices himself, he dies, and is reconciled with God.

Actually, all the forms of alienation are involved here. First, Christ alienates himself in taking on the human form (separating from God but while remaining in unity with God). This is neutral alienation. Next Christ takes upon himself the sins of humanity, the alienation that led to estrangement, to humanity's lack of unity with God. Then Christ alienates himself a second time—he sacrifices himself and gives up his life. This alienation overcomes estrangement—the antagonistic separation from God caused by sin. This alienation, we should notice, is very much like the heroism of service in which noble consciousness alienated itself, sacrificed itself up to the point of death, and created an estranged state power. Christ's alienation, however, which goes as far as his actual death, does not create an estranged power, but rather overcomes estrangement and reconciles absolute being with human self-consciousness (*PhS*, 470–2, 474–5/*GW*, IX, 414–16, 417–19). We will have to explain how alienation can have such opposite consequences—how alienation in one case produces estrangement and in the other overcomes it.

Neutral alienation is important for revealed religion because for it God and human self-consciousness are not and cannot be identical—the human being is not God. For Hegel, however, the implication of Christianity *is*, in fact, that human nature and divine nature are the same (*PhS*, 460, 471/*GW*, IX, 406, 415). Absolute knowing will be able to grasp this identity (*PhS*, 461/*GW*, IX, 406–7), but for religious picture thinking they must remain different. Thus, "it is the difference which, in pure thought, is immediately *no difference*" (*PhS*, 466/*GW*, IX, 411).

For revealed religion, then, while this difference must remain, it does not obscure recognition, for "spirit is knowledge of self in a state of alienation of self: spirit is the Being which is the process of retaining identity with itself in its otherness."[7] As human consciousness alienates itself, surrenders itself, and serves God, it does not lose itself to an other as it did when it served the state. It preserves itself in its alienation. This is a neutral alienation. Consciousness recognizes itself, its true self, its essence, in God. Self-consciousness knows itself in its alienation from itself because the substance that self-consciousness confronts is not an external substance. It is itself, its own alienation, its own essence.

In culture, the self alienated itself, gave up its essence to the state, which then took on a life of its own, reacted against, and began to form and culture the subject. It was the subject's own alienated essence that existed at the estranged level of the state, but the awareness that it was the subject's own essence was lost to the consciousness of the subject. When we reach religion, this lack of recognition is overcome. One sees that in one's relation to the object, in one's relation to God, one is related to one's own essence. One's relation to God is a relationship purely within spirit—purely within mind. Nothing in any way external stands between. Nothing obscures the relationship. It is a relationship purely in thought, though at this point only in pictorial thought.

So we can say that alienation produces estrangement when we are unable to recognize that it is our own alienation that produces the object, and thus when we do not recognize that the object is our alienated essence. But if our alienation does produce the object, and if we recognize the object as our own essence, then alienation overcomes the estrangement. Alienation which led to estrangement was necessary to form, develop, and universalize the state and culture, which then could mold, develop, expand, and universalize the consciousness of individuals. If this alienation goes far enough, to a total alienation, a total surrender of self, a total abandonment of self to the other, and if this alienation takes place at a high enough level, in religion, in absolute spirit, in absolute mind, then the alienation becomes transparent. We see that the other is our essence and that we are its essence—and thus alienation overcomes estrangement.

Alienation that has gone far enough is no longer a giving over of self as a loss of self, it is a giving over of self as a substantialization of self. As we began to see in "Unhappy Consciousness" and then again in belief's struggle with Enlightenment, alienation, the surrender of self, constructed God as our projection, which however remained a beyond in which we were lost. Total alienation, total surrender of self, constructs God as an absolute and total reality in which the self is not lost. The self finds its essence in God and becomes one with God. The self becomes real, substantial, and absolute.

Hegel does not want to claim that ordinary Christian believers see that their alienation constructs God, though they certainly do see God as their essence. Only some see that we construct God. In the "Moral View of the World," Hegel thought that this was the implication of Kant's postulates of practical reason.[8] Nonphilosophical believers, however, would not normally believe that their alienation constructs God; they would instead engage in religious picture thinking. It is only absolute philosophical knowing that finally sees ultimate reality as its own and can be fully at home with it, and it can do so because it sees that it has constructed it.

In religion, then, we do not yet get a pure identity with God. Neutral alienation remains. We are not God and God is not simply us. There is a difference within unity—a neutral alienation. Unlike the alienation that leads to estrangement, the unity here is recognized as much as the difference. The subject is aware of the substance as its own essence. Subjects see their unity with God. Thus recognition is regained and estrangement overcome. But religious picture thought cannot admit that we are identical with God, or God would collapse for religious picture thinking, and all we would have would be ourselves. And with only ourselves, without God, we would not have the totality and absoluteness we gain through religion. Human subjectivity must remain different from God—neutral alienation must remain. Human subjectivity must be distinguished from God within a transparent unity with God.

This reconciliation with God is a reconciliation in picture thought. Hegel says it is still burdened with a beyond—still something distant (PhS, 478/GW, IX, 420–1). Religion succeeds, then, in overcoming estrangement and the alienation that leads to estrangement, but the neutral alienation that remains still distances us from the deity in a way that is only overcome in absolute knowing. Picture thinking or Vorstellung, for Hegel, keeps things separate, fixes them, and places them over against each other.

This distance from the deity that prevents us from seeing that the deity is identical with us is still necessary, then, to prevent the sort of collapse that we saw in culture. Scientific reason, we saw earlier, did not have this problem. It too constructed its world, but it always confronted its world as an object, a limit, an it, that it could not dissolve into itself. It was simply unable to—and thus this prevented a collapse into solipsism. The cultural realm, on the other hand, stood in need of, and thus had to generate for itself, a certain amount of otherness and estrangement if it was to avoid collapse. The only problem was that such estrangement also meant domination and oppression. What we have been in need of, we have seen, is a way to end this estrangement, and thus domination and oppression, but without producing collapse—that is the problem culture left us with. The solution to this problem we finally achieve in religion. This is what neutral alienation gives us. There is no estrangement present. In confronting God we confront our own essence—we are free and at home. Yet there is enough alienation, neutral alienation that does not produce estrangement, to prevent collapse. God is other than us, but in essential unity with us.

At the start of "Absolute Knowing," the final chapter of the *Phenomenology*, Hegel tells us that to reach the absolute, all that remains to be done is to get past this form of picture thinking. To do so, consciousness must see that its object is nothing other than itself (*PhS*, 479/*GW*, IX, 422). Hegel writes that to surmount this object of consciousness we must see that

> it is the alienation of self-consciousness that posits the thinghood [of the object] and that this alienation has not merely a negative but a positive meaning.... The negative of the object, or its self-supersession, has a positive meaning for self-consciousness, i.e. self-consciousness knows the nothingness of the object, on the one hand, because it alienates its own self—for in this alienation it posits *itself* as object, or the object as itself, in virtue of the indivisible unity of *being-for-self*. On the other hand, this positing at the same time contains the other moment, viz. that self-consciousness has equally superseded this alienation and objectification too, and taken it back into itself so that it is in communion with itself in its otherness as such.[9]

Let me try to explain what I think this very obscure passage means. Hegel says that the alienation of self-consciousness has a dual significance, a negative and a positive significance. The negative significance is that self-consciousness alienates itself and establishes thinghood (it is an objectification). The self manifests itself, expresses itself, and produces an object or a thing (e.g., the emperor, the monarch, or the state). This alienation leads to estrangement where the object turns upon us and dominates us.

On the other hand, the positive significance of this alienation is that the alienation of self-consciousness cancels and supersedes this negative alienation and also objectification. This is possible only because alienation produced the thing as its alienated self in the first place. When this is seen, alienation that leads to estrangement is overcome. What we must notice at this point is that there are not really two different forms of alienation—alienation that leads to estrangement and alienation that overcomes estrangement—as if they were two different processes or forces. There is only one process. The very alienation that leads to estrangement is also the alienation that overcomes the estrangement. When we come to see that it was our own alienation that produced the object as our estranged self in the first place, the consciousness of this fact means that we have overcome the estrangement of the object. We no longer see it as other. We see it as our self, our own product, our own essence. We are at home with it.

What about the fact that this estranged object has been dominating us? If the object has developed to universality through our alienation and if the object has molded us and lifted us to universality through its domination, we should no longer see the domination as domination, but as our own development and discipline. Moreover, since the estranged object was our own alienation, we should see that this domination and discipline was a self-domination and self-discipline. In Hegel's view, this domination (say, in a rational state) comes to be seen as our own freedom—as rational self-determination.[10]

In the above quoted passage Hegel also says that objectification is overcome. Alienation is an objectification. It produces an objective, external thing by objectifying self-consciousness. It produces an estranged object like the state, which can turn upon us and dominate us, or, as in religious picture thinking, a God who is no longer estranged but is still other than us while being one with us in essence. So when self-consciousness supersedes alienation and objectification this certainly means that any estrangement is overcome, but it also means that the otherness of picture thinking is overcome. It ends the objective, independent, external, over-againstness of the thing. The relation becomes one purely within mind—within absolute spirit. It is a relation purely in thought, not an objective relation. Our relation to God then is immediate—nothing stands between us. Nothing mediates. We do not even have an other in the sense of a picture. We have erased the line between phenomena and noumena. Human nature and the divine nature are the same (*PhS*, 460, 471/*GW*, X, 406, 415). Hegel says, "God is attainable in pure speculative knowledge alone and *is* only in that knowledge, and is only that knowledge itself, for He is Spirit" (*PhS*, 461/*GW*, IX, 406–7). This is the absolute. God is one with self-consciousness. All of reality is immediately present to self-consciousness.

III. The Absolute and Its Deduction

Alienation and estrangement are crucial to understanding Hegel's deduction of the absolute. They explain the relation of the absolute to consciousness. The absolute is not a mere fantasy or illusion of individual consciousness. The absolute is an alienation of cultural consciousness. The absolute, it is true, is not real in the way that God was traditionally taken to be real, that is, independently of human consciousness. The absolute is a construction of human consciousness. The fact, then, that the absolute is not a metaphysical ontotheological entity should make it easier for most to accept, as long, that is, as they can avoid the opposite and equally mistaken conclusion that it is a mere illusion. It is no more an illusion than are a monarch, the state, or any number of other cultural institutions that are also constructed. The absolute, like the state or the government, is an alienation, not a mere idea. It *is* an idea, but it is also a power, a force, a reality. It has a life of its own. It dominates and disciplines us. We serve it to the point of death. It cultures us. It raises us to the universal—to the absolute. It is not an illusion. It is reality—indeed, Hegel thinks, our highest and most powerful reality.

The absolute is a reality that has made us what we are. We could not exist as a culture without it. To imagine that we could decide that the absolute was not real and somehow eliminate it (if that were actually possible), would mean that we would cease to be who we are. Without our laws, practices, institutions, government, culture, religion, God, that is, without the absolute, we would not be the people that knows what we know, values what we value, aspires to our goals, and finds reality meaningful in the way that we do. No doubt we could change some of the elements of our absolute, even drop some of them, but to eliminate the absolute completely or to change it radically would make us some other people that we would not recognize.

Moreover, if being an individual means drawing upon a larger cultural-religious source that gets crystallized—individualized—in our action, then without the absolute we could not be the individuals that we are. Furthermore, if the self is a bundle of potentialities with no determinate core, if there is no transcendental self, then we only achieve a stable self through alienation that produces cultural institutions like government and the state, and ultimately God and the absolute, with the power to give us stable recognition.

It is often thought that the *Phenomenology* has a weak ending—that the last chapter is brief, vague, and obscure. It is at least possible, however, that the ending seems weak because it does not give us what we expect, and the reason for that could be that we expect the wrong thing. If we expect the absolute to be demonstrated, proven in the ordinary sense, we are expecting the wrong thing, and such expectations are certainly not fulfilled in the last chapter. If, on the other hand, we realize that God and the absolute are cultural-religious constructions, then we must see that those constructions have for the most part already been established in chapters VI and VII on culture and religion, and thus what we should expect in the last chapter would be something more like a wrap up and summary, which, in fact, is what we do find.

Concerning ordinary proofs for the existence of God, Hegel, in the *Logic*, writes:

> Demonstration, as the understanding employs it, means the dependence of one truth on another. In such proofs we have a pre-supposition— something firm and fast, from which something else follows; we exhibit the dependence of some truth from an assumed starting-point. Hence, if this mode of demonstration is applied to the existence of God, it can only mean that the being of God is to depend on other terms, which will then constitute the ground of his being. It is at once evident that this will lead to some mistake: for God must be simply and solely the ground of everything, and in so far not dependent upon anything else. And a perception of this danger has in modern times led some to say that God's existence is not capable of proof. (*L*, 74/*SW*, VIII, 114)

Needless to say, this is not the sort of procedure that Hegel employs in the *Phenomenology* to prove the absolute. He continues in the same passage from the *Logic*:

> Reason, however, and even sound common sense give demonstration a meaning quite different from that of the understanding. The demonstration of reason no doubt starts from something which is not God. But, as it advances, it does not leave the starting-point a mere unexplained fact, which is what it was. On the contrary it exhibits that point as derivative and called into being, and then God is seen to be primary, truly immediate and self-subsisting, with the means of derivation wrapt up and absorbed in himself. Those who say: "Consider Nature, and Nature will lead you to God; you will find an absolute final cause:" do not mean that God is something derivative: they mean that it is we who proceed to God himself from another; and in this way God, though the consequence, is also the absolute ground of the initial step.... This is always the way, moreover, whenever reason demonstrates. (*L*, 74–5/*SW*, VIII, 114–15)

This is the way that Hegel proceeds in the *Phenomenology*. He gives us, as I have put it, a Kantian-style deduction of the absolute. We start from experience but we take it as derivative. We ask what makes that experience possible. We must account for the conditions of its possibility—the necessary presuppositions of that experience. We must be able to account for every sort of experience that can be brought up and we must be able to give the conceptual presuppositions necessary to explain and justify that experience. This procedure drives us to the absolute because nothing short of the absolute will explain the totality of our experience.

Hegel's strategy is to show us that all is constructed—government, culture, our very selves, as well as all order in nature, society, and religion. Even

God is constructed. The concept of all this constructed experience held together as an ordered totality is the absolute. If we agree that Hegel has shown us that all experience and its order have been constructed—and each step in the *Phenomenology* has tried to subvert any alternative—then we have a deduction of the absolute. We must accept it as a necessary presupposition of our experience. If we do not accept it, if we reject it, then we would be left with nothing—we would reject the possibility of our experience. But that is impossible. We cannot deny that we have experience. We cannot deny that we have ordered experience. We either accept that we have constructed it, we either accept this construction as constituting the possibility of our experience, or we would be left with nothing. And it is obvious that we do not have nothing. That is the deduction.

We can now see that the absolute is also a necessary presupposition for the possibility of historical experience. History appears only on the last pages of the *Phenomenology* with the rise of the absolute (*PhS*, 492/*GW*, IX, 433). The earlier stages of the *Phenomenology*, I have argued, were abstracted from the historical and temporal. Thus, the course traversed by the earlier stages of the *Phenomenology*, Hegel says, is "not to be represented as occurring in Time. Only the totality of spirit is in Time" (*PhS*, 413/*GW*, IX, 365). For history to be possible, Hegel thinks, all of these earlier, separate stages have to be recollected (*PhS*, 492/*GW*, IX, 433). Recollection—the German word is *Erinnerung*—implies a collecting together, an ordering, and an inwardizing. What we must see is that the concept of such recollection—the collecting together, ordering, and inwardizing of the preceding stages of the *Phenomenology*—is nothing but the concept of the absolute. The absolute is the concept of all of our experience, all of the previous stages of the *Phenomenology*, holding together as an ordered totality, as a totality which is grasped by absolute knowing, that is, inwardized or idealized. This must be further explained.

In the *Philosophy of History*, we have seen, Hegel thinks that history involves a relationship between individuals, nations, and God, that is, a relationship between individual consciousness, cultural consciousness, and religious or absolute consciousness. Without religious or absolute consciousness, which we abstract from until the last pages of the *Phenomenology*, we could not have history. We could not have a sense of an ordered totality of things, their course, and our objective place in that totality. Without the recollection that the absolute makes possible, we could not hold together all the details, all the thises, heres, and nows, all the bits and pieces of our social, cultural, and religious world. They would not form a connected and meaningful experience for us. They would not form our identity. We would not have a sense of where we were coming from and where we were properly going. Hegel's emphasis on history, time, and recollection (Erinnerung), I would like to suggest, takes us back to Kant's threefold synthesis of the imagination, which we discussed in chapter 1.

In what Kant calls the synthesis of apprehension, the imagination takes up impressions, apprehends them, and makes them modifications of the mind belonging to inner sense and thus subject to time (CPR, A98-100, A120). The synthesis of reproduction then retains, remembers, and reproduces these perceptions. We must be able to reinstate preceding perceptions alongside subsequent perceptions and hold them together in a temporal series (CPR, A100-1, A121). We must be aware that what we think is the same as what we thought a moment before (CPR, A103). Otherwise we would have nothing but disjointed chaos. We would not be able to connect earlier and later perceptions of an event or object—they would not belong together for us.

These representations, however, cannot be reproduced in any order just as they happen to come together accidentally. The reproduction, Kant thinks, must conform to a rule according to which a perception is connected with some one representation rather than another (CPR, A121). The concepts or categories of the understanding provide these rules—rules for the necessary reproduction of the manifold (CPR, A103, A106; see also B233–A201). A synthesis of recognition in a concept is necessary to determine the specific order, relation, and reproduction of representations. Without this concept we would not have an object, but merely a disjointed series of isolated, remembered sensations.

This threefold synthesis, for Kant, also requires a transcendental unity of apperception (CPR, A106–7). If not, then the diverse multitude of sensations, the temporal flux of experience, would not belong to a single consciousness and thus could not belong to me. The flux must be unified within a single self for experience to be possible—or else this flux of images would not be *my* flux of images. It would not be *my* experience. There would then be no experience—but "merely a blind play of representations, less even than a dream" (CPR, A112; see also A122, B132–3).

Hegel agrees with all of this, it is just that he does not think it can hold up at the level of perception. It can only hold up at the level of the absolute. This unity cannot be brought about by a transcendental self or transcendental unity of apperception—it cannot be brought about by individual consciousness. It can only be brought about by the self-consciousness of a culture. We must historically re-collect all the details of our natural as well as our social, cultural, and religious experience—we must apprehend them, hold them together, and reproduce them in a temporal sequence. Moreover, they cannot be held together in any old way—they must be held together in a meaningful and purposeful order. They must be regulated by a concept, paradigm, or idea. Only this can form *our* identity—*our* self-consciousness. Only this can give us *our* history, *our* meaning and significance, our world—otherwise it would not be a meaningful experience at all. Unless experience is re-collected, brought together in a coherent and purposive whole, unless a culture constructs it as its history, as its identity, it would simply be a chaos of unconnected data—"a blind play of representations, less even than a dream."

. It is the absolute that allows us to re-collect the details of our experience, order them as a meaningful and purposive totality, and form all of this into our identity as a culture. Without this idea, without the absolute, European culture would not have an identity that brought together scientific accomplishments, free political institutions, respect for individuals, universal moral principles, global aims and purposes, and so forth. Without the historical re-collection made possible by the absolute, our experience could not amount to even as much as the different stages of the *Phenomenology*, separate and unconnected steps laid out side by side. Our experience would be fragmented; it could not form a totality. We could certainly not have a whole world with aims, aspirations, and accomplishments. Only with the absolute can such steps be shaped into a historical narrative with an order, purpose, and necessity. Only then can we get a history that is coming from somewhere and going somewhere, with each scene grasping and expressing some essential step in a whole development. As this history moves toward the realization of its aims, it unfolds, actualizes, and realizes the absolute—it moves a culture toward its truth. What the absolute makes possible is a historical sense of identity, of having a course, of moving toward and realizing something valuable and significant. Moreover, this historical narrative includes all—all that is important, significant, valuable, and true.

For Hegel, as we have seen in chapter 4 (see "Culture and Estrangement"), freedom must have four moments. First, we must be subjectively free. The subject must not confront anything alien, other, or outside. What it confronts must be its own. Subjects must be able to act on their personal commitments, passions, and interests. But this is not enough. There are, after all, slaves and subordinates who do not question their subordination—they may even love their masters. Second, then, actions must be right. They must be rational. They must be universalizable. They must accord with a categorical imperative. But still this is not enough. This is mere abstract freedom. Freedom that has not been realized is not yet real freedom. It must be concretized, institutionalized, embedded in the world in which we live. Our laws, institutions, customs, traditions, and practices must also be rational so that our feelings, attitudes, interests, and thus our actions will actually be formed in accordance with reason. If we are to be free, reason cannot tyrannize over feelings as in the French Revolution. Reason, feeling, and action must accord and they must reinforce each other.

But even this is not enough. It is not enough that we merely act in accordance with the customs and traditions of our nation. The fact that we

were born in a particular nation with its customs and traditions is an accident. It is not enough even that our customs and traditions agree with
reason. Reason is perfectly capable of blindness, as when Enlightenment
reason attacks belief for doing much the same as what Enlightenment reason
itself does. Universalizability cannot tell us whether private property or communal property is right. We need a deeper ground than this. Our customs
and traditions, even our ability to reason and to embed this reason in our
institutions, is not enough. Like Antigone we need a sense of being right, not
just in agreement with custom, tradition, or reason. Our customs, traditions,
and reason must be able to find themselves objectively and absolutely right.
This is what God or the absolute provides. They give us the highest sense of
right that we can have.

This is not to say that the absolute gives us a place to stand outside or
above culture and reason. The absolute is arrived at and constructed
through the use of reason within particular cultures. Nevertheless, in
thinking as deeply as we can think in our culture, in pushing as far as we
can push, we can achieve, and we need to achieve, this sense of what is
absolutely right. Take as an example our own culture's conception of
equality, a conception that at the very least rules out slavery, unequal
treatment before the law, overt discrimination, and so forth. How do we
ground the rightness of this conception? Certainly not empirically. If we
look around us in our world, people are actually quite unequal. On the
other hand, our commitment to equality, we certainly could say, is the
outcome of our customs, traditions, and history. But can we admit to ourselves that it has no deeper ground than this, that with a slight change in
customs, traditions, and history we would not have been, or might not in
the future be, committed to anything like our conception of equality? Is it
even enough to ground our commitment to equality on reason? Hasn't
reason been capable of powerful and subtle arguments for inequality as
well as a lot of other objectionable things? Hegel certainly thinks so. A
commitment to equality needs a firmer ground than this—it needs a
ground that is more than merely rational. Hegel argues in many places
(e.g., PWHI, 54–5, 114–15/PW, I, 62–3, 136–7) that our commitment to
equality first begins in Christianity's notion of the equality of each person
before God and it then spreads and develops with the expansion of this
consciousness. In short, it is the absolute that ultimately grounds equality.
Without the absolute, our commitment to equality could not for-us
amount to more than an arbitrary, contingent, or lucky accident—and it
seems to me that we actually *do* have a commitment to equality that is
much stronger than that. Thus it seems we have a commitment to equality
that is more deeply rooted in our identity than can be accounted for without presupposing something like the absolute.

The absolute thus makes our cultural identity possible and gives us history as *our* history. Our history, moreover, is not just a series of events that happen to have happened to us. It has a meaning, a significance, and a purpose. Furthermore, it is not just a history of the goals and aspirations of our particular culture. It is a history that has objective value and significance as world history. It reveals the hand of God, the advance of civilization, our national destiny, or something of the sort—for our culture it is objectively and absolutely right, true, and good. Nevertheless, this absolute does not escape being culturally relative, and we will shortly have to address this fact.

Does any of this prove the absolute? It seems to me that it does establish the absolute as a necessary idea that we must presuppose to be able to explain how we are, have become, and will continue to develop as ourselves. And that is all we need for our deduction. The absolute is a conception that our culture needs to explain to itself the possibility and the reality of its experience.

To reach this absolute, however, Hegel thinks we must move beyond picture thinking (*PhS*, 478–9/*GW*, IX, 420–2). For Hegel, "God is attainable in pure speculative knowledge alone and *is* only in that knowledge, and is only that knowledge itself" (*PhS*, 461/*GW*, IX, 406–7).[11] If all we have is a picture-thought-of-the-absolute, then when we realize that we have constructed this picture thought, we might well decide that the absolute has not been proven, and so, one more time, the fact that we see we have constructed the thing will bring about its collapse. But if we get beyond picture thinking, if we get to pure speculative thought, then thought and being, thought and the absolute are one. Speculative thought does not picture, point to, indicate, or refer to an object beyond it or other than it. If the absolute *is* thought and thought *is* the absolute, when we come to see this, what is there that can collapse? Collapse occurs because we are not certain that our thought-of-the-thing and the thing are one. But in pure speculative thought we do not have, as we do in picture thinking, a thought over against a thing with which it must correspond or could fail to correspond.

It is relatively easy to see that the absolute is thought. We construct it. Our culture thinks it up. It is harder to accept the absolute as reality, all of reality with nothing outside. If readers doubt this, the only thing they can do is to work through the *Phenomenology* again, reexamine thinking's various attempts to push its object outside of thought, to establish something really out there beyond thought, and to rereflect on Hegel's attempts to show us that thought continually fails to set up an other than thought. And so, Hegel thinks, we must finally accept the absolute as all of reality *and* as thought.

At any rate, the absolute that we reach in chapter VIII is not merely one more experience, one more form of consciousness, one last step in the long series of stages that the *Phenomenology* takes up. The absolute in one sense is nothing new—it is simply the totality of what we have already been through in the *Phenomenology*. In another sense, however, it is quite new in that it is a different perspective on all that has preceded. It is the paradigm that allows us to re-collect, organize into a whole, and understand the connections between all that has preceded (*PhS*, 491–2/*GW*, IX, 432–3). It takes it all up, makes it a part of a whole, and leaves nothing out.

Moreover, like a scientific paradigm, the absolute cannot be directly proven or disproven, certainly not in the sense that we can measure it against external reality or by some other independent criterion. It is the paradigm itself that allows us to study reality, establish a measure, form a criterion, and we can do so only within the paradigm.

Moreover, if we reject, as Davidson has shown us we must, the notion that conceptual schemes can be applied to already existent, external, non-schematized contents, if schemes and contents cannot exist apart from each other,[12] this helps us to see why we cannot think of the absolute as a conceptual scheme apart from the totality of its contents. We cannot separate thought from being or idea from reality. If we accept the notion that conceptual schemes and their content cannot be separated, and if we have been driven by Hegel's arguments to accept the absolute as the conceptual scheme that must be presupposed to explain the possibility of our ordered experience, if we cannot get out of this, then we must accept the absolute as real. We cannot dismiss it as a mere idea without reality, thought without being, or scheme apart from content. There would be no content without this scheme, no reality without this idea, no being without this thought. The absolute and the world are inseparable. The absolute could not have arisen without the world and the world would not be the world we experience without the absolute.

If we do not want to accept the totalization involved in the absolute, if we cannot accept that the absolute is all of reality with no outside, we might instead think of the absolute as a continuous process of self-subversion. We have seen that in claiming to be absolutely all of reality, the absolute incites the other that has been excluded and marginalized—it provokes the other to subvert the absolute. A new absolute must then be constructed that includes the other at its center. Thus, the absolute can be thought of as a continuous process of pushing the other to subvert it—a continuous process of bringing all outside inside. It is a process in which the absolute is even willing to sacrifice itself for the other, that it might be resurrected in the other in truer form.

The absolute in any era is not a fixed and final actualization of all potentiality—certainly not for any later era. For a particular era, the absolute is the ultimate, all that era can possibly think. As soon as it can think beyond the absolute, as soon as it recognizes something other, the absolute begins to be subverted. As a culture works on its reality, constructs it, transforms it, sooner or later it will find that something that was inessential, marginal, and unreal becomes central, important, and quite real. If our paradigm, if the absolute cannot accommodate this new reality—and sooner or later it will not be able to—then the absolute is not all of reality, not the absolute. At that point we are in need of a new absolute and culture will set about constructing it. Hegel speaks of "the tragedy which the Absolute eternally enacts with itself, by eternally giving birth to itself into objectivity, submitting in this objective form to suffering and death, and rising from its ashes" (NL, 104/GW, IV, 458–9; see also PhS, 6/GW, IX, 14).

The absolute can be likened to a Kantian regulative idea, an idea of reason that makes it possible for us to conceive the world as a unified and consistent totality, a concept that we must have and cannot do without. For Hegel, however, the absolute is not a mere appearance and does not involve transcendental illusion. It is real. Moreover, the absolute is unlike a Kantian regulative idea in that it is not something we eternally seek but are nowhere near achieving, never will achieve, and must not achieve. This is not to say, for Hegel, that we have finally achieved the absolute in the sense that we have all its content in fixed and final form. We must even admit that as far as content goes, the process of the absolute's realization will never be completed. But by the absolute we do not mean any particular content or specific worldview that has become fixed and final; we do not mean a particular system that has triumphed over all others. By the absolute, we mean a general *concept* of totality with nothing outside—and we *have* attained the *concept*. We have attained the idea or paradigm of a unified totality of all truth as our *own*—truth embedded in our cultural institutions, practices, values, and conceptions. Moreover, we are even driven by this conception. If someone can show us an exception, we are obliged to accommodate it. Any exception subverts the absolute. Moreover, our absolute invites such subversion, though it will not die without being resurrected. As Burbidge puts it, "The only thing that is genuinely absolute, that is without any condition and any restriction, is not an entity identified by a noun but a living process in which each absolute realization of spirit is overturned in favour of another that is more truly absolute."[13] When it is said, "The king is dead, long live the king," what is meant is that a particular monarch has died, but that the nation's king continues on in the form of another holder of that office. So, when the absolute is subverted, we might say, "The absolute is dead, long live the absolute." What we took to be absolute, we have come to see, fell short of the absolute, but has now been resurrected as the absolute.

What are we to say then? Does the deduction of the absolute work? Merold Westphal does not think so. He argues that in the *Phenomenology* Hegel holds two different and irreconcilable positions. First Hegel holds in agreement with modernity that all thought and experience are inextricably caught up in their historical and cultural situation. At the same time, Hegel also holds that while philosophical thought can never free itself from this historical and cultural conditionedness it can transcend it without abandoning it. In the second half of the *Phenomenology*, Hegel attempts to trace the development of such a consciousness that finally transcends its historical-cultural conditionedness and relativity. In short, he attempts to reach the absolute. Westphal thinks he fails.[14]

It is not clear to me that Hegel does fail. What we see in the *Phenomenology*, and especially in its last half, is that absolute knowledge is a concept that grows up and is worked out in a specific culture—a culture that comes to believe that its knowledge is capable of being absolute. Is this to say that its knowledge really is absolute? Well, I think we can say that it really is absolute for-this-culture. But is it more than just this culture's vision of things? Well, yes, for-this-culture. We have a culture that believes its knowledge is absolute and takes this claim to be a noumenological claim. Of course, there is no way to establish this except within the phenomenological conceptions of this culture (*PWHI*, 108/*PW*, I, 128–9; *PhS*, 335/*GW*, IX, 298; *L*, 44/*SW*, VIII, 82). Isn't this to transcend historicism and cultural relativism without abandoning them? Why doesn't this satisfy Westphal? After all, what else is possible?[15]

I suggest that Hegel did not fail to reach the absolute, understood as most people who claim this failure understand the absolute, because he was never after such an absolute in the first place. We are all situated in a particular culture and in a particular historical period. From that location we can aspire to the absolute—and it is even important that we do so, if we are to develop. But that will always be to seek a truth on the horizon of culture, historicity, and relativism, not to leave these behind and actually get to an absolute beyond them. Hegel stands somewhere between the naive positivist who thinks that truth unmediated by culture or history is possible and the radical postmodernist who completely denies this and thinks the concept of truth should be dropped. For Hegel, truth can be approached only within a cultural paradigm, but what is approached can be truth. In the past, certainly, Hegel was interpreted as an extreme absolutist. More recently, he has been interpreted as a relativist. To correctly understand him, I think, we must hold together and refuse to let go of either of these sides. Hegel is simultaneously an absolutist and a relativist.

But is this acceptable? Can we admit that it is we ourselves who have constructed what we take to be absolute in and for itself? If there is no transcendental self, if the self is only an indeterminate bundle of deeds and potentialities, if it needs an absolute to recognize it, shore it up, and make it real, can it construct this absolute itself? Well, where else is the absolute supposed to come from? The absolute certainly cannot exist *for-us*, it cannot be our own, unless we construct it. We must see that this tells us something about ourselves. Despite the fact that we are mere indeterminate bundles of potentialities, we have the potentiality to construct an absolute that for-us exists in and for itself. If we recognize our potential, if we overcome our inferiority complex, we can see that we do have the potential to construct a reality that can recognize us and make us solid.

Besides, there is no other alternative. We have a radical reciprocal dependency here. The absolute depends on us and we depend on the absolute. There would be another alternative, it would be possible for us to dismiss the absolute as mere illusion, if we actually had solid, stable, fixed transcendental selves with which we had constructed the absolute—that is, if we were Kantians and took the absolute to be a mere regulative idea involving transcendental illusion. But in fact we have seen that we have no such selves. We have seen that the self cannot exist without recognition. If the self is unable to gain sufficient recognition for itself and its objectifications, if the self is a mere bundle of deeds and potentialities, as Hegel has tried to show us throughout the *Phenomenology*, then we cannot have a coherent self without an absolute to grant it absolute recognition. It is just that among the objectifications of this self must be counted that very absolute itself. To hold that the absolute is illusion would mean, if we accept that there is no transcendental self, that we have no way to explain a stable unified self—step by step the *Phenomenology* has tried to show us that no other explanation will suffice. Moreover, we cannot simply accept the absence of a stable unified self, as some postmodernists seem to think we can, because—we saw as early as the first section of chapter 1 above—in the transcendental deduction Kant shows us that without a stable unified self we cannot explain the possibility of organized and coherent experience. Without a unified self we would have no experience—less even than a dream. But we obviously do have organized and coherent experience. How, then, is such experience possible? The *Phenomenology* has tried to rule out all other explanations. It is only possible if there is an absolute, and an absolute is only possible if we have constructed it. That, it seems to me, is to give a deduction of the absolute.[16]

IV. A Culturally Relative Absolute

We can put it off no longer. We keep promising to take it up. We must finally face up to a discussion of cultural relativism. If the assumptions we make force us to presuppose the absolute, but those assumptions are culturally relative or ethnocentric, what sort of absolute do we end up with? If we claim that the absolute exists in and for itself, but yet always qualify this by adding that this is so for-us, what does it mean to say that the absolute exists in and for itself?

The first thing that must be said is that cultural relativism is often—if not usually—caricatured by those philosophers who attack it, thus making it easier for them to dismiss.[17] The relativist is supposed to hold that the values of one culture are no better than those of any another culture, that the "right" thing to do in any particular culture is whatever that culture says it is, that the values of one culture cannot legitimately be criticized by members of another culture, and thus that ultimately there is no real truth when it comes to values, merely what different cultures hold to be true.[18]

This is *vulgar* cultural relativism. A *serious* cultural relativist, I will try to argue, would not—or should not—hold any of these views. For example, one cannot hold that somehow every culture simply, straightforwardly, and without question establishes what is right for that culture. In our culture, at least, it is quite possible to disagree with values that others hold. It is even possible to completely reject the mainstream values of our culture. Nothing is more common in Western culture. We might even say that for Western intellectuals, mainstream values have been flatly rejected nearly as often as they have been accepted.

A serious cultural relativist—and I want to argue that Hegel is a serious cultural relativist—holds, or should hold, two things: first, that all consciousness is formed, developed, and influenced within a particular cultural context in a specific historical era, and, second, that such cultures and historical eras can differ significantly. We must notice immediately that these two commitments—that serious cultural relativism—in no way precludes the possibility that a particular culture may have access to real truth. After all, from the fact that there have been different scientific paradigms, must we conclude that there is no scientific truth or that one paradigm is just as good as another? Serious cultural relativism does not preclude truth, it just implies that we cannot have access to it unless we come to understand it in and through a particular cultural and historical context.[19]

I keep talking about what serious cultural relativists hold, or should hold because the caricature of relativism has become so pervasive among philosophers that people who sensibly hold to, and should hold to, what I call "serious" cultural relativism, can easily end up very confused because they take cultural relativism to mean what I call "vulgar" cultural relativism, and so they reject cultural relativism—despite the fact that they really *are* cultural relativists. I want to argue that we must clearly distinguish vulgar from serious cultural relativism and that we should reject only the former. Moreover, we should not only accept the latter but should come to better understand it—which the bogie of vulgar cultural relativism often prevents us from doing.

For example, Wood's assessment of Hegel on these matters is as follows:

> Hegel sees that the only possible way of really escaping ethnocentrism is gradually, through the actual self-development of reason, which is always rooted in a determinate cultural tradition. Of course, on this path there is always the danger that what the most progressive tradition calls rational may be a function of its own biases and limitations. No doubt its judgment of alien cultures and traditions will always be based to some extent on partial blindness and ignorance (as we can now see that Hegel's own judgments about non-European cultures often were). Yet a fallible, culturally conditioned, and historically limited reason is the only reason we have. Its unavoidable limitations do not take from it the right to comprehend and judge the world as best it can, while continuing to criticize and develop itself. Nowhere will we find anything with a better right.[20]

I am in basic agreement with this assessment. Moreover, I think that what Wood is describing here is serious cultural relativism and, thus, that what he is showing us is that Hegel is a serious cultural relativist. Wood, however, subscribes to the vulgar definition of cultural relativism. Thus he rejects cultural relativism and concludes that Hegel is not a cultural relativist: "Alternative doctrines such as...cultural relativism are not at all well suited to defending a tolerant and receptive attitude toward other cultures. Relativism dogmatically claims that the values of different cultures are all equally valid, each for its own members. From this it follows directly that if you happen to belong to a narrow-minded and intolerant culture, then you are positively *required* to be intolerant. Relativism falls into this self-defeating position because it denies that there is a standpoint above and outside all cultures and then (self-contradictorily) tries straightway to occupy such a standpoint."[21]

Suppose, as cultural relativists do, I claim that I do not believe in any standpoint above and beyond all cultures from which we can judge, assess, or make general claims about other cultures or culture in general. Have I just made a self-refuting claim—one that in fact implies a standpoint above and beyond all cultures from which I am able to see that there are no standpoints above and beyond all cultures? I do not think a serious cultural relativist can be so easily trapped. The serious cultural relativist is—or should be—quite aware that the rejection of a standpoint above all cultures, like any other claim, is a claim made from within a particular culture. And despite the fact that such a claim is made from within a particular culture, there is nothing that automatically precludes—unless we embrace vulgar relativism—this claim from being true. Cultures, as far as I can see—certainly our culture—can have a perspective on other cultures or on culture in general, and it could be true. It is still a perspective from within a particular culture. We could also, with some effort, take the time to enculturate ourselves into another culture, or in more than one culture. In this way we could begin to compare cultures and come to see that while we still believe there is no place to stand outside or above all culture, it is quite possible to develop a perspective that is bicultural, multicultural, or that represents a hybrid mixture of cultures. I fail to see anything self-refuting here. Indeed, I suspect the by now standard argument that cultural relativism must be self-refuting is a dogma that has not been thought through very carefully.

But suppose I could be convinced that cultural relativism is self-refuting. I still would not think that this was the real issue at stake here. The real issue is not whether or not it is self-refuting to deny the existence of a standpoint above all culture; the real issue is whether or not one can actually have a standpoint above all culture. And if one cannot, then anticultural relativists who think they can make valid judgments from a standpoint above all culture are the ones who have blundered here, despite the fact that they may remain unsullied by self-refutation.

What is especially objectionable, however, is to think serious cultural relativists would hold that if you live in an "intolerant culture, then you are positively *required* to be intolerant." Herskovits argues that no anthropological relativist known would sanction such a claim (CR, 66). In fact, if we stop to think about it, it is rather astonishing how many people consider it a knockdown argument against cultural relativism to point out that if cultural relativism were true then there would be no way to object to someone like Hitler—presumably because in Nazi culture Nazi values would simply have to be accepted as right. But clearly, one would not have the slightest difficulty in finding cultural resources—within German culture of the Nazi era—with which to criticize and reject Nazi values. To name only the most obvious resources: all of Christian morality, all of Kantian morality, a great deal of Hegel, Marx, and even Nietzsche. What could anyone have in mind in thinking that a German living in the Germany of the Nazi era could not criticize the values of that era?

The enemies of cultural relativism, however, even if they were to be presented with volumes of actual criticism directed at Nazi values, would respond, I suspect, that such criticism could not consistently claim to have shown that Hitler was *objectively* wrong, that if cultural relativism is taken to be true, such critics could only consistently claim to have produced criticism that was culturally relative. Well, yes, serious cultural relativists would respond, that is because we are all cultural beings, not gods. All views, for the cultural relativist, will be embedded in particular cultures (or, if we include bicultural or multicultural individuals, combinations of cultures). That does not mean they cannot be true. The attack of the enemy of cultural relativism has not given us any reason to think that serious cultural relativists cannot muster good arguments against Nazi values. In fact, enemies of cultural relativism often do not even seem interested in the details of such arguments themselves; what is objectionable is just that they are the arguments of cultural relativists. What such an attack amounts to is the claim that cultural relativists (whatever their arguments might be or however good they are) cannot claim some official stamp of objectivity gotten from some mysterious authority above and beyond all culture. But so what? Of course they do not have such a stamp. All that cultural relativists aspire to—and all they need aspire to—are good arguments. What else is there? If their arguments are good ones, then to think that a commitment to cultural relativism somehow undermines their arguments is just as bizarre as to think that a rejection of cultural relativism will itself make the arguments of the enemy of cultural relativism any better. Such views, when spelled out, are quite unconvincing, yet they seem to be implied in widespread and common attacks on cultural relativism.

If one is an enemy of cultural relativism, then, how might one go about combating it? Many contemporary thinkers will concede to cultural relativism that our thought, as Wood put it, "is always rooted in a determinate cultural tradition," that it is "fallible, culturally conditioned, and historically limited," and that in judging other cultures it will always "be based to some extent on partial blindness and ignorance."[22] As Rorty puts it, there are no skyhooks or supercultural observation platforms to allow us to escape from our acculturation (OR&T, 2, 213). Such thinkers will admit that the values of Western culture cannot, as they traditionally were, be taken as simply objective. Certainly such values cannot be forced upon others if we are to avoid being imperialistic. So far, we have nothing but serious cultural relativism. But if such thinkers fear cultural relativism because to them cultural relativism means only vulgar cultural relativism—which implies to them that their own values would be no better than any other values[23]—what can they do? One thing they might do is embrace ethnocentrism, simply insist without any objective ground that the values of their cultural tradition are superior. Rorty explicitly, self-consciously, and even brazenly takes this approach, while other tamer souls conceal the fact from us (and perhaps even themselves), but end up pretty close to this position also.[24]

Rorty's views are worth considering here. He wants to reject any sort of Kantian identification with a transcultural and ahistorical self and to replace it by a Hegelian identification with our own community understood as a cultural and historical product (OR&T, 177). At the same time, he takes up Davidson's attempt to avoid cultural relativism by attacking as incoherent the possibility of incommensurablility. Cultural relativism, Davidson thinks, implies incommensurable conceptual schemes. However, the notion of incommensurable conceptual schemes, Davidson tries to show us, is unacceptable. Therefore the possibility of cultural relativism cannot be sustained.

Conceptual schemes are supposed to be "ways of organizing experience;...systems of categories that give form to the data of sensation;...points of view from which individuals, cultures, or periods survey the passing scene. There may be no translating from one scheme to another, in which case the beliefs, desires, hopes, and bits of knowledge that characterize one person have no true counterparts for the subscriber to another scheme. Reality itself is relative to a scheme: what counts as real in one system may not in another."[25]

The dominant metaphor here, Davidson thinks, is that of different points of view. And he argues that different points of view can only make sense if there is a neutral and common coordinate system that lies outside all conceptual schemes on which to plot these different points of view. For Davidson, however, as for Rorty, there is "no chance that someone can take up a vantage point for comparing conceptual schemes by temporarily shedding his own." Indeed, Davidson rejects in general the very possibility of separating scheme from content. The claim that we can have an organizing system and something waiting to be organized is a dogma of empiricism that cannot be made intelligible. If we cannot establish such a common coordinate system outside all schemes, then we cannot make sense of different conceptual schemes. Moreover, if we can translate from one language into another, as Davidson tries to show we can, we must give up the notion of different conceptual schemes. Davidson concludes that we cannot "be in a position to judge that others had concepts or beliefs radically different from our own."[26]

Rorty agrees with Davidson that there is no God's-eye point of view, no skyhook that can free us from the contingency of having been acculturated the way we were (OR&T, 13). He also follows Davidson in rejecting a scheme/content distinction (OR&T, 9). And consequently he rejects the notion that we construct reality out of some indeterminate goo (OR&T, 5). Rational inquiry does not involve conceptual schemes that organize reality, but is merely the continual reweaving of a web of beliefs (OR&T, 26, 217). Cultural relativism requires incommensurable conceptual schemes and Rorty rejects this possibility (OR&T, 26): "Alternative geometries are irreconcilable because they have axiomatic structures, and contradictory axioms. They are *designed* to be irreconcilable. Cultures are not so designed.... The distinction between different cultures does not differ in kind from the distinction between different theories held by members of a single culture" (OR&T, 26). In different cultures we just have different webs of belief.

I must say that I find much of this misconceived. In the first place, an a priori argument against incommensurability just does not seem the proper way to go. We should study particular cases empirically and see to what degree we can actually translate conceptions from one culture to another. It is true that complete and total incommensurability is not very likely. We could, after all, search for someone who is bicultural, or we could spend twenty-five years enculturating ourselves into the other culture so as to become bicultural ourselves. We could, at the point at which we can understand both cultures as well as any ordinary person in each (which means, of course, that there would still be a lot that we would not understand), take a concept or set of concepts from one culture and actually see how difficult it would be to translate into the conceptual scheme of the other culture. It could be quite easy or it could be difficult and complex, requiring awkward, convoluted, and roundabout ways of expressing the concepts. It could be that the set of concepts from one culture can be roughly translated into a set of concepts in another culture but that the two sets do not have exactly the same range of connotations and nuances. And so when speaking at length in one conceptual system, what follows and makes sense easily and clearly may not at all follow and make sense as clearly or easily in the other conceptual system. At this point in our translation we might have to throw in some explanatory footnotes to explain the range of meaning of one set of terms and how it cannot be captured exactly by any set of terms in the other scheme. We might even have to write an article or even a book to fully explain this difficulty—in the extreme case we could spend up to twenty-five years enculturating others into the culture whose concepts we are trying to explain. Let me take a very simple example from an article by Spinosa and Dreyfus. They speak of a person who belongs to two different traditions within a single culture, a person who is both a committed Christian and a practicing psychologist:

> As a psychologist, she sees certain people who exhibit dysfunctional coping skills as the same people who, when engaged in Christian practices, she would venerate and call saints.
>
> If the Christian psychologist tries to merge her two sets of types, then she will get inconsistencies. Suppose, quite naturally, that the Christian defines the type *saint* as a person worthy of imitation because he manifests his love of God by not caring where his meals or clothing come from. Suppose, too, that as a psychologist our Christian defines the type *dysfunctional person* as a person to be cured of his irresponsible disregard for planning. Then, the Christian psychologist could easily see how the types *saint* and *dysfunctional person* would apply to the same person at the same time and also see that one could not consistently claim that the same person is one whose behavior is simultaneously to be imitated and to be eradicated; that is, the Christian psychologist would see that the types are inconsistent.[27]

And so with Davidson and Rorty I doubt that we are going to find, as we do not in this example, anything that we cannot finally translate from one scheme to another. Nevertheless, in disagreement with Davidson and Rorty, to the extent that we have difficulty in translating, I think that we do want to say, if not that we are left with a degree of incommensurability, at least that we have had difficulty in establishing commensurability. We certainly want to say that we can end up with *inconsistency*. And this Rorty and Davidson do not seem very willing to concede.

Second, in order to identify differences between conceptual schemes that might be more or less difficult to make commensurable, I do not at all agree that we need a neutral and common coordinate system outside all schemes. I agree that supercultural observation platforms, skyhooks, and God's-eye views are impossible. What I do not agree with is the notion that we need any such thing to pick out differences between conceptual schemes. To agree would be like holding that the only way to translate from German into English would be by using French. Our bicultural person does not need a third cultural perspective, let alone some supercultural perspective, to see differences between the two cultures. Each conceptual scheme can be viewed from the perspective of the other and differences will emerge.[28]

Moreover, I do not agree with the notion that from the fact that we cannot separate content from scheme, and thus that there are no neutral systems, supercultural observations platforms, or skyhooks outside all conceptual schemes, we should conclude that we must give up the idea of conceptual schemes. Anyone who understands two conceptual schemes, anyone who is bicultural, can see the difference between the schemes. And even if it is the case that there is no final and complete incommensurability, nevertheless, commensurability could be difficult enough to achieve that we would want to preserve the notion of different conceptual schemes. Furthermore, I do not think Davidson and Rorty have established enough to force us to give up a conception of serious cultural relativism. We certainly do not need final and complete incommensurability; we need no more than difficulty in establishing commensurability to need a conception of cultural relativism.

It is quite clear that the conceptions of one culture, even if they are not at all incommensurable with, even if they are easily understood by, another culture, can be quite at odds with that culture, and if accepted could produce radical change, could even be harmful and destructive of that culture. Imagine a traditional and communal nonmarket culture that finds capitalist consumerism imposed upon it. It may well understand capitalist consumerism or come to—there is nothing *incommensurable* here. Yet capitalist consumerism could well destroy the traditional and communal nonmarket culture. Or this society may understand capitalist consumerism, fear it, and reject it as the Great Satan. In either case, it seems to me, we do not have incommensurability, we have understanding and translatability, but we still have different conceptual schemes and cultural relativism. We may understand very well the ideals of another culture, yet find them incompatible with our own values in ways that are not like simple differences within one conceptual scheme.

Cultural relativism does not require incommensurability. One of the main functions, if not the main function, that the concept of cultural relativism is intended to serve is to alert us to the possibility that when dealing with other cultures and traditions it may require a great deal of work to get beyond an initial stage in which it will be an illusion to think we understand what is going on when we think we understand what is going on. Cultural relativism does not imply that we cannot get beyond this situation, it implies that it takes some doing.

If we are going to judge anyone, certainly if it is going to lead to blaming them, harming them, or punishing them, we are obliged at the very least to try to judge them accurately, and to do that we must know what they have actually done. To misjudge them could lead to serious immorality. The function of the concept of cultural relativism is to remind us how difficult it may be to avoid misjudging another culture's practices. For the concept of cultural relativism to be meaningful it is not at all necessary to hold that it is impossible to avoid misjudging the practices of another culture—it is not at all necessary to claim incommensurability. The concept of cultural relativism serves a necessary and valuable function if it simply warns us away from conceptual laziness, if it reminds us how much work we have to do to avoid misjudging another culture, if it teaches us that we must understand the other culture as well as we understand our own before we are likely to be able to judge its practices without misjudging them.

I have another disagreement with Rorty. When he rejects the notion of cultural construction on the grounds that it presupposes an indeterminate goo that is then shaped into reality, one wonders whether Rorty himself has forgotten his basic commitment to the Davidsonian principle that we cannot separate content from scheme. There is no indeterminate goo for the social constructionist. Reality always presents itself as already schematized, interpreted, or constructed. What was there before we interpreted, schematized, or constructed reality? Not indeterminate goo, but some *other* interpretation, schematization, or construction. This is to say that we can reinterpret, reschematize, reconstruct, we can change paradigms. And in doing so we can see the difference between two paradigms without a supercultural observation platform, simply by comparing the two. I do not see that conceptual schemes, paradigms, or cultural relativism have been eliminated.

At any rate, Rorty finds it far worse to be accused of relativism than ethnocentrism (*OR&T*, 30). In fact, he enthusiastically embraces ethnocentrism. Since there are no skyhooks to lift us out of our acculturation, our best chance "is to be brought up in a culture which prides itself on *not* being monolithic—on its tolerance for a plurality of subcultures and it willingness to listen to neighboring cultures" (*OR&T*, 14). It is best to admit that our Western belief in equality is just ethnocentric and to say, "So what?" (*OR&T*, 207). Rorty admits that our ideals may be local and culture bound, yet, nevertheless, claims they may be "the best hope of the species" (*OR&T*, 208).

Rorty also looks forward "to a time when the Cashinahua, the Chinese, and (if such there be) the planets which form the Galactic Empire will all be part of the same cosmopolitan social democratic community" (*OR&T*, 212). In discussing how these different cultural groups can get along, Rorty adopts a distinction set out by Lyotard, a distinction between *litige* and *différend:*

> He defines a *différend* as a case in which "a plaintiff is deprived of means of arguing, and so becomes a victim," one in which the rules of conflict resolution which apply to a case are stated in the idiom of one of the parties in such a way that the other party cannot explain how he has been injured. By contrast, in the case of *litige* ... both sides agree on how to state the issues and on what criteria are to be applied to resolve them. ... My general reply ... is to say that political liberalism amounts to the suggestion that we try to substitute litigation for *différends* as far as we can, and that there is no *a priori* philosophical reason why this attempt must fail. (*OR&T*, 216–17)

If Rorty's liberalism were able to make headway in this direction, it would be quite admirable. But a great deal, if not most, of what he says about interaction between cultures points in the direction of différend more than in that of litige. To be ethnocentric, Rorty claims, is "to say that beliefs suggested by another culture must be tested by trying to weave them together with beliefs we already have" (*OR&T*, 26). Rorty does not suggest, however, that it is necessary that our beliefs be tested by the other culture in a similar way. But if not, how will it be possible to move toward litige, which requires that *both* cultures agree on how to state the issues and on what criteria are to be applied to resolve them? In fact, one wonders whether, for Rorty, our culture is expected to do enough testing of the beliefs of others to move *us* toward litige. He says that we "cannot leap outside our Western social democratic skins when we encounter another culture, and we should not try. All we should do is to get inside the inhabitants of that culture long enough to get some idea of how we look to them, and whether they have any ideas we can use" (*OR&T*, 212–13).

Hasn't the commitment to litige disappeared here? Rorty even says that to "be ethnocentric is to divide the human race into the people to whom one must justify one's beliefs and the others. The first group—one's *ethnos*—comprises those who share enough of one's beliefs to make fruitful conversation possible" (*OR&T*, 30). In a footnote, Rorty discusses the others, among them "primitive tribespeople." The beliefs of "such people do not present...'real options' for us, for we cannot imagine going over to their view without 'self-deception or paranoia.' These are the people whose beliefs on certain topics overlap so little with ours that their inability to agree with us raises no doubt in our minds about the correctness of our own beliefs" (*OR&T*, 30–1 n; see also 38). Isn't such an attitude likely to lead to a situation in which the plaintiff will be deprived of means of arguing, and so become a victim, that is, to différend?

For Rorty, it seems that with some people even discussion, let alone litige, is impossible:

> To refuse to argue about what human beings should be like seems to show a contempt for the spirit of accommodation and tolerance, which is essential to democracy. But it is not clear how to argue for the claim that human beings ought to be liberals rather than fanatics.... I think we must grasp the first horn. We have to insist that not every argument need[s] to be met in the terms in which it is presented. Accommodation and tolerance must stop short of a willingness to work within any vocabulary that one's interlocutor wishes to use, to take seriously any topic that he puts forward for discussion.... The view that human beings are centerless networks of beliefs and desires and that their vocabularies and opinions are determined by historical circumstances allows for the possibility that there may not be enough overlap between two such networks to make possible agreement about political topics, or even profitable discussion of such topics. (*OR&T*, 190–1; see also 203–4)

This not only excludes litige but, I must confess, it sounds suspiciously close to an admission of *incommensurability*. That, however, is supposed to be ruled out. Cultural differences, for Rorty, are not supposed to be "different in kind from differences between old and ('revolutionary') new theories propounded within a single culture. The attempt to give a respectful hearing to Cashinahua views is not different in kind from the attempt to give a respectful hearing to some radically new scientific or political or philosophical suggestion offered by one of our fellow Westerners" (*OR&T*, 215). But, clearly, we do not, or should not, dismiss new scientific theories that come along as not worth discussing. We cannot, or should not, hold that because there is not enough overlap between two such theories to make agreement possible our theory need not take the other seriously. But this is what Rorty does suggest we should do with some other cultures.

Rorty moves in opposite directions. When propounding the ideal of liberalism and boasting about its superiority, Rorty shuns cultural relativism, rejects the very idea of incommensurability, and puts forth litige as an ideal that should be established. But when under attack by critics of his liberalism, when pushed for a justification of his views, he simply becomes an extreme ethnocentric. Western liberal views are just superior. They do not need justification. They cannot be justified to everyone. He forgets all pretense of litige, comes dangerously close to admitting incommensurability, and virtually accepts cultural relativism.

Hegel too, I will argue, is ethnocentric, but far less so than Rorty. Hegel's absolute, it is true, makes claims that are just as ethnocentric as Rorty's claims. The absolute claims that it is everything and the other nothing. It claims to be all of reality and denies the reality of the other, but in doing so, the absolute incites the other to subvert it. It sets up a situation in which the other can show itself to be something and thus the absolute not to be everything—thus, not absolute. We would be trying to make such subversion impossible if, with Rorty, we were unwilling to even listen to the other and felt no obligation to justify ourselves before the other. Rorty does not want to give the other a chance to subvert his ethnocentrism. He simply insists that it is legitimate for Western democracies to be ethnocentric because they are so liberal, decent, and tolerant.

Herskovits argues that ethnocentrism "is the point of view that one's own way of life is to be preferred to all others.... It characterizes the way most individuals feel about their own culture ... and is to be viewed as a factor making for individual adjustment and social integration." It is only "when, as in Euroamerican culture, ethnocentrism is rationalized and made the basis of programs of action detrimental to the well-being of other peoples that it gives rise to serious problems" (CR, 21). Rorty certainly rationalizes ethnocentrism, and it is impossible for us to deny that in the past it has been the basis of very detrimental action toward other peoples. Rorty does not deny this, but it seems to me he sidesteps it. If the history of Euroamerican culture is considered honestly, even its most radical critics would have to concede with Rorty that there is a lot of good to be found in it. And, clearly, when Rorty is in the throes of his ethnocentric enthusiasm this is the West he has in mind. But at the same time, if we are to remain honest, we must also admit that a very great deal of evil can also be found in Euroamerican culture. Rorty does admit this: "We Western liberals have had the Gatling gun, and the native has not. So typically we *have* used force rather than persuasion to convince natives of our own goodness. It is useful to be reminded ... of our customary imperialist hypocrisy. But it is also the case that we Western liberals have raised up generations of historians of colonialism, anthropologists, sociologists, specialists in economics of development, and so on, who have explained to us in detail just how violent and hypocritical we have been" (OR&T, 219).

Rorty, we must concede, does recognize that Western bourgeois democracies are often accused, with good reason, of being racist and imperialist. His response, however, is to point out that they are also very worried and very critical about being racist and imperialist. In other words, one gets the feeling that for Rorty the good West is to be taken as the true West and the evil West, while it cannot be denied, is to be taken as an unfortunate and accidental exception to the rule. In short, one begins to suspect that Rorty is covertly operating with a form of essentialism that his theory would otherwise prohibit.

For example, Rorty is very critical of Heidegger for looking beneath the narrative of the West for the essence of the West and concluding that Stalin's Russia and Roosevelt's America were, metaphysically speaking, the same.[29] But to ensure that liberal democracy is different from Stalin's Russia doesn't Rorty himself covertly have to separate the good West from the evil West, make the former the essential West, and the latter an accident or exception, such that while it might be granted that in some respects we are accidentally like Stalin's Russia it can nevertheless be held that we are essentially different from it?

And make no mistake about it, if Rorty is covertly appealing to an essence here, his whole theory risks coming apart. Rorty so fears cultural relativism, which he understands as vulgar relativism (that is, that no values are better than any others), that to avoid such relativism he makes ethnocentrism the center of his theory—he simply asserts the superiority of the West. While it is quite clear, and he admits it, that such ethnocentrism cannot be grounded or justified, nevertheless, he must at least allay our fears that such ethnocentrism might lead to rampant racism or imperialism. He has to assure us that ethnocentrism is safe for the West. He has to assure us, in short, that we are a good West. But if he has to resort to essentializing the West to do this, don't we have to dismiss his argument? Isn't he just reversing Heidegger and isn't his view just as naive and unacceptable? But if he cannot guarantee that the West is a good West, then how can he persuade us that ethnocentrism is safe for the West? And if he cannot establish this then his whole theory starts to come unraveled. We would have no good reason to believe the West better than anywhere else and the bogey of vulgar cultural relativism, which all of this was to avoid, would again raise its ugly head for Rorty.

How do we decide whether a nation is good or evil? Nations are big and complex entities in which we are always going to find a mixture of good and evil. We could certainly find a lot of good—certainly good people and good deeds—even in Hitler's Germany or Stalin's Russia. In fact, if we were to count only the mere quantity, the sheer number, of individual deeds, we might even find that there were more good deeds than evil ones in Hitler's Germany or Stalin's Russia. What makes such nations evil is that, besides the quantity of their evil, its quality—its depth and intensity—stands out, predominates, and outrages. If we reject essentialism, then there is going to be no way to argue that despite a great deal of evil of sufficiently outrageous quality, we can still consider a particular nation to be *essentially* good. And if this is so, then it is not at all clear that we would not have to admit that the United States—to use Ronald Reagan's infamous phrase—is an evil empire.

Not many nations, after all, can claim a record equal to ours. We begin as a nation by stealing land from and carrying out genocidal attacks on Native American Indians. We continue well into the second half of the nineteenth-century to hold slaves—indeed, our commitment to slavery was such that it led to a civil war, to date the bloodiest war we have fought. We are the only nation to have engaged in a superhuman effort to build an atomic bomb and to have actually used it, not once but twice, against the Japanese, while at home imprisoning without due process citizens of the United States of Japanese ancestry. We are also the only nation to have dropped napalm in a war, this time on the Vietnamese. We are a country with a long and ugly history of racism and imperialism, and it does not seem to me that even today we are sufficiently embarrassed by this nor have we done anywhere near enough to overcome it.

It is certainly the case that there have been many anthropologists, historians, philosophers, and what have you who have worried, complained, and been quite critical about all of this. That, however, does not seem to me to make the world safe for ethnocentrism. It certainly has come nowhere near erasing the legacy of racism or eliminating its continuation against blacks, Native American Indians, and others. To argue for ethnocentrism in such a society, to suggest that that is not only a safe thing to do, but "the best hope of the species" (*OR&T*, 208), is, it seems to me, to be buried a good bit too deeply in liberal ideology.

V. Hegel's Ethnocentrism and Racism

There is no denying that Hegel too is ethnocentric. As Houlgate puts it, Hegel holds "that certain civilizations are more advanced than others and that the culture and civilization of the Western Christian tradition is the most profoundly self-aware and thus most advanced in history." Houlgate, however, claims that this "involves no doctrine of 'cultural imperialism' or 'racial superiority.' (Hegel is not concerned with given racial differences between people because in his view human self-consciousness is what determines a civilization's character, and this self-consciousness can be changed and developed through education.)"[30] I think it is quite true that Hegel is not a racist in the strong sense—he is not a theoretical or scientific racist. And I will even try to argue that Hegel's ethnocentrism is not as bad as Rorty's. But to suggest that there is no significant racism or ethnocentrism to be found in Hegel's thought, if this is what Houlgate means, or that Hegel's view of European superiority is acceptable, is indefensible. Houlgate does not actually give us an argument that Hegel is not racist or ethnocentric. He uses a few scare quotes and rhetorical flourishes to avoid taking the issue on directly and then slides into a defense of Hegel's concept of freedom. We must face the issues squarely.

The course of history, for Hegel, is understood as one grand narrative concerning the realization of spirit. It is a narrative that does recognize, affirm, and respect cultural difference. At the same time, though, this narrative organizes different cultures into a historical and spiritual unity by ranking them. Cultures are ranked in terms of their level of awareness of the absolute, as well as according to their contribution to its development. Indeed, without the absolute there would be no ranking, or at least not the sort of ranking we find in Hegel, which puts northern European culture at the top. Perhaps any conception of historical development would imply some sort of ranking. If history is thought to be coming from somewhere and headed toward something, some will inevitably be found to be further along this course and others further behind. At any rate, to rank peoples in this way is not, for Hegel, to say that a backward nation may not prosper or realize its goals; it is just to say that it does not participate "in the life of the Idea" (*PWHI*, 60/*PW*, I, 69). That is, it does not rank highly according to the absolute—the ranking system of northern Europe.

Hegel, as I have said, recognizes and respects differences between cultures. He also thinks that each culture has a character that gives it an identity and forms its particular spirit—in short, he is an essentialist. Moreover, he describes the character of some peoples such that it is impossible to avoid the charge of racism. In the *Philosophy of Mind,* Hegel writes:

> Negroes are to be regarded as a race of children who remain immersed in their state of uninterested *naïveté.* They are sold, and let themselves be sold, without any reflection on the rights or wrongs of the matter. The Higher which they feel they do not hold fast to, it is only a fugitive thought. This Higher they transfer to the first stone they come across, thus making it their fetish and they throw this fetish away if it fails to help them.... They do not show any inherent striving for culture.... They do not attain to the feeling of human personality, their mentality is quite dormant, remaining sunk within itself and making no progress, and thus corresponding to the compact differenceless mass of the African continent (PM, 42–3/SW, X, 73–4; see also PWHI, 172, 174, 177, 179–81, 185, 190/PW, I, 212, 214, 218, 220–2, 227, 234).

In the introduction to the *Philosophy of History*, Hegel also writes, "Since human beings are valued so cheaply, it is easily explained why *slavery* is the basic legal relationship in Africa. The only significant relationship between the negroes and the Europeans has been—and still is—that of slavery. The negroes see nothing improper about it, and the English, although they have done the most to abolish slavery and the slave trade, are treated as enemies by the negroes themselves" (*PWHI*, 183/*PW*, I, 225). And he adds, "The negroes have no sentiments of regret at this condition of slavery. When the negro slaves have laboured all day, they are perfectly contented and will dance with the most violent convulsions throughout the night" (*PWHI*, 219/*PW*, I, 269).

Hegel makes it sound as if the main responsibility for slavery lies with Africans, while poor unappreciated England is the only one objecting to slavery. Here, it would seem, the dialectic has passed well beyond the stage of Bacchanalian revel—having drunk too deeply of the cup of prejudice it has fallen overboard. Hegel also says, "As regards the specific difference of the various national minds, in the African race this is insignificant in the highest degree; even in the Asiatic race proper it is much less apparent than in Europeans, in whom mind or spirit first emerges from its abstract universality to display the wealth of its particular forms. For this reason we propose to speak here only of the immanently varied character of the European peoples" (*PM*, 47/*SW*, X, 80).

This picture of Africans makes Hegel's ignorance of Africa quite clear. As Appiah has shown us, it is impossible to lump all Africans together as a single national mind with only insignificant variations or differences. It is wrong to assume that there is a cultural or linguistic homogeneity to Africa as a whole. In fact, there is an extraordinary diversity of peoples, cultures, religions, and languages. Appiah argues that whatever "Africans share, we do not have a common traditional culture, common languages, a common religious or conceptual vocabulary...we do not even belong to a common race."[31]

However, indigenous Americans fare even worse than Africans in Hegel's hands:

Although [the New World] did possess an indigenous culture when it was first discovered by the Europeans, this culture was destroyed through contact with them.... It was a purely natural culture which had to perish as the spirit approached it.... Nearly seven million people have been wiped out. The natives of the West Indian islands have died out altogether. Indeed, the whole north American world has been destroyed and suppressed by the Europeans.... Culturally inferior nations such as these are gradually eroded through contact with more advanced nations which have gone through a more intensive cultural development.... When the Jesuits and Catholic clergy first set out to acquaint the Indians with European culture and manners ... they went into their midst and prescribed their daily duties for them as if they were minors. ... I even recollect having read that a clergyman used to ring a bell at midnight to remind them to perform their matrimonial duties, for it would otherwise never have occurred to them to do so.... The negroes are far more susceptible to European culture than the Indians. (*PWHI*, 163–5/*PW*, I, 200–2)

Asians are ranked a bit higher: "In the Asiatic race ... mind is already beginning to awake, to separate itself from the life of nature. But this separation is not yet clear-cut, not yet absolute. Mind does not as yet grasp itself in its absolute freedom" (*PM*, 43/*SW*, X, 74–5). In Asia, spirit is still immersed in substantial existence and has not yet liberated itself to attain subjective freedom (*PWHI*, 199/*PW*, I, 245–6; see also *PH*, 111–12/*PW*, II, 267–9). In Hegel's view, "Orientals ... knew only that One is free ... the Greek and Roman world ... that Some are free," and the Germanic world will know "that All men as such are free, and that man is by nature free" (*PWHI*, 54–5/*PW*, I, 63). Due to the absence of subjective freedom, Hegel thinks that philosophical knowledge is impossible in the East (*ILHP*, 171/*EGP*, 231–2). Moreover, it is his view that India has made no cultural progress in over three and a half thousand years (*PWHI*, 13/*PW*, I, 5; see also *PRel*, II, 597, 602/*VPRel*, IIa, 492, 497). He thinks that China too is a static culture and that Chinese is an inferior language (*PM*, 216, 218/*SW*, X, 349, 351).

Arabs fare a good deal better. Among the "western Asiatics, especially the Arabs ... mind destroys the caste system and all its works which prevail in India, and every Mohammedan is free; despotism in the strict meaning of the word does not exist among them. Political life, however, does not yet achieve the form of a rationally organized whole, or a differentiation into special governmental powers" (*PM*, 44/*SW*, X, 76). Hegel also says of Islam that the "fanaticism of its adherents impelled them to conquer the world, but it was incapable of producing a state with a differentiated organic life and a system of laws framed in the interest of freedom" (*PWHI*, 111/*PW*, I, 132).

Hegel's attitude toward the Jews is quite ambiguous. It is Egyptian culture, for Hegel, that represents the transition from Asia to Europe, the latter beginning with ancient Greece. In his early theological writings, it is clear that Jewish religion ranks below Greek religion (*PCR*, 68–9, 154-7/*GW*, I, 282–3, 365–70). In the *Philosophy of History*, the spirit of Judaism even ranks below that of Egypt, which is seen as synthesizing various elements of Persian and Jewish spirit (*PH*, 198–9/*PW*, II, 460). In the *Lectures on the Philosophy of Religion* of 1824, however, it is clear that Jewish and Greek religion belong to the same stage.[32] In the *Lectures* of 1827, Jewish religion has even come to rank higher than the Greek (*PRel*, II, 669/*VPRel*, IIa, 561). In the *Lectures* of 1831, however, Jewish religion again comes to rank below the Egyptian and thus also below the Greek (*PRel*, II, 737–8/*VPRel*, IIa, 623–5).

When it comes to Greece, Hegel does not deny the origin of its religion and culture in Egypt and Asia. He does not, as other intellectuals of his era were beginning to do, claim that Greece was purely Aryan.[33] But Hegel does insist that the Greeks "so much changed, worked upon, turned around, and altogether made so different" this inheritance, that it became "essentially their own" (*HP*, I, 150/*SW*, XVII, 188). At any rate, we have entered the realm of European spirit:

> It is in the Caucasian race that mind first attains to absolute unity with itself. Here for the first time mind enters into complete opposition to the life of Nature . . . achieves *self*-determination, *self*-development, and in doing so creates world-history. . . . The principle of the European mind is, therefore, self-conscious Reason which is confident that for it there can be no insuperable barrier and which therefore takes an interest in everything in order to become present to itself therein. The European mind opposes the world to itself, makes itself free of it, but in turn annuls this opposition, takes its Other . . . back into itself . . . In Europe, therefore, there prevails this infinite thirst for knowledge which is alien to other races. The European is interested in the world, he wants to know it, to make this Other confronting him his own. . . . European mind . . . subdues the outer world to its ends with an energy which has ensured for it the mastery of the world. (*PM*, 44–5/*SW*, X, 76–7)

While Hegel denied that there were significant national differences to be found among Africans or Asians, this is definitely not his view of Europeans. Among Europeans he distinguishes different national characters and ranks them from lowest to highest in terms of their supposed degree of reflectiveness or intellect. Italians are at the bottom, then come Spaniards, the French, the English, and (you guessed it) Germans are at the top (*PM*, 47–50/*SW*, X, 81–7; see also *PH*, 420–1/*PW*, II, 886–7).

We have come to find it objectionable to lump people together in the way that Hegel does, to take a nation, culture, or race as having a common essence or character that will be expressed in each of its members. We find it especially objectionable if this leads to the assumption that individuals can represent, certainly that they can speak for their whole community, nation, or race. We would very definitely worry about letting Protestants speak for Catholics, southerners for northerners, right-wingers for left-wingers, or men for women.

Nevertheless, without losing sight of the need to recognize and respect difference, and without at all going back on it, we must at the same time agree with Hegel that there are national characters in some sense. We must concede that seventeenth-century Mexican culture will be different from twelfth-century Chinese culture and that both will be different from nine-teenth-century Canadian culture. Moreover, if we listen to members of one of these cultures at length, or read what they have written, we are not likely to mistake the culture they come from for one of the others. Moreover, while none of these cultures will be homogenous, while each will involve a great deal of difference, and despite cross-cultural similarities that may appear, nevertheless, we will find something common about nineteenth-century Canadian culture that will very clearly set it off from twelfth-century Chinese or seventeenth-century Mexican culture, though perhaps not so sharply from nineteenth-century culture in the United States. There is something to what Hegel is saying, despite the fact that he pushes it way too far, and especially so in the case of Africa and Asia.

At any rate, I think we must see that such ethnocentrism presupposes the absolute. For European mind to be able to view history as a long develop-ment culminating in itself as a highpoint, for it to be certain of the inferiority of others and of its own superiority, it must presuppose the absolute—or something very much like it. From his treatment of scientific reason out to conquer the world in chapter V of the *Phenomenology* to his ranking of cul-tures in the *Philosophy of Mind* and his treatment of the historical mission of Europe and America in the *Philosophy of History*, Hegel not only captures the ethnocentrism of Western culture but he shows us its philosophical under-pinnings. He reveals a drive to self-assertion, totality, and the marginalization of the other that appears over and over again in different forms of our experi-ence. He shows us how our conception of the absolute allows us to rank as objectively highest the qualities we have come to value as a culture. Without the absolute, all we would be able to say about ourselves would be that we are characterized by and especially value certain qualities: individuality, freedom, equality, rationality, and so forth. But it is not the case—certainly in the past and even for most people today—that we take these qualities merely to be qualities that many of us just happen to value, the mere result of cultural and historical happenstance. Rortian ethnocentrism—that is, ethnocentrism that is merely asserted without justification or ground—would not be adequate to explain our actual attitude toward these values. We rank them objectively as the highest qualities, we think they characterize us far more than they do others, and we think they raise us essentially above other cultures. For us to be able to think this—and we *do* think it—requires a presupposition very much like the absolute. Hegel's description of us as a culture that thirsts for knowledge as a totality, that is confident it will meet no insuperable barriers, that believes it will master the world, and that takes this as its mission, not only hits the nail on the head as a description, but implies the assumption of something like the absolute as a regulative idea. Hegel's absolute, I suggest, gives us a fairly accurate description and a reasonable understanding of ourselves, and thus is of significant value.

On the other hand, we cannot pretend that Hegel confines himself to merely describing Western ethnocentrism, imperialism, and racism. Unlike Houlgate, we must admit that Hegel actually endorses them and we must be clear that this endorsement is deeply objectionable. At the same time, however, it is something we should expect, if we think that Hegel has actually revealed to us the absolute of his age. If the absolute is all of reality self-enclosed, then in revealing it Hegel could not be giving us a mere description from outside. He could not give us a mere description that abstracted from involvement or commitment. Absolute knowing knows the truth of things and that includes their moral truth. And indeed nineteenth-century Europeans took their ethnocentrism, imperialism, and racism to be moral truths. Disagreement, of course, was not impossible, but it tended to be minimal.[34] Thus if we take Hegel to have revealed the absolute of his era, we cannot realistically expect him to have seen through it or gone beyond it to the extent that he could have described it but not endorsed it. Had he been able to really get beyond it, that would have implied a different era with a different and changed absolute, which then is the absolute we would expect him to have described—but then we could not expect him to have gotten beyond that absolute.

We must be clear, then, that Hegel endorses views that are ethnocentric and racist—some of them even horrific. We must object to these views and reject them. At the same time, however, in describing Western racism and ethnocentrism and in laying bare their philosophical underpinnings, Hegel gives us tools that will allow us to free ourselves from some of that ethnocentrism and racism. And, indeed, we have done so to some extent since Hegel's time. On the other hand, a good deal of the ethnocentrism and racism that we find in Hegel is still with us, and that too is something we should expect if Hegel has gotten the absolute right. We are not likely to have changed that much that soon.

How can we, anyway, compare one culture to another in order to establish superiority or inferiority? Cultures are far too complex to compare in any simple and straightforward way. Those who pretend to engage in such comparisons usually focus on a handful of concepts, values, or practices and decide on the basis of these few elements that one culture is lower, backward, or inferior and that the other is higher, more advanced, or superior. Moreover, what almost always happens (and maybe is even very difficult to avoid) is that the elements selected are ones that are central and significant in one's own culture while less central or significant in the other culture. Moreover, it almost always happens (and maybe is very difficult to avoid) that we emphasize what we take to be good about our own culture (while deemphasizing the bad) and we compare this to what we take to be bad about the other culture (while deemphasizing the good). I think it is rather clear that people from the other culture who were as knowledgeable about our culture as we are of theirs could give us a very different comparison, select different concepts, values, and practices, emphasize what is good in their culture and bad in ours, counter us point for point, and very possibly make as good a case for the superiority of their culture. To resist this, I suspect, will be to head toward an untenable form of essentialism—the *essence* of our culture is freedom and rationality whereas irrationality and aggression are the *essence* of their culture, or something of the sort. To identify essences in this way not only radically oversimplifies and is highly reductive, but there is no reason to believe that bias has been avoided in the selection of what is taken to be essential. Why is freedom rather than imperialism the essence of our culture? And why is irrationality and aggression rather than, say, concern for honor, the essence of the other culture?

If we decide that such essentialism is unacceptable, I think we will have to conclude that cultures are just too complex to effectively compare. We might imagine something like the following: two huge national libraries belonging to two different cultures, each library roughly equal in size and not containing more than a small number of the same texts. How would we compare the quality of these two libraries, let alone the rest of the two cultures? Scholars familiar with one library could spend decades (if not centuries) learning about and arguing with scholars from the other library. While this sounds like a very pleasant and fascinating project, it is not one that is likely to reach conclusive decisions. The scholars could very well achieve conclusive decisions as to which library contributed the most to the development of calculus, haiku, or the combustion engine, but they are not at all likely to agree as to what the value of calculus, haiku, or the combustion engine is or should be in the grand scheme of things, let alone how to understand the grand scheme of things. Serious cultural relativists do not argue that all cultures are equal, they simply think it extremely difficult if not impossible to work out comparisons in an impartial way (CR, 23 ff., 36, 267).

At any rate, we cannot deny that Hegel engages in such comparisons and rankings; we cannot deny that he is ethnocentric. Even if he does give us a philosophical explanation of Western ethnocentrism, his own endorsement of it is objectionable and unacceptable. We must firmly reject this aspect of Hegel's thought. But can we really do that? Can we simply reject his ethnocentrism while at the same time accepting other aspects of his thought? I suggest that if we were to reject Rorty's ethnocentrism, there would not be much left—certainly no justification for his views. Rorty, we have seen, simply insists on the values of his tradition; he simply and openly holds without objective ground or justification that the values of his culture are superior. If we reject such ethnocentrism, Rorty would have no argument left for preferring his own values, and thus Rorty's thought would dissolve into what he would perceive as the abyss of cultural relativism, that is, vulgar cultural relativism, which thinks it impossible to establish one view as better than any other. The question, then, is how deeply Hegel's ethnocentrism cuts. Is it essential to his thought and inextricable from it?

Hegel's ranking of cultures, his ethnocentrism, and his racism, I think, do not cut that deeply. We can reject them, disown them, and still find that most of the rest of Hegel's thought will remain largely unaffected. After all, his ranking of cultures as well as his explicit ethnocentrism and racism are found predominantly in later texts like the *Philosophy of Mind* and the *Philosophy of History*, not in earlier texts like the *Phenomenology*. Moreover, if we reject and drop Hegel's ethnocentrism, he will not fall into the abyss of vulgar cultural relativism, as Rorty would. What we would be left with for Hegel, I will try to show, would be a healthy, insightful, and serious cultural relativism capable of positively affirming the value of difference.

In the first place, then, to see that Hegel's racism does not cut as deeply as other forms of racism, we must notice that Hegel is not a scientific racist. He is a racist. He believes that races have different characters that rank them higher or lower in the historical scheme of things, but at the same time, we must see that he explicitly rejects a scientific justification for any of this.

To start with, Hegel states unequivocally in the introduction to the *Philosophy of History* that slavery "is unjust in and for itself, for the essence of man is freedom" (*PWHI*, 184/*PW*, I, 226). He does add, however, that the human being "must first become mature before he can be free. Thus, it is more fitting and correct that slavery should be eliminated gradually than that it should be done away with all at once." Human beings must attain "a higher ethical existence and a corresponding degree of culture [*Bildung*]" (*PWHI*, 184/*PW*, I, 226). Nevertheless, Hegel is explicit in the *Philosophy of Mind* that blacks "cannot be denied" this "capacity for education [*Bildung*]" (*PM*, 42/*SW*, X, 73–4). He also argues:

> With respect to the diversity of races of mankind it must be remembered first of all that the purely historical question, whether all these races sprang from a single pair of human beings or from several, is of no concern whatever to us in philosophy. Importance was attached to this question because it was believed that by assuming descent from several couples, the mental or spiritual superiority of one race over another could be explained, indeed, it was hoped to prove that human beings are by nature so differently endowed with mental or spiritual capacities that some can be dominated like animals. But descent affords no ground for

granting or denying freedom and dominion to human beings. Man is implicitly rational; herein lies the possibility of equal justice for all men and the futility of a rigid distinction between races which have rights and those which have none. (PM, 41/SW, X, 70–1)

Such natural or scientific arguments, for Hegel, are irrelevant. Moreover, Hegel argues that "the familiar proposition, All men are by nature equal, blunders by confusing the 'natural' with the 'notion.' It ought rather to read: *By nature* men are only unequal. But the *notion* of liberty...this single abstract feature of personality constitutes the actual *equality* of human beings. But that this freedom should exist...is so little *by nature*, that it is rather only as result and product of the consciousness of the deepest principle of mind, and of the universality and expansion of this consciousness" (PM, 265–6/SW, X, 412).

Thus, in the *Philosophy of Right*, Hegel claims that "all historical views of the justice of slavery and lordship, depend on regarding man as a natural entity pure and simple, as an existent not in conformity with its concept....The argument for the absolute injustice of slavery, on the other hand, adheres to the concept of man as mind, as something inherently free" (PR, 48/SW, VII, 111). Hegel goes on to say that we cannot regard humans as simply free by nature, but rather that mind or spirit is capable of developing this freedom (PR, 48/SW, VII, 111). He says that it "is part of education [*Bildung*]...that the ego comes to be apprehended as a universal person in which all are identical. A man counts as a man in virtue of his manhood alone, not because he is a Jew, Catholic, Protestant, German, Italian, &c. This is an assertion which thinking ratifies and to be conscious of it is of infinite importance" (PR, 134; see also 168–9 n/SW, VII, 286, 354–5 n).[35]

These texts clearly reject a scientific, natural, or theoretical fixing of races or peoples as inferior or superior. Such things are simply irrelevant. It is our concept of mind—a philosophical or cultural conception ultimately presupposing the absolute—that shows us that all are capable of education, development, culture, freedom, and equality. In this sense, Hegel is not a racist. On the other hand, Hegel definitely does not think that all races have actually developed to the same level as others, and because of this he ends up ranking them in an ethnocentric and racist way.

Appiah argues that many nineteenth-century thinkers held "that there are heritable characteristics, possessed by members of our species, which allow us to divide them into a small set of races, in such a way that all the members of these races share certain traits and tendencies with each other that they do not share with members of any other race. These traits and tendencies characteristic of a race constitute, on the racialist view, a sort of racial essence; it is part of the content of racialism that the essential heritable characteristics of the 'Races of Man' account for more than the visible morphological characteristics—skin color, hair type, facial features."[36]

If one thinks that such heritable characteristics establish more than skin color, hair type, or facial features, that is, that they establish moral or cognitive differences that could legitimate the unequal social treatment of different races, then one has scientific racism on one's hands.[37] It is clear in the passages quoted above from the *Philosophy of Mind*, the introduction to the *Philosophy of History*, and the *Philosophy of Right* that Hegel explicitly rejects such views. Such issues are not raised in the *Phenomenology*. However, we can look to Hegel's treatment of phrenology, physiognomy, and psychology in chapter V of the *Phenomenology*. If these sections do not simply reject as pseudoscientific all attempts to link moral character or cognitive capacities with heritable biological characteristics or external social conditions, they certainly call all such attempts into question. Phrenologists observe natural objects—skulls—from which they infer that certain bumps were produced by certain brain processes. From those brain processes they then make a leap to mind and infer specific traits of character. Psychologists move from outer circumstances to the inner individual and physiognomists from facial expressions to inner intentions. All of these attempts to infer inner character from outer and observable phenomena are rejected by Hegel in the *Phenomenology*. It would be difficult to imagine, then, that Hegel could turn around and accept as scientific the attempt to infer character or cognitive capacities from heritable racial characteristics.

We have to see, then, that insofar as Hegel thinks races have essences these essences are not understood in a natural, biological, or scientific manner. Rather, racial or national essences reside in mind or spirit. One might wonder what difference this makes. The answer would have to be that in the short term it would not make much difference at all, certainly not in terms of the amount of prejudice that could be expected. But in the long term it would make a difference because it is quite clear that mind or spirit cannot be seen as fixed and unchanging. It develops, evolves, and realizes itself. This means that all races are educable. The essence of mind is to be free—freedom is a potential waiting to be realized in all.

While it is certainly true that Hegel ranks peoples, races, and cultures, nevertheless, it is important to see that he also *includes* them. They are all part of mind or spirit and, as we have seen throughout our discussion of the *Phenomenology*, it is spirit that constructs the absolute. This is to say, I think, that all races and cultures have played a role in the construction of reality. It is true that Hegel thinks that northern Europeans are the ones who have taken this to its highest point. And it is also the perspective of northern European culture that it is the highest culture, that other cultures are less important and some of little or no importance, in short, it is its perspective that it is absolute. But, as we have seen, that only sets the stage for subversion by the other. Hegel even thinks that world spirit will soon pass on to the New World (*PWHI,* 170/*PW,* I, 209–10; A, II, 1062/*SW,* XIV, 355). Thus I think it essential that we understand the exclusion, rejection, or negation of other cultures dialectically. They cannot be simply or undialectically excluded. They are a part of spirit. As we shall see, they all contain truth. To try to exclude the other, to try to negate it, may well result in the sort of subversion the master undergoes at the hands of the slave.

Thus, each "national spirit represents a new stage in the conquering march of the world spirit as it wins its way to consciousness and freedom" (*PWHI,* 63/*PW,* I, 73). World spirit does not ultimately belong to any nation. The world spirit and a particular nation are identified for a time, but world spirit will go beyond that nation. It will even go beyond us. No culture, I suspect, can quite imagine world spirit moving past itself—no culture can but see such an event as tragic. But as world spirit reconstitutes itself from the ashes it will include at its center the other that had been excluded. Any culture, any absolute, any knowing excludes, distorts, reduces, and simplifies the other. Thus it is not only the other that needs a way in, but we need a way to disrupt ourselves, to undermine our prejudices, crack our narrowness, get outside ourselves. World spirit needs this to be realized—which is also to say that *we* need it as well as that the other needs it.

Thus, each nation that represents a new stage in the march of world history will look to the past, explain to itself where it is coming from, how it has gotten to where it is, and where it is going. It will weave all of its experience, values, and aspirations into a grand narrative, a narrative that without doubt will exclude, distort, and oppress the other, but a narrative that at the same time invites subversion and helps empower the other to go beyond it. Hegel says that it is only through heterogeneity that spirit acquires the power of realizing itself as spirit (*PH,* 226/*PW,* II, 535).

We must also say that despite Hegel's racism and his ranking of cultures he does not seem to put much emphasis on racial or cultural purity. In fact, consistent with his commitment to heterogeneity, he argues that most cultures that have been at the forefront of world history developed out of a racial-cultural mix. This is certainly Hegel's view of the Greeks and the Romans. In particular, he does not deny Greece's Egyptian origins, as Bernal shows us other Germans were soon to do (*PH,* 226, 283/*PW,* II, 535, 665; A, II, 1048/*SW,* XIV, 336).[38] Hegel also holds that the same sort of intermixture can be found in Italy, Spain, Portugal, and France. However, the Germanic nations, that is, Germany, England, and Scandinavia, "have maintained a consistent tone of uninterrupted fidelity to native character" and "*Germany Proper* kept itself pure from any admixture" (*PH,* 349/*PW,* II, 778). Hegel does not, it seems to me, push this any further, and he does not, as far as I can see, suggest that purity is better than admixture. In fact, the development of spirit would seem to require heterogeneity (*PH*, 226/*PW*, II, 535).

Moreover, I think we have to say that Hegel is a multiculturalist. If we were to ask ourselves what we would hope to see several hundred years down the road—a single world culture into which all particular cultures had been absorbed and assimilated, or many different cultures preserving distinct characteristics—it is quite clear that Hegel would prefer the second alternative to the first. He does not want one common global culture to which all peoples assimilate. As Hoy puts it, "Hegel is opposed to Kant's 'cosmopolitan' ideal of a universal history in which social and cultural differences are gradually dissolved as we try to produce a society in which everyone is like everyone else." Hegel "prefers an account that will identify the specific characters of different peoples and recognize differences between different times and places."[39] Despite the fact that he ranks cultures, I think we have to say that Hegel values and at least to some extent even respects their differences. He certainly wants to tolerate these differences. He even thinks that the modern nation ought to be pluralistic enough to tolerate Quakers, Anabaptists, and Jews without expecting them to assimilate (*PR*, 168, 168–9 n/*SW*, VII, 353–4, 354–5 n). Hegel holds to a concept of spirit in which all are inherently free (*PR*, 48/*SW*, VII, 111). Nevertheless, he does not want cultural identities absorbed into abstractions or submerged under universals. It is only within the spirit of one's particular culture, he thinks, that freedom can develop.

If, after all is said and done, we decide that Hegel's racism and ethnocentrism do not cut that deeply, then, when we go on to condemn and reject them, there should be no special reason why we could not still accept much of the rest of Hegel's thought. We certainly should be able to admit that he has shown us how the ranking of cultures has been central to Western thought and to the construction of a Western identity, and we should be able to accept this while at the same time we can and should refuse to accept Hegel's endorsement of this ranking and of the superiority of northern European culture. In rejecting his ethnocentric and racist bias in favor of northern European culture, we would end up with simple cultural relativism.

Let me try to put this another way. Let me distinguish between an everyday cultural perspective and a philosophical metacultural perspective. From the everyday cultural perspective, within one's own culture, when thinking and acting, it is perfectly normal to be ethnocentric—to prefer one's own practices, conceptions, and values. Herskovits even suggests that healthy individual adjustment and social integration require this (*CR*, 21). In fact, it is probably impossible to escape being ethnocentric. We are products of our culture. We think in its categories. Nevertheless, we can also adopt a philosophical metacultural perspective from which we see that our culture's practices, conceptions, and values are one particular way of viewing and relating to things and that there are other ways. We can compare different cultures. I do not wish to suggest that a metacultural perspective is a supercultural perspective. I do not think it can launch us outside our culture, give us a God's-eye view, or put us on a supercultural observation platform. The point I wish to make here is simply that while it is perfectly normal and most of the time relatively unproblematic to be ethnocentric at the everyday cultural level, it is a totally different thing to be ethnocentric at the philosophical metacultural level. The latter can even lead to imperialism and oppression.

Though Rorty certainly does not advocate imperialism or oppression, we must see that he is advocating ethnocentrism at the philosophical metacultural level. He holds that Western values are superior to those of other cultural traditions. I suggest that this is seriously problematic. At the same time, it cannot be denied that Hegel too advocates ethnocentrism, the ranking of cultures with northern Europe at the top, and that he too does this at the philosophical metacultural level. What I am suggesting is that we can reject Hegel's ethnocentrism at this level. Since it does not cut that deeply (for all the reasons I have given above), we can simply dismiss it. What we will be left with in Hegel will be an excellent description of ethnocentrism at the everyday cultural level—that is, an excellent description (as we have seen in earlier chapters) of how we construct our institutions and are shaped by them, how this forms our values, conceptions, practices, and identities, and how we take this to be absolute. Of course, we have to admit that European culture does also go on to think itself absolute at the philosophical metacultural level, superior to other cultures, and that as we have just said Hegel endorses this also. But this we can and should reject—and can do so without any serious problems. In fact, we might even suspect that Hegel had set it up that way for us. He knew that northern Europe's absolute would be subverted some day—he thinks America is the land of the future. If that is so, if that is a part of the structure of Hegel's thought, then how could it be inconsistent with his thought for us to take his absolute as now subverted and to reject it? And if we can and do reject ethnocentrism at the philosophical metacultural level, if we reject the superiority of Western culture to other cultures, what we would fall back to is only ethnocentrism at the everyday cultural level, that is, to a culture that at the everyday level does take its absolute to be true *in and for itself*, but which at the philosophical metacultural level we could only understand as something true *for-our-culture*. In other words, at the philosophical metacultural level, since we reject ethnocentrism at this level, we would be left only with serious cultural relativism, the recognition that all thought develops within a culture and that cultures differ, no longer an ethnocentric insistence on cultural superiority.

VI. Cultural Relativism and Truth

I would like to argue that we should come to accept and endorse serious cultural relativism. It is only vulgar cultural relativism that we should reject, and if we do so then we will not be driven to advocate ethnocentrism at the metacultural level in order to avoid the notion that all values are as good as any others. To begin to make this argument, then, we must be quite clear about what serious cultural relativism holds and what it does not. It does not hold, it is only vulgar cultural relativism that holds, that all cultures and all cultural values are simply equal or that one is just as good as another. Serious cultural relativism, we have seen, holds something quite different, merely that it is difficult, if not impossible, to impartially compare things as complex as cultures.

Furthermore, serious cultural relativism recognizes that there is nothing in the anthropological fact of cultural relativism alone from which we could necessarily deduce a moral obligation to be tolerant of, or to respect, another culture. That would be to try to deduce values from facts in an unacceptable way. Cultural relativism, as Ladd points out, can only supply us with ammunition we might use if we decide on other grounds that we should argue against cultural intolerance.[40] For example, it can show us that a particular case of cultural intolerance would involve a conceptual blunder. If all consciousness is formed and developed within cultures and cultures differ, it may very likely involve a conceptual blunder to make a judgment about another culture without clearly understanding that culture and the ways in which it is different from one's own. I will try to argue, then, that we should in fact reject cultural intolerance, that we should promote respect for cultural difference, and that serious cultural relativism can assist us to do so in a way that vulgar cultural relativism will not.

The claim that cultural relativism can assist us in making a case for the toleration and respect of other cultures is a claim that is widely made and equally widely attacked. I want to agree with the attackers that vulgar cultural relativism, that is, cultural relativism that does not embrace a conception of truth, will not effectively contribute to making a case for real toleration, and certainly not for toleration with respect. On the other hand, I want to disagree with the attackers and try to show that serious cultural relativism, relativism that can and should embrace a conception of truth, can effectively contribute to making a case for toleration and respect.

Let me start with an example. Let us imagine a group of Western anthropologists who visit a traditional and non-Western people. For the anthropologists to get close enough to this people to be able to study them effectively, the people will, very likely, have to feel that the anthropologists have sufficient respect for them, their values, their culture, and so forth. It is not likely that the anthropologists themselves will hold all the values these people do, but imagine that the anthropologists are able to feel respect for the values of this people because the anthropologists believe that all values are subjectively held commitments, not objective truths. Our imagined anthropologists will be able to respect the values of this people because our anthropologists, while they do not think any values are true in and for themselves, do think that the values of this people are just as true and important for-this-people as the anthropologists' values are for-the-anthropologists or Western values are for-Westerners. In short, our imagined anthropologists are vulgar cultural relativists (which is not to claim that any real anthropologists are).

If this traditional people is able to see what is going on here, I think it very likely that they will feel duped and possibly even offended. Such matters vary from culture to culture, but imagine that these people, like most, if not all, traditional cultures, are not subjectivists. They do not think their values are valuable simply because they are theirs. They do not feel that value is posterior to commitment, as Lomasky puts it.[41] For them, value is prior to commitment. However they might express this in their culture, language, or conceptual scheme, we would say that they simply take their values to be true. They do not take their values to be subjectively objective. They take them not just to be true-for-themselves, but true-in-themselves. They are ethnocentric at the everyday cultural level, as Herskovits suggests (CR, 21–2).[42] The anthropologists can only accept the values of this traditional culture at the everyday cultural level because at the philosophical metacultural level they are vulgar cultural relativists—for them no values are objectively true but only subjectively held commitments. This, I suggest, fundamentally subverts a basic commitment of this traditional people—what we would call the commitment to the objective truth of their values. Furthermore, if the anthropologists conceal these subjectivist commitments at the philosophical metacultural level from this traditional people so as to allow them to believe that they simply and objectively accept their values at the everyday cultural level, the anthropologists deceive them. If the anthropologists do not, it is possible that this traditional people will not accept the anthropologists.

In other words, in the interchange between these imagined anthropologists and this traditional people, the very first thing to go is the basic commitment of the traditional people. The very condition of the interaction is predicated on the rejection of the nonsubjective character of their values. And the first thing to be established, even if only covertly, is the imposition of Western subjectivism. This is not real toleration. It is certainly not respect. It is a subtle way of imposing oneself on others and it is also a subtle form of ethnocentrism.[43]

I want to contrast this with the view that all peoples or cultures have, or at least can have, their own access to truth—and not just subjective, but objective truth. This is not such a strange notion. After all, individuals who visit foreign cultures often find something objectively valuable and true in those cultures, even if it is not compatible with the values and conceptual scheme of their own culture. Moreover, this is a view that we can find in Hegel. For Hegel, all philosophies contain some truth. The latest philosophical system "is the result of all the systems that have preceded it" (*L*, 23/*SW*, VIII, 59) and different philosophical systems, for Hegel, constitute the "progressive unfolding of truth" (*PhS*, 2/*GW*, IX, 10). Hegel writes of the history of philosophy:

> Although it may be admitted that every philosophy has been refuted, it must be in an equal degree maintained, that no philosophy has been refuted, nay, or can be refuted. And that in two ways. For first, every philosophy that deserves the name always embodies the Idea: and secondly, every system represents one particular factor or particular stage in the evolution of the Idea. The refutation of a philosophy, therefore, only means that its barriers are crossed, and its special principle reduced to a factor in the completer principle that follows. Thus the history of philosophy, in its true meaning, deals not with a past, but with an eternal and veritable present: and, in its results, resembles not a museum of the aberrations of the human intellect, but a Pantheon of Godlike figures. (*L*, 160, 168/*SW*, VIII, 205, 215; see also *SL*, 580/*SW*, V, 9–10)

In Hegel's view, any philosophy is the expression of the absolute as it has taken shape in a particular culture and age:

> If the Absolute, like Reason which is its appearance, is eternally one and the same—as indeed it is—then every Reason that is directed toward itself and comes to recognize itself, produces a true philosophy.... For Reason, finding consciousness caught in particularities, only becomes philosophical speculation by raising itself to itself, putting its trust only in itself and the Absolute.... Speculation is the activity of the one universal Reason directed upon itself. Reason, therefore, does not view the philosophical systems of different epochs and different heads merely as different modes [of doing philosophy] and purely idiosyncratic views. Once it has liberated its own view from contingencies and limitations, Reason necessarily finds itself throughout all the particular forms.... The true peculiarity of a philosophy lies in the interesting individuality which is the organic shape that Reason has built for itself out of the material of a particular age. The particular speculative reason [of a later time] finds in it spirit of its spirit, flesh of its flesh, it intuits itself in it as one and the same and yet as another living being. Every philosophy is complete in itself, and like an authentic work of art, carries the

totality within itself. . . . In [any] culture the appearance of the Absolute has become isolated from the Absolute and fixated into independence. But at the same time the appearance cannot disown its origin, and must aim to constitute the manifold of its limitations into one whole. The intellect, as the capacity to set limits, erects a building and places it [between] man and the absolute, linking everything that man thinks worthy and holy to this building, fortifying it through all the powers of nature and talent and expanding it *ad infinitum*.[44]

The history of philosophy, for Hegel, is "the history of one, eternal Reason presenting itself in infinitely many forms" (*DFS*, 114/*GW*, IV, 31). Each culture has the absolute before it. The absolute is the expression of that culture and that culture is the expression of the absolute. A culture shapes and constructs its reality and this reality shapes and constructs it. Philosophy attempts to grasp and express its culture's absolute and in doing so contributes to its construction. The absolute incites philosophical thinking, shapes it, and is realized through that thinking. All such philosophical systems contain truth.[45]

Rorty wants to separate two ways in which human beings try to give sense to their lives by locating themselves in a larger context. In the first, they tell stories about their contribution to a community or culture. They exemplify solidarity. They are loyal to a web of beliefs. In the second, they describe themselves as standing in relation to a nonhuman reality—they exemplify a desire for objectivity and they seek truth (*OR&T*, 21). Rorty, who considers himself a Hegelian of sorts (*OR&T*, 177), would persuade us to abandon the second approach and be content with the first. This, we must see, is not Hegel's approach at all. Hegel attempts to fuse *both* of these approaches. Solidarity, embeddedness in one's culture, expression of a web of beliefs, in short, cultural relativism, is not to be opposed to, it is to be understood as compatible with objectivity and truth. Hegel is what I have called a serious cultural relativist.

I want to try to give at least a very brief sketch, then, of the view that all cultures have, or can have, their own access to truth. I think this is the only view which, at the same time, (1) will allow for real respect for the values of others and thus solidly ground difference, pluralism, and multiculturalism; (2) will not lead to vulgar relativism and the erosion of values, that is, to the view that values are posterior to commitment and thus that all values are as good as any others; and (3) also will not lead to ethnocentric arrogance, that is, either to the claim that only one's own values are important or to a subtler imposition of one's own values on others.

This view makes room for pluralism and multiculturalism, but only by eliminating vulgar relativism. The anthropologist example sketched above shows that, contrary to the belief of its supporters, vulgar relativism is at odds with pluralism. In fact, if we think about it, it is rather strange that vulgar relativists would claim that they are the most tolerant of other cultures. Most existing cultures in the world today tend to be traditional cultures, and this suggests that they are likely to be committed to nonsubjective values, however that might be expressed in their particular conceptual schemes. The way the vulgar relativist or subjectivist puts this is to say that those values are merely-true-for-them. That is unacceptable. It is even a subtle form of ethnocentrism—the projecting of one's own subjectivism onto a different culture. The members of most traditional cultures would not be likely to accept this "merely-for-them." They take their values simply to be true. I do not see how any value system that does not accept such nonsubjective values can exist in a relationship of tolerance and respect with most traditional societies. The spread of vulgar relativism and subjectivism brings an erosion of values and, in fact, is perceived as such by many traditional cultures.

On the other hand, the solution is certainly not an arrogant ethnocentrism either of the traditional sort which simply and unthinkingly takes its own cultural views to be true and theirs false or of the Rortian sort that openly admits that its ethnocentrism is just ethnocentrism. The value systems of different cultures obviously differ, and I do not see how it is possible for anyone to seriously respect another system which they cannot take to contain some truth, let alone one they simply take to be false. Moreover, I can even less imagine anyone feeling respected by someone who does not even think it possible for their values to be true because all values are subjectively held commitments. The only way out, then, is to try to hold, and to show, that all systems have, or at least can have, their own access to truth.

This view is not without its problems. Increasingly, contemporary intellectuals react in horror at the very mention of truth—it is totalizing and terroristic. One can distinguish, however, between different notions of truth. The traditional notion of truth implied in Plato's allegory of the cave, for example, is quite objectionable. Philosophers climb up out of the cave, see the forms, gather up what Virginia Woolf would call pure nuggets of truth,[46] and then return to the cave to rule over those at the bottom for the latter's own benefit. The philosophers claim to see what the shadows in the cave are really about in a way that those at the bottom cannot. The latter see illusion. The philosophers see truth and consequently can have little respect for those at the bottom of the cave.[47]

This imposition by the philosophers is obviously objectionable if their truth is not really truth, if it is only subjective truth-for-the-philosophers, or if it is false. But even if it is real truth, this imposition is still objectionable. It is objectionable because those at the bottom of the cave do not discover the truth for themselves. They are not assisted to climb up out of the cave—they are ruled at the bottom. This makes real virtue impossible for them, even as Plato understands real virtue. They are not ruled by their own wisdom. They do not lead a reflective life. They are not guided by their own reason. They are ruled by someone else.[48] To be virtuous, even for Plato, we must ourselves come to know what is right and we must do it because it is right. This is impossible for those at the bottom of the cave. Imposing the truth on others, even if it really is truth, turns truth against itself and frustrates its value.

But this is very different from the notion of truth found in Plato's *Symposium*. There, following Diotima, Socrates speaks of an Eros, a love or a yearning for the good, the beautiful, and the true—which qualities we can find in physical bodies, in the soul, in laws and institutions, and ultimately and most purely in the forms. All things participate in, are attracted by, and yearn for the good, the beautiful, and the true. We might, on our own, suggest that cultures do the same sort of thing, that truth attracts all cultures, that they seek it and attempt to express it, each in their own different way, and that different aspects of the truth are accessible through different cultures. Truth can be approached through any culture, but each culture offers a different embedding of, a different perspective on, a different construction of, the truth. The important point here—at least implied by Socrates and Diotima—is that we strive for the truth, but we never finally get there. And that is crucial. Because if we actually got there—as in the allegory of the cave—we would cease to strive. Only beasts who are ignorant and gods who actually possess the forms do not strive for them.[49] To be human means to strive and to cease to strive is to cease to be human.

The virtue of this model is that (1) it posits an objective truth that incites us to strive for it; (2) it allows us to envision all cultures as having access to, but different perspectives on, truth; and (3) it does not allow us to impose this truth upon others. Since we never finally arrive at the truth, since we never reach a supercultural observation platform, we cannot judge other cultures from an absolute perspective up outside the cave. Truth must be taken as a process or a project—a regulative ideal—not an achievement. Truth as authority and power over others is eliminated as much as for the vulgarist relativism, but truth as an empowering goal and as an ideal of unity is preserved. And most importantly, in so far as we are concerned with truth, other cultures are due our respect, not simply because they too have an access to truth, but because they have access to different aspects of the truth than we do.

We can hope, then, that each culture will learn from other cultures and thus come to value them. The point here is that it is crucial that all cultures strive for the truth in their own way, and each culture have a stake in preserving difference, the different access of other cultures to the truth, not just to benefit those other cultures, but to benefit themselves. To destroy another culture or to impose one's own views upon it would close a door to the truth.

Hegel, it is quite clear, holds a view much like this. In the "Tübingen Essay," he argues that those who take the religious beliefs of other nations to be absurd and their own insights to be higher do not know what religion is.[50] In the *Aesthetics*, he goes much further:

> Mythology must...be interpreted *symbolically*. For "symbolically" means here only that the myths, as a product of spirit (no matter how bizarre, jocular, grotesque they may look, no matter how much too of the casual external caprices of fancy is intermingled with them) still comprise meanings, i.e. general thoughts about the nature of God, i.e. philosophical theories....Creuzer especially has begun...to study the mythological ideas of the ancients not, in the usual manner, externally and prosaically...on the contrary, he has sought in them their inner rational meanings. In this enterprise he is guided by the presupposition that the myths and legendary tales took their origin in human spirit. This spirit may indeed make play with its ideas of the gods, but, when the interest of religion enters, it treads on a higher sphere in which reason is the inventor of shapes, even if it too remains saddled with the defect of being unable yet at this first stage to unfold their inner core adequately. This hypothesis is absolutely true: religion has its source in the spirit, which seeks its own truth, has an inkling of it, and brings the same before our minds in some shape or other more closely or more distantly related to this truthful content....If...we dig down for the inner truth of mythological ideas...we may then justify even the different mythologies. But to justify man in his spiritual images and shapes is a noble preoccupation. (A, I, 310–11; see also 20/SW, XII, 417–18, 44)

We can also find the sort of view I am after elsewhere. Consider the following passage from Husserl: "Science designates the idea of an infinity of tasks....These constitute at the same time the fund of premises for an endless horizon of tasks united into one all-embracing task....Scientific truth claims to be unconditioned truth, which involves infinity, giving to each factually guaranteed truth a merely relative character, making it only an approach oriented, in fact, toward the infinite horizon, wherein the truth in itself is, so to speak, looked on as an infinitely distant point."[51]

But to achieve an acceptable conception of truth, we must go even further. It is not enough that we always strive for the truth, but never reach it—never get a truth outside the cave or from the perspective of a supercultural observation platform. And it is not enough that we find other cultures or other conceptual systems that allow access to different perspectives on the truth. We must also say that it is not at all likely that these different truths will fit within one consistent conceptual system. We will find truths that are not compatible with our own truths. This obviously threatens the deep-seated commitment of Western philosophy to the consistency of truth. All truths must be consistent—they cannot be inconsistent. If one truth contradicts another truth, both cannot be truths. It seems to me that we must relax this commitment—or at least push it off to the far horizon. There are good reasons for doing so. Gödel's theorem, for example, has shown that it is impossible to prove that any self-consistent mathematical system can be complete—it cannot deduce all true mathematical propositions. In other words, there will be many true mathematical propositions that cannot be consistently derived from the system. There will be many truths inconsistent with the truths that the mathematical system will be able to establish.[52]

I also think that this notion of truth follows from the Kuhnian view of paradigms. Any given paradigm, sooner or later, is likely to discover anomalies. Another paradigm may be developed that can include and explain these anomalies, but they cannot be explained in the first paradigm. Insofar as any paradigm, sooner or later, will meet anomalies that only another paradigm will be able to explain, we can wonder about the possibility that no paradigm will ever be able to account for all anomalies—all truths. Certainly, scientists seek broader and broader paradigms that they hope will include and explain all truths. That, indeed, is the goal of science—on the far horizon. But it may well take a very long time to achieve, if it is ever achieved.

This suggests, then, that no one system, no one culture, is likely to possess all truths. If that is so, then we clearly need other cultures—and their differences. However, we must be careful here. Rorty attacks the notion that cultures are like geometric systems. The latter can be incommensurable—they are designed to be so. He does not think there is anything incommensurable about cultures (though, as we have seen, he tends in this direction when he does not want to take another culture seriously and thinks its views not worth listening to) (OR&T, 26, 30–1, 38, 190–1, 203–4). I certainly agree that cultures are not like geometric systems. Cultures do not have anything like the sort of rigorous unity and consistency expected in a geometric system. After all, it is quite possible to have a highly pluralistic culture—a culture capable of including a wide variety of different values and perspectives. It certainly does not follow from this, however, that the various beliefs and values of such a culture will be consistent. To deny that two systems are incommensurable, that is, to admit that by becoming bicultural we can explain one system to the other so that the same persons can understand both, does not at all mean that the two systems cannot still be quite inconsistent and irreconcilable, as we saw in our example of the Christian psychologist. At any rate, as I have said, I think the question of how much consistency we will be able to find is to be decided empirically.

If we suspect that all truths will not fit within one self-consistent system, and if we are always only approaching truth, then we can certainly argue about whether we are effectively on the way to truth, we can certainly work at getting closer to the truth, we can seek truth, but I do not think we can effectively, and certainly not with certainty, say that we are further along toward truth than all other cultures, paradigms, or conceptual systems. We can argue about it, we can treat the question critically, but we cannot be sure.

If we accept that while we seek truth we never finally reach it, and if we admit that it is not likely that all truth can consistently fit within one conceptual system, and especially if we admit that one single system is not likely to be the best approach to discovering all truths, it follows that different cultural perspectives become fundamentally important. Insofar as we value truth, we should not only tolerate but respect these other perspectives. We should want to preserve their different access to truth. It would be a tragedy to destroy other cultures, or to simply absorb them into our own and remake them in our own image, or even to merely tolerate them but ignore them. They have a real access to truth—a particular access we may not have.

Moreover, this respect for difference would not just be a paternalistic attempt to protect "inferior" others. They are a source of real truth. We ourselves want their otherness, for ourselves—yet not in the sense that we want to collapse them into our system or remake them in our image. That could put an end to their access to the truth, an access we do not have, which thus would be lost. We want the other to remain other for-itself, with its own integrity, dignity, and access to the truth. And we want this for-ourselves. I am not suggesting that the value of this other truth is simply the use it has for-us. I do not want to set up yet another hierarchy with our culture at the top. I am suggesting that other cultures, because they have an access to the truth, are ends in themselves—ends in themselves for-themselves, but also for-us. Truth is valuable for its own sake—it is an end in itself—for-others *and* for-us.

If we can find truth in another culture that will not fit consistently into our conceptual system or that our conceptual system is not as likely to discover, this should cause us to respect that other culture and its differences. Moreover, if we do not expect all truths to fit within one consistent system, then one set of truths and values is not as likely to erode another set. We would not need to project onto another culture our notion of subjective value holding. Subjectivizing the values of another culture not only works to erode and subvert them, but it means that we lose those truths as objective truths and thus have less reason to respect the other culture. Moreover, accepting the notion that the truths of other cultures, short of the far horizon, need not be consistent with our own conceptual system may well allow our culture to open itself to and welcome other cultures without eroding our own values and truths. It would not be necessary to subjectivize truths—our own or those of others—to handle the problem of inconsistency. We could accept their inconsistency and their truth. To grasp the truths of another culture, we must of course come to understand that culture seriously and thoroughly. That is a difficult thing to do and takes a good deal of time. But if we do this, that culture could come to have objective value for us.

Furthermore, if we are convinced that the other culture can be a source of truth, and if we seriously and thoroughly understand this other culture, it becomes legitimate to criticize it, and, of course, for other cultures similarly to criticize us. As Herskovits puts it, cultural relativism "does not imply unilateral tolerance of ideas other than one's own" (CR, 94).

Without the model of truth that I have been developing, however, criticism of another culture would tend to be understood in one of two ways. It might be understood on the allegory of the cave model, where criticism of another culture would mean the imposition of our own values, which we take to be objective, on another culture, which has not appropriated these values as its own, and thus (depending on the power relations involved) could tend toward the oppression of that culture. Or, if we reject this model, we could hold, as vulgar cultural relativists, that all values are subjectively held commitments that are merely true-for-their-holders (or neither true nor false), and then criticism of another culture would tend to appear groundless.

But criticism need not be either oppressive or groundless. If we recognize the other culture as a real source of truth, truth that will not necessarily fit consistently within our conceptual system, then criticism need not be an oppression from up outside the cave, the imposition of our truth on those who lack it. The other culture cannot so easily be dismissed—it is a source of real truth. Nor can the other culture be dissolved into mere subjectivism such that no criticism is possible—it is a source of actual truth. We must respect this other culture's truth, take it seriously enough to criticize it. That is certainly the way we act in our own culture. It is strong enough to take criticism and serious enough to demand it. To refrain from criticizing another culture would be to demean it. Though to criticize another culture, we must, of course, come to understand it thoroughly and seriously from inside.[53]

Resistance to criticism grows out of vulgar cultural relativism. If there is no objective truth, criticism can only be an attempt to have our own subjective values dominate. But if there is objective truth, criticism implies a respect for that truth and is a necessary tool for approaching it. In general, criticism should not be seen as an attempt to measure or fix truth from up outside the cave, but as a means that criticizers must use to draw themselves closer to the truth—approach it themselves.

Moreover, it is certainly not the case that everything a culture takes to be true is to be uncritically accepted as true. It is not the case "that if you happen to belong to a narrow-minded and intolerant culture, then you are positively *required* to be intolerant," as Wood thinks.[54] In any cultural system, there can be truths that no one has yet discovered, some things can be held to be true that are later seen to be false, and some things that are thought false can later be found to be true. For these reasons, criticism is most important. Moreover, it is certainly possible for one conceptual system to change another system's mind about what it takes to be true or false.

This gives us no absolute guarantees. Even in our own culture, criticism can do damage—it can harm those with less power. The same could happen to other cultures. Great care must be taken here. But it does not seem that vulgar relativism has a better answer. Vulgar relativism is more ethnocentric than the view I am arguing for—the projection of subjective values and subjective value holding onto another culture is ethnocentric. The view that other cultures have access to truth allows for more real respect for the other culture. And it seems to me that members of a traditional culture are more likely to respond positively to criticism from one who thinks their culture contains truth, from one who would therefore be willing to accept criticism from them, than to lack of criticism from one who thinks their values are mere subjective commitments. To be able to criticize without excluding, harming, or oppressing, it is necessary that the other, especially if they are not equal in power, at least have a real voice that is seriously heard. To hold that the other has access to objective truth leads in this direction more so than does subjectivism.

MacIntyre argues that any tradition must be open to the truths of rival traditions in a way that approaches, but, I think, falls short of, the view of truth that I am arguing for. MacIntyre writes:

> The possibility to which every tradition is always open . . . is that the time and place may come, when . . . it may encounter another alien tradition . . . and may discover that while in some area of greater or lesser importance they cannot comprehend it within the terms of reference set by their own beliefs, their own history, and their own language-in-use, it provides a standpoint from which . . . the limitations, incoherences, and poverty of resources of their own beliefs can be identified, characterized, and explained in a way not possible from within their own tradition.
>
> It follows that the only rational way for the adherents of any tradition to approach intellectually, culturally, and linguistically alien rivals is one that allows for the possibility that in one or more areas the other may be rationally superior to it in respect precisely of that in the alien tradition which it cannot yet comprehend. . . . Only those whose tradition allows for the possibility of its hegemony being put in question can have rational warrant for asserting such hegemony.[55]

For MacIntyre, traditions set out from posited norms that they defend and develop as true. If they interact with rival traditions, they can learn from them, they can merge with them, or they can swallow or be swallowed by them. For MacIntyre, it tends to be the case that the relationship between traditions, unless they ignore each other, is competitive. Each attempts to defend against the other, appropriate the other, swallow the other, or gain hegemony over the other. For MacIntyre, there seems to be no sense, or at least not a very developed sense, in which the other tradition can possess a different truth such that the other tradition is worth preserving as other.[56] And this is so despite the fact that all of the traditions that MacIntyre discusses in *Whose Justice? Which Rationality?* yearn for the truth—objective truth—and at least in part this truth is understood on the *Symposium* model, that is, that the truth remains a regulative ideal which they never finally achieve and thus cannot impose on others. This would make it conceivable for them to value other traditions as other—and to wish to preserve that otherness. Indeed, how could they not do so and still claim to be really concerned with truth.

I do not wish to suggest, however, that the only desirable relation to another tradition, culture, or conceptual system is to distance it as other. Syncretism, the incorporation of major aspects of other cultures, even the merging of cultures, can be perfectly legitimate and, as Clifford has shown, need not mean the corruption of a culture. It can even mean reinvigoration, the development of something new, and, on my view, a new perspective on the truth. In fact, the desire to preserve the purity of another culture, something we would not especially desire for our own culture, can even be paternalistic.[57] Moreover, criticism, or defense against criticism, need not be competitive in the sense that one tradition attempts to replace, suppress, or swallow another. Criticism can be a way of affirming the importance of the other, a form of empowering both traditions, not of gaining power for one over the other.

Let me give an example. Renato Rosaldo—an anthropologist who has written about the Ilongots, a group of headhunters from northern Luzon in the Philippines—tells us that despite his anthropological training and long discussions with the Ilongots, he was unable to put aside his Western disapproval of headhunting, "Despite my indoctrination in cultural relativism, headhunting seemed utterly alien and morally reprehensible."[58] Moreover, this became apparent to the Ilongots, at which point they began to criticize Western forms of warfare. This came up because Rosaldo was about to be drafted to fight in Vietnam. Rosaldo writes, "They told me that soldiers are men who sell their bodies. Pointedly they interrogated me, 'How can a man do as soldiers do and command his brothers to move into the line of fire?'" For the Ilongots, "This act of ordering one's own men (one's brothers) to risk their lives was utterly beyond their moral comprehension."[59] Headhunting, they implied, was not carried on in this way.

The point that I want to get at here is that this very alien culture, perhaps to many even a repulsive culture, even a bit repulsive to Rosaldo (and these are the very reasons why I choose this example), contains—in its very alienness—a truth that we are driven to accept for ourselves. They are right. There is something very ugly about our form of warfare, and the Ilongots—at least in part because of their experience as headhunters—were able to see this ugliness before Rosaldo (and before many of us). Rosaldo also writes:

> Through such encounters the possibility for reciprocal critical perceptions opened between the Ilongots and me. This encounter suggests that we ethnographers should be open to asking not only how our descriptions of others would read if applied to ourselves but how we can learn from other people's descriptions of ourselves. In this case I was repositioned through an Ilongot account of one of my culture's central institutions. I could no longer speak about headhunting as one of the clean addressing the dirty. My loss of innocence enabled me and the Ilongots to face each other on more nearly equal ground, as members of flawed societies. We both lost positions of purity from which to condemn the other, without at the same time having to condone what we found morally reprehensible in ourselves and in the other. Neither war nor headhunting, in deeply serious ways, has been the same for me since.[60]

Rosaldo's serious cultural relativism, his openness to the other, allows for the moment when his ethnocentrism can be punctured. Compare this to Rorty who brazenly holds up his ethnocentrism as a shield, who thinks it not worth trying to have discussions with some people (presumably, Ilongot headhunters would be prime candidates for such exclusion), and who thus closes himself off from criticism that could make for the recognition of new truths. Perhaps not everyone will agree with the Ilongot critique of our form of warfare or find it that impressive. That is not the point. Find a different example. The point is that a very alien culture, because of its very alienness, can show us something that is not only true, but that is a truth about ourselves that we had not been able to see on our own. And that truth can be the ground on which real respect can be built.

I am not suggesting that this will make us want to take up headhunting or decide that it is ethical, nor even that it is only through dialogue with headhunters that we can learn to be morally self-critical of our own institutions and practices. But the fact that headhunting allowed the Ilongots to achieve a moral insight that we had not yet achieved, I am suggesting, is reason enough for us to owe them respect. We need other cultures, not because they are like us in having merely subjective values that are as important to them as ours are to us, but precisely because they are different from us. It is this difference that should make us want to know the other culture—and not to paternalistically safeguard its pursuit of merely personal values, but for our own benefit. In my opinion, anthropologists ought to work to reveal the truths of other cultures, to begin to make them accessible to those who otherwise would not have access to that culture and those truths,[61] and especially to report their criticism of our culture's values, practices, and institutions. The existence of alien cultures is important for all other cultures—the human species—because other cultures can teach us about truth that we are yet unable to see for ourselves.

I would like to try to be even clearer here. What I want to suggest is that selfishness in some cases is more desirable than altruism. No one, for example, wants a lover who loves them merely out of a sense of altruism. To be loved in such a way would suggest that except for our lover's altruism we would not be found lovable. We all want lovers who love us with a certain degree of selfishness, who wants us for themselves, who wants us because we move or satisfy them personally. So also, to accept other cultures merely because we feel we have an obligation to tolerate or protect them—especially if we come from a culture that is a major power in the world—patronizes and demeans those other cultures. I am trying to argue that all cultures need other cultures. We need the insight they can give us about ourselves. We have an interest in them that is to a certain degree selfish—if wanting to move closer to truth can really be called selfish. This does not demean the other culture. It is a basis for real respect, real toleration, and real pluralism. We could also say that other cultures need us, need our truths, but given the way this has been understood in the past, and given the relations of power involved, one should be very careful here. After all, to claim that other cultures need our truths is more than a bit arrogant. This is not for us to say, but for others to say, if they decide to say it. At the same time, I do not want to set up a hierarchy in which other cultures are merely storehouses of truth to be used as means to our selfish ends. The truths of other cultures are ends in themselves, to be sought for their own sake, but also they are ends in themselves for-us.

There are many different arguments that could be made for multiculturalism. I would like to develop only one of them. Aristotle argued that human beings are political beings—that they are political by nature. Very similarly, Marx argued that human beings are species beings.[62] Hegel, I think, holds something only slightly different—that human beings are cultural beings. To say that human beings are cultural beings is to say that culture is fundamental to what human beings are. Without culture, we would not become human beings, or at least not fully human beings. Human beings only develop their distinctly human potentiality, their powers, capacities, talents, values, aspirations, and so forth, in culture. We do not develop except in and through a culture that provides us a language, a worldview, values, different sorts of knowledge, and a thousand other things, all of which, of course, we continually transform and reconstruct through our own ongoing cultural activity.

If we are to care about human beings, about the realization and development of their potential, if we are to respect what they *are*, we must be fundamentally concerned with, we must care about and respect their culture. In fact, if we were willing to risk provoking postmodernists, we could even say that culture is essential to what human beings are. Does anyone really want to argue that culture is not essential to what human beings are?

This particular essentialist argument, however, is unlike most essentialist arguments. It makes *difference* fundamental. Culture is essential to human beings. We do not have human beings without culture. But cultures differ. We cannot expect cultures to be the same—indeed, we expect near infinite variety among cultures. Even single cultures are not unified in any simple way. Western culture, for example, involves many different languages, worldviews, paradigms, sets of values, and so forth. They all overlap and share family resemblances, but they are also quite different and they compete with each other.

Difference, however, need not lead to a ranking of cultures. I do not accept this aspect of Hegel's thought—certainly not at the philosophical metacultural level. It is true that ethnocentrism at the everyday cultural level is very difficult, perhaps even impossible, to avoid. Everyone thinks their own culture is best—it is like being for the home soccer team. Even so, we all have to admit, and Hegel would certainly agree, that the human potential cannot be plumbed or exhausted by any one culture. Human beings are capable of much more than we can ever expect to find in a single culture. Other cultures afford the human species a range of potentialities it would not otherwise possess.

And so I think assimilationism is objectionable. Either remaking the world according to the measure of our own culture in imperialist fashion, imposing our culture upon others, or insisting that immigrants abandon their own culture and adopt ours is objectionable because it is reductive. It diminishes the human potential. It limits the realization of the human essence.[63]

Differences, then, are fundamental. We reduce the richness of the human species if we eliminate differences, if we force people to assimilate, or if the structure of our society makes the abandonment of different cultural traditions necessary for social acceptance. I have tried to argue that we should respect other cultures and their differences. I have also said that this does not mean that the only desirable relation to another tradition or culture is to distance it as other. Different systems can legitimately decide to incorporate aspects of other cultures or traditions, or even to fully merge with them. What is objectionable is to try to eliminate another culture, or even just to marginalize it. But if this does occur, we have another Hegelian model to call upon, that of the slave who subverts the master. We can have all the difference we want *within* the absolute, but any difference *from* the absolute means the absolute was not absolute and thus subverts it.

What we have in history is the realization of human spirit—not just my culture's spirit, but human spirit. Nevertheless, human spirit can be realized only through particular cultures and their spirit. It may be that human spirit, right now, is being especially and powerfully influenced by the spirit of my culture. It may even be that my culture sees itself as the high point of world spirit, sees little else of value besides itself, even perhaps thinks that its spirit simply *is* world spirit. Nevertheless, world spirit will move on past my culture. As Hegel puts it, every new philosophy asserts "that the others have not yet found the truth. It claims not only to be the true philosophy at last but to make good the deficiency of its predecessors. But to this philosophy too we can apply the words of the Apostle Paul to Ananias: 'See the feet of those who will carry thee out are already at the door'" (*ILHP*, 61/*EGP*, 90).

The absolute is taken to be closed, finished, and total—that is, it is taken to be absolute—by its culture. But this is to set the stage for tragedy, for the appearance of an other, who, as soon as it appears, as soon as we can recognize it, subverts the absolute. Hegel says that the "Absolute eternally enacts" tragedy "by eternally giving birth to itself into objectivity, submitting in this objective form to suffering and death, and rising from its ashes into glory" (*NL*, 104/*GW*, IV, 458–9). We can only make room for the other by going under ourselves, even if we began as an other. Tragedy, for Hegel, means a conflict between two goods and the emergence of an even higher good.

The absolute, then, not only includes a great deal of difference *within* itself, but it also incites difference *from* itself to subvert it and thus to be included within a new and more inclusive absolute. We cannot let ourselves focus only on the side of the absolute that embodies a drive for totality, mastery, and the negation of all that is other. We must also recognize that like the opposed pole of a magnet the absolute incites its other to deny its totality, protest against its imperialism, assert a difference, and finally to subvert it. Each of these drives incites the other. The absolute must be seen as a process that ultimately implies total openness. To think it closed, fixed, and final is only to see one side of it.

What must we finally say about the absolute? All of reality, Hegel has tried to show us, has been constructed by us. This does not mean that it is false, illusory, or even mere appearance. It can be constructed and be true. It can be constructed and be absolute. This truth will be the truth of a particular culture, it will be culturally relative, but again that does not mean, I have tried to show, that it cannot also be true. But can such truth be total—can it actually be *absolute?* It certainly can *for-this-culture.* This culture will be ethnocentric. It will take its truth to be true in and for itself. It is even likely that this culture will not countenance exceptions. It will not recognize differences. It may even use its power in masterly and imperial fashion to negate and marginalize alternatives. Nevertheless, at the same time, this culture will also *stake* itself on its absolute. It will go under, it will be subverted, if the other shows up with anything real that has not been included in its absolute. Despite the fact that the only thing we have here is an absolute that is true in and for itself *for-this-culture,* nevertheless, the absolute *can* be absolute for-this-culture *only* if the absolute *is true in and for itself.* If it is shown not to be, then it can no longer be absolute for-this-culture.

Notes

Introduction

1. In citing Hegel I will use abbreviations given in the list of abbreviations. I will cite an English translation followed by a German edition.

2. For a good discussion of Hegel's holism, see R. Stern, *Hegel, Kant and the Structure of the Object* (London: Routledge, 1990), 1–6.

3. I have used the N. Kemp Smith translation of Kant's *Critique of Pure Reason* and, for the German, *Kant's gesammelte Schriften* but simply cite the standard A and B edition pagination.

4. Others have held that Hegel's argument is similar to a Kantian transcendental deduction. See K. R. Westphal, *Hegel's Epistemological Realism: A Study of the Aim and Method of Hegel's Phenomenology of Spirit* (Dordrecht: Kluwer, 1989), 154–88; R. B. Pippin, *Hegel's Idealism: The Satisfactions of Self-Consciousness* (Cambridge: Cambridge University Press, 1989), 93, 102 ff., 132 ff; C. Taylor, "The Opening Arguments of the *Phenomenology*," in *Hegel: A Collection of Critical Essays*, ed. A. MacIntyre (Garden City, NY: Anchor, 1972), 151, 160; see also Taylor, *H*, 95–6; J. Stewart, *The Unity of Hegel's Phenomenology of Spirit: A Systematic Interpretation* (Evanston, IL: Northwestern University Press, 2000), esp. 14–31. M. N. Forster attacks this view in *Hegel's Idea of a Phenomenology of Spirit* (Chicago: University of Chicago Press, 1998), 162, 163–4 n. See also R. C. Solomon, *In The Spirit of Hegel: A Study of G. W. F. Hegel's Phenomenology of Spirit* (New York: Oxford University Press, 1983), 351–7.

5. B. Russell, *History of Western Philosophy* (London: George Allen & Unwin, 1948), 771–2.

6. Hegel himself makes this point in *SL*, 530 and *Wissenschaft der Logik*, ed. G. Lasson (Hamburg: Felix Meiner, 1969), II, 157. Some scholars think the absolute is logically deduced; see A. Kojève, *Introduction to the Reading of Hegel*, tr. J. H. Nichols, Jr. (New York: Basic Books, 1969), 82; J. Hyppolite, *Genesis and Structure of Hegel's Phenomenology of Spirit*, tr. S. Cherniak and J. Heckman (Evanston, IL: Northwestern University Press, 1974), 157; R. Norman, *Hegel's Phenomenology: A Philosophical Introduction* (New York: St. Martin's Press, 1976), 117–18; J. N. Findlay, "Forward," in *PhS*, vi–vii.

7. See J.G. Fichte, *Science of Knowledge (Wissenschaftslehre)*, tr. P. Heath and J. Lachs (New York: Appleton-Century-Crofts, 1970), 12, 24 and for the German, *Fichtes Werke*, ed. I.H. Fichte (Berlin: de Gruyter, 1971), I, 429–30, 443. See also W. T. Stace, *The Philosophy of Hegel* (New York: Dover, 1955), 89–115.

8. Fichte, *Science of Knowledge*, 25 and *Fichtes Werke*, I, 446.

9. *Republic*, 509d-516c; I have used the Bollingen edition of the *Collected Dialogues of Plato*, ed. E. Hamilton and H. Cairns (New York: Pantheon, 1961), but cite the column pagination so any edition may be used.

10. Kojève, 82; Hyppolite, 157; Stace, 54, 308–9; Norman, 16.

11. G. Lukács, *The Young Hegel*, tr. R. Livingstone (London: Merlin, 1975), 188; T. Pinkard, *Hegel's Phenomenology: The Sociality of Reason* (Cambridge: Cambridge University Press, 1994), 12; Stewart, *Unity of Hegel's Phenomenology*, 30–1; Forster, 186; J. Butler, *Subjects of Desire* (New York: Columbia University Press, 1987); D. P. Verene, *Hegel's Recollection* (Albany: State University of New York Press, 1985), 20–2, 64, 67. Also, D. Forbes rejects the notion of strict logical deduction; see introduction to *PWHI*, xxx–xxxi.

12. F. H. Bergmann, "The Purpose of Hegel's System," *Journal of the History of Philosophy* 2 (1964): 189–204, esp. 191. Solomon (206–9) argues a similar position.

13. On Hegel's method of presuppositions, see J. C. Flay, "Pragmatic Presuppositions and the Dialectics of Hegel's *Phenomenology*," in M. Westphal, ed., *Method and Speculation in Hegel's Phenomenology* (Atlantic Highlands, NJ: Humanities Press, 1982), 15–26.

14. S. Houlgate, *Freedom, Truth and History: An Introduction to Hegel's Philosophy* (London: Routledge, 1991), 71. See also W. Marx, "Dialectic and the Role of the Phenomenologist," in *G. W. F. Hegel: Critical Assessments*, ed. R. Stern (London: Routledge, 1993), 3:57–63.

15. S. Houlgate, *Hegel, Nietzsche and the Criticism of Metaphysics* (Cambridge: Cambridge University Press, 1986), 135 ff.

16. Taylor, *H*, 130. J. Butler, "Commentary on Joseph Flay's 'Hegel, Derrida, and Bataille's Laughter,'" in *Hegel and His Critics*, ed. W. Desmond (Albany: State University of New York Press, 1989), 175.

17. J. Walker, "Hegel and Religion," in *Hegel and Modern Philosophy*, ed. D. Lamb (London: Croom Helm, 1987), 198.

18. Norman, 12.

19. See also Hyppolite, 15; Stewart, *Unity of Hegel's Phenomenology*, 41 ff.

20. Pippin, 99–100.

21. *Hegel's Philosophy of Nature*, tr. M. J. Petry (London: George Allen & Unwin, 1970), I, 202 and *SW*, IX, 44–5; see also *SL*, 25/GW, XXI, 5.

22. M. J. Herskovits, "Cultural Relativism and Cultural Values," in *Ethical Relativism*, ed. J. Ladd (Belmont, CA: Wadsworth, 1973), 74, 76. See also J. Ladd, "The Issue of Relativism," in *Ethical Relativism*, 111–12.

23. See Walker, 214.

24. See, e.g., Butler, *Subjects of Desire.*

25. F. Jameson, forward to *The Postmodern Condition: A Report on Knowledge,* by J.-F. Lyotard, tr. G. Bennington and B. Massumi (Minneapolis: University of Minnesota Press, 1984), xix.

1. Consciousness and the Transcendental Deduction

1. Q. Lauer, *A Reading of Hegel's Phenomenology of Spirit* (New York: Fordham University Press, 1976), 42. Pippin, 118. See also M. S. Gram, "Moral and Literary Ideals in Hegel's Critique of 'The Moral View of the World,'" *Clio* 7 (1978): 376.

2. *CPR*, A97 (brackets in original).

3. D. Hume, *A Treatise of Human Nature,* ed. L.A. Selby-Bigge (Oxford: Clarendon Press, 1967), 251-63.

4. See also my "Kant and the Possibility of Uncategorized Experience," *Idealistic Studies* 19 (1989): 163, also 158–63. Allison also makes this point; see *KTI*, 141–2.

5. Postmodernists attack the notion of a unified self. But I do not think they can get away with simply rejecting Kant's notion of a transcendental unity of apperception. It is true that selves may have more than one identity they are torn between. They may also feel pressured toward a single identity as if it were supposed to be their "essence" and such that other parts of the self are repressed. Nevertheless, as Kant shows, there must be enough unity in the first place for this self to have experience sufficiently organized to then go on to say that it wavers between multiple identities or feels pressured toward one and marginalizes others. We cannot dismiss Kant, though we can decide that things are more complicated than he thought.

6. T. Rockmore, *Cognition: An Introduction to Hegel's Phenomenology of Spirit* (Berkeley: University of California Press, 1997), 39.

7. Plato, *Theaetetus*, esp. 182a–182e, 205c. Stern (*Hegel, Kant and the Structure of the Object*, 44) makes this point also.

8. Aristotle, *Metaphysics*, 1039^b–1140^a. I have used the Bollingen edition of the *Complete Works of Aristotle*, ed. J. Barnes (Princeton, NJ: Princeton University Press, 1984), but I cite the column pagination so that any edition may be used. Hyppolite (87) also points this out.

9. Pippin, 123. Generally speaking, Pippin as well as Rockmore (2) especially appreciate the degree to which Hegel's *Phenomenology* is following, criticizing, and trying to get beyond Kant.

10. For an interesting and valuable treatment of "Sense-Certainty," see K. Dulckeit, "Can Hegel Refer to Particulars?," in *The Phenomenology of Spirit Reader: Critical and Interpretive Essays*, ed. J. Stewart (Albany: State University of New York Press, 1998), 105–21.

11. Stern, *Hegel, Kant and the Structure of the Object*, vii, 1–2.

12. J. Locke, *An Essay Concerning Human Understanding*, ed. P. H. Nidditch (Oxford: Clarendon Press, 1975), 95, 175, 295–7.

13. For evidence that Hegel is aware of the importance of a synthesis of reproduction in imagination, see *PM*, 208–10/*SW*, X, 337–41; see also *FPS*, 219–21/*GW*, VI, 285–7.

14. Locke, 134–5, 137.

15. See also Stern (*Hegel, Kant and the Structure of the Object*, 36–8) for a very good treatment of these matters.

16. G. Berkeley, *The Principles of Human Knowledge*, reprint ed. (La Salle, IL: Open Court, 1946), 34–5.

17. Pippin, 126–7.

18. Stern, *Hegel, Kant and the Structure of the Object*, 13–14.

19. See also Hyppolite, 129–30.

20. D. Hume, *An Enquiry Concerning Human Understanding*, in *Enquiries Concerning Human Understanding and Concerning the Principles of Morals*, ed. L. A. Selby-Bigge, 3rd ed., revised P. H. Nidditch (Oxford: Clarendon Press, 1975), 22, 29–30, 42.

21. Fichte, *Science of Knowledge*, 13 and *Fichtes Werke*, I, 431.

22. Hegel makes a similar point with respect to the kingdom of laws. As we move beyond specific laws by subsuming them under higher level laws, the higher level laws become less specific and more general. We finally end up with the Kantian notion of a unity and consistency of nature as-if designed by a supreme intelligence, which might seem like a grand accomplishment, but in fact is quite superficial—nothing but the mere concept of law itself, merely the notion that all reality is conformable to law (*CPR*, A670–B701, A678=B706, A686=B715, A697–B726; *PhS*, 91–5/*GW*, IX, 91–5). This is nothing new and has no real content—as specific laws do. And nothing is more easily known.

23. H. E. Allison, "Transcendental Idealism: The 'Two Aspect' View," in *New Essays on Kant*, ed. B. den Ouden and M. Moen (New York: Peter Lang, 1987), 155; *KTF*, 3–4; *KTI*, 8.

24. Stern (*Hegel, Kant and the Structure of the Object*, 39–40, 108, 110–14) rejects the view that the Kantian subject constructs and unifies experience. Rather, he thinks, the absolute does this. See also R. R. Williams, "Hegel's Concept of *Geist*,"

in *Hegel's Philosophy of Spirit,* ed. P. G. Stillman (Albany: State University of New York Press, 1987), 1–20. The absolute is ultimately responsible for constructing and unifying reality, but, I will argue as we proceed, the absolute is a cultural consciousness constructed by a culture. And so we do construct reality, though not as Kantian individual subjects.

25. This is another reason why Hegel focuses on force. He says that force may be a universal principle, not just of physical nature, but even of spiritual nature; *JS,* 63–4/*GW,* VII, 60–1. We will see in the next chapter that self-consciousness is a force.

26. For an excellent and very interesting treatment of the inverted world, see Verene, 52–8.

2. Self-Consciousness and the Other

1. Allison argues that Kant's official position is that the subject of apperception is to be identified with the noumenal self: "Kant succinctly expresses this view in a frequently cited Reflexion when he remarks, 'The soul in transcendental apperception is *substantia noumenon*'" (*KTI,* 286). On Kant's deepest view, however, "the subject of apperception is distinguished from the noumenal self, indeed, from any kind of intelligible *object*" (*KTI,* 287). Insofar as we take the latter to be Kant's true position, however, it just makes things easier for Hegel. Kant's position slides more easily into Hegel's.

2. Kant usually uses the term *Erkenntnis* and Hegel *Anerkennen.* Kant also speaks of a *Synthesis der Recognition;* see *CPR,* A103–10; *PhS,* 111 ff./*GW,* IX, 109 ff.

3. R. R. Williams, "Hegel's Concept of *Geist,*" 1–2.

4. R. R. Williams, "Hegel's Concept of *Geist,*" 2–3.

5. Ibid.

6. See also Kojève, 3–7; Hyppolite, 160; J. C. Flay, *Hegel's Quest for Certainty* (Albany: State University of New York Press, 1984), 54.

7. Kojève, 6–7.

8. Kojève, 8.

9. I think it inappropriate, when referring to the master and the slave, to replace Hegel's language with gender-neutral language. I think the master and the slave are basically masculine in the way they have been conceived by Hegel.

10. D. Diderot, *Rameau's Nephew,* tr. L. W. Tancock (Harmondsworth: Penguin, 1966), 83, 121. Lordship and Bondage might also be compared to W. E. B. Du Bois's notion of double consciousness; see *The Souls of Black Folk* (New York: New American Library, 1969), 45–6.

11. G. Berkeley, *Three Dialogues Between Hylas and Philonous,* reprint ed. (La Salle, IL: Open Court, 1954), 64, 68, 97.

12. What does it mean to say that the unknown thing-in-itself serves as an anchor? The thing-in-itself, certainly on the standard two worlds view, is an entity, a *thing,* in a distinct ontological realm. Kant even says, "Knowledge has to do only with appearances, and must leave the thing in itself as indeed real *per se,* but as not known by us" (*CPR,* Bxx). After all, it would be "absurd," to hold "that there can be appearance without anything that appears" (*CPR,* Bxxvi–ii; also A251–2). Thus, "We must admit and assume behind the appearances something else which is not appearance, namely, things in themselves " (*F,* 69/KGS, IV, 451). If instead we insist that the thing-in-itself is *not* a thing, but a *mere* concept, a mere negative or limiting concept (*CPR,* A253–6), then Kant's position will slide into Hegelian idealism. To prevent this, an unknown thing in a different ontological realm is necessary. It is not necessary to ground the objectivity of experience, which is due to the universality and necessity of the categories, but it is necessary to "anchor" experience, that is, to prevent its implosion entirely into consciousness—into Hegelian idealism. After all, if no thing remains in a distinct ontological realm unknown to us, then in constituting experience, we constitute reality, not appearance.

13. F. Fanon, *Black Skin, White Masks,* tr. C. L. Markmann (New York: Grove, 1967), 220 n.

14. "Spinoza to J. Jellis," in *Chief Works of Benedict de Spinoza,* tr. R. H. M. Elwes (New York: Dover, 1951), 2:370.

15. T. Todorov, *The Conquest of America: The Question of the Other,* tr. R. Howard (New York: Harper & Row, 1984), 42.

16. There is no better example of this than Virgil's *Aeneid.*

17. Hegel also points out that the criterion of the true and the good for Stoicism, much as for Kant, is reasonableness, a reasonableness that contains nothing determinate, no desire, no particular interest, no concrete purpose (*PhS,* 122/GW, IX, 118).

18. *Sextus Empiricus: Outlines of Scepticism,* tr. J. Annas and J. Barnes (Cambridge: Cambridge University Press, 1994), 4–6.

19. Epicurus, "Letter to Pythocles" and "Letter to Menoeceus," in *The Epicurus Reader: Selected Writings and Testimonia,* tr. B. Inwood and L. P. Gerson (Indianapolis: Hackett, 1994), 19-20, 31. Lucretius, *On the Nature of Things,* tr. F. O. Copley (New York: Norton, 1977), 34–5.

20. Augustine, *Confessions,* tr. R. S. Pine-Coffin (Harmondsworth: Penguin, 1961), 169. See also Romans, 7:14–23.

21. *PhS,* 136 (brackets in original)/GW, IX, 130.

22. See my "Nietzsche, Skepticism, and Eternal Recurrence," *Canadian Journal of Philosophy* 13 (1983): 365–87.

23. See also *Prolegomena to Any Future Metaphysics*, ed. L. W. Beck (Indianapolis: Bobbs-Merrill, 1950), 100, 102/KGS, IV, 351, 354.

24. Practical reason gives us postulates, but that is not, for Kant, to constitute objects of experience or construct realities.

3. Reason in the World

1. Or, as Hegel puts it, consciousness has forgotten it (*PhS*, 141/GW, IX, 133).

2. Lauer, *A Reading of Hegel's Phenomenology*, 132–3.

3. Hyppolite, 244 (italics added).

4. Hegel writes, "But when we said that what is sensed receives from the intuiting mind the form of the spatial and temporal, this statement must not be understood to mean that space and time are only subjective forms. This is what Kant wanted to make them. But *things are in truth themselves spatial and temporal*; this double form of asunderness is not one-sidedly given to them by our intuition, but has been originally imparted to them by the intrinsically infinite mind, by the creative eternal Idea" (*PM*, 198 [italics added]/SW, X, 323).

5. See "idealism" in the *Cambridge Dictionary of Philosophy*, ed. R. Audi (Cambridge: Cambridge University Press, 1995), 355–7.

6. See note 12 of chapter 2 above.

7. Aquinas, *Summa Theologiae* (New York: McGraw-Hill, 1964), 1st Part of 2nd Part, 22–3.

8. Hegel summarizes Kant's "Refutation of Idealism" and critiques it in *HP*, III, 441–3/SW, XIX, 570–2.

9. *PhS*, 147 (translation altered)/GW, IX, 138.

10. We also find these concepts in Kant, even in his "Refutation of Idealism" (*CPR*, B339=A283, B274–8). We also find that Hegel started to examine these concepts as early as his discussion of the "kingdom of laws" (*PhS*, 90 ff./GW, IX, 91 ff.).

11. Hegel argues that this too is Kant's view; see *HP*, III, 443/SW, XIX, 574.

12. In his discussion of physiognomy, Hegel says we are considering the antithesis of practical and theoretical reason from the side of the practical aspect. We are looking at the individual's actual doing as opposed to the individual's making this doing its object (*PhS*, 191–2/GW, IX, 176–7). For a good discussion of physiognomy and phrenology, see A. MacIntyre, "Hegel on Faces and Skulls," in *Hegel: A Collection of Critical Essays*, 219–36.

13. However, in the *Critique of Judgment*, the ideal of artistic beauty, for Kant, requires the visible expression in bodily form of the moral ideas that rule us inwardly (*Critique of Judgment*, tr. J. H. Bernard [New York: Hafner, 1966], 72 and KGS, V, 235).

14. I prefer Baillie's translation of this passage: *PhM*, 369/*GW*, IX, 190.

15. Hyppolite, 233.

16. See also *KTF*, 39–40, 97, 102, 110–11; A. W. Wood, *Hegel's Ethical Thought* (Cambridge: Cambridge University Press, 1990), 146–8; K. R. Westphal, "Hegel's Critique of Kant's Moral World View," *Philosophical Topics* 19 (1991): 150; B. Herman, *The Practice of Moral Judgment* (Cambridge, MA: Harvard University Press, 1993), 12.

17. Lauer, *A Reading of Hegel's Phenomenology*, 157.

18. R. R. Williams, *Recognition: Fichte and Hegel on the Other* (Albany: State University of New York Press, 1992), 184.

19. K. Ameriks, "The Hegelian Critique of Kantian Morality," in *New Essays on Kant*, 194–7. *KTF*, 184–5. As Allison points out, Hegel at times does employ a rather crude model of the relation of duty to inclination (see *SCF*, 211/*HTJ*, 265–6; see also *R*, 164/*KGS*, VI, 176; *KTF*, 185).

20. Here I prefer Abbott's translation: *FP*, 15–16/*KGS*, IV, 398; see also *MPV*, 49–50/*KGS*, VI, 391.

21. *R*, 169 (first italics added)/*KGS*, VI, 181.

22. *MPV*, 47 (italics added)/*KGS*, VI, 389.

23. *R*, 87 (brackets in original)/*KGS*, VI, 95–6.

24. Lauer, *A Reading of Hegel's Phenomenology*, 158–9.

25. In the "Tübingen Essay" of 1793, Hegel thinks that folk religion is essential to the revival of Sittlichkeit. The qualities folk religion must have are: (1) that its teaching must be founded on universal reason; (2) that imagination, the heart, and the senses must not go away empty handed; and (3) that it must be so constituted that all of life's needs, including public and official transactions, are bound up with it. "Tübingen Essay," in *Three Essays, 1793–1795*, tr. P. Fuss and J. Dobbins (Notre Dame, IN: University of Notre Dame Press, 1984), 49 and *GW*, I, 103.

26. *PCR*, 154 (brackets and parentheses in original)/*GW*, I, 367–8.

27. See also in Luther's translation of the Bible, Ephesians 2:2.

28. Lauer, *A Reading of Hegel's Phenomenology*, 162–3; Hyppolite, 290. However, see Pinkard, 105–111.

29. Rockmore (100) sees the connection of "Virtue and the Way of the World" to Kant, but not to Kant's "Idea for a Universal History."

30. Also, see my earlier treatment of these matters in *Marx and Modern Political Theory* (Lanham, MD: Rowman & Littlefield, 1993), chapters 4–5.

31. A. Smith, *Wealth of Nations*, ed. E. Cannan (New York: Modern Library, 1937), 423.

32. Hegel was also influenced by Adam Smith and James Steuart. For a fuller treatment of these matters, see my *Marx and Modern Political Theory*, 123–30, 149–50 n. 36.

33. Hegel's rejection of reason's superiority to passion in the ethical sphere echoes a similar view in Hume; see *Treatise*, 413–18.

34. See also Onora (formerly Nell) O'Neill, *Acting on Principle: An Essay on Kantian Ethics* (New York: Columbia University Press, 1975), 84–9.

35. B. Williams, *Moral Luck: Philosophical Papers 1973–1980* (Cambridge: Cambridge University Press, 1981), 21–4.

36. It is certainly possible for real talent to go unrecognized, for artists, say, to be ahead of their time. But to hold that a talent that will never be recognized is still a talent is self-delusion.

37. Miller translates *die Sache selbst* as "'the matter in hand' itself," or elsewhere as "the heart of the matter." I think a better translation is simply "the fact itself."

38. Baillie's translation is clearer here: *PhM*, 431/GW, IX, 223. Hyppolite, 309.

39. I prefer Baillie's translation here: *PhM*, 435–6/GW, IX, 226–7.

40. This is not to say that significant work never goes unrecognized. A work that is significant and deserving of recognition can fail to gain that recognition. But from this we cannot conclude that public recognition should be dismissed altogether and that all an honest consciousness need be concerned with is its own work. Its work amounts to nothing unless it deserves recognition. Recognition is essential here. The fact that society does not grant recognition where it is deserved is a separate problem that we must take up later.

41. I prefer Baillie's translation here: *PhM*, 437–8/GW, IX, 227–8.

42. Pippin, 206–7. K. R. Westphal, *Hegel's Epistemological Realism*, 176. See also MacIntyre, "Hegel on Faces and Skulls," 220–1.

43. Kant might even agree with some of this. He claims that juridical legislation "must be derived from pathological grounds determining will, that is, from inclinations and disinclinations" (*MEJ*, 19/KGS, VI, 219).

44. M. G. Singer, *Generalization in Ethics* (New York: Knopf, 1961), 251–2.

45. Singer, 252; K. Westphal, "The Basic Context and Structure of Hegel's *Philosophy of Right*," in *The Cambridge Companion to Hegel*, ed. F. C. Beiser (Cambridge: Cambridge University Press, 1993), 252–3.

46. In *PR*, 90/SW, VII, 194, Hegel speaks of bringing a particular content under consideration.

47. D. C. Hoy makes an argument similar to mine in "Hegel's Critique of Kantian Morality," *History of Philosophy Quarterly* 6 (1989): 216 ff.

48. Of course, to decide whether a particular act is an act of murder or whether it is first- or second-degree murder might require a great deal of analysis and deduction. That murder itself is wrong, however, does not and should not.

4. Culture and Reality

1. Taylor, "The Opening Arguments of the *Phenomenology*," 151, 160; Pippin, chapters 7–8.

2. M. Westphal, *History and Truth in Hegel's Phenomenology* (Atlantic Highlands, NJ: Humanities Press, 1979), 36–7; T. L. Haering, *Hegel: Sein Wollen und sein Werk* (Stuttgart: Scientia Verlag Aalen, 1963), II, 479 ff.

3. R. R. Williams, *Recognition*, 1–2, 5, 254–5.

4. M. Westphal, *History and Truth*, 129.

5. K. A. Appiah, *In My Father's House: Africa in the Philosophy of Culture* (New York: Oxford University Press, 1992), 32, 174–5, 177.

6. A longer version of this section appeared as "Hegel, Antigone, and Women" in a volume devoted to "Feminism and Hegel's Antigone Revisited," *Owl of Minerva* 33 (2002): 157–77. The volume also included articles critical of mine: see P. J. Mills, "'Hegel's Antigone' Redux: Woman in Four Parts," 205–21, and H. M. Ravven, "Further Thoughts on Hegel and Feminism: A Response to Philip J. Kain and Nadine Changfoot," 223–31.

7. See P. J. Mills, *Woman, Nature, and Psyche* (New Haven: Yale University Press, 1987), 11. See also Mills's introduction to *FIH*, 4; P. J. Mills, "Hegel's *Antigone*," *Owl of Minerva* 17 (1986): 131–52; P. J. Mills, "'Feminist' Sympathy and Other Serious Crimes: A Reply to Swindle," *Owl of Minerva* 24 (1992): 55–62; H. M. Ravven, "Has Hegel Anything to Say to Feminists?," in *FIH*, 242–5; H. M. Ravven, "A Response to 'Why Feminists Should Take the *Phenomenology of Spirit* Seriously,'" *Owl of Minerva* 4 (1992): 65 ff; M. O'Brien, *The Politics of Reproduction* (Boston: Routledge & Kegan Paul, 1981), 69–73; K. Oliver, "Antigone's Ghost: Undoing Hegel's *Phenomenology of Spirit*," *Hypatia* 11 (1996): 72–3. However, Simone de Beauvoir argues that in certain respects the relation of master to slave especially applies to the relation of man to woman. *The Second Sex*, tr. H. M. Parshley (New York: Vintage, 1952), 73.

8. Oliver, 70.

9. M. O'Brien, "Hegel: Man, Physiology, and Fate," in *FIH*, 179. ✓

10. Ravven, "Has Hegel Anything to Say to Feminists?," 230–2.

11. I prefer Baillie's translation here: *PhM*, 478/*GW*, IX, 248–9.

12. I prefer Baillie's translation here: *PhM*, 481/*GW*, IX, 250.

13. J. Hodge, "Women and the Hegelian State," in *Women in Western Political Philosophy*, ed. E. Kennedy and S. Mendus (Brighton: Wheatsheaf Books, 1987), 127–58.

14. E.g., K. Popper, *The Open Society and Its Enemies* (Princeton, NJ: Princeton University Press, 1950), 225. Also R. Haym, *Hegel und seine Zeit* (Berlin: Rudolf Gaertner, 1857), 357 ff.

15. Norman, 82.

16. N. Tuana, *Woman and the History of Philosophy* (New York: Paragon, 1992), 100.

17. Here I prefer Baillie's translation: *PhM*, 474/GW, IX, 246.

18. R. R. Williams, *Recognition*, 182, also 184. M. Westphal, *History and Truth*, 131. Hegel's definition of love (see *PR*, 261–2/SW, VII, 237–8) is not a definition merely of sexual love. It would also include nonsexual love. Love is a form of recognition capable of producing a unity or bond that holds people together. This is similar to Aristotle who in his treatment of love or friendship also includes both sexual and nonsexual relations (*NE*, 1157^a). There are significant differences between sexual love and nonsexual love, but for my concerns here these differences can be left aside.

19. *SEL*, 126–7 (brackets in original)/SS, 35.

20. For further argument to this effect, see my "Hegel, Antigone, and Women," esp. 176 n.

21. This crucial point is ignored by Mills in her argument against my view that Antigone is like the slave; see "'Hegel's Antigone' Redux."

22. S. Benhabib, "On Hegel, Women, and Irony," in *FIH*, 40.

23. I prefer Baillie's translation here: *PhM*, 496/GW, IX, 259.

24. Of course, this is not to suggest that the *death* of Antigone is comic. It is the collapse of the *community* that can be viewed either as tragic or as comic.

25. Ravven, "Has Hegel Anything to Say to Feminists?," 225–52; O'Brien, "Hegel: Man, Physiology, and Fate," 177–207; S. N. Starrett, "Critical Relations in Hegel: Woman, Family, and the Divine," in *FIH*, 253–73; A. L. Brown, "Hegelian Silences and the Politics of Communication: A Feminist Appropriation," in *FIH*, 299–319.

26. The chaotic multiplicity of "Legal Status" does not, as postmodernists might want to think, eliminate a spiritual whole, totality, or the absolute. Rather, this chaotic multiplicity *is* totality, *is* the absolute, as it appears in this era. And so we should question whether the contemporary proliferation of difference is anything but the absolute as it emerges in the postmodern era.

27. *PR*, 165 (translation altered)/SW, VII, 348.

28. For an earlier treatment of Hegel's concepts of alienation and estrangement, which I follow and revise here, see my *Schiller, Hegel, and Marx* (Montreal: McGill-Queen's University Press, 1982), 40–52.

29. L. P. Hinchman, *Hegel's Critique of the Enlightenment* (Gainesville: University Presses of Florida, 1984), 109. Lukács, 492.

30. M. Westphal, *History and Truth*, 164–5.

31. *The German Constitution*, in *Hegel's Political Writings*, tr. T. M. Knox (Oxford: Clarendon Press, 1964), 150–1, 189, 216 and, for the German, *Werke*, ed. E. Moldenhauer and K. M. Michel (Frankfurt am Main: Suhrkamp, 1971), I, 469, 516, 548–9.

32. Hyppolite, 405.

33. Hinchman, 96.

34. I prefer Baillie's translation here: *PhM*, 514/GW, IX, 267.

35. I find Baillie clearer here: *PhM*, 539–40/GW, IX, 281–2. Diderot, 78, 83, 121.

36. Diderot, 33–4, 111.

37. R. R. Williams, *Recognition*, 1, 5, 255–6.

38. *PhS*, 296 (brackets in original)/*GW*, IX, 266.

39. I prefer Baillie's translation here: *PhM*, 547/GW, IX, 286.

40. For a very good treatment of the whole section on culture—from noble and base consciousness through Rameau's nephew—see Pinkard, 151–65.

41. Athenian democracy was possible because consciousness, though it did construct its reality, nevertheless, erased itself, its own doing; it took its laws to be "not of yesterday or today, but everlasting,/ Though where they came from, none of us can tell" (*PhS*, 261/GW, IX, 236).

42. For a fuller and more extended treatment of this issue, see my earlier *Marx and Modern Political Theory*, 123–51.

43. Even when the ideal nonestranged state is achieved, for Hegel a certain amount of alienation will still be necessary. We must not view the political constitution as something made, manufactured, the creation of its subjects. We must view it as divine (*PR*, 178, 287/*SW*, VII, 375, 376–7). The constitution *is* historically constructed by the subjects, but they must not view it as such if it is to have authority and command respect. Thus Hegel cannot accept full-fledged democracy (e.g., *PR*, 181–2, 195, 197/*SW*, VII, 382–3, 407, 411).

44. The term *fremd* was used there, but that is a much vaguer term than *Entäusserung* or *Entfremdung*. *Fremd* can simply mean "strange."

45. See *Marx and Modern Political Theory*, 342–6, esp. 345–6; *Schiller, Hegel, and Marx*, 50–1.

46. "Tübingen Essay," 44–5/GW, I, 99.

47. *PhS*, 328 (translation altered)/*GW*, IX, 292.

48. Hyppolite, 534, 541

49. Kojève, 167. Solomon (582 ff.) also argues that Hegel is essentially an atheist.

50. L. Feuerbach, *The Essence of Christianity*, tr. G. Eliot (New York: Harper & Row, 1957), 12–14, 33, 226–7.

51. *PhS*, 321 (brackets in original)/*GW*, IX, 286–7.

52. For fuller treatment of these matters, see my *Marx and Modern Political Theory*, 65–75.

53. F. Schiller, *On the Aesthetic Education of Man*, tr. E. M. Wilkinson and L. A. Willoughby (Oxford: Clarendon Press, 1967), 9, 11, 25, 215.

54. Diderot, 49, 70–1, 83, 85–7.

55. See especially *Discipline and Punish: The Birth of the Prison*, tr. A. Sheridan (New York: Vintage, 1979), 26–7; *The History of Sexuality: Volume I: An Introduction*, tr. R. Hurley (New York, Vintage, 1980), 85–91.

56. *Discipline and Punish*, 23–31, 224. See also *The History of Sexuality*, I, 3–35.

57. Hyppolite, 322; Lukács, 485–6; M. Westphal, *History and Truth*, 153; Norman, 24; Forster, 298-9; Stewart, *Unity of Hegel's Phenomenology*, 24–5, 291–2.

58. Lauer, *A Reading of Hegel's Phenomenology*, 108, 187; G. A. Kelly, *Hegel's Retreat from Eleusis* (Princeton, NJ: Princeton University Press, 1978), 38–9; K. R. Westphal, *Hegel's Epistemological Realism*, 174–5, 185.

59. Hyppolite, 462; F. Rosenzwieg, *Hegel und der Staat* (Munich: R. Oldenburg, 1920), I, 217–20.

60. Forster argues that this passage does not claim that the development of the *Phenomenology* is not temporal (300–1). But to make his case, at least in my view, Foster must ignore the passage as a whole and quote it only selectively.

61. Lauer, *A Reading of Hegel's Phenomenology*, 191; Lukács, 491.

62. M. Westphal, *History and Truth*, 161; Stewart, *Unity of Hegel's Phenomenology*, 317.

63. Kojève, 43–4, 47, 158–9 n, 160–1 n, 162–3 (see also A. Bloom's introduction to Kojève, vii–xii); F. Fukuyama, "The End of History?," *The National Interest* 16 (1989): 4–5; Pinkard, 331–2.

64. Bloom, introduction to Kojeve, x, see also xi.

65. Lukács, 454. Lukács quotes K. Rosenkranz, *Georg Wilhelm Friedrich Hegels Leben* (Darmstadt: Wissenschaftliche Buchgesellschaft, 1963), 214-15.

66. Lukács, 503–4. Forster (455) agrees with Lukács' view.

67. Hyppolite, 534, 541.

68. See the final section of chapter 2 above.

69. Allison too finds Kant's views on progress toward holiness and the highest good problematic (*KTF*, 172–3).

70. There are places where Kant thinks the moral law is compatible with God as supreme law giver; see *MPV*, 18–19, 27, 102, 157–8/*KGS*, VI, 219, 227, 440, 487–8; *R*, 3–5/*KGS*, VI, 3–5.

71. See Hyppolite (512–15), for a discussion of how Hegel's concept of the beautiful soul is based on similar conceptions in Schiller, Jacobi, and Goethe. See also Hinchman, 176–7. M. S. Gram, in "Moral and Literary Ideals in Hegel's Critique of 'The Moral View of the World,'" argues that Hegel has Novalis in mind rather than Schiller or Goethe.

5. Culture, Religion, and Absolute Knowing

1. Hyppolite, 541, 534.

2. *PhS*, 479 (translation altered)/*GW*, IX, 422.

3. Hyppolite, 542.

4. Lukács, 79.

5. I prefer Baillie's translation here: *PhM*, 756/*GW*, IX, 404.

6. *PhS*, 417 (brackets in original)/*GW*, IX, 369. See also *PhS*, 459, 490/*GW*, IX, 405, 431.

7. I prefer Baillie's translation here: *PhM*, 758/*GW*, IX, 405. See also *PhS*, 478/*GW*, IX, 420–1.

8. See last section of chapter 4 above.

9. *PhS*, 479 (brackets in original and translation altered)/*GW*, IX, 422.

10. This is something that Marx will especially disagree with; see *Economic and Philosophic Manuscripts*, in *Karl Marx Frederick Engels Collected Works* (New York: International, 1975–), III, 331 ff.

11. In the *Logic*, Hegel says, "God himself, exists in proper truth, only in thought and as thought" (*L*, 34, also 61, 126–7/*SW*, VIII, 70, 100, 169–70).

12. D. Davidson, "On the Very Idea of a Conceptual Scheme," in *Inquiries into Truth and Interpretation* (Oxford: Clarendon Press, 1984), 183–98.

13. J. Burbidge, "Hegel's Absolutes," *Owl of Minerva* 29 (1997): 33–4.

14. M. Westphal, *Hegel, Freedom, and Modernity* (Albany: State University of New York Press, 1992), 80–1. Also, see my review of Westphal's *Hegel, Freedom, and Modernity* in *Bulletin of the Hegel Society of Great Britain* 27/28 (1993): 73–6.

15. For a view similar to mine, see T. McCarthy, "Deconstruction and Reconstruction in Contemporary Critical Theory," in *Méta-Philosophie: Reconstructing Philosophy?*, *Canadian Journal of Philosophy*, Supplementary Volume 19 (1993): 258–60.

16. A postmodernist might argue that Hegel has not succeeded in giving us a deduction of the absolute because Hegel cannot really prove to us that it is necessary to presuppose such a concept in order to make sense of our experience. Postmodernists think we do not need and should completely reject such a concept. If postmodernism is right, if we can get along without a concept of the absolute, then it would not be necessary to assume such a concept to make sense of our experience, and thus Hegel's deduction would fail. We would have to admit this conclusion if it were the case that postmodernism can actually get along without a concept of the absolute. But can it? I suggest that it cannot; see note 26 of chapter 4 above. See also W. Maker, *Philosophy Without Foundations: Rethinking Hegel* (Albany: State University of New York Press, 1994), 131.

17. This point is also made by C. Geertz, "Anti Anti-Relativism," in *Relativism: Interpretation and Confrontation*, ed. M. Krausz (Notre Dame, IN: University of Notre Dame Press, 1989), 12. See also G. Harman, "Is There a Single True Morality?," in *Relativism: Interpretation and Confrontation*, 363–4. If one starts with a bizarre enough definition of cultural relativism, one can end up attributing to cultural relativists positions that it would be lunacy to hold; see, e.g., J. W. Cook, *Morality and Cultural Differences* (New York: Oxford University Press, 1999).

18. For a history of the concept of cultural relativism, see E. Hatch, *Culture and Morality: The Relativity of Values in Anthropology* (New York: Columbia University Press, 1983).

19. For a view that generally agrees with mine, though it is developed in a very different way, see D. B. Wong, *Moral Relativity* (Berkeley: University of California Press, 1984).

20. Wood, 204–5.

21. Wood, 204. See also R. Rorty, *OR&T*, 23. G. Harman thinks such self-contradiction can be avoided; see "Moral Relativism Defended," *Philosophical Review* 84 (1975): 3.

22. Wood, 204–5.

23. That this is Wood's view can be seen in the passage quoted above: Wood, 204. For Rorty's similar view, see *OR&T*, 23.

24. Wood (205, also 204) is very close to this position in the passage quoted above. See also Fukuyama, 3, 4, 9; Houlgate, *Freedom, Truth and History*, 36.

25. Davidson, 183.

26. Davidson, 184–5, 189, 190, 197. For a very good critique of Davidson, see Forster, 368–409.

27. C. Spinosa and H. L. Dreyfus, "Two Kinds of Antiessentialism and Their Consequences," *Critical Inquiry* 22 (1996): 753–4.

28. Bernard Williams argues this sort of point in *Ethics and the Limits of Philosophy* (Cambridge, MA: Harvard University Press, 1985), 17–18. See also T. Eagleton, *After Theory* (New York: Basic Books, 2003), 62.

29. Rorty, *Essays on Heidegger and Others: Philosophical Papers* (Cambridge: Cambridge University Press, 1991), II, 69.

30. Houlgate, *Freedom, Truth and History*, 36.

31. Appiah, 26, also 24.

32. *PRel*, II, 235–6 (also see editor's introduction, 17–18)/*VPRel*, IIa, 140–2.

33. M. Bernal, *Black Athena: The Afroasiatic Roots of Classical Civilization* (New Brunswick, NJ: Rutgers University Press, 1987), I, 1, chapters 6–7.

34. Even Marx, and at a later period, was unable to free himself from all endorsement of imperialism. See "British Rule in India," in *Marx Engels Collected Works*, XII, 132; "Future Results of British Rule in India," in *Marx Engels Collected Works*, XII, 222; *Marx and Modern Political Theory*, 273 ff.

35. Contrast the latter passage with *HP*, I, 443/*SW*, XVIII, 115–16.

36. Appiah, 13.

37. Appiah, 13 ff.

38. See also Bernal, *Black Athena*, I, chapters 6–7.

39. Hoy, 212.

40. J. Ladd, "The Issue of Relativism," 111–12; Hatch, 67–8; Wong, chapter 12, also 215.

41. L. E. Lomasky, *Persons, Rights, and the Moral Community* (New York: Oxford University Press, 1987), 49, 54.

42. See also A. Bloom, *The Closing of the American Mind* (New York: Simon and Schuster, 1987), 36.

43. Bloom argues that relativism is ethnocentric—a form of western prejudice (*Closing*, 36). I agree that vulgar relativism can be ethnocentric and I tend to agree with a good deal of Bloom's criticism of such relativism, but not with his solution to it. Bloom's book at times shows real insight, though it is always mixed with a great deal that is very objectionable. On relativism, see Bloom, *Closing*, 25–43.

44. *DFS*, 87–9 (all brackets in original except the last)/*GW*, IV, 10–13.

45. It is also the case for Hegel that all philosophical systems contain falsity (*PhS*, 2, 23, 27/*GW*, IX, 10, 30–1, 34–5), often by pushing their truths too one-sidedly.

46. V. Woolf, *A Room of One's Own* (New York: Harcourt, Brace & World, 1929), 3–4.

47. *Republic*, 514a–521c.

48. *Republic*, 442a–442b, 590c–590d.

49. *Symposium*, 201c–212a; see also *Apology*, 20d–23b.

50. "Tübingen Essay," 38/*GW*, I, 92.

51. E. Husserl, "Philosophy and the Crisis of European Man," in *Phenomenology and the Crisis of Philosophy*, tr. Q. Lauer (New York: Harper & Row, 1965), 162. See also J. S. Mill, *On Liberty*, ed. C. V. Shields (Indianapolis, IN: Bobbs-Merrill, 1956), 26, 64.

52. See E. Nagel and J. R. Newman, *Gödel's Proof* (New York: New York University Press, 1958), 58–9, 98. Also Margaret Mead argues that Ruth Benedict thought it was "possible to see each culture . . . as having selected from the great arc of human potentialities certain characteristics and then having elaborated them with greater strength and intensity than any single individual ever could do in one lifetime" and that Benedict did not believe "that any closed system could be constructed into which all human societies, past, present and future, would fit." See R. Benedict, *Patterns of Culture* (Boston: Houghton Mifflin, 1959), viii, and chapters 1–2.

53. See M. C. Nussbaum and A. Sen, "Internal Criticism and Indian Rationalist Traditions," in *Relativism: Interpretation and Confrontation*.

54. Wood, 204.

55. A. MacIntyre, *Whose Justice? Which Rationality?* (Notre Dame, IN: University of Notre Dame Press, 1988), 387–8. See also MacIntyre, *Three Rival Versions of Moral Enquiry* (Notre Dame, IN: University of Notre Dame Press, 1990), 173.

56. However, see MacIntyre, *Whose Justice? Which Rationality?*, 10–11.

57. J. Clifford, *The Predicament of Culture* (Cambridge, MA: Harvard University Press, 1988), chapter 12.

58. R. Rosaldo, *Culture and Truth* (Boston: Beacon, 1989), 62.

59. Rosaldo, 63.

60. Rosaldo, 64.

61. Some anthropologists do find truth in other cultures. See P. Stoller and C. Olkes, *In Sorcery's Shadow* (Chicago: University of Chicago Press, 1987), 239. See also

L. Dumont, *Homo Hierarchicus: The Caste System and Its Implications*, tr. M. Sainsbury, L. Dumont, and B. Gulati (Chicago: University of Chicago Press, 1970), 1-4.

62. Aristotle, *Politics*, 1252^a–1253^a. Marx, *Economic and Philosophic Manuscripts*, 275 ff.

63. Some philosophers argue that there are many things that are universal or common among cultures (see, e.g., M. C. Nussbaum, "Non-Relative Virtues: An Aristotelian Approach," in *Midwest Studies in Philosophy, Volume 13: Ethical Theory and Character* [Notre Dame, IN: University of Notre Dame Press, 1988], 47–9). No doubt there are, but this would not eliminate the fact that innumerable legitimate differences between cultures would still remain. Thus, this would not amount to a successful argument against multiculturalism or cultural relativism.

Bibliography

Allison, H. E. *Kant's Theory of Freedom*. Cambridge: Cambridge University Press, 1990.

――――. *Kant's Transcendental Idealism: An Interpretation and Defense*. New Haven: Yale University Press, 1983.

――――. "Transcendental Idealism: The 'Two Aspect' View." In *New Essays on Kant*, ed. B. den Ouden and M. Moen. New York: Peter Lang, 1987.

Ameriks, K. "The Hegelian Critique of Kantian Morality." In *New Essays on Kant*, ed. B. den Ouden and M. Moen. New York: Peter Lang, 1987.

Appiah, K. A. *In My Father's House: Africa in the Philosophy of Culture*. New York: Oxford University Press, 1992.

Aquinas, T. *Summa Theologiae*. 74 vols. New York: McGraw-Hill, 1964–69.

Aristotle. *The Complete Works of Aristotle*. Ed. J. Barnes. 2 vols. Princeton, NJ: Princeton University Press, 1984.

Audi, R., ed. *Cambridge Dictionary of Philosophy*. Cambridge: Cambridge University Press, 1995.

Augustine. *Confessions*. Tr. R. S. Pine-Coffin. Harmondsworth: Penguin, 1961.

Avineri, S. *Hegel's Theory of the Modern State*. Cambridge: Cambridge University Press, 1972.

Beck, L. W. *A Commentary on Kant's Critique of Practical Reason*. Chicago: University of Chicago Press, 1960.

Beiser, F. C., ed. *The Cambridge Companion to Hegel*. Cambridge: Cambridge University Press, 1993.

Benedict, R. *Patterns of Culture*. Boston: Houghton Mifflin, 1934.

Benhabib, S. "On Hegel, Women, and Irony." In *Feminist Interpretations of G.W.F. Hegel*, ed. P. J. Mills. University Park: Pennsylvania State University Press, 1996.

Bergmann, F. H. "The Purpose of Hegel's System." *Journal of the History of Philosophy* 2 (1964): 189–204.

Berkeley, G. *The Principles of Human Knowledge*. Reprint edition. La Salle, IL: Open Court, 1946.

————. *Three Dialogues Between Hylas and Philonous.* Reprint edition. La Salle, IL: Open Court, 1954.

Bernal, M. *Black Athena: The Afroasiatic Roots of Classical Civilization.* 2 vols. New Brunswick, NJ: Rutgers University Press, 1987.

Bloom, A. *The Closing of the American Mind.* New York: Simon and Schuster, 1987.

Booth, W. J. *Interpreting the World: Kant's Philosophy of History and Politics.* Toronto: University of Toronto Press, 1986.

Brown, A. L. "Hegelian Silences and the Politics of Communication: A Feminist Appropriation." In *Feminist Interpretations of G. W. F. Hegel,* ed. P. J. Mills. University Park: Pennsylvania State University Press, 1996.

Browning, G. K., ed. *Hegel's Phenomenology of Spirit: A Reappraisal.* Dordrecht: Kluwer, 1997.

Burbidge, J. "Hegel's Absolutes." *Owl of Minerva* 29 (1997): 23–37.

Butler, J. "Commentary on Joseph Flay's 'Hegel, Derrida, and Bataille's Laughter.'" In *Hegel and His Critics,* ed. W. Desmond. Albany: State University of New York Press, 1989.

————. *The Psychic Life of Power: Theories in Subjection.* Stanford: Stanford University Press, 1997.

————. *Subjects of Desire.* New York: Columbia University Press, 1987.

Clifford, J. *The Predicament of Culture.* Cambridge, MA: Harvard University Press, 1988.

Cook, J. W. *Morality and Cultural Differences.* New York: Oxford University Press, 1999.

Davidson, D. "On the Very Idea of a Conceptual Scheme." In *Inquiries into Truth and Interpretation.* Oxford: Clarendon Press, 1984.

de Beauvoir, S. *The Second Sex.* Tr. H. M. Parshley. New York: Vintage, 1952.

De George, R. T. "Social Reality and Social Relations." *Review of Metaphysics* 37 (1983): 3–20.

Denker, A. and M. Vater, eds. *Hegel's Phenomenology of Spirit: New Critical Essays.* Amherst, NY: Humanity Books, 2003.

den Ouden, B. and M. Moen, eds. *New Essays on Kant.* New York: Peter Lang, 1987.

Desmond, W. *Beyond Hegel and Dialectic: Speculation, Cult, and Comedy.* Albany: State University of New York Press, 1992.

————, ed. *Hegel and His Critics.* Albany: State University of New York Press, 1989.

Dickey, L. *Hegel: Religion, Economics, and the Politics of Spirit, 1770–1807.* Cambridge: Cambridge University Press, 1987.

Diderot, D. *Rameau's Nephew.* Tr. L. W. Tancock. Harmondsworth: Penguin, 1966.

Du Bois, W. E. B. *The Souls of Black Folk.* New York: New American Library, 1969.

Dulckeit, K. "Can Hegel Refer to Particulars?" In *The Phenomenology of Spirit Reader: Critical and Interpretive Essays,* ed. J. Stewart. Albany: State University of New York Press, 1998.

Dumont, L. *Homo Hierarchicus: The Caste System and Its Implications.* Tr. M. Sainsbury, L. Dumont, and B. Gulati. Chicago: University of Chicago Press, 1970.

Duquette, D. A. "Kant, Hegel, and the Possibility of a Speculative Logic." In *Essays on Hegel's Logic,* ed. G. di Giovanni. Albany: State University of New York Press, 1990, 1–16.

Eagleton, T. *After Theory.* New York: Basic Books, 2003.

Epicurus. "Letter to Menoeceus." In *The Epicurus Reader: Selected Writings and Testimonia,* tr. B. Inwood and L. P. Gerson. Indianapolis, IN: Hackett, 1994.

———. "Letter to Pythocles." In *The Epicurus Reader: Selected Writings and Testimonia,* tr. B. Inwood and L. P. Gerson. Indianapolis, IN: Hackett, 1994.

Fackenheim, E. L. *The Religious Dimension in Hegel's Thought.* Boston: Beacon, 1970.

Fanon, F. *Black Skin, White Masks.* Tr. C. L. Markmann. New York: Grove, 1967.

Feuerbach, L. *The Essence of Christianity.* Tr. G. Eliot. New York: Harper & Row, 1957.

Fichte, J. G. *Fichtes Werke.* Ed. I. H. Fichte. 11 vols. Berlin: de Gruyter, 1971.

———. *Science of Knowledge (Wissenschaftslehre).* Tr. P. Heath and J. Lachs. New York: Appleton-Century-Crofts, 1970.

Findlay, J. N. Forward to *Phenomenology of Spirit,* by G. W. F. Hegel, tr. A. V. Miller. Oxford: Clarendon Press, 1977.

Flay, J. C. *Hegel's Quest for Certainty.* Albany: State University of New York Press, 1984.

———. "Pragmatic Presuppositions and the Dialectics of Hegel's Phenomenology." In *Method and Speculation in Hegel's Phenomenology,* ed. M. Westphal. Atlantic Highlands, NJ: Humanities Press, 1982.

Förster, E., ed. *Kant's Transcendental Deductions.* Stanford, CA: Sanford University Press, 1989.

Forster, M. N. *Hegel's Idea of a Phenomenology of Spirit.* Chicago: University of Chicago Press, 1998.

Foucault, M. *Discipline and Punish: The Birth of the Prison*. Tr. A. Sheridan. New York: Vintage, 1979.

———. *The History of Sexuality: Volume I: An Introduction*. Tr. R. Hurley. New York: Vintage, 1980.

———. *Power/Knowledge*. Tr. C. Gordon, L. Marshall, J. Mepham, K. Soper. New York: Pantheon, 1980.

Fukuyama, F. "The End of History?" *The National Interest* 16 (1989): 3–18.

Gadamer, H.-G. *Hegel's Dialectic*. Tr. P. C. Smith. New Haven, CT: Yale University Press, 1976.

Gauvin, J. "Entfremdung et entäusserung dans la *Phénoménologie de l'Esprit* de Hegel." *Archives de Philosophie* 25 (1962): 555–71.

Geertz, C. "Anti Anti-Relativism." In *Relativism: Interpretation and Confrontation*, ed. M. Krausz. Notre Dame, IN: University of Notre Dame Press, 1989.

———. *The Interpretation of Cultures*. New York: Basic Books, 1973.

Goldmann, L. *Immanuel Kant*. Tr. R. Black. London: NLB, 1971.

Gram, M. S. "Moral and Literary Ideals in Hegel's Critique of 'The Moral View of the World.'" *Clio* 7 (1978): 375–402.

Gray, J. G. *Hegel and Greek Thought*. New York: Harper & Row, 1968.

Habermas, J. *Knowledge and Human Interests*. Tr. J. J. Shapiro. Boston: Beacon, 1971.

Haering, T. L. *Hegel: Sein Wollen und sein Werk*. 2 vols. Stuttgart: Scientia Verlag Aalen, 1963.

Harman, G. "Is There a Single True Morality?" In *Relativism: Interpretation and Confrontation*, ed. M. Krausz. Notre Dame, IN: University of Notre Dame Press, 1989.

———. "Moral Relativism Defended." *Philosophical Review* 84 (1975): 3–22.

Harris, H. S. *Hegel: Phenomenology and System*. Indianapolis, IN: Hackett, 1995.

———. *Hegel's Development: Night Thoughts (Jena 1801–1806)*. Oxford: Clarendon Press, 1983.

———. *Hegel's Development: Toward the Sunlight, 1770–1801*. Oxford: Clarendon Press, 1972.

———. *Hegel's Ladder*. 2 vols. Indianapolis, IN: Hackett, 1997.

Hatch, E. *Culture and Morality: The Relativity of Values in Anthropology*. New York: Columbia University Press, 1983.

Haym, R. *Hegel und seine Zeit*. Berlin: Rudolf Gaertner, 1857.

Hegel, G. W. F. *Aesthetics: Lectures on Fine Art*. Tr. T. M. Knox. 2 vols. Oxford: Clarendon Press, 1975.

———. *Einleitung in die Geschichte der Philosophie*. Ed. J. Hoffmeister. Hamburg: Felix Meiner, 1959.

————. *Faith and Knowledge.* Tr. W. Cerf and H. S. Harris. Albany: State University of New York Press, 1977.

————. *First Philosophy of Spirit.* In *System of Ethical Life (1802/3) and First Philosophy of Spirit,* tr. H. S. Harris and T. M. Knox. Albany: State University of New York Press, 1979.

————. *Gesammelte Werke.* Ed. Rheinisch-Westfälischen Akademie der Wissenschaften. Hamburg: Felix Meiner, 1968–.

————. *Hegel and the Human Spirit.* Tr. L. Rauch. Detroit, MI: Wayne State University Press, 1983.

————. *Hegel's Lectures on the History of Philosophy.* Tr. E. S. Haldane and F. H. Simson. 3 vols. London: Routledge & Kegan Paul, 1968.

————. *Hegel's Philosophy of Mind.* Tr. W. Wallace. Oxford: Clarendon Press, 1971.

————. *Hegel's Philosophy of Nature.* Tr. A. V. Miller. Oxford: Clarendon Press, 1970.

————. *Hegel's Philosophy of Nature.* Tr. M. J. Petry. 3 vols. London: George Allen & Unwin, 1970.

————. *Hegel's Philosophy of Right.* Tr. T. M. Knox. Oxford: Clarendon Press, 1967.

————. *Hegel's Political Writings.* Tr. T. M. Knox. Oxford: Clarendon Press, 1969.

————. *Hegel's Science of Logic.* Tr. A. V. Miller. Atlantic Highlands, NJ: Humanities Press International, 1969.

————. *Hegel: The Letters.* Tr. C. Butler and C. Seiler. Bloomington: Indiana University Press, 1984.

————. *Hegels theologische Jugendschriften.* Ed. H. Nohl. Frankfurt am Main: Minerva, 1966.

————. *Introduction to the Lectures on the History of Philosophy.* Tr. T. M. Knox and A. V. Miller. Oxford: Clarendon Press, 1985.

————. *Lectures on the History of Philosophy: The Lectures of 1825–1826.* Vol. 3. Tr. R. F. Brown and J. M. Stewart with H. S. Harris. Berkeley: University of California Press, 1990.

————. *Lectures on the Philosophy of Religion.* Tr. R. F. Brown, P. C. Hodgson, J. M. Stewart, with J. P. Fitzer and H. S. Harris. 3 vols. Berkeley: University of California Press, 1984–87.

————. *Lectures on the Philosophy of World History: Introduction.* Tr. H. B. Nisbet. Cambridge: Cambridge University Press, 1975.

————. *Natural Law.* Tr. T. M. Knox. Philadelphia: University of Pennsylvania Press, 1975.

————. *On Christianity: Early Theological Writings.* Tr. T. M. Knox. Gloucester, MA: Peter Smith, 1970.

————. *Phenomenology of Mind.* Tr. J. B. Baillie. New York: Harper & Row, 1967.

————. *Phenomenology of Spirit.* Tr. A. V. Miller. Oxford: Clarendon Press, 1977.

————. *Philosophy of History.* Tr. J. Sibree. New York: Dover, 1956.

————. *Sämtliche Werke.* Ed. H. Glockner. 26 vols. Stuttgart: Frommanns, 1927–57.

————. *Spirit of Christianity and Its Fate.* In *On Christianity: Early Theological Writings,* tr. T. M. Knox. Gloucester, MA: Peter Smith, 1970.

————. *System der Sittlichkeit.* Ed. G. Lasson. Hamburg: Felix Meiner, 1967.

————. *System of Ethical Life (1802/3) and First Philosophy of Spirit.* Tr. H. S. Harris and T. M. Knox. Albany: State University of New York Press, 1979.

————. *The Difference Between Fichte's and Schelling's System of Philosophy.* Tr. H. S. Harris and W. Cerf. Albany: State University of New York Press, 1977.

————. *The Encyclopaedia Logic: Part I of the Encyclopaedia of Philosophical Sciences.* Tr. T. F. Geraets, W. A. Suchting, H. S. Harris. Indianapolis, IN: Hackett, 1991.

————. *The German Constitution.* In *Hegel's Political Writings,* tr. T. M. Knox. Oxford: Clarendon Press, 1964.

————. *The Jena System, 1804–5.* Tr. J. W. Burbidge and G. di Giovanni. Montreal: McGill-Queen's University Press, 1986.

————. *The Logic of Hegel.* Tr. W. Wallace. Oxford: Oxford University Press, 1968.

————. "The Positivity of the Christian Religion." In *On Christianity: Early Theological Writings,* tr. T. M. Knox. Gloucester, MA: Peter Smith, 1970.

————. *Three Essays, 1793–1795.* Tr. P. Fuss and J. Dobbins. Notre Dame, IN: University of Notre Dame Press, 1984.

————. "Tübingen Essay." In *Three Essays, 1793–1795,* tr. P. Fuss and J. Dobbins. Notre Dame, IN: University of Notre Dame Press, 1984.

————. *Vorlesungen über die Philosophie der Religion.* Ed. W. Jaeschke. Vols. 3–5 of the *Vorlesungen: Ausgewählte Nachschriften und Manuskripte.* Hamburg: Felix Meiner, 1983–.

————. *Vorlesungen über die Philosophie der Weltgeschichte.* Vol. 1. Ed. J. Hoffmeister. Hamburg: Felix Meiner, 1955.

————. *Vorlesungen über die Philosophie der Weltgeschichte.* Vols. 2–4. Ed. G. Lasson. Hamburg: Felix Meiner, 1968.

————. *Werke.* Ed. E. Moldenhauer and K. M. Michel. 20 vols. Frankfurt am Main: Suhrkamp, 1969–71.

————. *Wissenschaft der Logik.* Ed. G. Lasson. Hamburg: Felix Meiner, 1969.

Herman, B. *The Practice of Moral Judgment.* Cambridge, MA: Harvard University Press, 1993.

Herskovits, M. J. "Cultural Relativism and Cultural Values." In *Ethical Relativism,* ed. J. Ladd. Belmont, CA: Wadsworth, 1973.

———. *Cultural Relativism: Perspectives in Cultural Pluralism.* Ed. F. Herskovits. New York: Random House, 1972.

Hinchman, L. P. *Hegel's Critique of the Enlightenment.* Gainesville: University Presses of Florida, 1984.

Hirshman, A. O. *The Passions and the Interests.* Princeton, NJ: Princeton University Press, 1977.

Hodge, J. "Women and the Hegelian State." In *Women in Western Political Philosophy,* ed. E. Kennedy and S. Mendus. Brighton: Wheatsheaf Books, 1987.

Hollis, M. and S. Lukes, eds. *Rationality and Relativism.* Oxford: Blackwell, 1982.

Homer. *The Iliad.* Tr. R. Lattimore. Chicago: University of Chicago Press, 1951.

———. *The Odyssey.* Tr. R. Lattimore. New York: Harper & Row, 1967.

Houlgate, S. *Freedom, Truth and History: An Introduction to Hegel's Philosophy.* London: Routledge, 1991.

———. *Hegel, Nietzsche and the Criticism of Metaphysics.* Cambridge: Cambridge University Press, 1986.

Hoy, D. C. "Hegel's Critique of Kantian Morality." *History of Philosophy Quarterly* 6 (1989): 207–32.

Hume, D. *An Enquiry Concerning Human Understanding.* In *Enquiries Concerning Human Understanding and Concerning the Principles of Morals,* ed. L. A. Selby-Bigge. 3rd ed., rev. P. H. Nidditch. Oxford: Clarendon Press, 1975.

———. *A Treatise of Human Nature.* Ed. L. A. Selby-Bigge. Oxford: Clarendon Press, 1967.

Husserl, E. "Philosophy and the Crisis of European Man." In *Phenomenology and the Crisis of Philosophy,* tr. Q. Lauer. New York: Harper & Row, 1965.

Hyppolite, J. *Genesis and Structure of Hegel's Phenomenology of Spirit.* Tr. S. Cherniak and J. Heckman. Evanston, IL: Northwestern University Press, 1974.

Inwood, M. J. *Hegel.* London: Routledge & Kegan Paul, 1983.

Jameson, F. Forward to *The Postmodern Condition: A Report on Knowledge,* by J.-F. Lyotard, tr. G. Bennington and B. Massumi. Minneapolis: University of Minnesota Press, 1984.

Kain, P. J. "Hegel, Antigone, and Women." *Owl of Minerva* 33 (2002): 157–177.

—————. "Hegel, Reason, and Idealism." *Idealistic Studies* 27 (1997): 97–112.

—————. "Hegel's Critique of Kantian Practical Reason." *Canadian Journal of Philosophy* 28 (1998): 367–412.

—————. "Hegel's Political Theory and Philosophy of History." *Clio* 17 (1988): 345–68.

—————. "Kant and the Possibility of Uncategorized Experience." *Idealistic Studies* 19 (1989): 154–73.

—————. *Marx and Modern Political Theory*. Lanham, MD: Rowman & Littlefield, 1993.

—————. "Nietzsche, Skepticism, and Eternal Recurrence." *Canadian Journal of Philosophy* 13 (1983): 365–87.

—————. "Review of M. Westphal's *Hegel, Freedom, and Modernity*." *Bulletin of the Hegel Society of Great Britain* 27/28 (1993): 73–6.

—————. *Schiller, Hegel, and Marx*. Montreal: McGill-Queen's University Press, 1982.

—————. "Self-Consciousness, the Other, and Hegel's Dialectic of Recognition: Alternative to a Postmodern Subterfuge." *Philosophy & Social Criticism* 24 (1998): 105–126.

—————. "The Structure and Method of Hegel's *Phenomenology*." *Clio* 27 (1998), Special Issue: *H. S. Harris and the Vocation of a Scholar*: 593–614.

Kainz, H. P. *Hegel's Phenomenology. Part 1, Analysis and Commentary*. Tuscaloosa: University of Alabama Press, 1976.

—————. *Hegel's Phenomenology. Part 2, The Evolution of Ethical and Religious Consciousness to the Absolute Standpoint*. Athens: Ohio University Press, 1983.

Kant, I. *Critique of Judgment*. Tr. J. H. Bernard. New York: Hafner, 1966.

—————. *Critique of Practical Reason*. Tr. L. W. Beck. Indianapolis, IN: Bobbs-Merrill, 1956.

—————. *Critique of Pure Reason*. Tr. N. Kemp Smith. New York: St. Martin's Press, 1965.

—————. *Foundations of the Metaphysics of Morals*. Tr. L. W. Beck. Indianapolis, IN: Bobbs-Merrill, 1959.

—————. *Fundamental Principles of the Metaphysic of Morals*. Tr. T. K. Abbott. Indianapolis, IN: Bobbs-Merrill, 1949.

—————. "Idea for a Universal History." In *On History*, ed. L. W. Beck. Indianapolis, IN: Bobbs-Merrill, 1963.

—————. *Kant's gesammelte Schriften*. Ed. Königlich Preussischen Akademie der Wissenschaften. 26 vols. Berlin: Georg Reimer, 1910–55.

—————. *Metaphysical Elements of Justice: Part I of the Metaphysics of Morals*. Tr. J. Ladd. Indianapolis, IN: Bobbs-Merrill, 1965.

————. *Metaphysical Principles of Virtue: Part II of the Metaphysics of Morals.* Tr. J. Ellington. Indianapolis, IN: Bobbs-Merrill, 1964.

————. *Perpetual Peace.* In *On History,* ed. L. W. Beck. Indianapolis, IN: Bobbs-Merrill, 1963.

————. *Prolegomena to Any Future Metaphysics.* Ed. L. W. Beck. Indianapolis, IN: Bobbs-Merrill, 1950.

————. *Religion Within the Limits of Reason Alone.* Tr. T. M. Greene and H. H. Hudson. New York: Harper & Row, 1960.

Kaufmann, W. *Hegel.* Garden City, NY: Doubleday, 1965.

Kelly, G. A. *Hegel's Retreat from Eleusis: Studies in Political Thought.* Princeton, NJ: Princeton University Press, 1978.

————. *Idealism, Politics, and History.* London: Oxford University Press, 1973.

Kennedy, E., and S. Mendus, eds. *Women in Western Political Philosophy.* Brighton: Wheatsheaf Books, 1987.

Kojève, A. *Introduction to the Reading of Hegel.* Tr. J. H. Nichols, Jr. New York: Basic Books, 1969.

Krausz, M. *Relativism: Interpretation and Confrontation.* Notre Dame, IN: University of Notre Dame Press, 1989.

Kuhn, T. *The Structure of Scientific Revolutions.* 2nd ed. Chicago: University of Chicago Press, 1970.

Ladd, J., ed. *Ethical Relativism.* Belmont, CA: Wadsworth, 1973.

————. "The Issue of Relativism." In *Ethical Relativism,* ed. J. Ladd. Belmont, CA: Wadsworth, 1973.

Lamb. D., ed. *Hegel and Modern Philosophy.* London: Croom Helm, 1987.

Lauer, Q., ed. *Phenomenology and the Crisis of Philosophy.* New York: Harper & Row, 1965.

————. *A Reading of Hegel's Phenomenology of Spirit.* New York: Fordham University Press, 1976.

Locke, J. *An Essay Concerning Human Understanding.* Ed. P. H. Nidditch. Oxford: Clarendon Press, 1975.

Loewenberg, J. *Hegel's Phenomenology: Dialogues on the Life of the Mind.* La Salle, IL: Open Court, 1965.

Lomasky, L. E. *Persons, Rights, and the Moral Community.* New York: Oxford University Press, 1987.

Lucretius. *On the Nature of Things.* Tr. F. O. Copley. New York: Norton, 1977.

Lukács, G. *The Young Hegel.* Tr. R. Livingstone. London: Merlin, 1975.

Luther, M., tr. *Die Bibel.* New York: Amerikanische Bibel-Gesellschaft, 1854.

Lyotard, J.-F. *The Lyotard Reader.* Ed. A. Benjamin. Oxford: Basil Blackwell, 1989.

————. *The Postmodern Condition: A Report on Knowledge*. Tr. G. Bennington and B. Massumi. Minneapolis: University of Minnesota Press, 1984.

MacIntyre, A., ed. *Hegel: A Collection of Critical Essays*. Garden City, NY: Anchor, 1972.

————. "Hegel on Faces and Skulls." In *Hegel: A Collection of Critical Essays*, ed. A. MacIntyre. Garden City, NY: Anchor, 1972.

————. *Three Rival Versions of Moral Enquiry*. Notre Dame, IN: University of Notre Dame Press, 1990.

————. *Whose Justice? Which Rationality?* Notre Dame, IN: University of Notre Dame Press, 1988.

Maker, W. *Philosophy without Foundations: Rethinking Hegel*. Albany: State University of New York Press, 1994.

Marcuse, H. *Reason and Revolution*. Boston: Beacon, 1960.

Marx, K. *Economic and Philosophic Manuscripts*. In *Karl Marx Frederick Engels Collected Works*, Vol. 3. New York: International, 1975–.

————. *Karl Marx Frederick Engels Collected Works*. Tr. R. Dixon, et al. 50 vols. New York: International, 1975–.

Marx, W. "Dialectic and the Role of the Phenomenologist." In *G. W. F. Hegel: Critical Assessments*, Vol. 3. Ed. R. Stern. London: Routledge, 1993.

————. *Hegel's Phenomenology of Spirit*. Tr. P. Heath. New York: Harper & Row, 1975.

McCarthy, T. "Deconstruction and Reconstruction in Contemporary Critical Theory." In *Méta-Philosophie: Reconstructing Philosophy? Canadian Journal of Philosophy*, Supplementary Volume 19 (1993): 247–64.

McDonald, H. *The Normative Basis of Culture: A Philosophical Inquiry*. Baton Rouge: Louisiana State University Press, 1986.

Mill, J. S. *On Liberty*. Ed. C. V. Shields. Indianapolis, IN: Bobbs-Merrill, 1956.

Mills, P. J., ed. *Feminist Interpretations of G. W. F. Hegel*. University Park: Pennsylvania State University Press, 1996.

————. "'Feminist' Sympathy and Other Serious Crimes: A Reply to Swindle." *Owl of Minerva* 24 (1992): 55–62.

————. "Hegel's Antigone." *Owl of Minerva* 17 (1986): 131–52.

————. "'Hegel's Antigone' Redux: Woman in Four Parts." *Owl of Minerva* 33 (2002): 205–21.

————. *Woman, Nature, and Psyche*. New Haven: Yale University Press, 1987.

Molière. *Le Bourgeois Gentilhome*. In *The Miser and Other Plays*, tr. J. Wood. Baltimore: Penguin, 1968.

Nagel, E., and J. R. Newman. *Gödel's Proof*. New York: New York University Press, 1958.

Bibliography

🦢 305

Nell, O. *Acting on Principle: An Essay on Kantian Ethics*. New York: Columbia University Press, 1975.
Norman, R. *Hegel's Phenomenology: A Philosophical Introduction*. New York: St. Martin's Press, 1976.
Nussbaum, M. C., and A. Sen. "Internal Criticism and Indian Rationalist Traditions." In *Relativism: Interpretation and Confrontation*, ed. M. Krausz. Notre Dame, IN: University of Notre Dame Press, 1989.
———. "Non-Relative Virtues: An Aristotelian Approach." In *Midwest Studies in Philosophy, Volume XIII: Ethical Theory and Character*. Notre Dame, IN: University of Notre Dame Press, 1988.
O'Brien, M. "Hegel: Man, Physiology, and Fate." In *Feminist Interpretations of G. W. F. Hegel*, ed. P. J. Mills. University Park: Pennsylvania State University Press, 1996.
———. *The Politics of Reproduction*. Boston: Routledge & Kegan Paul, 1981.
Oliver, K. "Antigone's Ghost: Undoing Hegel's *Phenomenology of Spirit*." *Hypatia* 11 (1996): 67–90.
Paton, H. J. *The Categorical Imperative*. London: Hutchinson, 1965.
———. *Kant's Metaphysic of Experience*. 2 vols. London: George Allen & Unwin, 1970.
Pinkard, T. *Hegel's Phenomenology: The Sociality of Reason*. Cambridge: Cambridge University Press, 1994.
Pippin, R. B. *Hegel's Idealism: The Satisfactions of Self-Consciousness*. Cambridge: Cambridge University Press, 1989.
Plant, R. *Hegel*. Bloomington, IN: Indiana University Press, 1973.
Plato. *Collected Dialogues of Plato*. Ed. E. Hamilton and H. Cairns. New York: Pantheon, 1961.
Popper, K. *The Open Society and Its Enemies*. Princeton, NJ: Princeton University Press, 1950.
Priest, S., ed. *Hegel's Critique of Kant*. Oxford: Clarendon Press, 1987.
Putnam, H. *The Many Faces of Realism*. Lasalle, IL: Open Court, 1987.
———. *Reason, Truth and History*. Cambridge: Cambridge University Press, 1981.
———. *Representation and Reality*. Cambridge, MA: MIT Press, 1988.
Ravven, H. M. "Further Thoughts on Hegel and Feminism: A Response to Philip J. Kain and Nadine Changfoot." *Owl of Minerva* 33 (2002): 223–31.
———. "Has Hegel Anything to Say to Feminists?" In *Feminist Interpretations of G. W. F. Hegel*, ed. P. J. Mills. University Park: Pennsylvania State University Press, 1996.
———. "A Response to 'Why Feminists Should Take the *Phenomenology of Spirit* Seriously.'" *Owl of Minerva* 24 (1992): 63-8.
Reiss, H., ed. *Kant's Political Writings*. Cambridge: Cambridge University Press, 1992.

Riedel, M. *Between Tradition and Revolution: The Hegelian Transformation of Political Philosophy*. Tr. W. Wright. Cambridge: Cambridge University Press, 1984.

Riley, P. *Kant's Political Philosophy*. Totowa, NJ: Rowman & Littlefield, 1983.

———. *Will and Political Legitimacy*. Cambridge, MA: Harvard University Press, 1982.

Ritter, J. *Hegel und die französische Revolution*. Frankfurt: Suhrkamp, 1965.

Rockmore, T. *Cognition: An Introduction to Hegel's Phenomenology of Spirit*. Berkeley: University of California Press, 1997.

Rorty, R. *Essays on Heidegger and Others: Philosophical Papers*. Vol. 2. Cambridge: Cambridge University Press, 1991.

———. *Objectivity, Relativism, and Truth: Philosophical Papers*. Vol. 1. Cambridge: Cambridge University Press, 1991.

Rosaldo, R. *Culture and Truth*. Boston: Beacon, 1989.

Rosenkranz, K. *Georg Wilhelm Friedrich Hegels Leben*. Darmstadt: Wissenschaftliche Buchgesellschaft, 1963.

Rosenzwieg, F. *Hegel und der Staat*. 2 vols. Munich: R. Oldenburg, 1920.

Rousseau, J.-J. *Œuvres complètes*. Ed. B. Gagnebin and M. Raymond. 4 vols. Paris: Gallimard, 1959–95.

———. *On the Social Contract*. Tr. J. R. Masters. New York: St. Martin's, 1978.

Russell, B. *History of Western Philosophy*. London: George Allen & Unwin, 1948.

Russon, J. *The Self and Its Body in Hegel's Phenomenology of Spirit*. Toronto: University of Toronto Press, 1997.

Saner, H. *Kant's Political Thought*. Tr. E. B. Ashton. Chicago: University of Chicago Press, 1973.

Schacht, R. *Alienation*. London: Allen & Unwin, 1971.

Scharfstein, B.-A. *The Dilemma of Context*. New York: New York University Press, 1989.

Schiller, F. *On the Aesthetic Education of Man*. Tr. E. M. Wilkinson and L. A. Willoughby. Oxford: Clarendon Press, 1967.

Sextus Empiricus. *Sextus Empiricus: Outlines of Scepticism*. Tr. J. Annas and J. Barnes. Cambridge: Cambridge University Press, 1994.

Simpson, P. *Hegel's Transcendental Induction*. Albany: State University of New York Press, 1998.

Singer, M. G. *Generalization in Ethics*. New York: Knopf, 1961.

Smith, A. *Wealth of Nations*. Ed. E. Cannan. New York: Modern Library, 1937.

Smith, N. K. *A Commentary to Kant's "Critique of Pure Reason."* 2nd ed. Atlantic Highlands, NJ: Humanities, 1962.

Solomon, R. C. *In The Spirit of Hegel: A Study of G. W. F. Hegel's Phenomenology of Spirit.* New York: Oxford University Press, 1983.

Spinosa, C., and H. L. Dreyfus. "Two Kinds of Antiessentialism and Their Consequences." *Critical Inquiry* 22 (1996): 735–63.

Spinoza, B. "Spinoza to J. Jellis." In *Chief Works of Benedict de Spinoza*, Vol. 2. Tr. R. H. M. Elwes. New York: Dover, 1951.

Stace, W. T. *The Philosophy of Hegel.* New York: Dover, 1955.

Starrett, S. N. "Critical Relations in Hegel: Woman, Family, and the Divine." In *Feminist Interpretations of G. W. F. Hegel*, ed. P. J. Mills. University Park: Pennsylvania State University Press, 1996.

Stein, S. "Wittgenstein, Davidson, and the Myth of Incommensurability." In *Méta-Philosophie: Reconstructing Philosophy? Canadian Journal of Philosophy*, Supplementary Volume 19 (1993): 181–220.

Stern, R., ed. *G. W. F. Hegel: Critical Assessments.* 4 vols. London: Routledge, 1993.

———. *Hegel, Kant and the Structure of the Object.* London: Routledge, 1990.

———. "Unity and Difference in Hegel's Political Philosophy." *Ratio* 2 (1989): 75–88.

Stewart, J. "The Architectonic of Hegel's *Phenomenology of Spirit*." In *The Phenomenology of Spirit Reader: Critical and Interpretive Essays*, ed. J. Stewart. Albany: State University of New York Press, 1998.

———, ed. *The Phenomenology of Spirit Reader: Critical and Interpretive Essays.* Albany: State University of New York Press, 1998.

———. *The Unity of Hegel's Phenomenology of Spirit: A Systematic Interpretation.* Evanston, IL: Northwestern University Press, 2000.

Stillman, P. G., ed. *Hegel's Philosophy of Spirit.* Albany: State University of New York Press, 1987.

Stoller, P. and C. Olkes. *In Sorcery's Shadow.* Chicago: University of Chicago Press, 1987.

Strawson, P. F. *The Bounds of Sense.* London: Methuen, 1966.

Swindle, S. "Why Feminists Should Take the *Phenomenology of Spirit* Seriously." *Owl of Minerva* 24 (1992): 41–54.

Taylor, C. *Hegel.* Cambridge: Cambridge University Press, 1975.

———. "The Opening Arguments of the *Phenomenology*. " In *Hegel: A Collection of Critical Essays*, ed. A. MacIntyre. Garden City, NY: Anchor, 1972.

———. *Philosophy and the Human Sciences: Philosophical Papers 2.* Cambridge: Cambridge University Press, 1992.

Todorov, T. *The Conquest of America: The Question of the Other.* Tr. R. Howard. New York: Harper & Row, 1984.

Tuana, N. *Woman and the History of Philosophy.* New York: Paragon, 1992.

Tuschling, B. "*Rationis societas*: Remarks on Kant and Hegel." In *Kant's Philosophy of Religion Reconsidered*, ed. P. J. Rossi and M. Wreen. Bloomington: Indiana University Press, 1991.

Verene, D. P. *Hegel's Recollection*. Albany: State University of New York Press, 1985.

Virgil. *Aeneid*. Tr. A. Mandelbaum. New York: Bantam, 1971.

Walker, J. "Hegel and Religion." In *Hegel and Modern Philosophy*, ed. D. Lamb. London: Croom Helm, 1987.

Westphal, K. "The basic context and structure of Hegel's *Philosophy of Right*." In *The Cambridge Companion to Hegel*, ed. F. C. Beiser. Cambridge: Cambridge University Press, 1993.

———. "Hegel's Critique of Kant's Moral World View." *Philosophical Topics* 19 (1991): 133–176.

———. *Hegel's Epistemological Realism: A Study of the Aim and Method of Hegel's Phenomenology of Spirit*. Dordrecht: Kluwer, 1989.

Westphal, M. *Hegel, Freedom, and Modernity*. Albany: State University of New York Press, 1992.

———. *History and Truth in Hegel's Phenomenology*. Atlantic Highlands, NJ: Humanities Press, 1979.

———, ed. *Method and Speculation in Hegel's Phenomenology*. Atlantic Highlands, NJ: Humanities Press, 1982.

Williams, B. *Ethics and the Limits of Philosophy*. Cambridge, MA: Harvard University Press, 1985.

———. *Moral Luck: Philosophical Papers 1973–1980*. Cambridge: Cambridge University Press, 1981.

———. *Morality: An Introduction To Ethics*. New York: Harper & Row, 1972.

Williams, R. R. "The Concept of Recognition in Hegel's *Phenomenology of Spirit*." In *Hegel's Phenomenology of Spirit: New Critical Essays*, ed. A. Denker and M. Vater. Amherst, NY: Humanity Books, 2003.

———. "Hegel's Concept of *Geist*." In *Hegel's Philosophy of Spirit*, ed. P. G. Stillman. Albany: State University of New York Press, 1987.

———. *Recognition: Fichte and Hegel on the Other*. Albany: State University of New York Press, 1992.

Wilson, B. R. *Rationality*. Evanston: Harper & Row, 1970.

Wolff, R. P., ed. *Kant: A Collection of Critical Essays*. Garden City, NY: Anchor, 1967.

Wong, D. B. *Moral Relativity*. Berkeley: University of California Press, 1984.

Wood, A. W. *Hegel's Ethical Thought*. Cambridge: Cambridge University Press, 1990.

Woolf, V. *A Room of One's Own*. New York: Harcourt, Brace & World, 1929.

Index